# Madam C. J. Walker's

## GOSPEL OF GIVING

## THE NEW BLACK STUDIES SERIES

Edited by Darlene Clark Hine and
Dwight A. McBride

*A list of books in the series appears
at the end of this book.*

# *Madam C.J. Walker's*
# GOSPEL OF GIVING

## BLACK WOMEN'S PHILANTHROPY
## DURING JIM CROW

*TYRONE MCKINLEY FREEMAN*

FOREWORD BY
*A'LELIA BUNDLES*

**UNIVERSITY OF
ILLINOIS PRESS**
Urbana, Chicago, and Springfield

Publication of this book was supported by funding from the Indiana
University Lilly Family School of Philanthropy Faculty Research Fund.

Excerpts appear from "The Collectivist Roots of Madam C. J. Walker's
Philanthropy" by Tyrone McKinley Freeman on *Black Perspectives* (the
blog of the African American Intellectual History Society), May 20, 2019,
https://www.aaihs.org/the-collectivist-roots-of-madam
-c-j-walkers-philanthropy/. Reprinted by permission of *Black
Perspectives*.
Portions of chapter 5 originally appeared in T. Freeman, "The Big-
Hearted Race Loving Woman: Madam C. J. Walker's Philanthropy While
Living in Indianapolis, Indiana, 1911–1914," in *Hoosier Philanthropy:
Understanding the Past, Planning the Future*, edited by Greg Witkowski
(Bloomington: Indiana University Press, forthcoming). Reprinted by
permission.

Library of Congress Cataloging-in-Publication Data
Names: Freeman, Tyrone McKinley, 1973– author.
Title: Madam C. J. Walker's gospel of giving : black women's
    philanthropy during Jim Crow / Tyrone McKinley Freeman ;
    foreword by A'Lelia Bundles.
Description: Urbana : University of Illinois Press, 2020. | Series: The new
    black studies series | Includes bibliographical references and index.
Identifiers: LCCN 2020013474 (print) | LCCN 2020013475 (ebook) | ISBN
    9780252043451 (cloth) | ISBN 9780252085352 (paperback) | ISBN
    9780252052330 (ebook)
Subjects: LCSH: Walker, C. J., Madam, 1867–1919. | African American
    women executives—Biography. | Women philanthropists—United
    States—Biography. | Cosmetics industry—United States—History.
Classification: LCC HD9970.5.C672 F74 2020 (print) | LCC HD9970.5.C672
    (ebook) | DDC 338.7/66855092 [B]—dc22
LC record available at https://lccn.loc.gov/2020013474
LC ebook record available at https://lccn.loc.gov/2020013475

*To Michelle, Olivia, and Alexander.*

*For all of*

*the generous churchwomen-clubwomen-educator-philanthropists*

*who have raised, taught, and loved me, especially Mom.*

# Contents

Foreword *by A'Lelia Bundles*    ix

Acknowledgments    xiii

Introduction    1

1   Making Madam C. J. Walker    25

2   Opportunity    55

3   Education    83

4   Activism    105

5   Material Resources    143

6   Legacy    165

Conclusion    185

Epilogue: Madam C. J. Walker and African American
Philanthropy in the Twenty-First Century    201

Notes    209

Bibliography    253

Index    269

*Photographs follow page 129*

# Foreword

A'Lelia Bundles

Tyrone McKinley Freeman's philanthropic biography of Madam C. J. Walker significantly expands our knowledge beyond her well-known role as an early-twentieth-century hair-care entrepreneur and places her on the continuum of black philanthropy from Colonial American benevolent societies to the transformative twenty-first century giving of billionaire Robert Smith.

In *Madam C. J. Walker's Gospel of Giving: Black Women's Philanthropy during Jim Crow*, Freeman sets out to redefine "who counts as a philanthropist and what counts as philanthropy." He questions conventional wisdom and asks us to reconsider the boundaries that have constricted our understanding of a vaunted American tradition.

As "a philanthropic foremother of black generosity," Freeman shows how Walker emulated traditional nineteenth-century African American philanthropic practices and then created her own model by seeding early-twentieth-century fundraising in her community with leadership gifts once she had the means to do so.

While placing Walker within the historical context of American philanthropy, Freeman challenges us to reexamine the criteria that rely almost exclusively on wealthy white nineteenth-century male benefactors as standard bearers. He argues that a singular focus on industrialists like Andrew Carnegie skews our analysis and casts a "vast philanthropic shadow." By this metric, Madam Walker's accomplishments are obscured and erased when compared with the philanthropy of men whose lives were not circumscribed by the sexism and the racist Jim Crow laws and customs she endured.

While "one *cannot* study the history of African Americans without encountering their philanthropy," Freeman notes, "it is unfortunate that one *can* study the history of philanthropy without encountering African Americans."

He seeks to correct this record and to "capture the richness" of African American volunteering, collective action, and financial contributions while dispelling the notion that African Americans "are primarily recipients of philanthropy" rather than "agents of it." Indeed, income inequality—and disposable income for philanthropy—in America remains stark. In 2016 the typical black family's net worth of $17,100 was about one-tenth that of a white household, according to *The Dynamics of the Racial Wealth Gap*, a 2019 study by two Federal Reserve Board economists. Focusing solely on the monetary value of a philanthropic gift, Freeman writes, reinforces the notion that African Americans "have a tradition of being *helped* but not a tradition of *helping*."

By centering the origins of Walker's philanthropy on her membership at St. Paul's African Methodist Episcopal Church in St. Louis during the late 1800s, Freeman links her to black philanthropy's roots in African societies as well as to black women's traditions of collective giving in missionary societies, fraternal orders, and national advocacy organizations that benefited black women and families.

Freeman shows how Walker's philanthropy evolved from small charitable gifts to larger, more transformative contributions that both connected her to her philanthropic forebears and set her apart from her contemporaries. As a poor widowed mother and washerwoman when she first arrived from Louisiana in 1888, she was a recipient of the largesse of others. Later, as a member of St. Paul's Mite Missionary Society, she helped collect pennies and nickels. As she became more prosperous, she gave to orphanages, retirement homes for the formerly enslaved, and needy neighborhood families near her Indianapolis factory. As a wealthy woman, she amplified the original giving model by hosting events for black suffragists, sponsoring war-bond drives during World War I, helping to retire the mortgage on Frederick Douglass's home in the Anacostia neighborhood of Washington, DC, and commissioning paintings by William Edouard Scott and John Wesley Hardrick, two renowned black Indianapolis artists.

Her annual convention of Walker Beauty Culturists provided an opportunity to advance her business as well as her philanthropy and political activism. She prioritized financial giving by awarding monetary prizes to the sales agents whose local clubs had contributed the most to charity. Despite their limited personal financial resources, Walker helped them use their activism, advocacy, and service as a gateway to giving. Today we call this "time, talent, and treasure."

"I want my agents to feel that their first duty is to humanity," Walker told her delegates in 1917, as large numbers of African Americans were migrating from the rural south to northern cities. "I shall expect to find my agents taking the lead not only in operating a successful business, but in every movement in the interest of our colored citizenship."

Over time, sales of her hair-care products became the platform and financial engine for a more ambitious goal: to empower black women and make them less dependent on the whims of white employers and, in some cases, deceased or unreliable spouses.

"I am not merely satisfied in making money for myself for I am endeavoring to provide employment for hundreds of women of my race," she told a reporter.

Even the August 1918 opening of Villa Lewaro, her estate in Irvington-on-Hudson, New York, became a forum for political advocacy. In today's terms, one might see this "conference of interest to the race" as what philanthropy professionals now call a "cultivation" event. Whenever she was not explicitly raising funds, she was seeking access so that she could influence the treatment of black soldiers who then were stationed in France during World War I.

A full inventory of Walker's philanthropy is yet to be compiled. *Madam C. J. Walker's Gospel of Giving* helps pave the way for additional research and an even more detailed analysis of the range of gifts from casual, spontaneous charity to strategically planned philanthropy. Freeman rightfully urges those who wish to understand Walker's impact to look beyond the two contributions for which she is best known: her $1,000 gift to the Indianapolis YMCA and her $5,000 gift to the NAACP's antilynching fund.

In her will, Walker earmarked $100,000 for causes, organizations, and individuals. More than $80,000 went to women and women's organizations, of which $29,500 went to women and girls who were employees and relatives. Another $20,000 went to the young sons of women friends, $16,000 to schools founded by women, and $17,500 to organizations that addressed the needs of women and children.

Freeman broadens the definition of philanthropy and pushes its boundaries. He is working to create frameworks and criteria that will provide alternatives to the model that centers primarily on wealthy givers.

He has brought a scholar's eye and analysis to the conversations that flourished on panels and at plenaries during the first decade of the twenty-first century at the National Center for Black Philanthropy's annual conferences and that continue today among members of the Association of Black Foundation Executives.

When my book, *On Her Own Ground: The Life and Times of Madam C. J. Walker*, was published almost two decades ago, I hoped there would be other scholars who would expand on what I had written. I intentionally included voluminous endnotes with citations and primary sources as breadcrumbs for those who wished to learn more and who had the curiosity to dig more deeply.

Freeman has exceeded my expectation by exploring new dimensions of Walker as a philanthropist and as an educator. His work opens the doors for a more inclusive and more meaningful analysis so that black philanthropy is a feature rather than a footnote of American philanthropy.

# Acknowledgments

The pathway that has led to this book began years ago in the churches of my family. As the son, grandson, nephew, and cousin of black Baptist preachers, first ladies, Sunday school teachers, ushers, deacons, missionaries, and trustees, I was immersed in communities of generosity and surrounded by true philanthropists. They embodied the spirit and meaning of philanthropy to their core, inside and outside of the church, seven days per week. My parents, Rev. William McKinley Freeman and First Lady Carolyn Cooper Freeman, and the members of my home church, Union Baptist in Orange, New Jersey, are the first philanthropists I've ever known. Indeed, I am who I am because of the love and generosity of generations of Freemans, Coopers, Union members, and extended family—known and unknown—who have given me so much. And the dynamic adults of my hometown of South Orange, New Jersey, gave us kids a community of nurturing and models of success for which I am very grateful.

My Historic Black College and University experience at Lincoln University of the Commonwealth of Pennsylvania was marked by the power of the gift of words and education as professors, peers, and the parade of history makers who regularly visited campus spoke positivity, possibility, challenge, and love into my life. My faculty made me want to be like them, and they planted seeds and nurtured the abilities in me to fulfill that desire. I am grateful to have matriculated under the presidency of the great anthropologist Dr. Niara

Sudarkasa, whose work on West African family and community structures influences my thinking about black philanthropy today. Dr. Judith A. W. Thomas introduced me to the Paula Giddings classic, *When and Where I Enter*. And many others, from administrators to peers, helped me to catch a glimpse of who I could become. I am eternally grateful to Dr. Sheila M. Foor, who, in 1995, took me, as a senior, to two academic conferences to present papers I wrote in her classes, which gave me the chance to rub elbows with Henry Louis Gates Jr. and Houston Baker. I still have the photos I took with those intellectual giants as well as my autographed copy of her book about Charles Dickens in which she inscribed how much she looked forward to one day reading my book. Well, Dr. Foor, here you go!

The late Dr. Linda Keys recruited me away from the East Coast to the Midwest for graduate school. She believed in me and taught me new ways of thinking about community. I regret that she passed away before we had a chance to write that book we used to talk about together. I remain a Keys Kid through and through. Dr. Natasha Flowers was the first graduate professor to flat out tell me I was a scholar after reading one of my papers. She said it with such conviction and meaning that I had to believe her, which spurred me to look into PhD programs. While working full-time as a fundraiser for Dr. Khaula Murtadha, I entered my doctoral program with her blessing and mentorship, and, later, walked across the commencement stage with the Kente stole she gave me.

All my colleagues at the Indiana University Lilly Family School of Philanthropy have been incredibly supportive by providing not only funding and time in support of this project but audience and encouragement, too. It is an honor, privilege, and pleasure to be building the world's first school of philanthropy in our field of philanthropic studies with you. I extend my gratitude, especially, to Dean Amir Pasic, Patrick Rooney, Una Osili, Deb Mesch, Lehn Benjamin, Gene Tempel, Tim Seiler, and Dwight Burlingame. I also thank the Indiana University–Purdue University Indianapolis E.M.P.O.W.E.R. Program for funding in support of this project.

Nancy Marie Robertson is an incredible historian, mentor, and friend. This book would not exist without our many conversations and her ongoing support. Her encouragement through the lowest moments and her celebrations through its highs are hallmarks that I will forever treasure. Richard Turner has read various versions of this manuscript and provided valuable feedback and companionship during this journey. Many conversations with Modupe Labode lent insight and direction. Andrea Walton's courses shaped my thinking about who and what counts in philanthropy. Marybeth Gasman's service on my committee meant the world to me. And many communities of scholars have contributed to this project through panels and discussions at meetings of groups like the Association for Research on Nonprofit and Voluntary Action, the Association for the Study of African American Life and History, the Indiana Association of Historians, and the History of Education Society.

Ten years ago, I met with A'Lelia Bundles, Madam Walker's great-great granddaughter, to share my idea for what has become this book. She affirmed the need for deeper understanding of Madam's philanthropy, and made her family archive available to me. She introduced me to colleagues, sat on panels with me, and readily engaged in critical conversations about Madam Walker and history. I'm grateful for her support.

I am indebted to the late Wilma Moore, archivist extraordinaire, whose stewardship of the Walker Collection at the Indiana Historical Society (IHS) helped make this book possible. I thank the IHS staff for their hospitality while I virtually lived in the collections. I also appreciate IHS giving me the opportunity to help shape the *You Are There 1915: Madam C. J. Walker, Empowering Women* exhibit, which opened in 2019. I thank all of the archivists around the country who had a hand in some element of this project from Chicago to New Haven, Connecticut. And I thank the Brownsburg Public Library in Indiana for being the primary refuge for writing this book.

This project would be nothing without the community of scholars known as black women's historians. I deeply value the relationships and conversations that I have developed with this community. Thank you for your scholarship, commitment, and struggle. I hope you will find honor in what I have done with the gift of knowledge you have given to this world. In particular, I want to thank Darlene Clark Hine, Tiffany M. Gill, Noliwe Rooks, and Tanisha C. Ford, whose work and conference panel commentary influenced my approach to studying Madam Walker.

For encouraging conversations about and moral support for this project, I want to thank Emmett Carson, Susan Batten, Wayne Hilson, Lilya Wagner, Judy Ransom-Lewis, Olivia McGee-Lockhart, Dr. Rose Mays, Judith Thomas, Thomas Ridley, Ebonie Johnson Cooper, Natalie Madeira Cofield, Paul Mullins, Susan Olsen, Suzann Lupton, Amanda Moniz, Kim Williams-Pulfer, Tiara Dungy, Kisha Tandy, Susan Hall Dotson, LaTasha Sturdivant,

Kyle Malone, Ben Soskis, Maribel Morey, David King, Winterbourne La-Pucelle Harrison-Jones, Nancy Butler, Katie Herrold, Greg Witkowski, and many others. To my students over the years—and all my colleagues who have invited me into their classrooms to speak to their students—thanks for your interest, questions, and ideas that have helped me learn how to talk about Madam Walker and black philanthropy with others.

Dawn Durante at the University of Illinois Press is an incredible editor. From the moment I met her I knew I wanted to work directly with her and with this press. I really appreciate the way she conducted this process, but I most value her enthusiasm and love of books. I thank the reviewers who pushed me and this book to new levels, and I thank the press board and staff for their excitement and support.

I end where I began, with family. I honor the memories of my grandparents Rev. Roscoe D. Cooper Sr., First Lady Virginia White Cooper, David M. Freeman, Ruth Freeman, Henry Vicks, and Claudine Vicks, and my father-in-law Michael Jefferson. Thanks to my sister Dr. Lanniece Hall and her family. My love and appreciation to all my in-laws, Selma Dry, B. J., Brian, Tonya, and all my aunts, uncles, cousins, nieces, and nephews.

My wife, Michelle, is a precious gift in my life and the one who sustained me throughout this process. You are forever my Lincoln Love and Soulmate. My children, Alexander and Olivia, were in elementary school when this project began, and now, at its release, are in college and high school respectively. I love you dearly and am so proud to be your daddy.

And thank you, Heavenly Father, for life, love, peace, trust, ideas, curiosity, creativity, and, most of all, generosity.

MADAM C. J.
WALKER'S
GOSPEL OF GIVING

# Introduction

"I am unlike your white friends who have
waited until they were rich and then help
but have in proportion to my success, I have
reached out and am helping others."
—Madam C. J. Walker, 1914[1]

Black. Female. Daughter of slaves. Orphan. Child laborer. Widowed young
mother. Penniless migrant. Poor washerwoman. Philanthropist. Before
she became known as "the first self-made female millionaire" in the United
States, Madam C. J. Walker (1867–1919) lived a devastatingly difficult life
in the emerging Jim Crow South after the end of Reconstruction in the
late nineteenth century. But she resolved early to help herself and black
people by being generous any way she could, with what she had, no matter
the circumstances. Ultimately, Walker worked to give to black people—
particularly black women—some of what Jim Crow had taken away from
them. In the process, she became a significant American philanthropist and
a foremother of black philanthropy today.

She was born Sarah Breedlove on December 23, 1867, to Owen and Minerva Breedlove, their fifth but first free-born child, on a cotton plantation
in Delta, Louisiana. Young Sarah would not have much time with her parents. Sarah's parents died by the time she was seven, and her older sister,
Louvenia, cared for her. They moved around the South in search of better
opportunities, and Sarah, while barely a teen, began working as a washerwoman. She married, had a daughter at seventeen, and lost her husband

quickly to death. Life was cruel. But in her early twenties, Sarah and her young daughter, Lelia, began to turn their lives around after arriving in St. Louis, Missouri, around 1889 with less than $2 in hand. They connected with a local African Methodist Episcopal (AME) church and received aid through its network of social services for black migrants that was largely operated by black women. Sarah's work as a washerwoman along with other odd jobs eventually enabled her to put her daughter through Knoxville College in Tennessee and attend night school herself, for the aftermath of slavery and rise of Jim Crow had originally denied her an education.

By 1910, after many more struggles and movement through other cities such as Denver and Pittsburgh, Sarah made her home in Indianapolis and incorporated the Madam C. J. Walker Manufacturing Company of Indiana (the Walker Company), which sold hair-care and beauty products. The company's success would make her one of the wealthiest black women in the country, causing her to become known as the "first self-made female millionaire."[2] Adopting the initials and surname of her third husband, Charles Joseph Walker, Sarah forged an entrepreneurial and philanthropic identity as Madam C. J. Walker and directed her giving to black social service and educational causes dear to her, important to her business, and vital for her people, especially black women.

As a race woman, Walker's guiding philosophies were racial uplift and independence for black women, and she used philanthropy to express them throughout her life generally, and specifically through the Walker Company and her agents. Although she died in 1919 at the age of fifty-one from stress-related illness, she enjoyed the fruits of her labor. At the height of Jim Crow, Walker's success enabled her to travel the country promoting her business in her own personal automobiles. She also owned several pieces of real estate, including a $250,000, thirty-four-room mansion that she built in the wealthy white neighborhood of Irvington-on-Hudson, New York, where nearby residents included John D. Rockefeller, the famous oil magnate and philanthropist, and Helen Miller Gould Shepard, the finance heiress and philanthropist. She regularly achieved things that simply were not supposed to happen for black folks under Jim Crow America's severe constraints, and she gave regularly and generously to others, in numerous forms, along the way.

*Madam C. J. Walker's Gospel of Giving: Black Women's Philanthropy during Jim Crow* charts this generosity across her lifespan and afterward through her agents and her estate. It challenges deeply held assumptions that continue to inform scholarly inquiry and public perception of philanthropy today. They include that generosity is strictly a numbers game and a matter of scale; that philanthropy is the singular domain of the social elite; that women's giving is grounded in leisure and inheritance; and that whites are the primary agents of philanthropy and blacks are mainly its recipients. This book provides a different view of who counts as a philanthropist and what counts as philanthropy in the discourse dominated by the works on and perspectives of white wealthy elites. It reclaims and names black women as philanthropists using Walker as their exemplar.

## Madam C. J. Walker's Gospel of Giving

With few exceptions, the historiography on Walker has prioritized her entrepreneurial achievements in beauty culture and has rarely placed philanthropy at the center of her story.[3] Walker's philanthropy has mostly been addressed through tangential references or momentary detours en route to other important ideas and arguments about black women, beauty culture, and black business.[4] Such sparse attention has left us with philanthropic anecdotes about her rather than analysis. Walker is generally known to have made numerous financial gifts to organizations serving the cause of black racial uplift during the tumultuous Jim Crow period and to have left a sizable estate with generous charitable provisions. Her 1911 pledge of $1,000 to the colored YMCA of Indianapolis and her last will and testament are two of the most frequently cited examples to document her giving.

Confining Walker's philanthropy to specific financial examples prevents us from seeing the whole because, although money was important, it was not the full extent. A broader notion of philanthropy as "voluntary action for the public good" places Madam Walker's activities in a more appropriate context.[5] In the African American experience, philanthropy did not originate in wealth, but rather in resourceful efforts to meet social needs in the face of overwhelming societal constraints and impositions. It was less concerned with the exact form of gift giving than with the intent and appropriateness of the gift in responding to need. These distinctions evolved from a historical experience in which racial and gender oppression were rampant and circumscribed every aspect of black people's daily lives. As a result, African American philanthropy is better defined as a medley of beneficent acts and gifts that address someone's needs or larger social purposes that arise from a collective consciousness and shared experience of humanity.[6]

In this context, limiting our understanding of Madam Walker's philanthropy to the aforementioned regularly cited financial gifts fails to show the depth and breadth of her giving then and why it remains important today. It obscures her larger significance and casts her in a light all by herself because of the moniker "first self-made female millionaire." This distancing removes her from the broader normative giving structures among black women and African Americans more generally, from which she emerged and alongside whom she gave. Walker knew why and how she gave, and a particular statement she wrote in a 1914 letter made this clear: "I am unlike your white friends who have waited until they were rich and then help but have in proportion to my success, I have reached out and am helping others."

Through this sentence, Walker meant to clarify the context for a $300 gift she was planning to make to a school that had attracted national attention and her admiration for its educational work. She offered $50 each for five students and $50 for general operations. Around that time, average tuition was approximately $98 per pupil, so this gift could have alleviated half the cost of attendance for its beneficiaries, who would then earn the rest of their keep in other ways. In earlier correspondence, the school's principal and chief fundraiser had cast doubt on the utility of her prospective gift and suggested that more money would be required to help the cause. Urging donors to upgrade their gifts to higher levels was a common practice among organizations reliant on donations and, indeed, is considered a best practice in modern philanthropic fundraising. To Walker, however, it was insulting. In that moment, she was offering support and felt that the principal essentially told her it was not good enough.[7]

Walker was making about $3,000 per month, which was a far cry from the average American worker's annual wage of $800 at the time and even further from the $2 she had when she had first migrated to St. Louis twenty-five years earlier.[8] She had far more than most black women, but her resources were still finite. She explained to the principal, "I thought by giving scholarships . . . I was not only helping the student[s] but the school as well. If these scholarships do not help the school I have missed my mark."[9] She stated that she could not cover the full cost of attendance for five students but had hoped that $50 each would be useful. Later in the letter, she referred to an ongoing conversation about the school's adopting her beauty culture curriculum to prepare students to work in her professional field.[10] Walker offered that if the school agreed and the program was successful, "I could not only give hundreds of dollars . . . but [t]housands of dollars."[11] She wanted the principal to understand both the limits and the potential of her financial support because, while she aimed to do more, she had to start with what she had at the time.

She did not have the wealth of some of the school's other donors, but her emerging success story of rising from the depths of a southern plantation system adorned the pages of the black press frequently largely because of her own fierce marketing prowess. She had already defined herself in a segregated beauty culture marketplace within a larger discriminatory economy not designed for her success, and so correcting the principal's misperception of her was easy, though annoying. Her letter described the Walker Company as being large, but she noted that its increase in size had incurred greater expenses. The implication was for the fundraiser not to assume that she had unlimited means. The fact that the fundraiser was Booker T. Washington and the school was Tuskegee Institute made the need for correction even more urgent. She revered Washington, found his story to be inspirational, and would later remark that the grief and regret she felt by his death in 1915 surpassed that felt for any other person in her life—family or friend.[12] It was important to her that he really understood her and treat her as she expected to be treated.

Attempting to upgrade the gift was not unreasonable and was part of Washington's long view of how to do fundraising. In his 1901 autobiography, *Up from Slavery*, he had recounted the importance of patience and continuous cultivation in successful fundraising, noting that the $50,000 he eventually received from white railroad magnate Collis P. Huntington started with $2 given years before.[13] Washington was well aware of Walker's $1,000 gift made to build the colored Senate Avenue YMCA in Indianapolis three years earlier. He celebrated that gift when Walker spoke at his National Negro Business League annual meeting the year before. And when he visited Indianapolis in 1913 for the grand opening of that same YMCA building, Walker hosted his stay at her home, accommodations that the local black newspaper described as unsurpassed in terms of "elegance, comfort, and convenience."[14] Further, she had already spent time on the Tuskegee campus. So the two were not strangers, but Walker felt the need to clarify further.

When Walker pointed out she was not like Washington's "white friends," she was referring to a leading member of Tuskegee's board, the steel magnate Andrew Carnegie, who had single-handedly seeded Tuskegee's endowment with $600,000.[15] Further, John D. Rockefeller, Julius Rosenwald, and several major white millionaire industrialists had cast their philanthropic favor upon Washington and Tuskegee. These donors' gifts were regularly touted and criticized in the media of the day. In his autobiography, Washington had been clear that what looked like mere favor to others had required serious labor on his part to obtain. It had taken Washington years to cultivate Carnegie's interest. That said, Walker had no intention of competing with such donors or even being like them—she could not anyway. She genuinely valued the education Tuskegee provided and wanted to support it. She even modeled the curriculum at her own beauty school after it. More practically, she knew that Washington's blessing of her work was a political stamp of approval that carried favor in the black business world and black community. So, when Washington responded to Walker nearly three weeks later and declined her offer of curriculum by citing his board's disapproval of the idea, it was undoubtedly disappointing. She would eventually overcome that objection and secure Tuskegee's support on the matter. For now, the victory was in regard to how Washington was to view both her donations and her role as a donor. Washington, who had previously affirmed the value of "small gifts" even while pursuing the larger ones, conceded to Walker that "What you send will certainly help [the students] in a most satisfactory and appreciable way."[16] Like many other donors who initially rejected all or part of Washington's solicitations, Walker would subsequently give more to Tuskegee at higher levels, but on her own conditions and within her own time frame. In this moment, she had made Washington explicitly affirm his respect for who she was as a donor and the value of this gift.[17] She donated on her own terms and, in the process, she articulated what I call her *gospel of giving* that claimed her brand of black women's generosity as a distinctive American tradition that demands our attention.

The differences Walker noted about herself to Washington were not idiosyncrasies. They were indicative of an ethos of giving and sharing among African American women that had developed over time in response to their treatment and conditions under slavery and Jim Crow. As an approach to generosity, Walker's gospel of giving was grounded in this tradition, diverse in scope, and gradually unfolded. In this context, our view of Walker as an entrepreneur who happened to be charitable changes to one as a significant

American philanthropist who applied her generosity to the needs of her race and gender, as she understood them, through the means available to her at any given time, which eventually included entrepreneurship and wealth. This approach can be best understood as having emerged out of her experiences as a poor, black, female migrant from the Jim Crow South dependent on a robust philanthropic infrastructure of black civil society institutions and black women in the Midwest who cared for and mentored her and enabled her to become a financially independent yet community-minded donor and entrepreneur.

Walker took the example of her black female mentors and translated it into a gospel of giving based on three tenets: (1) give as you can to be helpful to others, (2) spare no useful means that may be helpful to others, and (3) give more as your means increase to help others. Walker had learned and begun practicing the first tenet of this gospel of giving in St. Louis, and she applied the second and third tenets later through her agents and her company, which she created and operated to pursue commercial and philanthropic goals concurrently. These goals included improving black women's personal hygiene and appearance; increasing their access to vocational education, beauty culture careers, and financial independence; and promoting social bonding and activism among her agents through Walker clubs.

In her own words to Washington, Walker effectively staked her position in the philanthropic landscape of early-twentieth-century America. She directly told him—and now us—not to focus on the prevailing white philanthropists of the day and their approaches to philanthropic giving in order to understand her—and black women by extension—but to look at her directly. This book takes such a view and argues that Madam C. J. Walker was not simply a charitable entrepreneur, but rather a great African American and American philanthropist who practiced a distinctive racialized and gendered approach to giving that simultaneously relieved immediately felt needs in her community and thwarted the systemic oppression of the Jim Crow regime—thus making her a historical progenitor of today's black philanthropy.

As previously discussed, African American philanthropy has historically found expression through a medley of channels because of an expanded definition and practice of what constitutes giving. Walker is useful for examining implications of this definition because she laid claim to both the more easily recognizable forms of financial charitable giving to organizations *and* to black women's activist community work focused on racial uplift, which included various types of voluntary actions, programs, and services. Walker deployed monetary and nonmonetary gifts, such as time, but she also gave employment, education, pride in personal appearance, inspiration, food, and tangible goods. Consequently, her company, schools, agents and Walker clubs, and life story stood alongside her time and money as key philanthropic resources put in service to racial uplift. She expanded the ways in which she gave according to the growth in means she experienced. Her last will and testament then became a tool for ensuring that these gifts were continued in their various forms and were complemented by new ones, such as real estate and provisions for the proper and dignified burial of family and friends. After her death in 1919, Walker's legacy accrued significant meaning as the Walker Company and Walker clubs used it to inculcate philanthropic values into sales agents, beauty-school students, and customers. Her legacy was, however, larger than Walker employees could ever imagine as African Americans, especially black women, embraced Walker as a cultural hero whose life story was a gift of inspiration to successive generations—one that refuted Jim Crow's racist and sexist narratives about black life and potential.

Her gifts position Walker as a significant early-twentieth-century American philanthropist who sought to inspire others by modeling giving and philanthropic sensibilities in support of individual development, racial uplift, and social change oriented around black women. She used the means available to her to give donations that made opportunity and hope accessible to everyday African Americans so they could fulfill their potential in spite of Jim Crow America's horrific and unfair circumstances; which, in turn, moved the country closer toward its professed ideals. To be sure, her philanthropy had practical value for her company as well. It helped her gain access to leading social and political circles of influence in black America and positioned her favorably among her customer base. For Walker, however, business and philanthropy were not in tension, as our twenty-first-century sensibilities might lead us to suspect. The presence of multiple motivations and effects need not discount a larger orientation toward generosity and helping others, and this book explores such a relationship.

Walker's gospel of giving was vital to her identity as a woman. It was through her philanthropy that she blended her identity as a churchwoman, clubwoman, race woman, fraternal woman, and businesswoman with that of being a mother and a friend. Through her giving, Walker expressed her greatest aspirations for herself, her race, and her gender. She affirmed the dignity and humanity of African American men, women, and children by directly and indirectly providing much-needed social services and economic and educational opportunities so they could navigate a treacherous racialized and gendered landscape. Through her philanthropy, she connected working-class black women to each other through associationalism to bond and leverage their collective power in support of a better quality of life for themselves, their families, and their communities. She affirmed her ties with family, friends, and community by making provisions for continuity in their care after her death. Together, these actions created a philanthropy that enabled Walker to celebrate social relationships and define her public role and voice in the liberation of black women and all African Americans.

As a result, Madam C. J. Walker is a philanthropic foremother of black generosity as we know and understand it today. She did not create African American philanthropy, but she *embodied*—and, therefore, represents—a significant historical culmination of major threads of African American philanthropic practice as they were evolving in the late nineteenth and early twentieth centuries. Her approach was distinct from the dominant racialized and gendered paradigms of the rich white male and female philanthropists of her era, while being representative of black women's norms of giving. Consequently, when told in this manner, her story provides a historical window for viewing and documenting the deep historical rootedness of black women's philanthropy as it existed then and as it is practiced today. It expands our knowledge of her giving by integrating investigation of her financial gifts and generosity with her associational networks and business operations. It builds on our knowledge of the causes she supported by contextualizing in greater depth the motivations and influences behind her giving. In the process, the influence of race, class, and gender on the practices of giving is exposed, so that by understanding Madam Walker's philanthropy more fully, we better understand African American women's philanthropy; and by better comprehending black women in this manner, the history of American philanthropy becomes enlarged, clearer, and more complete.

## Madam C. J. Walker and Philanthropy Scholarship

It is certainly tempting to compare Walker to John D. Rockefeller, Andrew Carnegie, and other white male contemporaries to contextualize her philanthropy in the early twentieth century.[18] Scholars and donors have viewed Carnegie, for instance, as the archetypal philanthropist of the era, and his presence and activities have been historical markers for the evolution of philanthropy in America.[19] The comparison is problematic because it yields specious conclusions. When Walker is compared to Carnegie, she emerges either as a great exemplar of his philosophy of "a gospel of wealth" because she felt a responsibility to use her affluence to help the less fortunate or as a poor contrast because her total giving was an infinitesimal fraction of that of Carnegie.[20] In addition, Walker's sense of obligation to others and commitment to philanthropy did not originate with her acquisition of wealth; it was inculcated and meaningfully acted on earlier in her life when she had meager resources, and it expanded over time.

Or instead of Carnegie, we might turn to New York's Olivia Sage (widely known as Mrs. Russell Sage), the prototypical female donor of the period, to contextualize Walker.[21] Walker and Sage were contemporaries as wealthy female philanthropists who used their money to support social and educational causes. This juxtaposition falls short equally because, although they shared the same gender, Sage's inheritance, race, and class gave her a starkly different historical experience that does not explain or relate to Walker as a black woman or a philanthropist. Unlike Sage, Walker *created*—rather than inherited—her wealth to rise out of poverty. Furthermore, she was still black and female, a distinctive position in American history. We must understand her specific social experience—along with its historical consequences—on its own terms.

Walker's lack of similarity to the most widely known models of philanthropy of her day has caused her own legacy of generosity to be obscured at worst or only partially recognized at best. As an individual who, for generations, has been publicly known as "the first self-made *female* millionaire" and who gave to many charitable causes, Walker is, ironically, missing from the major histories of philanthropy and public conversations driving giving today. She does not fit the philanthropic mold crafted by media, scholars, and donors alike to explain philanthropy and identify it when seen because she was a black female who lived during a historical period not associated with the agency of African Americans or women. Instead, a narrative has evolved today that African Americans were mostly recipients of philanthropy by whites and not agents of it themselves. Such constant portrayal of African Americans as having great philanthropic need reinforces the idea that they have a tradition of being *helped* but not a tradition of *helping*. The resultant typecasting compounds the strength of limited elite definitions of philanthropy and perpetuates the cycle of obscurity for Walker and other donors of color like Clara Brown (1800–1885), Thomy LaFon (1810–93), Colonel John McKee (c. 1821–1902), Annie Malone (1869–1957), and Sarah Spencer Washington (1889–1953), to name a few.[22]

Leading scholarship on the history of philanthropy exacerbates these problems for reviewing a donor like Madam Walker. Major historical works in this area from the past few decades have not significantly engaged women or people of color as philanthropic agents or have done so in limited ways. For instance, Walker is included in compendium works on American philanthropy, such as encyclopedias and almanacs.[23] In such instances, it is very important that she appears alongside the more storied white philanthropists of America as part of the narrative, but typically without the kinds of historical and cultural contexts that explain what she represents beyond the trope of the wealthy giving to the poor. In addition, numerous biographies have taken up the lives of the best-known white male philanthropists in ways that offer little insight into Walker or anyone beyond such narrowly prescribed slices of elite giving based on wealth.[24]

In other cases, Walker is absent altogether, especially in synthetic texts or those that historicize philanthropy across time periods or within her era.[25] As a cultural, political, economic, and social force, American philanthropy is frequently presented as a combination of the "big money" philanthropy of the wealthy elite (especially through foundations) and the small giving of the American masses. This perspective is helpful in many ways for illuminating some larger developments in philanthropy over time, but it limits the ability to locate within it Walker specifically and African Americans more generally. Walker would not qualify as an elite giver by such standards because her financial gifts were not of sufficient magnitude to pass a threshold defined as hundreds of thousands to millions of dollars. Further, although she did make several "small gifts," the overall arc of her giving exceeded the capacity of millions of everyday Americans regardless of their race, gender, or class. So, with "big money philanthropy" residing on one end of the spectrum of American philanthropy's historical narrative and mass or retail giving existing at the other, Madam C. J. Walker falls short of the threshold for the former and exceeds that of the latter, leaving her floating unseen somewhere in the middle.

Similarly, the history of women's philanthropy has not left much room for a woman like Walker because the elite and middle-class white women featured in it had a fundamentally contrasting relationship to philanthropy that was differently circumscribed by gender, being derived from leisure and inheritance and boosted by racial and economic advantages simply beyond the realm of possibility for black women. This historiography has, indeed, helped us understand how some white women traditionally utilized their philanthropic gifts of time, skills, and money to forge power structures outside their domestic spheres that paralleled men's private and public spaces of paid labor and politics. Doing so allowed them to assert themselves in public and quasi-public realms to generate social and political change. Pursuing their own philanthropic agendas and engaging in gendered approaches to institution building enabled them to overcome previous exclusion from specific arenas, such as the arts and social welfare, and assume leading roles in some of the nation's top museums and social movements.[26]

Other work in this space has charted the influence of gender and class on shaping political and social reform and deconstructed the complexity of women's evolving identities and self-actualization through their benevolent work in associations.[27] Various types of women's associations and spaces, such as exchange networks and marketplaces in the antebellum and post–Civil War eras have been explored, as have the rise and fall of women's associations in the Progressive Era. Biographies have placed at the center the philanthropic lives of women such as Abby Aldrich Rockefeller, Olivia Sage, Alva Vanderbilt Belmont, and Mary Elizabeth Garrett, who, as contemporaries of Madam Walker, made tremendous contributions to the arts, social services, education, the environment, and women's suffrage.[28] But even as this scholarship carved out the philanthropic roles and influence of women, it was inordinately focused on the endeavors of white middle- and upper-class women. Further, these women married into or inherited the wealth that they later distributed philanthropically, and they understood their own generosity through the lens of leisure. Consequently, their models, though challenging of deeply held notions about who engages in philanthropy, still do not fit Walker—as an independent business owner who worked her entire life and whose philanthropy was not beholden to any of her three husbands—or deepen our intellectual engagement with the women she represents.[29] Walker's experiences as an entrepreneur further distanced her from these women by placing her in different relationships to wealth, to the economy, and to the masculine spaces of commerce and politics.

If we think that the literature exclusively on African American philanthropy would offer the relief we seek and bring Madam Walker's giving into clear view, we would be surprisingly mistaken; it has not engaged her either. This oversight is due largely to its focus on the collective rather than the individual—that is, on the institutional contexts and communal practices of giving rather than particular givers. It has raised to the fore the institutions and social movements that created the kinds of social change that we understand as philanthropic in the black experience but has placed little emphasis on the individuals who funded and drove those institutions and movements. Considerable emphasis has been placed on churches, fraternities, sororities, fraternal orders, voluntary associations, women's clubs, and advocacy and social service organizations as vital philanthropic institutions in the black community. But although this scholarship similarly contributes to the problem, it has the distinction of informing a solution.

On the whole, a very small, multidisciplinary and exploratory body of literature has begun to explore the history of African American philanthropy. It has not yet coalesced into an intellectual field itself, but strong foundations were laid down in the 1990s that remain relevant today. Historian Darlene Clark Hine's "'We Specialize in the Wholly Impossible': The Philanthropic Work of Black Women" was an early treatment of black clubwomen's work as philanthropy. Economist Emmett Carson's *A Hand Up: Black Philanthropy and Self-Help in America* was an early attempt at a brief synthetic history of African American philanthropy from colonial times into the 1970s. Historian Adrienne Lash Jones's "Philanthropy in the African American Experience" went further by sketching out a periodization of black philanthropy as it evolved across four historical eras unique to the black experience. These works had the distinction of not merely describing black philanthropic action across time but attempting to historicize and theorize it. Subsequent work by historians Bettye Collier-Thomas and Iris Carlton-LaNey offered gendered analyses of black women's community work and healthcare giving as philanthropy through the purview of the fields of black education and black social welfare rather than philanthropic studies.[30]

*Madam C. J. Walker's Gospel of Giving* is indebted to these scholars in particular because their work provided three important constructs on which it builds. First, they recognized African American philanthropy's origins in West Africa and its importance as part of black adjustment to the Atlantic

World, which positions it as being inclusive of, but larger than, reactions to what happened to black people in America. Second, they expanded definitions of philanthropy grounded in the historical circumstances of the African American experience, which provided the proper scope for making Walker's giving visible on her own terms. And third, they situated black philanthropy within the collective consciousness of African Americans, which meant that giving was not just a skill or an activity but a phenomenon fundamentally anchored within *black identity* and *black bodies*. This last construct, in particular, led me to black women's history in an effort to bridge the gap between the philanthropy scholarship and Madam C. J. Walker. Because of their unique historical experience and social position in the United States of America, black women are the quintessential philanthropists in this tradition. Their history and ways of being offer the best entrée into it. A problem, however, is that philanthropy as a term or concept has not been regularly applied to black women as historical agents despite some important specific efforts to do so.

## Reclaiming and Naming Black Women as Philanthropists

In 1894, while the settled migrant Sarah Breedlove was being mentored by the black churchwomen and clubwomen of her St. Louis community, black journalist, activist, and intellectual Gertrude E. H. Bustill Mossell of Philadelphia published *The Work of the Afro-American Woman*, which has been described in recent times as the *When and Where I Enter* of the 1890s.[31] She argued for a broad depiction of black women's work that included achievement in the professions, ministry, the arts, and business. Mossell dedicated more than half the volume's title essay to philanthropy, which she saw as a particular form of black women's work: "Perhaps the effort that is most unique and yet entirely consistent with the character of the race has been done along the line of philanthropic work . . . [many] of our women have turned aside from laboring for their individual success and given thought to the condition of the weak and suffering classes."[32] Mossell's articulation of philanthropy included women's efforts in both starting and running missions, orphanages, schools, hospitals, colleges, and working girls' clubs, as well as in funding the same through living and estate gifts. She lifted up Ida B. Wells as the exemplar: "Perhaps the greatest work in philanthropy yet accomplished by any woman of the race is that undertaken and so successfully carried out at the present hour by Miss Ida B. Wells."[33] She highlighted the way Wells used her journalistic writing and her voice through lectures to raise global consciousness about the evils of lynching and facilitated organized responses for reform.

Mossell's use of Wells, a woman she had already discussed earlier in the text as a successful journalist, indicated that she did not think of philanthropist as an either-or category set apart from these other fields and arenas of black women's labor, but one embedded across them all. It was accessible to all black women. According to Mossell, this work required no education or wealth and was largely "carried on by faith."[34] Further, while she saw the era's new but limited educational and industrial opportunities for black woman as portals conducive to philanthropic engagement, she also laid claim to a deeper, historical, and cultural tradition, stating about black women that "They have shown that the marvelous loving kindness and patience that is recorded of the native women of Africa [was] not crushed out by the iron heel of slavery but still wells up in their bosoms and in this brighter day overflows in compassion for the poor and helpless of their own down-trodden race."[35] This idea that generosity and compassion traversed the Atlantic along with other forms of African cultural genius within black bodies via the slave trade is astounding in light of the conditions under which the enslaved suffered and grounds black people's philanthropic expression in something more enduring than their North American horrors. Mossell closed her celebration of Wells with a push toward the universal by asking "Who shall say that such a work . . . shall not place her in the front rank of philanthropists, not only of the womanhood of this race, but among those laborers of all ages and all climes?"[36] It is fitting that this observation about the deep rootedness of black women's philanthropy—and the importance of naming it as such—comes from the annals of black women's intellectual history, another vibrant field that was initially overlooked and is challenging to trace. But Mossell's observations were not meaningfully taken up by scholars for another hundred years.

At the beginning of the twenty-first century, a handful of historians directly and eloquently explored the specific connection between black women and philanthropy. Darlene Clark Hine identified black women, mostly church and clubwomen, as philanthropists by connecting their quest for racial uplift and respectability to philanthropy as a vehicle for upholding virtuous womanhood. She positioned the National Association of

Colored Women as the "institutionalization of black women's voluntarism and philanthropy" and described black women's philanthropy as reproductive work because it reclaimed and restored downtrodden black individuals as agents in their own lives and in the larger ongoing struggle for freedom. Bettye Collier-Thomas highlighted the womanist nature of black women's philanthropy, observing that it was generally for the race, but expressly for black women, grounded in their collective consciousness and central to their identities and positionality. She located black women's philanthropy across numerous sites, including schools, clubs, churches, hospitals, and orphanages. Later, she pinpointed black women's foreign and domestic missionary agendas inside black religious denominations as philanthropy. Joan Marie Johnson extended black women's philanthropy even further through lodges, parent-teacher associations, and social clubs and related fundraising as "the most striking aspect of black women's philanthropy." She further conjoined it to black women's advocacy and activism work, particularly in relation to lynching. And Tiffany Gill asserted that philanthropy was central to the emerging professional identities of twentieth-century black women beauty culturists. She associated it with their activism for civil rights. As noted, however, these are the exceptions. The specific work done by these significant scholars to claim philanthropy on behalf of black women has not been meaningfully and consistently advanced by the broader field. Instead, black women's history has preferred other descriptive terms and valuable frameworks for interpreting black women, which are useful for this investigation of Walker, but not wholly sufficient.[37]

For instance, the political and social work of black clubwomen has largely been interpreted as a form of activism in relation to the state.[38] In these works, black women's spaces and activities—namely clubs and federations—were bases from which to navigate systems of oppression and to advocate for governmental action and protections, such as women's suffrage.[39] This activism was also asserted within black institutional contexts and communities to leverage black women's power in managing gender authority through auxiliaries and conventions in places such as the black church.[40] Such work cut across class divisions as black middle-class and working-class women advocated for themselves and their communities on the basis of their own understandings of respectability and racial uplift. It also spanned every geography that black women traversed, whether northern, midwestern, or southern. What is more, these political and social activists not only worked at the local, state, or national levels but extended themselves and their concerns globally in ways that connected the African American struggle for freedom with that of people of color around the world.[41] These works and this activist lens provide important ways of seeing black women as agents who staked claims for their own humanity and citizenship in the face of seemingly impossible odds.

Community work or uplift is another framework for understanding black women.[42] In this view, black clubwomen, churchwomen, educators, and others built community institutions of various kinds at various levels—local, state, regional, national, even international—to address their communities' social needs created by discrimination and racial hatred. Sometimes referred to as institution building or reform, this work included the creation, funding, and maintenance of schools, orphanages, old folks' homes, homes for girls, kindergartens and day nurseries, mothers' clubs, settlement houses, medical care facilities, and a full array of educational, cultural, and developmental programming offered through the same spaces. Their clubs, churches, and other voluntary associations, such as fraternal orders, frequently served as the hubs for these endeavors. Accordingly, this community work and activism were not mutually exclusive. Indeed, the former frequently gave rise to the latter, as public resources were sought to sustain programs and services when local community or other donor resources were exhausted. The community work perspective has recognized how the depth of black women's identities as women and mothers informed such work and how they publicly asserted themselves in numerous ways. As a form of black women's labor, it was integrated into how they thought of themselves, their responsibilities to others, and how they organized their time. The work was a continuation of their employment outside the home and their household labor.[43]

Last, black women's fundraising prowess has been recognized in their mastery of generating financial resources for their racial uplift work across generations.[44] Through raffles, galas, baby contests, sports competitions, balls, fairs, bake sales, bazaars, craft-making sales, penny drives, and direct solicitation of individuals and foundations, black women successfully raised money to support their institution-building, reform, and activist efforts throughout the nineteenth and twentieth centuries—but not without cost. It is important to remember that during Walker's time, fundraising was an important skill but also a nuisance. For black women like Mary McLeod

Bethune, Nannie Helen Burroughs, Charlotte Hawkins Brown, and Jane Edna Hunter, fundraising was exhausting, never-ending, anxiety-producing work, especially when they had to step out into white communities to do it. Hunter once remarked to Burroughs, "Somehow I wish that you, Mary Bethune and myself could give up raising money and could devote all our strengths and spiritual life to the building of God's kingdom. This money getting business destroys so much of one's real self, that we cannot do our best, feeling that we need money all of the time."[45] Fundraising was a stark reminder of the dependency of askers and the authority of donors, particularly when it came to black female solicitors interacting with white donors. John D. Rockefeller's term for fundraisers, "honorable beggars," emphasized these inherent social relations and tensions.[46] So, although fundraising is a vital part of philanthropy and may be a useful starting point for exploring black women's philanthropy, it has serious limitations. Focusing on it obscures the deeper values and moral imagination that drove the need for funding in the first place and that defined the larger ends to which the resources were put on behalf of the race.

*Madam C. J. Walker's Gospel of Giving* reaffirms Mossell's conclusions and embraces and advances the insights of scholars of black women by coalescing the full range of black women's voluntary actions under the rubric of philanthropy. It is not an argument for replacing activism, community work, and fundraising, which were firmly entrenched in black women's lives; on the contrary, it is a powerful addition. Applying the constructs of philanthropy and philanthropist to black women amalgamates their diverse voluntary actions regardless of the social, political, or communal realms in which they occurred. It grounds these efforts in—and gives access to—black women's moral imaginations as expressions of their complex intersectional identities. It casts broader light on their overall work that moves them beyond the existing depictions of simply being recipients of white people's charitable giving, or as fundraisers dependent on other people's responsiveness to their solicitations, or even as activists making demands on the social and political systems controlling their lives.

Most important, it makes claims for black women's generosity in ways that *activist, community worker,* and *fundraiser* simply do not. It bridges the gap between narrowly focused self-help within segregated black communities and a wider notion of public and common good for all American society, even the world. It extends mutual aid beyond the boundaries of family and neighborhood to the brotherhood and sisterhood of humankind.[47] In so doing, it gives voice to the heart of generosity at the core of black women's embodied actions, commitments, and identities. It unifies the full range of black women's *intersectional philanthropy*—the diverse means, methods, and motivations through which black women redefined womanhood, uplifted their race, and transformed a country.

When Madam Walker is viewed through the limitations of the aforementioned philanthropy scholarship, which has centered on elite white male and female models of charitable giving, she appears either as rare and imitative or interesting but inconsequential. But when viewed through the lens of black women's history, her giving presents as ubiquitous yet distinctive, powerful, and transformative. For Madam Walker, her agents, and her peers, these were not auxiliary actions engaged in only when leisure time and surplus resources allowed—they were fundamental aspects of their daily lives and identities regardless of wealth or station.

For the past half-century, scholars have argued that black women need to be taken seriously as historical agents who have contributed their whole selves—physically, intellectually, emotionally, and spiritually—to American life.[48] In putting forward Madam C. J. Walker's gospel of giving, I apply the same argument to black women as philanthropists by tracing the life Walker lived to unveil the roots, meanings, and expressions of giving in this tradition.

## Madam Walker's Philanthropic Biography

This book presents a critical examination and excavation of Madam Walker's philanthropic actions by using historical methods and archival research. Walker did not publish texts about her giving as did a small number of her white philanthropic contemporaries.[49] Walker biographer and descendent A'Lelia Bundles has suggested that perhaps Walker—who worked and traveled constantly to build her business right up until a few weeks before her death—was too busy to write about her philanthropy in such a manner.[50] Or it may have been the case that giving and sharing were so ubiquitous and widely understood in her community that writing about it seemed unnecessary. Regardless of the reasons, if she did not write extensively about her giving, she certainly lived it. She spoke about it in public venues, she referred to it in company marketing promotions and internal communications, and she corresponded with her attorney, Freeman B. Ransom, about it. In essence, her life was her treatise on philanthropy. Consequently, my analysis of Walker's correspondences and speeches, company records and marketing materials, newspaper accounts, and other primary sources enables this story of her gospel of giving and situates her within the broader philanthropic landscape of the early twentieth century. The result is a philanthropic biography focused on giving across Walker's lifespan as well as its legacy thereafter.

Studying Madam Walker's philanthropy presented an intriguing twist on the typical archival challenges that accompany historical inquiry into the black experience. First, the simple illegality—by statute or custom under slavery and Jim Crow—of black assembly, literacy, and association prevented many black lives, organizations, and activities from being documented because they had to move in secrecy or under constraints. Further, problems of storage and maintenance over time and across generations sometimes led to the catastrophic loss of surviving documents from natural disasters or man-made destruction (e.g., fires, floods, tornados, inadvertent and intentional disposal). The powerful are better prepared to maintain and bequeath archives to posterity than the powerless, which has the effect of transmitting their prejudices to the future too. Along with preserving the substance of memory, archives preserve the prevailing power structures of the places and times they represent by privileging certain people and perspectives. Consequently, scholars who have engaged the black experience, particularly that of black women, have had to contend with the absences from the historical record of source materials that are either missing or fragmented, or biased when present. Jenny Shaw has observed that such absences "proliferate as silences" that further conceal black voices and lives. By engaging the lived experience of black people, historians have been able to overcome, or at least to challenge, such archival absences, silences, and other limitations. Shaw's solution, in part, required "reading around [her subjects'] experiences" and "reading [primary and secondary] sources alongside one another." Marisa Fuentes has similarly demonstrated how black lives and experiences can be reconstructed, which in its own right is a form of not only recovery but also protest and subversion.[51]

In a similar vein, this work is one of protest against the prevailing definitions of philanthropy that obscure the generosity of black people. Walker left behind a voluminous archive, and elements of her philanthropy were well documented through receipts, letters, memos, and other records. In this situation, it is not necessarily the case that Walker's archives are incomplete, fragmented, or skewed because of the power dynamics of their creator, it is that the leading definitions of philanthropy, during Walker's time and our own, were not nimble or imaginative enough to accommodate her (or black women's) philanthropic vision, resources, and approaches as being constitutive of giving. The question was not so much what is missing from her archives—though it was certainly far from complete—because it offers more than many collections by and about black women. The question became, How do I read and interpret what was present?

The answer required tools and perspectives from outside my field of philanthropic studies. A quest for Walker's philanthropy was not hindered for lack of sources, but for lack of appropriate definitional contexts to read against and to guide interpretation. Borrowing from Fuentes's assertion that "history is a production as much as an accounting of the past, and that our ability to recount has much to do with the conditions under which our subjects lived," I constructed the appropriate lenses for viewing Walker's lived experiences that would bring to light what was hidden in plain sight.[52] Because the financial dimensions of Walker's giving were so readily identifiable and documented—and, therefore, focused on and written about by others—a comprehensive view of her philanthropy has remained unseen until now. I used frameworks from across historical fields—including black women's, black business, and black social welfare—to create a lens for interpreting Walker as philanthropist through her words, motivations, relationships, and actions as manifested in her daily life. Through this study, historians' contention that attending to the lived experiences of marginalized subjects overcomes, or at least challenges, the inherent biases of archives, has also borne an interrogation of the constricting definitions that perpetuate the perspectives of the powerful over the powerless. The result is a view of Walker's philanthropic life not as one enriched by a set of leisurely activities engaged only when surplus resources availed themselves, but rather one grounded in the fierce urgency of the times and in the lifeblood of generosity itself.

This book is composed of six chapters, which explore in depth Walker's story through particular types of gifts she made while simultaneously illustrating the broader cultural contexts and philanthropic practices that informed black women's lives and giving. These giving practices were not

Walker's alone, for she was socialized into this mode of giving specifically by black women and generally by the cultural and religious ethos among African Americans that set expectations about one's responsibility to others and to the race. Although she did not originate them, Walker put her own stamp on these norms and amplified them through her unique personality, evolving resources, and national networks of women. The end result is an articulation not only of Walker's gifts but also of those of other black women as a long-standing, deeply rooted historical tradition of philanthropy that is alive and well today.

Chapter 1 presents the early life experiences that influenced Walker's sense of responsibility to others and informed her philanthropic life. It shows how she was socialized into respectability, a racial uplift ideology, generosity, and philanthropic giving by a group of black St. Louis church-women and clubwomen and how a robust black philanthropic social infrastructure enabled her to change her life course. By situating her within networks of women and the culture of the AME Church, chapter 1 reveals her formation of a moral imagination that integrated business and philanthropy, embraced particular causes, and forged diverse means for giving. Chapter 2 discusses the Walker Company as both a commercial and a philanthropic enterprise for giving opportunity to a people who were locked out of discriminatory labor markets and struggled to care for basic family needs. I argue that the opportunity for employment, in this context, became a philanthropic gift because of the broader private market and governmental failures that were deliberately negligent of African Americans and viciously acted to make their lives unnecessarily burdensome. The chapter studies the structure and practices of the Walker Company to reveal how she blended the philosophies of self-help and racial uplift into a brand of entrepreneurship that held commerce and philanthropy in a reciprocal relationship rather than in tension. It explains how the company effectively became a third "C" that Walker added to the church and the club as platforms for black women's racial uplift activities. The result created avenues of opportunity on a large scale for black women to develop financial independence and serve their race, and each other, along the way.

Chapter 3 focuses on Walker's gift of education through her national network of beauty schools as a model of urban industrial vocational education at the same time that Booker T. Washington's southern rural model of industrial education was prominent. Washington's approach has been critiqued as unsuccessful in addressing black educational needs despite its proliferation because it appeased the white South and focused on the fading agricultural economy. Walker's beauty schools, in contrast, offered an urban alternative for migrating black women to earn credentials, enabling their gainful employment in the emerging industrial economies of the North, Midwest, and South. This gift of education aligned Walker with other educator-philanthropists of her era, such as Mary McLeod Bethune, Lucy Laney, and Charlotte Hawkins Brown—whose schools she also funded. The chapter reinterprets the historical relationship between industrial philanthropy and black education and the value of industrial vocational education in urban black communities. Chapter 4 examines Walker's gift of activism. In a manner reflective of leading black women's clubs and fraternal organizations of the day, Madam Walker organized her agents into a national association to legitimize beauty culture as a profession and to enlist her agents in doing charity and advocacy work in their communities that would last after her death. The National Beauty Culturists' and Benevolent Association of Madam C. J. Walker Agents, Inc., developed a model of associationalism, ritualism, and activism that galvanized Walker agents to serve their communities and the cause of racial uplift. The chapter reviews Walker's unique ability to interact with black women across class differences within her own clubs and across others at the national level. Through her clubs and their rituals, Walker agents staked claims for themselves as respectable professionals, performed charitable works in black communities, and used their formidable numbers to speak out against lynching and Jim Crow.

Chapter 5 presents a range of material resources that Walker gave to black individuals and organizations as an expression of her generosity. Administered by her closest adviser, black attorney Freeman B. Ransom, these particular gifts reflected Walker's motivations for giving during a period of significant financial growth for her company in the early 1910s. Drawing insights from the types of gifts given and the kinds and locations of recipients supported, chapter 5 demonstrates how black women's philanthropy flowed through black communities around the country. As a result, social needs were met, and a national infrastructure of organizations and networks was gradually constructed to navigate the stigmas and debilitating effects of Jim Crow, and, eventually, dismantle the institution. Chapter 6 tells the full story of Walker's last will and testament, which has been used by scholars to document her generosity because of its numerous charitable provisions. To date, scholars have missed the discrepancy between Walker's intended charitable provisions and those actually executed by her daughter, Lelia, as executor.[53] Consequently, only one-tenth of Walker's estate ultimately went to charity rather than her intended one-third, a reduction explained in part by Walker's own exorbitant spending during her lifetime and that of her daughter afterward. Walker lived during a transitional period in which women's wills were rare—but becoming more common—and African American wills were historically restricted. Nevertheless, she used testamentary documents to navigate her social position with respect to race, class, and gender and asserted her identity as an honorable, respectable, God-fearing, and generous black female business owner under the absurdities and indignities of Jim Crow. They documented for succeeding generations how she wished to be remembered and signaled women's and African Americans' increasing use of testamentary tools to preserve their property rights.

The chapters of this book tell the story of the origins and evolution of one woman's generosity, but it was (and is) not her story alone. It is also the story of a people and how their generosity helped them navigate and ultimately overcome powerful and externally imposed constraints. Through this analysis, Madam C. J. Walker provides a window into the evolution of black women's philanthropy during the critical turn-of-the-century period, which set the stage for the coming civil-rights movement of the midtwentieth century and provides the historical grounding for giving by African Americans today.

# 1
## Making Madam C. J. Walker

I was considered a good washerwoman and
laundress. I am proud of that fact.
—Madam C. J. Walker, 1917[1]

In the history of no people has [the
washerwoman's] example been paralleled,
in no other figure in the Negro group can be
found a type measuring up to the level of this
philanthropic spirit in unselfish service.
—Carter G. Woodson, 1930[2]

In 1912 an interviewer from the *Indianapolis Freeman* newspaper visited
Madam C. J. Walker's home in the city. By this time, about seven years after
the founding of her business, Walker's wealth and fame were accelerating.
She earned up to $2,000 per month and valued her home and its adjacent
laboratory at $12,000. In her house adorned with the accoutrements of suc-
cess, Walker was reflective. She looked back over her forty-five years of life
and humble beginnings and told her visitor about the importance of early
experiences in shaping her generosity, particularly those from her time in
St. Louis. The paper reported, "The habit of giving long since became a part
of her. From her youth up she has felt to give—the widow's mite, at least,
when she could do no more. She speaks of giving as a joy—a result of a
Christian duty, as well as an inborn inclination. She holds the belief that
the Lord prospers her because of her giving."[3] Walker felt a responsibility to

God and a passion for her people that led her to be generous in spirit and deeds. These values were inculcated into her from an early age, shaping her moral imagination and the ways in which she gave to others.[4]

The moral imagination enables philanthropists to consider the suffering of others and name that suffering as a reality that needs to be changed. In the process, they imagine new realities in which that suffering is alleviated, and they are moved to take action to bring those visions into existence. An individual's moral imagination is shaped by many forces, including identity, ethnicity, culture, experience, political and historical context, and religious and moral values. Consequently, analysis of someone's philanthropic action provides insights into elements of that person's moral imagination. Several important factors influenced Madam C. J. Walker, but her philanthropy can be best understood as having emerged out of her experiences as a poor, black, female migrant moving around the South dependent on a robust philanthropic infrastructure of black civil society institutions and black women who cared for her during the most difficult period of her life. This story does not begin with Madam Walker, however, but rather with Sarah Breedlove.

## The Early Years of Sarah Breedlove

Sarah's first few breaths of life on December 23, 1867, were taken as a free person, unlike those of her parents, Owen and Minerva Breedlove, and her older siblings, who had been enslaved on the Burney plantation in Delta, Louisiana.[5] Having been freed from the bondages of slavery by a range of advocacy, military, presidential, and legislative actions—which included the antebellum Abolitionist movement, the Civil War from 1861 to 1865, President Abraham Lincoln's Emancipation Proclamation in 1863, and the states' ratification of the Thirteenth Amendment in 1865—Owen and Minerva were likely proud of the fact that their infant would not have to know the horrors of the US slave system as they had. Born free, Sarah Breedlove was set on a different trajectory than the nearly four million African Americans who were just beginning to breathe the new air of freedom. But even her hopeful parents likely never imagined what their newborn would achieve later in life.

Although their exact birthdates are unknown, Owen and Minerva had been part of the Burney plantation since 1847. Few details are known about their specific experiences there, but Louisiana was known for its particularly brutal form of slavery. In this context, Owen and Minerva had four children before Sarah—Louvenia, Alexander, James, and Owen Jr. Solomon was born two years after Sarah. Although marriages and other familial relationships were not recognized by the system of slavery, Owen and Minerva officially married early in their emancipation, along with thousands of other formerly enslaved people, because this essential relationship was recognized by the Bureau of Refugees, Freedmen, and Abandoned Lands (Freedmen's Bureau), the federal agency charged by Congress to help the mass of newly freed people. The Breedlove family was part of the Pollard Church of Delta, Louisiana, a Baptist church pastored by Reverend Curtis Pollard, a man who was a political leader in the reconstructed state government of Louisiana.[6]

Owen and Minerva did not have much time to enjoy their new freedom or their legally recognized marriage and family. Both died within a few years of Sarah's birth. Minerva died first. Owen remarried, but he also succumbed within a few years. By the age of seven, Sarah was orphaned and in the care of her older sister and brother-in-law, Louvenia and Jesse Powell.[7]

Sarah was born during a moment of freedom in US history commonly known as Reconstruction, but she had barely reached ten years of age before that new reality began to unravel at the hand of an avenging, belligerent, and resentful white South determined to restore order by retaking control of its state governments and returning African Americans to positions of subordination and peonage. The Civil War had ended, the enslaved people had been emancipated, and the bloodied yet preserved union was trying to piece itself back together. Four million freed people were trying to comprehend and execute their recently acknowledged liberties. A collection of massive governmental, religious, and philanthropic actions led to new policies and reforms toward the goal of engaging freed people as citizens.

The government ratified the Thirteenth (1865), Fourteenth (1868), and Fifteenth (1870) Amendments to the US Constitution and passed a series of Reconstruction Acts (1867), which abolished slavery, affirmed black citizenship, extended voting rights, and established military rule in the South to safeguard the black population and reinforce reforms. Black males were enfranchised and many black officials were elected to state and federal offices. The federal Freedmen's Bureau implemented a range of programs to aid blacks in areas related to housing, labor, health care, education, and participation in the court system. Black scholar and activist W. E. B. DuBois noted that the bureau had spent an estimated $18 million on the freedmen and called the effort "an extraordinary piece of work," but he viewed the effort as largely unsuccessful because of inherent structural flaws in its design and implementation.[8] Religious responses by white denominations involved missionary programs to provide educational, health, and social services to black people, including the establishment of schools and colleges. Philanthropic actions by whites also came out of the first formal foundations that would become important players in addressing education for the newly freed people, such as the Peabody Education Fund (1867) and the Slater Fund (1882).[9]

Black philanthropic responses were especially prevalent and were mostly led by women. After a long period of involvement in abolition and other forms of resistance, several black women and black women's organizations continued their establishment of initiatives and institutions to meet the needs of their people. They created churches, schools, colleges, old folks' homes, orphanages, businesses, social services, fraternal organizations, and a range of advocacy associations. Along with such organized efforts, many interpersonal practices of giving and sharing were staples in their survival mechanisms as they collaborated with each other to navigate the difficulties of life as free persons.[10] The dynamics of this period not only provided important context for the social, political, economic, and cultural environment into which Sarah was born, but also delimited the contours of the black experience in America for decades to come. The expansion of Jim Crow and the acceleration of migration placed a premium on the creation of black institutions. As a result, black women continued their institution-building and service-provision efforts well into the twentieth century.[11]

The situation for black people was dire during early Reconstruction. On the whole, they had no wealth, property, or education, and upwards of 90 percent were illiterate. Their family members had been dispersed by slavery across the South. They were legally freed, but that freedom had to be operationalized in an American society that was rebuilding itself. During Reconstruction, black people asserted their newly found freedom under the protection of twenty thousand federal troops stationed throughout the South. Historian Eric Foner has noted how the situation began to improve: "By the early 1870s, biracial democratic government, something unknown in American history, was functioning effectively in many parts of the South."

Before the war, black men could vote in only a small number of northern states, and black elected officials were nonexistent. After the war and because of Reconstruction, black men could vote and as many as two thousand black officials held elected office. As such historic gains were achieved, white Southerners began to feel powerless and resorted to terrorist tactics to protest the apparent rise of blacks to power. At least 10 percent of black elected officials were victims of threats and assaults, and at least thirty-five were murdered by the Ku Klux Klan, a white supremacist group founded in Tennessee in 1866 whose membership was swelling across the South. Groups such as the White Brotherhood and the Knights of the White Camelia added to the violence. Individual acts of violence evolved into mass mobs through which entire towns were devastated as blacks or their white sympathizers were run from their homes or lynched. In 1873 Colfax, Louisiana, a town less than two hundred miles from Sarah's home in Delta, was the site of a mass lynching in which more than fifty black militia members were killed by a white mob. Such violence along with the emergence of Jim Crow, local laws and statutes enacted by white Southerners to counteract the effects of Reconstruction, created hostile living conditions for black people and slowly pushed them into a dehumanized second-class citizenship with extraordinary restrictions on their rights, movements, and opportunities.[12]

On the heels of the 1876 election, the demise of Reconstruction was secured when political maneuverings led the new president, Rutherford B. Hayes, to recognize the Democrats' control of the South and discontinue Reconstruction efforts. The end of Reconstruction brought many changes for African Americans and would mark the beginning of what historian Rayford Logan called the nadir of African American history. Historian Kenneth Stampp further summed it up: "As for the Negroes, they would have to struggle for another century to regain what they had won—and then lost—in the years of radical reconstruction." For African Americans, the aftermath of Reconstruction's end resulted in an increase in violence and terror, political disenfranchisement, second-class citizenship, and denial of equal opportunity.[13]

For the members of the Breedlove family, these events were not distant occurrences. They were happening in their own community of Delta. The demise of Reconstruction in Louisiana began in 1871 as a result of a range of local reactionary activities by whites and increasingly difficult living conditions. With nearby lynchings, poor labor conditions, and boll weevil devastation of local crops, there was not much reason to stay in Delta. Sarah's parents were deceased and her older brothers had already gone to St. Louis, Missouri, in search of better opportunities. In 1878, at the age of eleven, Sarah left Delta with Louvenia and her husband Jesse for Vicksburg, Mississippi, just on the other side of the Mississippi River, in search of jobs and in flight from white terror, economic hardship, and a yellow fever outbreak. It was during her time in Vicksburg that Sarah's life course was changed by important events, some of which became hallmarks of the story Madam Walker would later tell audiences about her humble beginnings.[14]

During this time, young Sarah began working as a washerwoman, also called a laundress, in Vicksburg. More than thirty years later, this life as a washerwoman loomed large in the moral imagination of Madam Walker as evidenced by her use of it as a staple in her speeches. In a 1912 speech before Booker T. Washington's National Negro Business League, Madam Walker asserted, "I have been trying to get before you business people and tell you what I am doing. I am a woman that came from the cotton fields of the South; I was promoted from there to the wash-tub . . . and from there I promoted myself into the business of manufacturing hair goods and preparations." Having been a laundress was an essential part of Madam Walker's identity, and her experience of such laborious, low-wage work was the inspiration for a different life. The job served as a basis for Walker's personal narrative of ascent and as a constant reminder of the troubled state of employment for black women characterized by few options, horrendous working conditions, and meager remuneration. Working as a laundress was backbreaking labor. Laundresses spent the better part of the workday hunched over a tub of boiling water breathing in, and having their skin irritated by, the chemical fumes from cleaning agents used to sanitize clothing. Washerwomen typically gathered laundry loads from two or three white families on Mondays to begin the weeklong process of washing dozens upon dozens of sheets, towels, pillowcases, and clothing. This strenuous routine continued week after week, and Sarah seldom made more than $1.50 per day.[15]

Little is known about Sarah's washerwoman experience, but washerwomen were fixtures in black communities during the late nineteenth and early twentieth centuries. In 1890, 151,540 black women worked as washerwomen and their numbers increased to 218,227 by 1900.[16] Black washerwomen were cornerstone figures in their communities who labored with great love and sacrifice for their families and communities. Historically, they derived from enslaved women who maintained household duties for their masters' wives and from free women in the antebellum North who supplemented their husbands' diminished earning power through their labor. In the former case, enslaved washerwomen were heads of household whose family units were constantly shifting at the whims of their masters as a result of the selling and breeding of enslaved males. For the latter, free washerwomen were frequently the breadwinners because their husbands were locked out of labor unions and other trades. Tenuous as freedom was after Emancipation, washerwomen again became breadwinners, providing their families with money or food bartered for their services. As economic agents, they frequently took the lead in buying family homes, paying children's tuitions, supporting their husbands' professional training, and funding business capital for new enterprises that offered the hope of employment in the community. What is more, washerwomen regularly gave money to help the less fortunate despite their own great need. Although their numbers were plentiful at the turn of the century, their numbers would gradually decrease as the twentieth century began. More than a decade after Madam Walker's death in 1919, historian Carter G. Woodson lamented the black washerwoman as a vanishing figure in the rapid industrial, economic, and technological forces that automated her services. He further memorialized the black washerwoman: "In the history of no people has [the washerwoman's] example been paralleled, in no other figure in the Negro group can be found a type measuring up to the level of this philanthropic spirit in unselfish service." The black washerwoman's sacrificial toil and unbounded generosity made her the quintessential philanthropist among African Americans.[17]

Washerwomen's generosity was surpassed only by their creativity. Challenging work conditions and low wages made their lives difficult. To compensate, washerwomen and other black women domestic workers resorted to scavenging, borrowing, bartering, and pan toting in lieu of money.[18] These practices procured food, clothing, and other items desperately needed that the women shared among themselves to provide for their families. The social networks among working women catalyzed the creation of formal networks and institutions, such as churches, secret societies, mutual aid and benevolent organizations, labor unions, and political leagues.[19] That is, the highly educated, middle-class black clubwomen and churchwomen of the era were not the only black women organizing. These networks helped washerwomen and other working-class women support each other through sickness, tragedies, and other life challenges. Further, once the informal networks became formal organizations, they frequently offered death benefits and other forms of financial assistance leveraged from the dues paid by members. But such networks and organizations also helped working-class black women to speak out, become politically engaged, and advocate for themselves and their communities.[20]

For instance, washerwomen in Atlanta, Georgia, created *washing societies* in the late nineteenth century, and communities of washerwomen in other portions of the South engaged in public protest of their working conditions. In 1866 washerwomen in Jackson, Mississippi, protested their harsh labor conditions by organizing and informing the mayor that they were going to institute uniform pricing to enable them to make an honest living and afford the bare necessities for their families. In 1877 around the same time that Sarah first began working as a washerwoman in Vicksburg, a group of working women in Galveston, Texas, organized their own protest to demand an increase in pay. And in 1881 members of the washing society in Atlanta, Georgia, staged their own strike in order to set a uniform pay rate to protect themselves from low wages. In the process, the washing society created effective funding and recruitment mechanisms to support its protests, all of which grew out of what historian Tera Hunter termed "the communal work of laundry." These organizations and mechanisms would later help washerwomen in Atlanta stave off threats from industrialized laundries and unjust court fines and taxation proposals.[21]

Little is known about the specific community of black washerwomen in Vicksburg (and later in St. Louis, Missouri) that Sarah was a part of during the late nineteenth century. But this historical background provides a basis for understanding washerwomen as a community network of influence and support that likely aided and inspired Sarah during this most difficult time in her life. Particularly, black washerwomen were inclined to give, share, and pool their resources collectively to meet each other's needs and their communities' needs. While remembering the experience near the end of her life, Walker stated, "I was considered a good washerwoman and laundress. I am proud of that fact."[22] She certainly disliked being a washerwoman, but it was likely the case that local washerwomen in Vicksburg and St. Louis helped her to survive, influenced her moral imagination, and shaped her ideas about creating employment for black women.

Within three years of arriving in Vicksburg, Sarah married a man named Moses McWilliams. Sarah married McWilliams in order to get away from her abusive brother-in-law, Jesse, and to establish a home of her own.[23] McWilliams fathered Sarah's daughter, Lelia, who was born in 1885 when Sarah was seventeen. This new family experience for Sarah was short-lived; McWilliams died before the end of the decade. By the age of twenty-two, Sarah had married, birthed a child, lost her husband, and found herself a single mother in the Deep South—a devastating sequence of events.

Although living in Vicksburg under such circumstances was certainly challenging, it afforded Sarah exposure to an emerging black civil society that likely captured her imagination. The developing black community of Vicksburg attracted black migrants from neighboring states and consequently a robust gamut of black benevolent and social organizations evolved, which is typical of migration patterns. Churches were among these groups, but many other groups flourished as well. The Order of Colored Knights of Pythias, the Negro Masons, and the Grand United Order of Odd Fellows were particularly active and known for their vibrant parades, which were always communitywide spectacles.[24] These benevolent organizations were composed of men, but they also had women's auxiliaries that were very active. Sarah would have observed these men and women in action serving their community. These types of civic and community activities were not unique to Vicksburg; they occurred throughout the South as black people, particularly women, created organizations to meet their social, educational, religious, and political needs in a frenetic explosion of voluntary activity during the post-Reconstruction era.[25] These organizations in Vicksburg were likely Sarah's first meaningful exposure to the black self-help ethos that was pervasive during the national failure of Reconstruction and increasing white hostility toward black people. Lynchings were happening throughout Mississippi and across the South. Left widowed with a child, Sarah fled Vicksburg for St. Louis, Missouri, just like tens of thousands of southern black people known as "exodusters" who had headed west away from the terror of the South a decade earlier.

## Mentored Migrant and Budding Philanthropist in St. Louis

The Great Black Migration out of the South into the North is commonly considered to have started on the eve of World War I, and it continued for decades. But its roots trace back to the late nineteenth century when people like Sarah, in much smaller numbers, moved around the South before eventually leaving for good. Early migration patterns in the 1880s were incremental and reactive as black people moved laterally from town to town fleeing repression in search of safety before finally heading north and west. Such conditions certainly explained Sarah, Louvenia, and Jesse's movement from Delta, Louisiana, to Vicksburg, Mississippi, in 1878. But Sarah's departure from Vicksburg to St. Louis, Missouri, in 1889 finds context in an earlier episode in black migration history.[26]

Starting in 1879, between four and five thousand black exodusters left the South for Kansas in search of new communities befitting their new freedom. The largest single wave of black migrants arrived in Kansas in the early 1880s, and the trend continued such that the state's black population more than doubled to more than forty-three thousand by the 1890s. Arkansas and other contiguous states saw similar black population trends.[27] Sarah's movement from Delta to Vicksburg in 1878 preceded the start of the exoduster minimigration by a few months. Sarah likely heard about Kansas and St. Louis from the exodusters who left from or passed through Vicksburg, which was a primary point of departure because of its location on the Mississippi River. St. Louis was a main way station en route to Kansas and was only five hundred miles north along the river. Historian Nell Irvin Painter captured the lure of St. Louis for the Exodusters:

> St. Louis occupied a pivotal position in the mythology of the Exodus. It linked the two parts of the idea, negative and positive, slavery and freedom. The first step, and the most decisive, took Exodusters out of the South, beyond the grasp of re-enslavement. Arriving in Kansas, where there had never been any slavery and where salvation awaited, represented the final step. If they only got out of the South, Exodusters would automatically reach Kansas on the strength of their belief in the idea. The crucial point was St. Louis. When Exodusters reached that city they were out of danger: they had done their part. St. Louis was like the Red Sea, explained an Exoduster, drawing a parallel between Southern Black people and the Israelites.[28]

Sarah was not an exoduster herself, but her 1889 entry into St. Louis was greatly influenced by the exodusters, whose overwhelming and impecunious presence in the city over the preceding decade had caused St. Louis's black churches and benevolent organizations to rally resources and supportive services for them. Relief activities for black migrants arriving in St. Louis began in March 1879, when Sarah was about twelve years old, as Charlton

H. Tandy, a local black politician, appealed to the city for funds. His appeal was initially denied, even though help was being administered to other, nonblack, migrants. Eventually $100 was granted by the city for all the black migrants, but this sum greatly paled in comparison to the amounts of up to $300 each that were given to white migrant families passing through the city.[29] After this denial of support, the local black community organized a fundraising appeal and began housing arriving migrants with local families.

St. Paul African Methodist Episcopal (AME) Church hosted a meeting on the question of how to help the migrants, and a group called the Committee of Twenty-Five emerged as the Colored Relief Board to coordinate the black community's response to the migrants. St. Paul's and two local Baptist churches became shelters for the exodusters and housed 150–350 migrants.[30] Using donations of food and money, the local black community supported the exodusters for more than a month before word spread across the country and charitable donations were sent by black and white donors. The Colored Relief Board evolved into the Colored People's Board of Emigration of the City of St. Louis and expanded its activities to include sending representatives to Kansas to ensure the migrants who had passed through their city were faring well despite the lack of social services on the ground. Tandy traveled the country raising money for the board, but interest in the exodus was short lived. The board continued to operate into the 1880s but faced increasing hostility from local public officials who did not want black migrants settling in St. Louis. Although the board did not continue indefinitely, the churches and other community groups remained active in receiving and caring for migrants. A decade later, Sarah was greeted by this same black civic, religious, and philanthropic infrastructure, and it made a tremendous difference that was to have lasting impact on the widowed single mother who wanted a better life for herself, her daughter, and her people.

If black migrants left the South in search of greater opportunity, Sarah's brothers, Owen, Alexander, James, and Solomon, found it in St. Louis. The Breedlove brothers opened a barbershop in the black St. Louis neighborhood anchored by the St. Paul AME Church.[31] Not wealthy by any means, the Breedlove men were able to provide for themselves in ways that Delta and Vicksburg had not allowed. Sarah's experiences in St. Louis provide important insights into the origins and motivations of Madam Walker's philanthropy.

In 1889 Sarah and Lelia arrived in St. Louis with more hope than money. She connected with her family and resumed working as a washerwoman. But as a widow with a child, more support was necessary. Sarah was welcomed into the city by the social infrastructure undergirded by St. Paul AME Church and its many female members as well as local black clubwomen and social-service and benevolent organizations. St. Paul AME Church was the entry point and primary connector of Sarah to this social network. Founded in 1841, the church had an active base of churchwomen, who ran internal ministries and auxiliaries, and clubwomen, members who participated in community clubs outside the church, within its membership.[32] Sarah was embraced by these women.

One of the first support services the church connected Sarah to was the St. Louis Colored Orphan's Home, which had recently opened. The home was one of hundreds across the country founded by black women to care for two of their own most vulnerable populations, children and the elderly. Both old folks' homes and orphanages proliferated in black communities in the years after the Civil War and Reconstruction. Although black families had taken in both blood and fictive kin in the aftermath of Emancipation, these old folks' homes and orphanages were founded as key social institutions to meet the widespread needs of the black community presented by the sheer volume of children and elderly in need and the blatant aggression, discrimination, and neglect exhibited by the white social service agencies that refused to serve them.[33] Frequently founded by black fraternal orders or by black clubwomen, orphanages provided training and moral development for children who were not only neglected but frequently labeled delinquent by white legal authorities and faced threats of imprisonment. In particular, black clubwomen viewed their child welfare work as an important component of their overall social-reform efforts to improve the race alongside their schools, mother's meetings, day nurseries, kindergartens, and other educational and youth-focused efforts.[34]

The St. Louis Colored Orphan's Home was founded in 1888 by Sarah Newton Cohron, a black graduate of Oberlin College, who was concerned about the lack of services for black orphans. She worked with local religious organizations to raise awareness and launched a campaign to start the home. It was built on land purchased by black Civil War veterans and undertook the work of caring for orphans.[35] St. Paul AME Church was a founding partner in the home.

The St. Louis Colored Orphan's Home enabled Sarah to work knowing her daughter was being cared for properly. In addition to serving parentless children, the home also served children of single parents and provided them with educational and religious instruction, food, recreation, and sleeping accommodations. Lelia stayed at the home a few days each week while Sarah worked.[36] The staff at the home also connected Lelia with the local elementary school when she was of age so that her formal schooling could begin. The home's support was tremendously helpful to Sarah and gave her a firsthand view of the power of the self-help ethos among black people to address community needs despite the widespread neglect and exclusion by the dominant white social service providers and larger society.

It was also through St. Paul's that Sarah became connected with the Court of Calanthe, the auxiliary of the black fraternal organization the Colored Knights of Pythias. Founded as a white fraternal organization in 1864, the Knights of Pythias had denied access to black men. After the organization denied a petition in 1870 by a group of black men from Pennsylvania to be accepted, the Colored Knights of Pythias was founded in Vicksburg, Mississippi, ten years later. The Colored Knights of Pythias became one of the largest black fraternal orders, and it offered life, burial, and sickness insurance and operated old folks' homes and orphanages. In 1883 the Colored Knights of Pythias created the Independent Order of Calanthe, which offered sickness benefits at a cost of $1 to $4 per week. The Court of Calanthe's membership was composed of knights and their female relatives, including spouses, mothers, and siblings. Calanthes were very invested in doing charitable works and, similarly, pooled resources via dues structures to fund projects. From Vicksburg, the organization expanded across the South and northward.[37]

Jessie Batts Robinson was the friend who introduced Sarah to the Court of Calanthe and convinced her to join. Robinson was a member of St. Paul AME Church and was married to Christopher K. Robinson, who held numerous leadership positions with the order. His involvement afforded high visibility, and he reportedly had regular audiences with white public officials and civic leaders. Jessie and Sarah became very close friends, and through Jessie, Sarah gained exposure to a new world of literature, etiquette, and culture that was in stark contrast to what she had seen in Delta and Vicksburg.[38]

Along with the Court of Calanthe, Sarah experienced the St. Paul's Mite Missionary Society. Through this society, a group of St. Paul women worked on various community projects to help needy families. During the waves of migration, such projects frequently revolved around black migrants' arrival in the city. Sarah's experience with the women of the Mite Missionary Society was transformational because it positioned her to be of service to others. Having known the experience of being new in an unfamiliar city with no money, Sarah could relate to the migrants. The church, the orphan's home, and the Court of Calanthe had all given her access and exposure to new friends, new resources, and new ways of being from her close proximity to—even from the tutelage of—black women who were educated, had social standing, and were very involved in the local community.

They influenced Sarah and her view of herself, her people, and her world. According to a newspaper interview from 1912, Madam Walker once recalled personally knocking on doors during this time in her life to raise money and collect food to help an elderly man who had great difficulty in caring for his family:

> It was in St. Louis that the madame [sic] learned that it was truly her mission to relieve the poor and the distressed according as she was able. She read in the *St. Louis Post-Dispatch*, a publication of that city, of an aged colored man with a blind sister and an invalid wife depending upon him for support. The incident touched her heart. Without an acquaintance of any kind with the family, she went among her friends in the behalf of the distressed people, succeeding in collecting [money], which she gave to them. She was so pleased with the joy manifest by the giving that she felt herself not only well paid in the instance, but well enough to enlist her future sympathy. She felt it was her duty to do even more for the poor people spoken of. She arranged for a puppy party through which means groceries in abundance were given, also a purse of $7.50.[39]

The account reveals much about the influence of the St. Louis women on young Sarah and the origins of Walker's gospel of giving. First, it shows her engaging literacy in ways not possible in Delta and Vicksburg during her troubled, underresourced youth and lack of schooling. The women connected not only her daughter with education but Sarah as well. Second, while under the influence of these women, Sarah transitioned from being a recipient to a donor. She, too, was empowered to help others just as she had been helped simply by giving "according as she was able." Third, the joy that Walker experienced and articulated gave different language to the giving process than early-twentieth-century philanthropists typically used, enough to "enlist her future sympathy" as a lifelong commitment to help others.[40] It is clear, as historian Bettye Collier-Thomas pointed out, that black women's church-based societies, auxiliaries, and conventions were "significant nonpartisan bases of power" that "constituted the backbone of black community philanthropy" during this period.[41] Young Sarah learned that the ability to give and be helpful to others was contingent on the willingness to do so rather than financial wealth; thus she birthed the early expressions of Walker's gospel of giving.

During this time, Sarah also experienced important changes that affected her family while in St. Louis. In 1893, when Sarah was twenty-five, her brother, Alexander, died from an intestinal illness. A year later, she married a man named John Davis, who, by the personal accounts of family and friends, was not a good provider, was frequently unemployed, and was fond of alcohol and other women. She endured his abuse and infidelities for several years. Later, in 1902, Sarah's brother James died of heart disease, followed by Solomon, who died a year later from tubercular meningitis. These losses were no doubt devastating for Sarah, who had already lost her parents at an early age. To compound the situation, her eldest brother Owen had previously abandoned his wife and left for New Mexico, and her sister, Louvenia, had stayed behind in Mississippi. Sarah thus found herself with her widowed sisters-in-law in St. Louis, married to an abusive husband. While grieving the demise of her siblings, Sarah separated from John Davis but did not formally divorce him. While in St. Louis she eventually met a young man named Charles Joseph Walker, who was a charming, energetic salesman. His experience would later become very important for Madam Walker's enterprise during its early years.

Even with a new relationship, Sarah's life was turbulent. She and Lelia had changed residences constantly. Their transient lifestyle was due largely to the instability of urban life, Sarah's tumultuous family life, and meager financial resources. It was partly this transient, unstable existence along with her increasing exposure to new people, ideas, and organizations that led Sarah to put Lelia into boarding school at Knoxville College in Tennessee in 1902. Founded in 1875, the school offered industrial education and normal training for teachers at high school and collegiate levels. Lelia studied arithmetic, geography, physiology, sewing, English, elocution, and handwriting.[42] While Lelia was away at school, Sarah continued working as a washerwoman, participating in church, and dealing with family concerns. She enrolled in a local night school to improve her own education. Thanks to resources created and managed by local black women, she was developing a new sense of herself, her possibilities, the world, and her place in it. The women of St. Paul's were anchors for Sarah during this most troubling time in her life. They showed her how life could consist of more than pain and struggle. But Sarah was not just the object of the programs and services of her middle-class "uplifter" women mentors. She was learning from them, but she was also developing her own ideas about who she was and what she wanted for herself, Lelia, and black people.[43]

## Evolving AME Churchwoman

An example of the significant and ubiquitous self-help and philanthropic institution building among African Americans during the late nineteenth century, St. Paul AME Church stood at the center of the woman-powered organizational and interpersonal network that enabled Sarah and Lelia to survive. St. Paul's provided a cocoon of supportive educational and social services that enveloped Sarah and Lelia. It positioned them on a new path that, though still fraught with the disadvantages of black urban life in Jim Crow America, offered examples of self-help and collective action to navigate such social ills and a sense of possibility for a future very different from the one offered by the Burney plantation in Delta, Louisiana. But St. Paul's offered Sarah more—it gave her a spiritual base that won her devotion and sparked her moral imagination even further. As a religious institution, St. Paul's introduced Sarah to the AME Church in a powerful way that would cause her to convert from her Baptist upbringing and spend the rest of her life living in accordance with the AME Church's doctrines and practices.

The AME Church had a history of self-help and voluntary action; print and oral cultures focused on literacy; educational and international missions programs; charitable giving teachings and practices; and active auxiliaries run by women that were very likely attractive to and influential on Sarah during her twenties and thirties. Through these mechanisms, Sarah became anchored in what historian Martha S. Jones articulated as black women's public culture, which "encompassed a realm of ideas, a community of interpretation, and a collective understanding of the issues of the day."[44] The black church was a particular site for this public culture, especially during Sarah's time in St. Louis as the disappointments that black men experienced after Reconstruction led them to reassert their claims to authority in lieu of their lost enfranchisement in the 1890s. They reasserted control in the sanctuary, leading to many internal institutional conflicts and struggles with women based on gender. That said, Jones observed that "women did not abandon public culture. Instead, they founded autonomous women's clubs as vehicles for their continued exercise of public authority and standing. By the century's end, ideas about women's place in public life had been transformed. Women were influential and independent forces in causes ranging from temperance to the campaign against lynching and from missionary work to party politics."[45] These dynamics explain much of what was happening around Sarah and the churchwomen in relation to the organizations they started, the specific history of the church, and its articulation of problems and solutions for the race.

The AME Church had its beginnings in protest against discrimination by white Methodists, and its history demonstrates African American philanthropy's grounding in the colonial era. In 1789 Richard Allen (1760–1831) and Absalom Jones (1746–1818), two black members of St. George's Church in Philadelphia, Pennsylvania, were physically accosted and forced to leave a whites-only seating section while they were in the midst of prayer. In protest, Allen, Jones, and several other black members left the church and began holding their own services. They first created the Free African Society as a benevolent association—one of the first voluntary associations created by black people in America—that engaged in economic, social, and religious activities and enabled them to hold services. According to its by-laws, the Free African Society's founding ideal was "free and autonomous worship in the Afro-American tradition, and the solidarity and social welfare of the black community." Among its main objectives were the provision of weekly financial support to members' widows and the poor and the provision of education for the children of deceased members. In 1793 the Free African Society provided five hundred volunteers for burial and nursing services to assist with Philadelphia's deadly yellow fever outbreak, which killed nearly five thousand people. As many as four hundred black people died during the epidemic, among them many who served in this voluntary capacity. For this service, the mayor of Philadelphia praised Allen and the black volunteers.[46]

In 1794 Allen and associates constructed Bethel Church but found themselves under the aegis of the white Methodist Conference for a significant period of time. In 1816, after a legal battle that went to the Pennsylvania Supreme Court, Allen and other black Methodist leaders met in Philadelphia to form their own independent denomination and called it the African Methodist Episcopal Church. Allen was elected its first bishop.

To this day, Allen stands as a revered figure in the AME Church and his life story has been handed down through the generations. His biography has been regularly conveyed to successive generations as a narrative of ascent in which Allen arose from slavery nearly one hundred years before Frederick Douglass and Booker T. Washington. The veneration in which Allen was held is evident in early-twentieth-century church literature, which heralded him as the first person, of any race, "to boldly proclaim and practice the 'Fatherhood of God and the Brotherhood of Man' in a manner inclusive of all, especially black Christians" as well as "the first American to put the principle of self-help in the so-called Negro Problem." Sarah, who had her own humble beginnings and had come from an enslaved family, was undoubtedly exposed to the story of Richard Allen and likely was inspired by it as well. Common church narratives about Allen emphasized how he gained his freedom by "industry and thrift" and was such a persuasive preacher that he reportedly converted his own master to Christianity, which was what enabled him to purchase his own freedom. In addition, church lore described Allen as one of the wealthiest black men in Philadelphia. He was regularly heralded for his respectability, prominence as a citizen of Philadelphia, and ingenuity as an owner of three businesses while serving as minister and bishop of the church. Allen's emphasis on self-help was repeatedly highlighted in church literature, including that he "instructed his people that the only way to be free is to be self-supporting." Further, the example of the Free African Society loomed large as a mutual-aid self-help organization out of which the AME Church was born. By establishing the AME Church, Richard Allen and his colleagues achieved an impressive feat in the face of the oppression of slavery and the legal and cultural prohibitions against black literacy, associationalism, interstate travel, and communication. Their accomplishments included producing the first black Protestant bishop in America, the first black interstate organization in America, and the first black ordained elders in Methodism. As a member of the AME Church, Sarah would have been constantly surrounded by such aspirational narratives focused on leadership, self-help, entrepreneurship, property ownership, achievement, associationalism, and progress.[47]

These ideals were not exemplified only by the leadership and history of the AME Church; they were engrained into its very operation. The AME Church had a rich print culture and tradition of literacy, education, advocacy, and sociopolitical commentary through denominational publications. The church produced numerous publications that covered religion, literature, art appreciation, science, child rearing, moral development, international missions, and other matters the church believed were related to racial uplift. Two in particular, the *Christian Recorder* (1853) and the *AME Church Review* (1884), became major national publications. When AME Church membership exploded from twenty thousand in the 1850s to more than four hundred fifty thousand by the end of the 1890s, the circulation of these two literary vehicles kept pace, placing them among the leading black periodicals nationwide and attracting church and national authors, including W. E. B. DuBois and Booker T. Washington.[48]

These publications enabled the AME Church to engage in a historicization process by producing publications that affirmed black life and success. The process included the framing of slavery and emancipation in biblical terms that identified black people with scriptural themes and stories of captivity and liberation and casting the Civil War and Reconstruction as the upward arc of historical and divine processes sympathetic to the plight of black oppression. The AME Church used its writings to create what historian Julius Bailey described as "narratives that simultaneously [engaged] the past and present and [portended] particular futures." In this manner, the church was able to ground its membership, and the broader black community, in a meaningful history that offered possibilities that ran counter to the prevailing and restrictive myths about black people promoted by white society to justify its superior status and treatment of them. The historical consciousness of the publications found confirmation and relevance in the daily operations of the AME Church as an institution created and managed by black people with complete autonomy and authority, which had great beneficial effect in black communities across the country and overseas. Women figured largely in such efforts, particularly in the South, as churchwomen and clubwomen used their programming to counter the Lost Cause narrative of confederate sympathizers and develop curricula to rear black children with pride and a sense of responsibility and possibility for the race. Through these combined efforts, the AME Church "shaped the identity of the race and empowered those of African descent to reach for and achieve greater heights." As a member of St. Paul's, Sarah had access to these publications. She likely became a subscriber herself—a common practice for members—once her employment became steady and her own literacy increased through the night school she attended.[49]

The AME Church believed that part of black suffering came from the lack of publicly available role models of black individuals in high positions of authority to serve as examples of a different future. Consequently, it emphasized leadership opportunities for members. In fact, Bishop Daniel Payne, who was leading the church when Sarah joined it, said the church provided the race with a "space to rise . . . [as] every office in the gift of this Church was accessible, and the most meritorious obtained it."[50] AME church leaders believed that seeing black people in leadership roles provided "ocular proof" to its membership of the race's innate intelligence, abilities, and potential and, therefore, had a powerful inspirational and educational effect.[51] As was custom, local AME churches like St. Paul's were frequently visited by bishops, officers, and other leaders, who preached sermons, presided over events, and brought news of church achievement from across the country and overseas. For Sarah, public culture within the AME Church opened up a new way of understanding and engaging the world.

To reinforce this visual display of black potential and leadership, the AME Church implemented an aggressive agenda in education and international missions. Founding Bishop Richard Allen believed in education as an important component of Christianity and liberation. But it was Daniel Payne, the sixth AME bishop, in office from 1852 to 1893, who shaped the church's educational agenda by overseeing the creation of AME ministerial training, schools, and colleges for the black population. When Sarah joined St. Paul's, Payne's education agenda was already in motion; nine universities had been founded, including Wilberforce University (1856) in Ohio, Allen University (1870) in South Carolina, and Morris Brown College (1881) in Georgia.[52] After leading the AME takeover of Wilberforce University, Bishop Payne became its president, thereby also becoming the first black president of a college in America. The church was also developing schools in Africa as part of its missionary outreach. As one who could not go to a school as a child and who felt the daily limitations associated with not being able to read, Sarah was now a part of an international black organization that was building schools across her native South and abroad. Her moral imagination was bustling.

The AME Church's international work extended to many countries. Bishopric visits to Africa began four years after the church was founded. By 1830 similar missionary initiatives had produced two churches in Haiti, with more to follow in Canada, Liberia, Sierra Leone, and across the Caribbean.[53] The AME Church's overseas work was not limited to the traditional kinds of missionary outreach and proselytizing done by most white Christian denominations, however. The AME Church's overseas agenda was steeped in a plural nationalist political ideology that focused on racial awareness and pride along with collaboration and cohesion to fight oppression in the global context. The AME Church had detailed engagement and debates over social and political issues in countries like Spain, Russia, Philippines, Ireland, France, and Japan and across Africa. The church had, as described by historian Lawrence Little, "a foreign agenda that sought a global application of American liberty by globalizing issues of oppression and identifying with oppressed people around the world, regardless of race."[54] Sarah may have taken note of the church's activities in Africa more broadly and South Africa more specifically, which had received widespread attention during her first decade of membership. And she, too, would later develop an international consciousness that shaped her view of racial oppression.

Just as education and international missions were important to the AME Church from its founding, charitable giving was emphasized as well. The AME Church believed that giving to the poor was so characteristic of Jesus Christ that charity should be equally normative for those who follow him. Church founder Allen wrote of Christian charity that it

> is pure and disinterested, remote from all hopes or views of worldly return or recompence from the persons we relieve. We are to do good and lend, hoping for nothing again. In its extent it is unlimited and universal. . . . [It] takes in all mankind, strangers as well as relations or acquaintances, enemies as well as friends, the evil and unthankful, as well as the good and grateful. It has no other measure than the love of God to us, who gave his only begotten Son, and the love of our Saviour, who laid down his life for us, even whilst we were his enemies. It reaches not only to the good of the soul, but also to such assistance as may be necessary for the supply of the bodily wants of our fellow creatures.[55]

Madam Walker's aforementioned 1912 newspaper interview about her early socialization into becoming a donor while living in St. Louis despite having meager resources and constant crises echoed Allen's exact teachings. The "good of the soul" identified by Allen was described by Walker in the interview as the "joy" she experienced from giving to others. But there are larger consequences of his church teaching on charity.

Traditionally, Western conceptions of philanthropy assume great distance between the giver and the receiver.[56] Allen, however, had situated friends and family alongside strangers and even enemies as objects of charity; thus, he made charity comprehensive and inclusive without stipulation. Allen described the extent of charity as "unlimited and universal" and he presented God as charitable for having given his only son, Jesus Christ, as a gift for the salvation of humanity. In turn, Christ gave his life to secure that salvation. In this Christian tradition, both God the Father and God the Son had made their gifts out of love. Consequently, Allen believed that AME Church members also should demonstrate love and generosity through giving. To that end, Christ's followers were to use whatever means were at their disposal to exhibit his love through their giving. Church literature described the expectation of member financial support as contributing "their earthly substance, according to their ability for the support of the gospel, church, poor, and the various benevolent enterprises of the church."[57] This institutional expectation also included giving to promote the uplift of the race.

Sarah, and later as Madam Walker, gave in ways that agreed with the AME Church's teachings on Christian charity. In 1914 the *Indianapolis Freeman* described her as possessing "the gift and spirit for the charity work. She takes great stock in the theory that the Lord loves a cheerful giver. She gives bountifully and cheerfully."[58] This biblical reference finds context in 2 Corinthians as the Apostle Paul conveyed his experience with churches in Macedonia, where he observed people in severe poverty giving voluntarily, abundantly, and generously of the little they possessed. Walker felt compelled to give and enjoyed being generous toward people known and unknown and by using diverse forms of gifts to be of assistance. This approach to giving was taught by the church and embodied in the lives of Sarah's women mentors as they navigated a harsh racialized and gendered world and expressed their intersectional identities. They taught her well, and her own moral imagination would carry her far beyond their teachings in this regard.

Of all the aspects of life in the AME Church that Sarah was exposed to, the most far-reaching in influence was undoubtedly the example of women lay leaders in the church whom she came to know through St. Paul's Mite Missionary Society and the choir. The AME Women's Parent Mite Missionary Society (WPMMS) was formally organized at the denominational level in 1874 out of the preexisting work of Dorcas Societies and women's groups that conducted charity relief work for the poor. Church law dictated that only male ministers could initiate local mite missionary societies, and many men opposed their creation over fears of competition from women. In spite of this opposition, members of the all-female WPMMS board regularly advocated for autonomy within this environment. By 1894, all AME district conferences and regions had their own missionary societies, which were simply called Mite Missionary Societies, a name that referred to the ways in which the aggregate of women's "mites"—their small gifts of money— created important funding streams for missions activity.[59]

As a national body, WPMMS effectively became the AME Church's missionary department. WPMMS was committed to world evangelism and, through partnership with other AME home and foreign missionary groups, to sending a missionary to Haiti, which eventually happened in 1877. At the national level, WPMMS was vying for leadership of the denomination's home and foreign missionary activities, while at the local level, Mite Missionary Societies, like the one at St. Paul's, raised money for home and foreign mission activities, provided support to local churches, and aided ministers and their families. The term "home missions" generally meant activities within the United States and included visiting sick and incarcerated individuals and giving food, clothing, and other assistance to the local poor. This combination of home and foreign missions activity "often fused evangelism with political and social reform" and extended throughout local black American communities and overseas to Haiti, Africa, the Dominican Republic, Canada, and South Africa. Consequently, black religious denominations gave African American philanthropy concurrent domestic and international foci from its earliest evolutions, and black women frequently led the way as their church numbers increased. There were more than thirty thousand black women organized into church-sponsored missionary auxiliaries around the turn of the century, and that number grew to more than half a million by the middle of the twentieth century.[60]

Such numbers, however, did not initially result in women's representation in the church's male-dominated hierarchical leadership structure. Even though women were present from the beginning, having joined Allen and Jones in leaving St. George's Church, their participation did not immediately translate into power. Women's groups within the AME Church enabled women to acquire three important sources of power—membership, organization, and resources—through which to challenge male dominance without destroying the denomination or distracting from their assistance to black communities.[61] Although black women had to contend with racism and sexism from whites in society, they also battled with sexism from black men and black institutions. Within the AME denomination, sexism took the form of what historian Bettye Collier-Thomas called "hegemonic masculinity," a force that relegated black women to auxiliaries in order to maintain male control over women's actions and funding.[62] However, such auxiliaries were catalytic in developing black women's autonomy.

Women's missionary societies and conventions—in both black and white denominations—provided the necessary infrastructure for women to launch national efforts to promote and advocate for their rights. In the AME Church, women obtained political and civic skills and the social capital necessary to create national networks and organizations to reform society. Women's auxiliary groups also served as mechanisms for social discourse, socialization, and education as AME women discussed important issues and shared information; learned about daily church operations; held offices; and served as teachers, exhorters, evangelists, class leaders, and even preachers. Further, such participation enabled black women to develop both the material resources (real estate, labor, and finances) and the nonmaterial resources (denominational knowledge, formal education, community leadership, service experience, reputational credibility, and spiritual credibility) they used to advocate for their rights within the denomination. Consequently, at the start of the twentieth century, the AME Church, which had been founded without any provisions for women, had three denominational positions specifically for women and two autonomous women's missionary societies.[63]

AME women's advocacy occurred outside the denomination as well. AME women used their societies to engage with national networks, such as the National Association of Colored Women (NACW), that were protesting racism and sexism around the country. These relationships were clearly evidenced by the NACW affiliation of many of the women Sarah interacted with at St. Paul's, such as Lavinia Carter, board member of the St. Louis Colored Orphans' Home, and Maria Harrison, who was Sarah's neighbor at one point. In 1904 the World's Fair Exposition was held in St. Louis and lasted several months. Controversy soon arose over the representation of African Americans in the exhibition as well as their access to activities. But the event also brought the NACW to town for its fourth biennial meeting. which was hosted at St. Paul AME. Two hundred NACW delegates represented the organization's fifteen thousand female members at the event, Black women with national reputations, such as orator Hallie Quinn Brown and Margaret Murray (Mrs. Booker T.) Washington, were also NACW members and participated in the biennial meeting. Because Sarah was not a NACW member at this time as a result of class divisions among African Americans, it is unlikely that she would have been involved in any meeting-related activities, but she likely would have known about them and learned more about NACW's activities in founding orphanages, retirement homes, kindergartens, tuberculosis camps, and resisting alcoholism and prostitution. In witness to its power to affect the world, Sarah would have likely heard about NACW's protest of the World's Fair for its denial of employment opportunities for some of its members as well as its valiant fight against lynching.[64]

Sarah observed these women not only performing good works in the community, but also challenging the strictures of race in society and gender in their own church. These women were exactly like the churchwomen historian Bettye Collier-Thomas described as embracing "a commitment to religion and racial uplift, by combining evangelism with their reform efforts and making them the central elements of their activism."[65] This religiously inspired self-help ethic and concomitant local and national infrastructure enabled black women's philanthropic action across the country. Sarah found herself right in the middle of this fervent activity. Later, her efforts would greatly resemble some of the structures and practices known to have been developed and nurtured by black clubwomen and churchwomen in general and the women of the AME church and NACW in particular. This impact was fitting; historian Martha S. Jones asserted that as black women "moved between the many sites of public culture—from Sunday sermon to Tuesday evening literary society meeting . . . they carried the ideas generated in each of those venues with them."[66] Sarah's exposure to and deep engagement with the AME Church broadly gave her examples of language, leadership, organization, and processes that would become critical to Walker's business empire and evolving practice of philanthropy—her gospel of giving—more than a decade later.

To be sure, the AME Church, like many churches, was never free from blemish. Historians have documented the AME Church's paternalistic and imperialistic motivations overseas, its condescending views of Southern freed people after Emancipation, its subordinate treatment of women, and the elitism and cultural arrogance of the denomination's middle-class membership with respect to the "black masses."[67] But on the whole, through the AME Church, Sarah, and later as Madam Walker, was exposed to an ambitious, visionary, action-oriented institution that was created, funded, and managed by black people during a time when US society made little room for them and regularly erected barriers to impede and complicate daily living. She became a churchwoman and a clubwoman—with her own evolving vision of service—and stayed close to the AME Church, never forgetting the women of the Mite Missionary Society.

## Virtuous Woman Entrepreneur

The first five years of the new century were filled with many pressures for Sarah, including sending her child away to school, grieving the deaths of her brothers, dealing with separation from her second husband, and working as a washerwoman while attending night school. She also began working for a black woman from Illinois named Annie Turnbo (who later became Annie Malone through marriage), who owned the Pope-Turnbo Company (later named Poro) in St. Louis, which sold hair treatment products. Sarah's hair had begun to thin and fall out. As a result of the contemporary state of hygiene and medicine, hair loss was common in response to sickness, scalp disease, low-protein diets, poor hair treatments, and inadequate washing.[68] The stress of urban life was taking its toll on Sarah, but the experience also led to an opportunity.

In a newspaper interview in 1917, Walker described the process by which she developed the formula for her hair care products. She asserted that while experiencing her severe hair loss, she prayed for heavenly guidance and her prayer was answered: "For one night I had a dream, and in that dream a big black man appeared to me and told me what to mix for my hair.

Some of the remedy was from Africa, but I sent for it, mixed it, put it on my scalp and in a few weeks my hair was coming in faster than it had ever fallen out. I tried it on my friends; it helped them. I made up my mind I would begin to sell it."[69] The moment was clearly a turning point in Sarah's life, and as Madam Walker later recounted the same dream time and time again through various speeches around the country. Undoubtedly delivered with dramatic flair, the story of this dream served as a point of separation and transition, a dividing line between Sarah Breedlove's humble beginnings and continuous struggle and the emergence of Madam C. J. Walker. The dream helped to recast Sarah's identity. No longer just a lowly washer-woman, Sarah was now a divinely inspired woman of God who claimed to be given specific instructions on how to produce a product that would not only change her life but put her in a position to change the lives of others through her gifts. Tutored in the ways of respectability and virtuous black womanhood, she now had her own vision of how to live and how to be in an unforgiving racialized and gendered world.

In 1905 Sarah left St. Louis for Denver, Colorado. Although Sarah's exact employment during this time is unknown, she reportedly sold Pope-Turnbo products and worked as a cook to pay for her expenses while she developed her own products. Sarah canvassed neighborhoods for her own customers instead of for Pope-Turnbo's. This period later became a cause of contention between Madam Walker and Annie Malone that resulted in a sustained rivalry over the origins and quality of their products and a fierce battle in the marketplace for market share.[70]

In Denver, Sarah joined the Shorter Chapel AME Church, where her sister-in-law, Lucy, was a member. She also joined the church's Mite Missionary Society and the Columbine Chapter of the Court of Calanthe. Her beau, C. J., joined Sarah by year's end, and they lived in a thriving black neighborhood that formed a strong black business district composed of barber shops, fraternal halls, shoe-repair shops, recreation outlets, churches, funeral homes, and medical and dental offices. The two married on January 4, 1906. It was during this time that Sarah began using the moniker Mrs. C. J. Walker in newspaper advertisements for her hair products. Simultaneously, C. J.'s penchant for sales and marketing began to show as he staged numerous events to draw attention to the products.[71]

The year 1906 was a critical one for Sarah as she constantly promoted her services, and business began to dramatically increase. For six months, she advertised weekly in local papers, even using communication from competitors to warn her customers not to utilize other products that did not have the same quality ingredients or results. But by the end of the summer, the "Mrs. C. J. Walker" promoted in weekly ads suddenly became "Madam C. J. Walker," a title commonly used by hairdressers and other women working in fashion and beauty. Against what she would later report as her husband's objections, she began traveling around Colorado promoting Madam Walker's Wonderful Hair Grower. Not only was she selling products, she was also training women through classes on how to grow their own hair. She reportedly instructed groups as large as forty-five at a time. Walker charged a modest fee for her class. Her daughter Lelia joined her and helped to manage a new shop they opened together in Denver.[72]

Walker's business was very successful and Annie Turnbo (Malone) took notice, placing ads that challenged Walker's assertions about her products and noting that she had trained Walker. Turnbo (Malone) sent an agent to Denver to set up shop just a few blocks away from Walker, and their rivalry ensued. After approximately two or three years, Madam Walker left Denver, in search of larger markets of black customers. Traveling had caused Walker to realize the potential in southern and northern cities with developing black populations. Within two years, Madam Walker's income went from $300 per year to $3,652 per year, and her new life was well under way.[73] Although her marriage to C. J. would not last, the orphaned-widowed-migrating-washerwoman-mother, who was socialized into respectability by black philanthropic women, had created and activated a new vision for her life and stepped onto a new trajectory of triumph that would reverberate across time, leaving a legacy for generations.

Sarah Breedlove gave birth to Madam C. J. Walker out of a moral imagination shaped by the harsh racialized and gendered realities of her circumstances and the hopeful racialized and gendered supports of the women around her. As someone born at the developing dawn of Reconstruction in the Deep South, but who came of age during its disappointing dusk as it was replaced by Jim Crow, Sarah was a long-suffering washerwoman who, instinctively, wanted something better for herself and her daughter. As an orphan, Sarah had not had the benefit of parental influence to inculcate philanthropic values. Instead, she was socialized within black civil society institutions and networks created, funded, operated, and led by black women focused on uplifting their race. They filled that parental void and helped Sarah do the same for her daughter, Lelia. From them and their example, Sarah acquired the wherewithal to not only dream but to actualize that dream so that it became not only about a better way for her and Lelia, but also for black and other oppressed people around the world.

For Sarah, the St. Paul AME Church stood at the heart of these nurturing and inspiring black women's networks. It represented a place of connection and caring as she was embraced by the churchwomen, introduced to much-needed social services, and led to join organizations run by them. Her social sphere expanded and she began to learn about the social and political issues affecting black life, the strategies of racial uplift and self-help as means to their amelioration, and the centrality of black women in securing freedom for her people.

Madam Walker's moral imagination, which was grounded in the experiences of Sarah Breedlove, acquired numerous outlets for expression with Walker's gradual accumulation of resources. No longer consumed with the struggles of a washerwoman, Madam C. J. Walker had answers to those struggles. Though she was still black, female, and subject to the larger structures of Jim Crow America, Walker's growing wealth and potential provided just enough insulation to enable her to dream even bigger dreams than Sarah had. Madam Walker's dreams included building an international company, employing thousands of black women, and engaging a type of philanthropic giving that called on a range of resources at her disposal to make gifts to uplift the race, empower black women, and make life better for others.

# 2
## Opportunity

I am in the business world, not for myself
alone, but to do all the good I can for the
uplift of my race.
—Madam C. J. Walker, 1912

In 1911 Maggie Wilson, a black woman from Pittsburgh, Pennsylvania, became an agent of the Walker Company. She worked hard to grow her business with a very lucrative clientele base selling Walker products in her community. Her involvement with the company lasted at least thirteen years, and she credited Madam Walker with opening up "a trade for hundreds of our colored women to make an honest and profitable living and where they make as much in one week as a month's salary would bring from any other position a colored woman can secure. . . . I advise all who have not 'learned the trade' or tried her wonderful goods to start at once."[1] Similarly, an unnamed agent in Cleveland, Ohio, reported to the *Indianapolis Freeman* newspaper that she had transitioned from unemployment with no income to employment as a Walker agent earning $900 per year within three years. A woman identified only as Mrs. Robert Walker from Ithaca, New York, became an agent in 1917. She started with two customers and eventually served between forty and fifty regular clients. She informed the company that "I have had wonderful success since I have been doing the work. . . . [M]y business has been constantly increasing. . . . Sometimes I wonder how I can accommodate them all." These three agents were not unique, but were representative of thousands of black women whose lives were changed by their affiliation with the Walker

Company. In 1911 the *Denver Statesman* observed that Walker "has made possible the way for many colored women to abandon the washtub for more pleasant and profitable occupation." Madam Walker gave her agents three ways to generate income and financial stability: (1) perform beauty treatments, (2) sell products, and (3) refer and train agents. Additional support from the company through training and incubation of beauty shops caused black women to become eager to work for Walker and grateful for the opportunity her business presented them.[2]

Just as Madam C. J. Walker was the physical embodiment of Sarah Breedlove's moral imagination, the Walker Company was the institutional manifestation of the commitments and dreams that formed her visions of the good life and the good society as Sarah and, later, as Madam Walker. Scholars have rightly taken to Walker as an early-twentieth-century example of a prominent American success. Her story has been used in a variety of ways to inform the historiography of many fields. In the process, scholars have acknowledged Walker's facility in merging individual and collective interests with corporate and community goals.[3] In such analyses, however, the Walker Company has typically been in the background, providing context for investigation but rarely the main subject of inquiry. Separate investigations of Walker's newspaper advertising strategy, national networks of beauty schools, and agent clubs have yielded insights into aspects of her company's operations. Blending and building on them frames this comprehensive view of the company as an instrument of Walker's commercial and philanthropic ethos that provided the gift of opportunity through employment to black women.

Scholars have tended to treat these elements of Walker's enterprise separately, but there is good historical reason not to do so. The idea of American society comprising three separate sectors—the market, the government, and the nonprofit sphere—was largely a late-twentieth-century construction that gathered momentum in the 1970s after the federal Filer Commission's delineation of nonprofit action as being distinctive from the other two.[4] Historically, however, rather than being distinct unto themselves, the three areas have typically overlapped, and intersections and interrelationships have resulted in a blurring of the lines between them from the earliest days of the country.[5] In the African American historical experience, the notion of three separate sectors has not always worked well because oppression has been pervasive and the three sectors have colluded in that oppression. During Walker's lifetime, African Americans were either locked out of the private market or locked into its most menial and worst-paying jobs; their rights were denied, acknowledged, and denied again by the government, which had previously legalized their enslavement; and their social-service needs were largely neglected by agencies. African Americans did not have the luxury of thinking in such a sector-based compartmentalized manner. They needed to be creative and adaptive, which required thinking across the boundaries of markets, governments, and social services and using any available means of meeting their own needs and working for societal change. The practice of self-help evolved to compensate for these failures, which meant that black institutions—whether schools, businesses, fraternal lodges, churches, or service agencies in name—would have to serve multiple purposes in practice.

Madam Walker the entrepreneur was a "race woman," meaning a black woman dedicated to serving the African American struggle for liberation.[6] She envisioned her company as facilitating an agenda that was simultaneously commercial and philanthropic for the benefit of the race. She intentionally conducted business to actualize this dual framework. Here, historian Elsa Barkley Brown's method of uncovering southern entrepreneur and race woman Maggie Lena Walker's (1867–1934) womanist philosophy of collective economic development is germane: "the clearest articulation of her theoretical perspective lies in the organization she helped to create and in her own activities. Her theory and her action are not distinct and separable parts of some whole; they are often synonymous, and it is only through her actions that we clearly hear her theory."[7] Placing the internal dynamics of the Walker Company, as directed by Walker, in the foreground reveals how the enterprise became a "race company,"[8] one owned and operated by a black woman and that simultaneously served commercial goals and pursued philanthropic values in service to the race. These dynamics involved particular recruitment practices and employment opportunities offered by the company, which addressed black women's unique status in the labor market, educational opportunities (through the national network of Walker beauty training schools), and activism (through Walker's national organization of agents)—the latter two to be discussed in later chapters.

All these corporate activities were focused on Walker's trust in Freeman B. Ransom, her general manager and legal counsel. Their relationship, which has not been previously examined in depth, reveals their partnership in operating the company for both commercial gain and philanthropic uplift and implementing her gospel of giving. Before examining these dynamics, however, it is important to define the historical basis for viewing the Walker Company as a commercial and philanthropic institution as well as the labor status of black women in the US marketplace.

## Dual Motives

At least two features of the African American historical experience identify the Walker Company as a commercial and philanthropic institution—that is, they explain why it was not just a money-making entity. First, black institutions have historically been characterized by their versatility and multipurpose functions. The ideology of self-help as practiced by African Americans in the late nineteenth and early twentieth centuries required deployment of any available means to uplift the race out of its destitute condition, whether private—meaning individual action conducted interpersonally to help others and collective action through privately run organizations and businesses—or public—meaning political action taken to use the law and make demands on government for policy and social change. This core requirement emerged from the sense that when almost everything had been taken away from African Americans (e.g., human rights; social, political, economic opportunities), anything else they possessed, slowly built, or acquired became a tool for recovering what was lost or for creating something new. Thus, activities and institutions in the white mainstream that traditionally had one primary purpose looked very different and assumed multiple roles and functions in the marginalized black experience. For instance, the black church has never been simply a religious institution. As a result of the broader condition of African Americans, the black church assumed social, cultural, economic, political, and educational roles and purposes along with its religious characteristics.[9] This versatile nature of black institutions was an adaptation for survival and it extended into black entrepreneurship as well.

Black businesses were subject to the hostility of white-controlled governments, white-owned businesses, and white consumers, which placed them on the frontlines of the struggle for equality and required a level of adroitness to navigate. Restrictive policies, exclusionary practices, and violence were regular obstacles. Such a volatile environment often required clandestine entrepreneurship, creativity, and continual adjustment by black women. On the labor side, many black businesses recognized the agency, acumen, and intelligence of black women and employed them in positions not available to white women in white-owned companies.[10]

In this context, black business was not just about making money. It had a major role to play in meeting community needs. Black women's entrepreneurship merged creativity, resource management, and sales to address the economic, social, and political contexts in which black women found themselves. Thus, there was a reciprocal relationship between black women entrepreneurs' social activism and their businesses. Walker constructed her use of entrepreneurship to provide avenues of opportunity on a large scale for black women, who would develop financial autonomy for themselves and their families and serve their race along the way. Education scholar Chery A. Smith confirmed this interaction: "Activism was used to make money, and money was made to support activism and social service and advance the cause of full citizenship for all Black people" because black women entrepreneurs "sold their products, their work, and their services for profit and for the betterment of the lives of Black women and Black people in general." Smith specifically added that Walker used "business as activism and activism as business." In addition, historian Tiffany Gill highlighted Walker as a pioneer of black women's use of beauty culture to do race work. The same collective consciousness that informed black philanthropy also informed black business. Before and after Walker, black business was rooted in the self-help tradition that gave it license to serve broader social purposes in the long-suffering struggle for freedom and equality.[11]

Second, black social and philanthropic institutions have historically placed significant emphasis on personal health and hygiene in their racial uplift work, particularly in the late nineteenth and early twentieth centuries. The substantial rural poverty of black farmers in the South and the large concentrations of black people in northern urban centers created by migration frequently led to squalid living conditions that were compounded by the effects of industrial racial discrimination (e.g., substandard housing, limited access to healthcare, hunger and inadequate nutrition, poor sanitation).[12] After observing black farming families with pigpens near water wells, dilapidated housing, and disheveled personal appearances, Booker T. Washington made health and hygiene an early emphasis of Tuskegee Institute's extension programming in Alabama. His efforts started in the 1890s and culminated with his National Negro Health Week campaign that contin-ued well after his death in 1915. In particular, his movable schools—which were initially horse-drawn covered wagons stocked with farming equipment and instructional materials—were sent out among black farmers to provide on-site instruction for improving their farming practices, personal hygiene, and sanitation regimes.[13] The Tuskegee Women's Club, organized in 1895 by educator Margaret Murray (Mrs. Booker T.) Washington, regularly sent members out into local homes to teach women housekeeping and child-rearing techniques. Later, it operated a sex hygiene committee to instruct women on the role of cleanliness and moral conduct in preventing venereal disease. In 1908 educator Lugenia Burns Hope founded the Neighborhood Union in Atlanta, Georgia, a social-services organization whose program-ming included surveying disease and sanitation and teaching black women hygienic practices related to bathing, caring for the sick, cleaning homes, and protecting well water.[14]

Although black institutions acknowledged the role of racism in creating poor health and hygiene in black communities, many blacks—as a result of Victorian perspectives on moral conduct—also thought poor blacks contrib-uted to their own squalid conditions through their behavior. Middle-class black clubwomen—including those who were in the NACW—emphasized moral conduct, purity, hygiene, and home maintenance in their pursuit of a Victorian model of womanhood through initiatives targeted at working-class black female migrants gathering in cities. Emphases on hygiene con-tinued as black clubwomen's programs expanded into social settlement houses, homes for the aged and orphans, and responses to tuberculosis outbreaks.[15] The National Urban League, founded in 1911, also emphasized hygiene, health, and personal appearance in its application of social science methods to black communities in northern cities. The league frequently conducted scientific surveys of black neighborhoods to assess housing and sanitary conditions and inform responsive strategies. In a local response to arriving black migrants, the Chicago Urban League distributed handbills that urged moral behavior, cleanliness, civility, and health during the orga-nization's first and second decades. Similarly, the New York Urban League believed personal hygiene was important as a cultural tool that had to be taught to newly arrived black migrants to help them adapt to the city. As a result, the organization distributed lists of do's and don'ts to migrants that promoted hygienic practices. The organization believed that maintaining one's personal appearance and engaging in appropriate behaviors enhanced one's self-esteem, reflected well on the race, and positioned blacks for social acceptance by whites.[16]

As a result of these activities and many more, black clubwomen and black organizations engaged in hygiene work that should be viewed as philanthropy because they prioritized confidence building and psychosocial development as pathways for personal and community development. In a Jim Crow society determined to assault black sensibilities and contain black aspirations, these efforts were essential countermeasures. Within this context, Madam Walker's use of beauty culture to create economic opportunities for herself and black women by improving black women's personal hygiene assumed added meaning and function. It was not just meeting a need in the marketplace for a particular set of goods. It was enhancing black women's self-esteem, personal appearance, and financial independence, thereby fulfilling an important goal of black women's racial uplift and philanthropic programs.[17]

To the church, the club, and the school, Walker added business as a location for black women's uplift work. She built her company as a platform to extend her version of the kinds of collaborative philanthropic activities churchwomen and clubwomen were doing. Whereas many black women raised funds and volunteered through their clubs, churches, and schools to provide the same race programs and services, Madam Walker sold products through her business to build a self-sustaining funding base that supported similar work and goals. As historian Kate Dossett observed, in doing this race work, "Walker was mothering the race" and the Walker Company was "a missionary outpost on a quest for racial advancement."[18] In such ways, Walker was part of the larger history of economic cooperation among African Americans that W. E. B. DuBois documented in 1907. He defined the tradition broadly as involving the economic and social pooling and distribution of resources and the building of institutions that "combined in some sort of mutual aid." He traced it from Africa through the colonial era into the twentieth century and placed a diverse range of institutions within its context: churches, schools, beneficial and insurance societies, banks, real-estate development companies, cooperative businesses, hospitals, banks, even the Underground Railroad.[19] Black women were a definitive part of these practices for pursuing economic and uplift goals as evidenced, for example, by the many enterprises of Mary Ellen Pleasant (1814–1904) in

San Francisco, California, and the Independent Order of St. Luke run by Maggie Lena Walker (1864–1934) in Richmond, Virginia.[20] Through beauty culture, Madam C. J. Walker—and others, like Annie Malone and Sarah Spencer Washington—leveraged a profitable business model that gave her a freedom and flexibility in addressing the needs of the race that her peers, who depended on fundraising—and frequently white donors—did not have.

It is crucial to remember the definition of African American philanthropy as a medley of beneficent acts and gifts that address someone's needs or larger social purposes based on a collective consciousness and shared experience of humanity. In this light, the roles of social institutions, entrepreneurship, hygiene, and cooperation in the African American experience provide the basis for Walker's blending of commerce and philanthropy without tension. The company provided opportunities to address the socioeconomic needs of black women specifically and the black community generally within the larger context of a hostile society and inimical labor-market conditions.

## The Walker Company and Black Women's Desolate Economic Landscape

Madam Walker incorporated the Walker Company in Indianapolis, Indiana, in September 1911. According to its articles of incorporation, its purpose was "to manufacture and sell a hair growing, beautifying and scalp disease-curing preparation and clean scalps with the same."[21] The company had as its officers Madam Walker, her husband C. J., and her daughter Lelia. Madam Walker retained the services of Freeman B. Ransom, a newly minted black attorney in Indianapolis, as legal counsel. Empowered by Walker to provide corporate counsel, Ransom called the business a "race company"[22] because it was created, owned, and operated by African Americans for the benefit of the black community. Along with shampoo for hair cleansing, the company's four earliest products were Temple Grower, for developing growth along the hairline; Tetter Salve, for relieving itching from scalp diseases such as eczema; Hair Grower, for strengthening weak hair; and Glossine, for moisturizing and adding sheen to hair.[23]

Madam Walker started her business activities during a time of growth in black businesses. In 1893, as Sarah had settled into St. Louis and dreamed of a better life for herself, there were seventeen thousand black-owned businesses in America. By 1903, that number had increased to twenty-five thousand as Sarah began selling products for Annie Malone and would soon develop her own products to sell in Denver. Ten years later, just two years after the incorporation of the Walker Company, there were forty thousand black-owned businesses.[24] But such numbers could not completely overcome the hostile policies and racist practices governing employment.

During the late nineteenth and early twentieth centuries, the employment prospects for black women were bleak, even though their rates of participation in labor markets greatly exceeded those for white women.[25] Black men and women during this period were effectively working-class in their relationship to production. On average, approximately 30 percent of black women over the age of ten were earning wages in the labor markets of major urban centers.[26] During and after Emancipation, the legacy of slavery forced blacks into the unskilled labor markets characterized by very low wages. Black women's rates of labor participation were three times as high as those of white women, and married black women's labor participation was six times as high as that of married white women, trends that continued well into the twentieth century. The large presence of black women in the labor market was attributed to the high unemployment and mortality rates for black men and low overall nonlabor income for black households, conditions also linked to blacks' historical oppression. As unskilled, low-wage earners, black women worked more intensively outside the home than white women and largely occupied domestic positions as cooks, servants, laundresses, and seamstresses. The experience of slavery had the additional effect of socializing black women to labor outside the home such that the late nineteenth-century stigmas against working for pay found among poor and working-class white women were much less prevalent among black women.[27] Black women's employment outside the home was critical for the maintenance of black households, especially when their men could not earn enough income.[28] But scholar Leith Mullings observed that "African American women had neither the protections of the household nor the conditions that allowed them choice about labor force participation."[29] Black women, having labored through slavery without pay, continued working after Emancipation and endured unfair, hostile work conditions, even as their migration patterns had begun taking them out of the South.

Black women were "an exclusive servant caste in the South,"[30] largely because of white women's refusal to work in positions associated with black women. To further exacerbate relations between the two, white women frequently refused to work alongside black women, which led to segregated and unsanitary work conditions for black women within northern factories. This refusal sometimes produced labor strikes by white women against their employers for hiring black women. When they were not fending off racialized attacks from white women, many black women (and the men in their lives) feared for their sexual exploitation by white male employers. This anxiety was particularly prevalent among black women domestic workers. By having to work inside their employers' homes, black women were frequently subjected to the sexual advances of white men. This omnipresent threat caused many black women domestic workers to forego higher wages, in an effort to protect their bodies and dignity, by refusing employers' offers to live in the residences. Further, black women domestic workers were frequently lured into their positions by advertised promises of particular wage levels, only to be shorted on payday as a matter of standard practice.

At the time when Walker incorporated her business, the racial dynamics of the labor market for black women were difficult. Black women were being paid as much as 60 percent less than white women, whose wages were already depressed because of their gender oppression. Further, there was no reprieve from such challenges to be found in white-collar work. Between 1870 and 1920, black women were excluded from the emerging professional, clerical, managerial, and sales positions that white women were entering. Major trade unions also directly prohibited membership to white and black women. Before Madam Walker and the other Mesdames in black beauty culture, labor in the manufacturing sector was largely closed off to black women save for the menial positions associated with cleaning factories.[31] The Walker Company's opportunity for employment was an oasis for black women in such a desolate economic landscape and was consistent with other racial uplift efforts.

The black beauty culture industry in the early twentieth century was an "ethnic niche economy" that enabled black women to navigate racial discrimination and their unskilled, low-wage labor status. As a "protected market," black beauty culture emerged as a result of black women's exclusion from the mainstream labor force, denial of services to them by majority merchants, their spatial concentration in segregated urban black communities, their "social distance" from whites, and their unique cultural attributes (e.g., hairdressing needs) that were difficult for external white merchants to understand. Beauty culture was a very attractive option for unskilled black female southern migrants arriving in the North. It had low barriers to entry and a hierarchical structure that yielded opportunities for advancement in that black women could start practicing in their homes and eventually open shops. Consequently, black beauty culture provided black women with unemployment protection, social and economic mobility, and the flexibility to blend gainful employment with familial responsibilities.[32]

This flexibility was important to black female wage earners whose self-concept as workers took a back seat to their more prominent identities as women, mothers, and race women. Black women's sense of their own work included occupational efforts to earn wages and community activism, marriage, and motherhood. In these ways, many black women often had a "triple day," that is, a full workday in the public sphere of employment, one in their private households, and a third day of activism, advocacy, and service provision to meet their communities' needs. The value they attributed to this work found meaning in its utility within a hostile society. They were able to financially support the black church and other organizations. They could meet their familial, social, and cultural obligations to serve others in need.[33] The employment opportunities created by Madam Walker thus provided a pathway for black women to autonomy and pride.

The Walker Company offered positions inside the company for administrative and manufacturing duties as well as contractual arrangements for sales agents, traveling agents, and salon owners, which paid a range of wages and salaries. Payroll reports from 1915 to 1917 indicate employees who worked in the office and factory of the company made between $1.50 per week and $25 per week. Some temporary or part-time workers were at the lower end of this range, and Walker's closest confidants were at the higher end. For instance, Alice Kelly, Walker's assistant and tutor, made $15 per week in 1915 and had received increases that amounted to $25 per week by 1917. Violet Davis, Walker's secretary, was paid $15 per week by 1917. As Walker's general manager and counsel, Freeman B. Ransom's pay exceeded the salary range. He earned $8,000 per year in 1918, which rose to $13,000 per year in 1919 after he assumed leadership of the company after Walker's death.[34] Walker also gave her staff shares in the company valued at $10 each, which added to their total compensation and gave them a stake in the company's success.[35]

Walker employed a cadre of special traveling agents charged with creating new markets, teach the "art of hair culture" curriculum, promote the company, and sell goods. The compensation for these individuals varied. Harry D. Evans of Indianapolis was paid $125 per month along with a 50 percent commission on new customer orders and a 25 percent commission on refills of existing customer orders. He and traveling agent Janet Johnson focused on getting Walker products on the shelves of pharmacies. Louis W. George of New York was paid for each one-dozen case of products he sold to merchants. Rather than sell goods, Alice Burnett was paid for recruiting agents and delivering her presentations in emerging southern urban markets. These special traveling agents maintained arduous schedules that covered multiple cities in short spans of time.[36]

In terms of her sales agents, Madam Walker did not believe in salaries. Because the active cultivation of a clientele base was so important, Walker remarked, "I don't think it a good idea to pay salaries; it is better to let them work up their own business."[37] And so she devised a wholesale agreement for agents to purchase Walker products from the company in bulk in cases of half-dozen or one dozen products that they could retail for a profit. The hair grower, shampoo, and Tetter salve products were sold wholesale to agents for $3.50 per dozen and retailed at 50 cents per container. The 42 percent margin netted a profit of $2.50 per dozen for the agents. The Glossine and Temple Grower products wholesaled for $2.75 per dozen and retailed at 35 cents each. The 35 percent margin produced a profit of $1.45 per dozen for the agents. Records show agents regularly ordered up to ten dozen cases of products multiple times per year. These profits complemented those earned from hairdressing and performing other beauty culture personal hygiene services, such as facial massage.[38]

Black beauty culture already had low barriers to entry, but Walker frequently reduced them further or completely for the most destitute among the prospective agents and salon owners she recruited. To become an agent required payment of a $25 fee and some initial training. This fee entitled the new agent to starter cases of products, pricing sheets, a Walker Company uniform, and authorization to buy Walker Company products wholesale and sell them retail. Many women signed up and paid the fee either directly before or after participating in Walker's demonstrations of beauty-culture techniques. The orientation was sufficient to get the women started selling products and offering services out of their homes or door to door. Walker was largely successful in collecting the $25 registration fee, but on occasion, she brokered discounts with women who could not pay it in full.

In such instances, Walker's reduction of the $25 fee was a mix of her compassion for others and her competitive drive to defeat her business rivals. Having been a washerwoman, Walker identified with the struggling women, who were wives, mothers, and caretakers in need of better economic opportunities to fulfill their responsibilities. Simultaneously, Walker knew that Annie Malone and many other beauty culture proprietors were actively recruiting agents every day. The businesses were in a race to achieve the highest possible volume of sales, which was directly proportional to the number of agents actively selling in the field. The combination of compassion and competition was evident in Walker's communications about her recruitment efforts.

For example, while in St. Louis in March 1918, Walker signed up a new agent whom she described in a letter to Freeman B. Ransom as "a poor woman who lost her all by fire." This tragic circumstance was clearly a point of sympathy for Walker. She continued, "I am letting her sell but making her [sign a contract] for our protection you take whatever [precaution] you think best. Don't send outfit."[39] Although she was empathetic toward the woman, Walker remained cognizant of the risk as well, for she noted Ransom should not send the customary Walker outfit and should continue to monitor the situation. In another letter sent to Ransom within a week, Walker stated, "I am making the offer of fifteen [dollars] to agents where ever I go and if they can't pay that, take what they can pay you until they can. Let them pay in installments, as I am going after the fifty-eight thousand agents."[40] This ten-dollar reduction in the registration fee reflected Walker's desire both to be helpful and to be competitive. The fifty-eight thousand agents reference was a goal to grow her workforce, which reportedly consisted of approximately twenty thousand agents at the time.[41] One week later in Chicago, Illinois, Walker noted that she was able to attract Annie Malone's agents to her speaking engagement, with some even turning in their training certificates from Malone's Poro Company as they switched over to the Walker system. Perhaps the fee reduction further enticed those agents to defect, because Walker noted, "Some of the Poro girls came directly from the [Poro] college to take my work and paid some money on the trade. I have a Poro diploma to return into the office. Many more are going to take."[42] Walker had figured that reaching her goal of more than doubling her agent workforce would require not only recruiting new women into beauty culture but also converting other companies' agents over to the

Walker method. If these Poro agents were convinced by Walker's presentation to "take" to the Walker method and become agents, Walker surmised that others would as well.

Walker also extended support to prospective salon owners by providing initial capital that did not always have to be repaid. In April 1918, Walker directed Ransom to make rent payments on behalf of a new shop opening in Columbus, Ohio, without reference to any repayment agreement.[43] Sometimes Walker provided partial support, as in the case of Florence Moss Blackwell, to whom she gave $50 toward the $175 start-up cost for a beauty parlor in Savannah, Georgia. A widow, Blackwell approached the company to take its training and quickly opened a shop. A month after providing the money, traveling agent Alice Burnett, who visited Georgia to check in on agents, reported that Blackwell was "getting along fine."[44] In another case involving a shop that Walker apparently funded completely, she contracted with a Mrs. Shelton to manage the parlor and keep profits but make fixed monthly payments until the cost of the parlor was recouped.[45]

For Walker, more agents could equal more revenues and greater profits, but agents had to produce in order for this calculation to work. There was still great risk to Walker in either wholly or partially subsidizing new agents, particularly those already struggling to make ends meet. Walker had been making such arrangements on a case-by-case basis at least since 1915, but she did not want it publicized. When confusion arose over the case of Carrie B. Harris, Walker confirmed for Ransom in a letter that "I remember her coming to me and I think I had her sign up a contract. She doesn't care to do the work and in fact she is not able to. She is almost an object of charity and if she hasn't her contract please send it to her. I am simply giving her that much making her an agent but she shouldn't go out telling it."[46] Though Harris's exact circumstances and motivations are unknown, in this instance, Walker's compassionate side seemed to outweigh the competitive one. She clearly lacked confidence in Harris's ability to perform, but, nonetheless, felt inclined to work with her. Still, Walker's compassion seemed to have limits, for she clearly was frustrated by Harris.

The sentiments expressed by Walker about Harris could certainly be dismissed as merely good business because of the gain Walker stood to experience for having as large of a workforce as possible, but they also reflect a generous attitude toward her employees and prospective employees, which, at a minimum, coexisted with other self-interests. Once a struggling, widowed migrant with a child herself, Walker had never forgotten the difficulties of her own earlier experiences and the help she received. Her company offered a chance to overcome such struggles, and she wanted as many black women as possible to have the option. In this respect, her company represented a philanthropic ideal.

Floyd Snelson, an African Methodist Episcopal (AME) minister who built churches worldwide, praised Walker as a great "Benefactress of Her Race," but not because of her financial gifts to organizations.[47] For Snelson, Walker's employment of the unemployable in a hostile land and labor market was her claim to the "benefactress" moniker. This sentiment was later echoed in the 1950s when the black trade periodical *Beauticians Journal* described the Walker Company as "Unparalleled in its historic growth as the big pioneer in beauty culture and undisputed as the foremost philanthropic institution among Negro Americans."[48] Madam Walker's moral imagination gave the company this philanthropic character, and Freeman B. Ransom, at her direction, operationalized it on a daily basis and at a national scale.

## Freeman B. Ransom, de Facto Philanthropic Adviser

In a 1931 letter to a reporter for the *Inter-State Tattler* newspaper working on a story about the Walker Company, Ransom fondly remembered Walker as "a woman with wonderful ideas." Ransom first met Walker in 1910 six months after starting his practice in Indianapolis, at a time when, in his own words, Walker "was struggling to get a foundation. At the time she was taking in roomers, cooking for them, manufacturing her own preparations in a back room, then doing heads in another room for the rest of the day; she did her washing at night."[49] Ransom experienced Walker as a driven, resourceful, workhorse visionary, who, in frenetic fashion, used every means possible—from taking in boarders to cooking and cleaning for them—to generate capital to advance her fledgling business. She knew she needed more to make her company thrive and she began seeking out the professional expertise necessary to be successful. Ransom's colleague, Robert Brokenburr, drafted articles of incorporation for her business, and Ransom drafted contracts for employing sales agents. From there, Ransom's counsel to her extended to all matters professional and personal, from managing her corporate finances to filing her divorce papers.

If Walker was the workhorse visionary with big dreams and ideas, Ransom was the pragmatic translator of those dreams into organizational form. "I think I helped most in shaping those ideas for her, in putting a good number of things into legal form, in reorganizing her bookkeeping system—or rather, establishing a bookkeeping system for her; in protecting her from the unscrupulous of all types and kinds," he wrote to the newspaper reporter.[50] He formalized and systematized the details of Walker's ideas so they could be implemented. The record of Walker and Ransom's mail correspondence during her extensive travel periods reveal the kinds of assignments she gave to him and the activities on which he advised and reported back to her. He processed the contracts of new agents, developed stereopticon slides for her public presentations, scheduled her travel itineraries, created advertising content, negotiated contracts with vendors, recorded and fulfilled charitable gift pledges, updated and managed product inventories, hired and terminated personnel, managed payrolls and compensation reviews, maintained all financial records and forecasted budgets, monitored agent performance, and followed up on business referrals. An attorney who grew up in the racially oppressive South, he quickly became indispensable.

Ransom was born in Grenada, Mississippi, in 1882. In 1908 he graduated from Walden University, formerly Central Tennessee College, in Nashville. He followed up his study of law at Walden with two terms in law at Columbia University in New York. He came to Indianapolis in 1910 and established a law office. One year later, he was admitted to the Marion County Bar, and he would become a prominent African American citizen of Indianapolis over the next four decades. In 1915 the *Indianapolis Freeman* newspaper described Ransom as "the only colored corporation lawyer in the state," who had also provided counsel for the local National Association for the Advancement of Colored People (NAACP), the Frederick Douglass Life Insurance Association, the Colored Young Men's Christian Association (YMCA), Dr. Perkins' Foot Soap Manufacturing Company, and for several private individuals whose estates he tended.[51]

Throughout his life, Ransom was a race man "identified with movements for the betterment of his people."[52] He was very active in serving many civic and philanthropic institutions in the community. He was a member and trustee of Indianapolis's Bethel AME Church. He was an avid Mason and held leadership positions in other fraternal organizations such as the Knights of Pythias—the parent lodge of Madam Walker's Court of Calanthe—and the Sisters of Charity No. 1. He served as president of Flanner House, a black-serving settlement house in Indianapolis, and sat on its board for much of his adult life. He served on the local boards of the

Alpha Home for Colored Folks and the Senate Avenue YMCA, both favorite charities of Madam Walker. He chaired the Management Committee of the Senate Avenue YMCA as well as the building committee that oversaw construction of the Phyllis Wheatley YWCA in 1929. Ransom also led the fundraising campaign that retired the debts of these two Y institutions. Politically, Ransom was the president of the Fifth Ward Republican League and was elected to the Indianapolis City Council in the 1930s.[53]

In 1918, when Walker's annual income was more than $275,000 and she determined that she could no longer effectively fulfill all the responsibilities she had assumed, she made provisions for Ransom to leave his legal practice and run the company full time.[54] He continued to run the company for many years after her death and managed affairs for Walker's successor, her daughter, Lelia, who had little interest in or acumen for the task.[55] After Ransom's death in 1947, his long-time friend and legal associate, Robert Brokenburr, succeeded him as head of the company. Ransom's life and career were distinguished by a commitment to his community, which started with his work for Madam Walker.

During this time, it was becoming common practice for well-known industrial philanthropists to rely on key advisers to administer their benevolence. Having noted the extraordinary physical and mental toll formal gift-making had taken on them, they would employ such people to render their giving manageable. John D. Rockefeller had Frederick T. Gates. Olivia Margaret Slocum Sage had Robert de Forest. Julius Rosenwald had Edward Rogers Embree. Andrew Carnegie had John Ross, Lord Shaw of Dunfermline, and a complex of boards to advise his giving, and three personal secretaries—James Bertram, Robert Franks, John Poynton—to process some four hundred to seven hundred solicitations received by mail daily. And Madam C. J. Walker had Freeman B. Ransom.[56]

But unlike the advisers specifically hired by the aforementioned philanthropists to run charitable foundations or manage daily activities associated with charitable giving, Ransom was not initially hired to do philanthropy. He was hired to run the Walker Company as general manager and legal counsel. But, as a result of the manner in which Madam Walker operated, Ransom's oversight of her philanthropic giving came as a natural extension of his original charge. The close personal and professional relationship between Walker and Ransom created a bond of loyalty until her death in 1919 that Ransom continued to honor until his own death, some twenty-eight years later.

Ransom did not simply write the charitable gift checks as directed by Madam Walker, he protected and advised her so she could achieve her goals and not outspend her resources. Just as Ransom helped Walker give form to her business, he gave order to her philanthropic giving. Her philanthropy became documented and institutionalized largely because of his efforts, a fact echoed in his obituary: "As a result of his great leadership, the Madam C. J. Walker Manufacturing Company did more than just make money, pay high salaries and build great buildings. It gave thousands of dollars for Y.M.C.A.'s, Y.W.C.A.'s, churches, schools and scholarships."[57] Ransom was Walker's primary, trusted adviser whose influence was particularly felt in his roles as financial manager and protector, which provide significant insight into how the Walker Company achieved its commercial and philanthropic goals.

Ransom had a large job in managing Madam Walker's finances. In this role, he completed many routine duties such as tracking receipts and expenses, making payroll, balancing the books, forecasting budgets, producing reports, and managing relations with banks and vendors. And the challenges associated with his responsibilities were exacerbated by Walker's extensive travel schedule and exorbitant spending.

Walker typically traveled for several months at a time demonstrating her products, recruiting new agents, checking in on existing agents, and promoting the company. It was normal for her to visit multiple cities and cross several states in less than thirty days using her personal automobile. For instance, in February 1918, Ransom sent Walker a pending itinerary for March and April projecting visits throughout Illinois, Indiana, Kentucky, Ohio, and Pennsylvania while she was completing a tour through Iowa:

> Now I hope to arrange your itinerary as far as Chicago on the 11th, Gary on the 12th, Ft. Wayne on the 13th, and then to Indianapolis. . . . I can arrange for you to run out to Marion, Indiana, and Terre Haute, and from Terre Haute to Indianapolis, and [then] you can make Louisville on April 3rd and it appears to me that you ought to go from Louisville to Cleveland, and from Cleveland to Columbus, Chillicothe, and Pittsburgh.[58]

Such a frenetic schedule required constant communication between Walker and Ransom.

For Ransom, keeping track of Madam Walker's spending was aided by their regular mail correspondence, but urging Madam Walker to spend less and save more was a challenge. Over a two-year period, he even engaged Lelia in his personal campaign to convince Madam Walker to be careful.

In a series of correspondence from 1913 to 1915, when Walker's income soared from an average of $48,000 annually to nearly six figures,[59] Ransom recruited Lelia for this effort:

> Madam has just bought six lots in Gary, and a 1913 seven passenger Cole Motor Car. Oh, it's the [latest] thing in autos, so you see you are quite an heiress, I want you to join me in urging Madam from this day on to bank a large portion of her money to the end that it be accumulating and drawing interest for possible rainy days. Madam is in a fair way to be the wealthiest colored person in America, I am ambitious that she be just that, you will help me won't you?[60]

Lelia's response to him is unknown, and it was unclear whether the letter's appeal to her own self-interest as an heiress had any effect during that time. More than a year later, however, Ransom felt compelled to reiterate the argument in relation to Madam's growing interest in moving from Indianapolis to New York and building a large home there:

> it will take quite an income to maintain a building of that kind and in the style that your mother lives, there are those who say live while you are living, but I can imagine no greater disgrace than to be known as your mother is known, and in the end give your enemies a chance to rejoice in the fact that you died poor, this of course, will never be if Madam's business keeps up, but who knows that it will keep up. You must therefore join me in urging that Madam not move to New York until she has paid all debts, I mean present debts, and piled up a snug sum for rainy days.[61]

Despite these early arguments, Ransom's challenge in reining in Madam's spending continued, and so did his campaign. Less than a year later, Lelia closed a business correspondence with a postscript that read: "I think mama will be careful in her spending."[62] It is not clear what specifically prompted this statement, but Ransom was determined to protect Walker's present-day solvency and long-term legacy. But even Lelia had her limits and frustrations. Three years later, after Madam Walker completed the move into her newly built palatial estate, Lelia noted for Ransom, almost with a sense of exasperation, "You know mother is a very reckless spender, far more so than I am. She spends $20.00 here, $15.00 there, etc. not realizing how much she is spending. She orders things like a drunken sailor, and when I tell her she has spent a lot of money she is shocked."[63] It was no small task for Ransom to manage company finances with a spender like Walker at the helm.

Additional difficulties surrounding Walker's spending emerged from her use of the company for both her personal spending and business accounts. As George S. Olive, an Indianapolis accountant, noted in an audit report of Walker's estate in 1919, "It was the custom of Mme. Walker during her life time to withdraw funds from the Company without any formal action on the part of the Board of Directors. Instead of declaring dividends on the stock of the Company and then paying such dividends from the Company's funds, Mme. Walker withdrew money at her own pleasure."[64] Upon receipt of a letter from Walker while she traveled, Ransom never knew what to expect when he opened it. In one instance, she asked him to quickly send $200 because her host had made no plans for her arrival.[65] In another letter, she reported a donation: "Have just drawn a check for $100.00 on the Fletcher [bank account] to the order of Palmer Memorial Institute at Sedalia, N.C., [noted educator] Charlotte Hawkins Brown's school."[66] Brown was Walker's friend through NACW and other circles. Several months earlier, her school had lost two buildings to fire. Walker had sent donations earlier in the year to help rebuild and continue her support. In still another letter to Ransom, Walker reported, "Am sending to Mrs. Robinson a check for $50 to distribute to my charities in St. Louis." As her mentor and friend, Jessie Batts Robinson maintained organizational ties for her through St. Paul's network of organizations.[67] Many such instances abound in their correspondence, for personal, business, and charitable expenses.

After years of such exchanges, Ransom must have had enough, because he put her on a $1,000 per month spending budget in January 1919 and urged her to observe it.[68] Walker did not like this restriction and countered a higher amount. Two weeks later, Ransom wrote to her, "I am afraid that the business is of such that it will not stand for such amount." But not wanting to risk further ire from his boss but still trying to remain firm, Ransom offered a compromise: "I am getting out my monthly report as well as having book balanced and what I shall do is to send you every cent that can be spared after I see just what the situation is."[69] Although Walker's inclination to consume made it difficult for her to abide by Ransom's advice on her personal spending, she heeded it in matters of business and philanthropy because she trusted him, as evidenced by her later making provisions for him to lead the company after her death.

On numerous occasions, Ransom's advice helped to protect Walker from what he perceived to be unscrupulous people and organizations she would have done best to leave alone. In 1918, when Madam Walker sent him a solicitation letter from the National Race Congress, Ransom admitted that he knew little about the organization but recommended she instead continue her support of the NAACP because of its reputation and focus, as well as his preference for it over newer organizations.[70] When Madam Walker's mail became overridden with solicitation letters from individuals and organizations, Ransom became the point person for determining which to respond to and which to discard. Office staff had strict protocols for directing such mail to Ransom and keeping it away from Walker so that she would not be overwhelmed.[71]

As the person who minded the business while Walker traveled, Ransom was also keenly aware of protecting her reputation. He regularly directed questionable characters and business interests away from Walker and the company, and he also directed Walker herself away from specific entanglements. His protective tendencies were most evident in correspondence related to Madam Walker's support of a group she cofounded, the International League of Darker Peoples (ILDP).[72]

Walker had a history of convening race leaders and community members to address matters of racial uplift. In 1912 Walker had invited friends, including women from the Equal Suffrage Association of Indiana, to her Indianapolis home to discuss a proposal to create a permanent fund that would provide aid to the poor and homeless during the winter. An unnamed organization was reportedly established during the meeting, with Walker announced in the newspaper as its president and Ransom as its secretary.[73] In 1914 Walker hosted a group of women and girls at her home who were interested in forming a local YWCA in Indianapolis.[74] In 1915 Walker hosted Eliza Peterson, a black woman from Texas who headed the Colored Division of the Women's Christian Temperance Union (WCTU), at her home. Peterson organized fifty children into a group called the Walker Loyal Legion—a play on WCTU's typical practice of forming groups of youth around the country to inculcate a commitment to Christianity and temperance—who signed WCTU's pledge not to consume alcohol or tobacco during their lifetimes and to never take the Lord's name in vain.[75] After she had moved to New York, her interest in convening increased as her mansion became the site for numerous meetings for organizations, including the ILDP.

In 1918 black leaders wanted black representation in the US delegation to the upcoming Paris Peace Conference, which was to decide punishments for Germany as WWI's chief aggressor. Numerous black organizations lobbied the federal government for representation and put forward their own delegates despite fierce resistance from the Wilson administration. In January 1919, Walker hosted A. Phillip Randolph, Marcus Garvey, Adam Clayton Powell Sr., Ida B. Wells, and others at her New York mansion, Villa Lewaro, to discuss these issues. They cofounded the ILDP to unify these interests and connect the African American struggle for liberation with similar struggles globally, much in the way the AME Church had begun doing when young Sarah was living in St. Louis. Such an approach was attractive because of frustrating domestic events like the 1917 East St. Louis race riots and President Wilson's neglect of the US treatment of blacks. The ILDP's agenda included independence for African colonies, especially those held by Germany; acceptance of racial equality worldwide; and equal representation of people of color in world governments. Walker was elected treasurer, and she agreed to pay the costs of travel to Europe for the group to participate in the peace talks.[76]

Ransom objected to Walker's involvement in the ILDP from the start. He thought it was a ploy to get to Madam's money. He viewed its agenda as "impractical, revolutionary, and foolish" and feared it would hurt the business and Walker's reputation by attracting the ire of the government. He did not want her associated with a socialist like Randolph or a nationalist like Garvey. He repeatedly advised her to remove herself. Ransom was an NAACP man. The NAACP, NACW, and National Urban League were very suspicious and dismissive of many of the global black nationalist groups that developed during this time, which resulted in tensions. Ransom felt that blacks needed to support one organization, namely the NAACP, so a concerted effort could be brought to bear on the race's problems. In his mind, there were too many organizations seeking attention, and they diluted energy. He was also concerned that Madam Walker's usefulness to the race would be diminished if she affiliated with too many organizations.[77]

After Walker sent him a list of radical activists affiliated with ILDP, he dramatically noted, "I have not written you on this matter before today because I have been trying to wait until I could write you calmly." He then pressed, "You must always be watchful lest you be charged with seeking cheap notoriety. We who know you and have learned to love you know that you are not of this type or kind by any means, but the world does not know it and will judge you naturally by your acts and associates."

Upset that Walker had convened the group in her home, he urged her that "one's home is sacred and it should never be made the place for gathering of theorists, propagandists, etc." Walker wanted to remain involved with ILDP but later relented; "I am very much hurt over your opinion of the International League and am sorry now that I had anything to do with it." She resigned from the organization. But by this time, Walker had already supported Randolph and Garvey by placing ads in their newspapers. In addition, Walker donated to Garvey's Universal Negro Improvement Association and helped to purchase his meeting facility in New York. Ransom's concerns were warranted, for such entanglements caused Walker to be placed under government surveillance and ultimately resulted in denial of her passport for travel to Paris.[78]

During this period, black men regularly formed their gendered identities in opposition to black women,[79] but such does not appear to have been the case with Ransom and Walker. Black men and black women frequently battled over the best approaches for uplifting the race. These tensions played out in numerous organizations and publications as leaders, orators, and writers from both genders criticized the other for failing them. Historian Deborah Gray White observed that black men attacked black women's morality and chastity, while black women accused their men of failing to honor, respect, and protect them.[80] Ransom never attacked Walker's character; he worked to protect it. He was steeped in fraternal life, which was known for connecting "production, patriarchy, respectability and manliness."[81] Madam Walker and the Walker Company were major parts of his identity and remained so until the end of his life. His partnership with Walker was more egalitarian than one would expect for the era. He was not always able to assert influence over her as he would have liked. Simultaneously, she valued his counsel and would concede on occasion. They developed an understanding between them that worked. He clearly disagreed with some of her approaches to racial uplift, like the ILDP, and felt a need to correct them. As a college-educated man and attorney, Ransom may have felt a responsibility for protecting Walker as an uneducated female. He may also have seen himself as having a greater capacity than Walker to protect herself and the company because he was male and educated. He certainly respected her ideas and her abilities, but he viewed himself as having to bring order to those ideas to keep them manageable. Ransom was dutiful and loyal to Walker, and a mutual respect existed between the two.

He was her friend, a dear friend who cared deeply for her and invested himself in her success with little demand for attribution.[82] Their bond extended to their families. Ransom's children referred to Walker as "Mother Walker," and she regularly inquired about their well-being in her letters to him. They routinely exchanged gifts on holidays, and, after she moved away to New York, Madam Walker joined the Ransom family for meals when visiting Indianapolis. In December 1918, Ransom captured the nature of their relationship when he wrote to Madam Walker,

> When Christmas comes around, I am always reminded of the number of years that I have known you and looking back over your remarkable career, I take a peculiar pride in the fact that I have had the pleasure of watching you develop in business and also your broadening along all lines and then I congratulate myself of having the honor of knowing you and representing you in a small way. I, of course, am writing in the hope that God will continue to smile on you and that you will continue to bless and help the less fortunate.[83]

One week later, Walker returned the sentiment: "The little gift from you and Nettie [Ransom's wife] is greatly appreciated and I understand to the fullest degree, all the love that came with it. But best of all, was the really beautiful letter you wrote and which I hope to always keep, as a reminder of an association of which I shall ever be proud."[84] The Walker-Ransom relationship was close and personal, focused on matters of business within a context of mutual love and respect. Their relational chemistry enabled the Walker Company's dual commercial and philanthropic goals to coexist and thrive in providing the gift of opportunity to thousands of African American women.

## Critiques of the Walker Company

Critics attacked Walker and her company for promoting white standards of beauty based on a perception that she was straightening black women's hair. Walker went to great lengths to dispel the perception, but it persisted. She drew a distinction when she said near the end of her life, "let me correct the erroneous impression held by some that I claim to straighten the hair. I deplore such impression because I have always held myself out as a hair culturist, I grow hair. I have absolute faith [in] my mission. . . . I want the great masses of my people to take a greater pride in their personal appearance and to give their hair proper attention." She was less interested in *how* black women styled their hair and more interested in making sure that they *had* hair to begin with that was full and healthy. She stated as much: "[I]n the next ten years it will be a rare thing to see a kinky head [of] hair and it will not be straight hair either." Her original four products—Temple Grower, Tetter Salve, Glossine, and Hair Grower—had little to do with straightening hair, but rather with soothing and healing scalp disease, moisturizing the hair and scalp, and providing for cleanliness and sheen.[85]

She knew the public was skeptical and knew the challenge involved in earning its trust in her products: "the principal obstacle I had to deal with was the traditional distrust and incredulity of the public, owing to their having [often] been deceived with worthless preparations, the sole merit of which was the audacity with which they were advertised and fostered upon the public; but with great faith in the merit of my goods I at last convinced the public that they were just as represented." In early 1919, Walker announced a new line of products, including a cold cream, cleansing cream, face powders, and witch hazel. She pushed these products as being helpful for basic cleansing, sunburn, aftershave, and protection from sun rays. She did not push a message of skin whitening or lightening, though her ads were occasionally juxtaposed with other companies' ads promoting that very thing. She reportedly developed the products in response to feedback from agents in the field, noting, "I have always made it a rule to never offer the public anything unless I thought that I was in position to give value received." Walker was clear in her intent to offer options to black women: "I make no superlative claims for my new toilet articles, while I naturally think they are the best and I know there is none better on the market. I shall let my goods make their own reputation. All I ask [is] that they be given a fair trial."[86]

In a competitive marketplace where multiple beauty companies used very light-skinned models and openly advertised skin-bleaching products, it was easy to ascribe ulterior motives to Walker. The charges reflected larger social and cultural anxieties among blacks about their place in America and the extent to which they could express themselves. Still, Walker bucked the trend by placing herself—a very dark-skinned woman with African-like facial features—in her company's marketing campaigns: "I want everybody to know that for years I had practically no hair at all and what I had was short and stubby. I want them to know that I used every remedy on the market I read about and to which my attention was called, but I obtained no result until I discovered [m]y preparation and upon using it my hair grew long and beautiful." A well-circulated advertisement juxtaposed a "before" picture of a short-haired Walker with an "after" picture of her with shoulder-length hair. The "after" photo was meant to dramatize the length of her hair after treatment with Walker products, not its straightness. Walker used herself as a model to convey a critical message that built the foundation of her brand. "I am not experimenting on the public to see what my preparations will do; I know what they will do and guarantee them when used as directed."[87] Certainly, no one could look at Walker and accuse her of attempting to make herself over as white.

Scholars have debated the point, noting that although the company may have denied accusations that it was assimilating white standards of beauty during Walker's lifetime, its product offerings, marketing strategies, and selling instructions to agents after her death suggest otherwise. Similarly, scholars have emphasized that white beauty companies definitely used their marketing to negatively critique black women's appearances and draw them into products used by white women, but black beauty culturists focused on the health and maintenance of hair. Beyond Walker, sentiments varied from beautician to beautician about the ultimate end of beauty culture, and a desire on the part of black women to use cosmetics did not necessarily constitute a desire to "be white." Furthermore, the aesthetics of black beauty were still being negotiated, as these were times when black women were trying to determine how to shape their own ideals of feminine beauty. Regarding the commodification of beauty, historian Kathy Peiss noted that "beauty images simultaneously promise and withhold, elevate and degrade." Although the influence of marketing was strong, Walker customers had the agency and autonomy to make decisions for themselves about which products to purchase, how best to wear their hair and present themselves.[88]

Scholars have also examined direct-selling organizations and mail-order businesses in the twentieth century. Madam Walker's company predated Mary Kay Cosmetics by more than half a century, but not the California Perfume Company (eventually Avon Cosmetics), which was founded in the 1880s by a man. Direct-selling organizations, like Avon, evolved from colonial peddlers who traversed the country pitching wares on behalf of merchants but then faded out of fashion as mass merchandising developed in the middle 1800s. They saw a resurgence in the early twentieth century as manufacturers sought an advantage in competing with retail department stores and, by the 1920s, direct-selling organizations were multilevel complex operations. Legitimate sales professionals had to wrestle with the stereotype of selling "snake oil" because of the history of abuses by con men, but the business opportunity that direct-selling organizations offered to their sales agents—who were increasingly women—was serious and significant.[89]

Similarly, the Walker Company was a tremendous opportunity for black women. This is not to say that there were not disgruntled agents, because there were some who were upset, for instance, at the company's logistics and distribution networks, which, periodically, struggled to deliver product orders on time. Ransom helped Walker address those situations, and one of the reasons she later organized her agents into clubs was to strengthen relations between them and the company. There is no evidence of the company abusing its agents, but rather a record of Walker and Ransom's concern over agent troubles. The United States Postal Service did investigate the Walker Company, along with Sears and Roebuck, for mail fraud in 1919, as part of a larger crackdown on the growing mail-order business sector, but that was a matter of consumer protection against suspected false marketing claims for mail-order products, all of which Ransom resolved to the company's benefit.[90]

⁕⁕⁕

Entrepreneurship did not distinguish Madam Walker from the dominant white male industrial philanthropists of the day, but it did distinguish her from the white women philanthropists and from most of the notable race women philanthropists of her era. Olivia Sage and other white women of leisure did not know the daily grind of work for pay. Walker was distinct from them because she never left the trenches of work for pay despite her wealth, which gave her a different relationship to the resources she used for philanthropy and the issues she addressed. Walker and her race women sisters were all clubwomen and churchwomen. Many of them were educators, political leaders, and journalists, like Nannie Helen Burroughs, Mary McLeod Bethune, and Ida B. Wells. The difference for Walker, however, was entrepreneurship. To the church, club, and school, Walker added *company* as a third "c." It was her platform for meeting the needs of her race. It enabled her to bring particular resources to bear on the struggle for justice and equality—resources that other race women had to navigate and negotiate white power structures or gendered hierarchies of black institutions to demand. Walker was able to circumvent these systems, establish her own efforts, and use her own resources to develop human capital in the black community without permission from anyone else.

In this way, opportunity was part of the medley of beneficent acts and gifts in the African American philanthropic tradition that Walker made through the platform of her race company. By employing laborers abused and undesired by the white mainstream labor markets and focusing on hygiene as a means of personal development and public pride, the Walker Company was simultaneously commercial and philanthropic. Shortly after Walker incorporated the company, a newspaper reported, "Indianapolis feels proud of this business woman, as well as of the opportunity for employment this corporation offers her boys and girls, and this city is proud of her for yet another reason, proud of her great, big, generous and race-loving heart." These dual characteristics emerged from the broader context of black suffering during Jim Crow, Madam Walker's moral imagination, and Walker's personal and professional relationship with Freeman B. Ransom, who invigorated her ideas.[91]

As a platform for commerce and philanthropy, the Walker Company was the hub of Walker's gospel of giving. It was the autonomous space through which she pursued her agenda rather than through some other male-approved parallel sphere. Walker competed head on with men like Anthony Overton of Overton Hygienic Manufacturing in Chicago and operated on a par with black male leaders of the race. So, rather than being in tension, Walker's dual purposes were reciprocal because the business of black business has never been about just business.[92] The commerce fueled and enabled the philanthropy, and the philanthropy gave meaning and moral legitimacy to the commercial. These dual purposes provided a base from which Walker launched a major initiative to address one of the most vexing issues facing African Americans under Jim Crow—education.

# 3

# Education

My ambition is to build an industrial school
in Africa—by the help of God and the
cooperation of my people in this country,
I am going to build a Tuskegee Institute in
Africa.
—Madam C. J. Walker, 1912

Given the magnitude of her
accomplishments, why aren't the decades
between 1890 and 1920 referred to as the Age
of Madam C.J. Walker, or perhaps the Age
of Booker T. Washington and Madam C.J.
Walker?
—Darlene Clark Hine, 1996

On Friday, August 23, 1912, Madam C. J. Walker, now a wealthy forty-five-year-old African American manufacturer of beauty-care products, stood before an audience of approximately two thousand that had filled a church on the South Side of Chicago, Illinois, to participate in Booker T. Washington's thirteenth annual meeting of the National Negro Business League (NNBL). Washington, the prominent black leader and advocate for black industrial education, had organized the group twelve years earlier to serve as a network for promoting black economic development in Jim Crow America. It quickly became popular and well attended by black business owners and professionals from across the country. Washington stood close to Walker that day, but he was chagrined because she was not a scheduled speaker. After months of trying to get Washington's attention through letters and recommendations made on her behalf by mutual friends, Walker was fed up with Washington's inattention and refusal to put her on his program.[1] So she commandeered the floor from him and demanded to speak.

Madam Walker wanted to share her story and gain Washington's respect and endorsement. Her company was growing. She had overcome much and wanted to help other black women conquer similar obstacles. She had a clear strategy for doing so through the Walker Company. She believed she was an entrepreneur deserving of respect with as much to share, if not more, as the packed slate of speakers who had dominated the meeting for nearly three days. She admired and identified with Washington, who had made it out of slavery to become a national leader, and she viewed her own life as having a similar ascending trajectory. At this point, she could endure his slights no more.

Madam Walker's disruption of the program began with her defiant declaration "Surely you are not going to close the door in my face" as she got up from her seat and walked to the front near a stunned Washington. She proceeded to outline the case to the audience for her speaking by highlighting her struggles as a poor washerwoman, the legitimacy of the beauty-culture industry and her business, the size of her staff and physical plant, her income, and the accoutrements of her success, such as her two automobiles. The crowd interrupted Walker's speech with great applause, but she urged them to stop so she could continue, not knowing how much Washington could stand before cutting her off. For the climax of the presentation, Walker left the audience with a particular statement with great implications for the history of black education and black women's philanthropy: "Perhaps many of you have heard of the real ambition of my life, the all-absorbing idea which I hope to accomplish, and when you have heard what it is, I hope you will catch the inspiration, grasp the opportunity to do something of far-reaching importance, and lend me your support. My ambition is to build an industrial school in Africa—by the help of God and the cooperation of my people in this country, I am going to build a Tuskegee Institute in Africa."[2] The audience applauded loudly as Walker resumed her seat. They loved her idea and her overall message. Washington tried to recover by quickly moving onto the next agenda item with little acknowledgment of Walker's presentation. But she had had her moment.

Her impromptu and forceful speech has been used by scholars to document her legacy as a black female entrepreneur,[3] but not so much as a philanthropist, educator, and supporter of industrial education. This model of education focused on the teaching and learning of "basic agricultural and trade skills" to promote "the dignity of labor" as a pathway to economic and then political empowerment for African Americans after Emancipation.[4] At the time, Washington's conceptualization of industrial education was lauded by white northern industrial philanthropists such as Andrew Carnegie, who promulgated it across the South through a significant investment of their resources, which was vehemently critiqued by W. E. B. DuBois, William Monroe Trotter, the black press, and many others as being detrimental to the race. As a result of these tensions, historiography in the past forty years has been very critical of Washington and his motives, model, and institution as not serving the interests of black people.[5] Yet here was an independent black woman using her voice to advance the contentious philosophy, too, as part of her gospel of giving. Walker's direct engagement with industrial education started well before she made her speech at the NNBL meeting and would continue to play out for years to come. Her dream of building a Tuskegee Institute in Africa represented not only her whole-hearted embrace of Washington's controversial educational philosophy, but perhaps one of the most significant philanthropic gifts she gave to others—education.

Throughout history, African Americans have pursued education as a prime aspiration. As a resource that had been both denied and pursued, education represented a linchpin for securing hope for individuals and freedom for the race. During slavery, the cultural and operating practices of southern plantations and the legal statutes of many southern states prohibited providing even the bare rudiments of literacy for enslaved people, let alone formal schooling. But, under secrecy and the constant threat of punishment, many enslaved people aggressively developed their literacy.[6]

This impulse for learning expanded after Emancipation. African American efforts to establish free communities especially emphasized education and the creation of schools. Washington's early observation of the formerly enslaved peoples' fervor for literacy after Emancipation informed his own desire to start Tuskegee:

> it was a whole race trying to go to school. Few were too young, and none too old, to make the attempt to learn. As fast as any kind of teachers could be

secured, not only were day-schools filled, but night-schools as well. The great ambition of the older people was to try to learn to read the Bible before they died. With this end in view, men and women who were fifty or seventy-five years old would often be found in the night-school. Sunday-schools were formed soon after freedom, but the principal book studied in the Sunday-school was the spelling-book. Day-school, night-school, Sunday-school, were always crowded, and often many had to be turned away for want of room.[7]

The demise of slavery and the rise of Reconstruction may have done away with laws against educating blacks, but African Americans still had to engage in a long-suffering struggle to assert their freedom and control their own lives. An ideological system of second-class education emerged for them through the efforts of southern white-led governments and northern white industrial philanthropists who sought to maintain the status quo of black racial oppression. In spite of such opposition, educational historian James Anderson observed that blacks created a "unique system of public and private education" in the decades after Emancipation because they "viewed literacy and formal education as means to liberation and freedom."[8]

Because the legally sanctioned denial of education was foundational to slavery and Jim Crow, it has been both a principal object of and an instrument for black women's engaging in philanthropy. As an objective, education motivated the voluntary actions of black women, who were especially adept at educating children, women, and families through their churches, benevolent associations, clubs, fraternal orders, literary societies, and normal and industrial schools. The provision of education for the masses was a goal of their philanthropy. They raised funds and ran educational programs. But education itself is a form of philanthropy.[9] The process of teaching and learning is a melioristic act, one that supports participants in acquiring, creating, and using new knowledge, skills, and dispositions—philanthropic gifts—that can dramatically change their relationship to the broader world.

The view of education as philanthropy has been elemental in black women's philanthropy. When black clubwomen at the beginning of the twentieth century set up their educational programs, they were not just providing education as a service, they were using teaching and learning itself to change the minds, lives, and conditions of African Americans through literacy, child-rearing, hygiene, and other academic and vocational subjects they deemed important for freedom. When black women teachers, who held positions of esteem in their communities because of the premium placed on education, worked in underresourced and dilapidated Jim Crow schools, they mentored their students and engaged in community work above and beyond the expectations of their paid positions, because education itself was viewed as an important instrument for uplifting the race. In these ways and more, educating others not only marked a significant aim of black women's philanthropy, it was a philanthropic act itself.[10] The gift of education supported the definition of African American philanthropy and expanded Walker's gospel of giving.

As early as 1908, Walker began creating a national chain of beauty schools that made her a major provider of industrial education. After selling products on her own for a few years, her growth strategy relied on employing others to sell along with her. Although she always had some training to offer, standardizing a curriculum and scaling up through schools in cities would further develop beauty culture as a respectable profession. The industrial education model was perfect for beauty culture because of its emphasis on skill development and reliance on demonstration and practice. Expanding through a network of schools would accelerate acceptance of her field, help her remain competitive with Poro, and extend education to black women, particularly migrants, as they settled in urban communities. As historian Glenda Gilmore observed, "Because education represented the key to class mobility, African Americans came to see it as nothing less than sacred, a spiritual duty that fell more heavily on women because of motherhood."[11] In taking up this mantle, Walker went further by giving philanthropic support to black industrial schools in the South to increase educational and economic opportunities for black women. After investigating curriculum from the early years of Walker's beauty schools and correspondence between Walker and the southern black industrial schools she supported, it is clear that Walker fully embraced an industrial educational strategy for racial uplift and emerged as a significant provider and funder of industrial education in the early twentieth century who empowered black women with financial independence so they could take voluntary and political action to improve black communities.

Not only does this analysis highlight Walker's use of education as a philanthropic gift, it provides a perspective on the relationship between industrial philanthropy and black education different from perspectives in the extant historiography. Philanthropists, who in the literature were mainly prominent white men of the late nineteenth and early twentieth centuries, are understood as having used their gifts to underwrite industrial training curricula in black schools as a means of maintaining social control of the black population and denying blacks civil rights. A more nuanced view of this historical relationship that moves beyond hegemonic explanations emerges when we investigate the agency of Walker as a wealthy black woman donor and educational provider and her recipient institutions.[12]

## The Problem of Black Education

After slavery and the Civil War ended, the question of what do with the 4 million newly freed people became central for the fractured South and the victorious North seeking to rebuild US society. Education was a battleground for the debate, and the Hampton-Tuskegee idea of industrial education became a dominant force for showing blacks their place in postbellum America.[13] Both black and white interest in black industrial education dated back to the early eighteenth century, but traction was not gained until well after the Civil War when southern whites and northern white philanthropists declared industrial training to be the model for black education. They believed industrial education was the best method for preserving the racial hierarchy and social order of the South. The Hampton-Tuskegee model of industrial training was created in Virginia by Samuel Chapman Armstrong in 1868 at Hampton Institute and promulgated by his pupil, Booker T. Washington, at Tuskegee Institute in Alabama after 1881. The model gained prominence in the eyes of white Southerners and began to dominate the funding agendas of white northern industrial philanthropists.

Washington believed that only industrial education could properly prepare blacks for life after Emancipation because it was better suited for helping them make the "connection between school and life" in practical ways through an emphasis on developing skilled labor rather than intellectual abilities as offered by classical liberal education. As a result of the partnership between Washington and northern white industrial philanthropists, the Hampton-Tuskegee idea rapidly reproduced numerous industrial schools across the South. The proliferation was not limited to small privately funded schools. The 1890 land-grant schools established by states for blacks adopted the Hampton-Tuskegee model too.[14]

But historians have shown that this mode of industrial education was flawed from its inception. James Anderson stressed that instead of

preparing blacks for work in particular skilled trades, the Hampton-Tuskegee model developed a work ethic among blacks so they could stay in the
agricultural southern economy. Donald Spivey and Roy Finkenbine affirmed
that this focus resulted from widely held views that blacks had to be taught
work as a moral virtue to overcome their inherent laziness, which would in
turn contribute to the South's economic prosperity. Rather than producing
a skilled workforce for the devolving agricultural economy, let alone the
emerging urban industrial economy, more than anything, the Hampton-
Tuskegee model produced a cadre of teachers whom Anderson described
"as missionaries of the Puritan work ethic in Southern black communities"
and "common laborers" for menial work in the southern railroad, coal, and
cotton-oil mill industries.[15]

Hampton's program comprised an academic curriculum to develop students' teaching abilities; a manual labor system to engage them in daily,
routinized, and unskilled work; and a code of conduct to mold their character.
Students' schedules were dominated by manual work, which often consumed
five times the number of hours spent in academic pursuits and did not focus
on the kind of trade skills that would yield meaningful employment in the
labor market. Eventually, Hampton offered specific training in skilled trades
near the turn of the century, but the preparation of teachers dominated its
efforts. Washington replicated the Hampton model at Tuskegee, including a
code of discipline that prescribed how students should stand, speak, and eat.
Some of his students were critical of Tuskegee, and many rebelled against
their treatment. Although student rebellion against educational institutions
was not uncommon, some Tuskegee students also expressed great dissatis-
faction at what they viewed as the low-quality and insufficient instruction
in useful skills and the institution's overt focus on their behavior.[16]

Washington urged blacks to stay in the South and not migrate northward because whites would lock them out of urban labor markets. Racism
in southern urban labor markets stifled opportunities for blacks and trade
unions prevented their membership. Similarly, blacks' lack of access to land
and the prominence of sharecropping and tenant farming made agricultural work a dubious endeavor. Consequently, graduates of these programs
were moderately prepared to teach and conduct menial unskilled labor. The
Hampton-Tuskegee idea of industrial education overwhelmingly focused on
teacher training and manual labor and did not open up economic pathways
into skilled professions for black graduates.[17]

The white northern industrialists had mixed motivations, but the driving impetus behind their push for black industrial education was fear and racism. For instance, the white board members and agents of the Slater Fund, a leading funder in this space from its founding in 1867, operated from a base of stereotypical assumptions about blacks despite characterizing themselves as "benevolent reformers." Other industrial philanthropists, such as John D. Rockefeller Sr., Anson Phelps Stokes, William Baldwin, and Robert Ogden, used their resources to socially engineer the "Negro problem" to avoid disrupting the existing southern racial order so essential to their commercial dominance. Arguments have been made that rather than being exclusively driven by racial animus, these funders were more motivated by fear of white opposition in the South. Thus, they implemented policies and funding decisions that avoided confrontation with the South and focused more broadly on public education for all. They ignored black concerns and criticisms and prioritized their own plans over the aspirations of those they sought to help. Consequently, historian William H. Watkins pronounced that the educational agenda prescribed for southern blacks differed greatly from blacks' own educational agenda. Not content to receive the charity of others, blacks collectively donated millions of dollars to fund their own schools and educational initiatives across the South. Throughout their experience in the United States, they have worked as philanthropists in the political and social struggle for education.[18]

Historians have inordinately focused, however, on the white industrial philanthropists. The extant historiography has pigeonholed whites in the role of philanthropists and blacks in the role of passive recipients to be educated by those philanthropists; but new understanding emerges when those conventions are upended. When black people, instead of being viewed as the victims of the philanthropic and educational ideologies of others, fulfill the roles of donor and recipient, provider and student, their actual agency, unseen before, completely changes the narrative. My analysis of Madam C. J. Walker provides the chance to explore these contexts and yields another view of how the relationship between industrial philanthropy and black education played out. Unlike Washington, Walker embraced urbanization and modernization.[19] As a former penniless migrant and low-wage washerwoman, she knew firsthand the challenges presented by both southern and northern labor markets for blacks; but she believed she had something to offer her race in spite of them—the gift of beauty-culture education through the industrial model.

## The National Madam C. J. Walker Beauty School Chain

In 1908, while living in Pittsburgh, Pennsylvania, Madam Walker established Lelia College, a training school in beauty culture. Named for her
daughter, the college was managed by Lelia—a graduate of Knoxville College—to enable Madam Walker to travel, sell her products, and refer black
women to the college for training. Lelia College became one of two leading
beauty schools for black women in the early twentieth century—the other
was Annie Malone's Poro College.[20] Lelia opened another location in Harlem
after she left Pittsburgh for New York City in 1913. The acclaim of Lelia
College and its reach was largely because it offered a $25 correspondence
course, through which students could learn beauty culture at home. Those
students who completed the course received a diploma signed by Walker
and were permitted to sell products on behalf of the company.

Despite its early success, the Lelia College beauty-school brand did not
last, but several Madam C. J. Walker Beauty Schools developed and lasted
for decades after Walker's death in 1919.[21] Over time, with locations in places
such as St. Louis, Dallas, Washington, Indianapolis, Chicago, and Kansas
City, these beauty schools trained thousands of black women in Madam
Walker's system of beauty culture and catapulted them into careers that
enabled them to support themselves and their families. As an extension
of the Walker Company, the beauty schools were an important aspect of
Walker's overall organizational strategy.

Walker had multiple rationales for starting a chain of beauty schools. She
needed agents in order to successfully compete in the densely populated
landscape of black beauty culturists. National companies, like Poro in St.
Louis and Overton Hygienic Manufacturing in Chicago, were in various
stages of their own evolution but had significant presences in the marketplace. There were also dozens of local competitors in northern and southern
markets. Though significantly smaller than Walker's primary rivals, the
local competitors sometimes acted as free riders who used the likeness and
substance of the Walker brand to peddle their own products.[22] Walker was
particularly frustrated by these impostors who repackaged and resold her
formulas, and thus undercut her own brand and profits. A Walker-branded
educational credential helped customers distinguish company agents in the
field from the competitors and impostors. A beauty school, thus, became a
means of maintaining brand integrity and developing and deploying more
hairdressers and agents in such a competitive landscape.

In support of Madam Walker's staffing objective, beauty schools further reduced beauty culture's low barriers to entry. Few capital resources were needed to be successful in beauty culture. It could be practiced out of one's home and products could be sold door to door.[23] The primary requirement was acquiring the knowledge, skills, and products so one could work. Walker personally traveled the country "making agents"—as she called it—through on-site training in church basements and other familiar locales in conjunction with her speaking engagements. As previously mentioned, she also employed a cadre of traveling agents who did the same. But Walker and these individuals could be in only a certain number of places and train only a limited number of people at a time. Lelia College and the subsequent chain of Walker Beauty Schools institutionalized the process and dispersed it geographically in major US cities so that "making agents" became routine and occurred on a larger scale.

The beauty schools also enabled Walker to substantiate her claims for beauty culture as a profession by establishing a recognized educational credential and a loyal workforce. Dubbed by the company a "passport to prosperity," the credential was a source of pride for working-class black women with limited options in the labor market. They could be immediately rewarded by employment through affiliation with the company, either as an agent, independent salon owner, or salon employee. In 1915 Mabel Marble announced her graduation in the *Indianapolis Freeman* newspaper, which described her as "the proud possessor of a diploma." Marble became an agent for the Walker Company and, two years later, taught the Walker method to students at black industrial colleges in the South on behalf of the company. The beauty credentialing process trained black women in the art and science of beauty culture and the appropriate use of products and techniques, but it also obligated them to use only Walker products, which protected Walker's market share and guaranteed a workforce.[24] Regarding black beauty-culture education, historian Tiffany Gill observed that "While their work was considered unskilled labor by some, they were credentialed and, eventually, licensed professionals." Madam Walker's schools made this possible. They represented Madam Walker's embrace of industrial education, at least in part, as one of many means for blacks to achieve economic self-sufficiency and the rights of citizenship.[25]

Although the original curricular materials that Walker used have not survived, the Walker Company published a training manual shortly after

Walker's death to guide coursework. Entitled *The Madam C. J. Walker Beauty Manual: A Thorough Treatise Covering all Branches of Beauty Culture*, the 208-page text detailed the fundamentals of the Walker system of beauty culture.[26] From its beginning, the text set a tone that invoked the presence and legacy of Madam Walker for students. It began with a history of Walker's life, company, and benevolence. The history was presented in triumphant fashion, clearly meant not only to inform but also to inspire Walker students, gain their loyalty to the Walker legacy and company, and convince them to see themselves in Walker's story. By chronicling the depths of Walker's difficult life and the heights of her success, the narrative sought to convince students that, just like Madam Walker, their success was in their own hands, and the Walker Company could help them achieve it.

The triumphant narrative began opposite a page that contained pictures of the small, run-down slave quarters on the Delta plantation on which Sarah Breedlove was born in 1867 juxtaposed with a picture of the extravagant thirty-four-room mansion named Villa Lewaro that Madam Walker built in Irvington-on-Hudson, New York, between 1916 and 1918.[27] The pain and struggle of Sarah's early life was conveyed through references to her as an "orphan" and "widow" who endured "hardships and much toil" and faced "many discouragements and obstacles," including friends who did not believe in her dreams of a better life. Walker's students would have had similar disappointments, particularly in a world where segregation and discrimination were the law and backbreaking menial work rarely covered their family expenses.

Despite such despair, the text reminded students that Madam Walker was "determined and felt inspired" as she was guided by her religious beliefs. The text created a vivid image of Madam Walker in partnership with Jesus Christ, noting that "by placing her hand in His," she set out with the potential to "convert the world by the wonderful good she would do for her people." The reference clearly delineated Walker's African Methodist Episcopal religious faith in a just God who would help the downtrodden and guide the efforts of those seeking to improve themselves and serve others. This kind of faith and service to others marked the text's point of departure for Sarah's struggles.[28]

The narrative began its ascent as the early days of Sarah's business in Denver and Pittsburgh were recounted, leading to the building of a factory in Indianapolis, agents and goods being sold in every state, and advertisements published overseas in four languages. Walker was portrayed as enjoying the fruits of her labor, including her ability to build "the finest home owned by any member of the race in this country," a reference to Villa Lewaro. The text reminded students that these fruits resulted from Walker's efforts and informed them that self-improvement was very important because Walker "read everything in sight, including the Bible, which she called her main guide." She hired a tutor, read classical literature, and studied relentlessly after business hours. Walker's self-improvement not only focused on the typical liberal arts elements of learning thought to increase knowledge and build character, but also the rudiments of business. The text noted, "As her business grew she made up her mind to develop with it, to that end she took lessons in commercial and business courses until she developed into a well-informed business woman." It was unknown exactly when and where Walker would have taken such courses, but the message was clear that success as a Walker Beauty School student and eventual beauty culturist required dedicated physical work in the matters of business and intellectual work in the matters of education and continual self-improvement. Even still, a work ethic and educational development were only part of the story.[29]

The opening biographical section of the text concluded with a history of Madam Walker's benevolence. The text recounted Walker's monetary gifts to charities, in-kind gifts to poor families, and her estate bequests. The text described the influence of Walker's giving, which "served not only to encourage others, but aroused them to a true high sense of duty." Naming Walker a "race woman," the text tied her business acumen and success to her generosity and faith by emphasizing that the company's dual commercial and philanthropic purposes were based on the principle of unselfish service that should be "emulated by others who are in a position to help the race and racial enterprises."[30] The school taught future agents to be generous, committed to the race, and loyal to the brand.

In racially hostile times such as those of the early twentieth century, Madam Walker's story had a philanthropic quality and currency to it that amounted to a gift amid a larger societal narrative that ridiculed black life as inhuman and worthless. In this way, the text extended her life story forward to succeeding generations as a counternarrative that emphasized the humanity, self-determination, resilience, and generosity of black life. This narrative showed how Walker overcame life's obstacles through faith, perseverance, hard work, and a philanthropic commitment to "the betterment of humanity and her race."[31] As a text in the beauty school, this story sought to inculcate the same values in students and build their loyalty so that they would use the Walker system to achieve their own independence and dreams, which also benefited the company financially and its efforts to uplift the race.

The curriculum presented a diverse range of topics and techniques. The foundations of beauty-culture practice included sterilization of instruments, hygiene, sanitation, and substantial coverage of the physiology, anatomy, and genetic composition of hair. The human scalp and the diagnosis and treatment of scalp diseases received significant attention, along with shampooing and other hair-processing techniques such as pressing, cutting, dyeing, bleaching, waving, and curling. Nail manicuring, facial massage, cosmetics, skin care, diet, and weight control were additional services agents could offer. Last, with an eye to Walker's intent to develop entrepreneurs, aspects of beauty-shop operations, including marketing, recordkeeping, and customer relations, were taught to promote effective management.

The exact character of the early educational culture of Lelia College and the Walker Beauty Schools is unclear, but later in the 1920s, 1930s, and 1940s the schools assumed a broader approach by offering an extended curriculum and extracurricular activities that suggested something more than only the imparting of vocational skill was taking place. For instance, the Walker Beauty School in Kansas City offered "Practical Classes" and "Theory Classes."[32] In the practical classroom, students wore uniforms in a clinical laboratory with equipment and stations set up for servicing customers. Some students stood at the stations and conducted various beauty-culture treatments on customers—who may have been other students, volunteers, or members of the public. There were typically five stations for doing hair, at which students practiced using dryers, curlers, and other implements on their customers. There were also manicure and facial massage stations where students hunched over their customers' hands and heads to perform various services or apply electric rotating scrub brushes to their customers' skin. In the theory classes, students also wore their uniforms but sat in traditional rows. Atop their wooden desks lay their textbooks and notepads as their instructor lectured from the front of the classroom. The Walker beauty manual text was well suited for both types of classes, in that it contained meticulous technical descriptions of beauty-culture techniques for the practical classes and scientific contexts for understanding scalp disease, anatomy, and other biological and physiological concepts for the theory classes.

Outside the classroom, the schools offered extracurricular activities that may have varied by location. There were basketball teams, swimming classes, social events, Christmas parties, and mock wedding events. There was also a sorority for beauty culturists named Lambda Alpha Phi that was dedicated to benevolent and educational activities. Socially, the students elected a queen and assigned superlatives to each other such as "most dramatic," "most talkative," "most faithful," and "best athlete." In these ways, the Walker Beauty Schools engaged students in studies and activities beyond skill development and toward broader intellectual and personal development.[33] The schools were also deeply instilled with black women's philanthropic values related to education as a key vehicle for uplift. The curriculum emphasized philanthropy and the expectation that agents would continue Walker's legacy of generosity and racial uplift. This instruction helped to imbue graduates with Walker's commercial and philanthropic values, ensuring that they would continue to exist into the future.

Enrollments from the earliest days of Lelia College and the Walker schools are not available, but numbers from the 1940s indicated regular graduating class sizes of nearly one hundred in multiple cities. Ultimately, Walker's beauty schools endured into the 1970s and prepared black women, and some men, for employment with the company or in the field. During Walker's lifetime, these schools were in a handful of cities, but Walker also wanted to connect with other black industrial schools to further legitimize her field and develop black women as agents. So she made monetary gifts to encourage the schools to adopt her curriculum.

## Walker's Philanthropy to Southern Black Industrial Schools

Supporting black education was essential to Walker's gospel of giving. She funded scholarships at institutions like Tuskegee, but she also made gifts for curriculum and facility renovation contingent on a specific proposal she believed would support the educational missions, build the credibility of beauty culture as a profession, open new markets, attract agent recruits, and generate income for both the institutions and the Walker Company.

On March 27, 1917, Madam Walker mailed a batch of letters to several black colleges in the South introducing the proposal. In view of the "great demand for beauty culture among our people" for both personal beautification and employment purposes, Walker had proposed that the colleges offer her hair-growing curriculum as a course of study. With such demand evident in her $175,000 income that year, Walker sought to establish beauty culture "as an industry, as we believe the proper care of the scalp and hair adds much to the personal appearance of the individual, and is as necessary as the training of the mind and development of the body." The course was entitled "The Art of Hair Growing," and Walker informed the colleges that it was already established at Tuskegee Institute, Roger Williams University, and Wiley College. By this time, Booker T. Washington was dead, but Walker had previously won him over on beauty culture. She had long supported Tuskegee with donations, and so this new proposal promised to scale up her support of black schools.[34]

To encourage their adoption of her curriculum, Walker offered the schools $100 donations to renovate rooms that could serve as clinical laboratories for the training program. Walker asked that the labs be furnished in white, in keeping with her own practice for salons, and prescribed a list of necessary equipment, including oak dressing tables, mirrors, and other articles. To staff the course, Walker asked the colleges to incur the travel expenses and $40 registration fee to send a representative to Lelia College in New York City in order to be trained in the Walker method. In return for the fee, the representative would receive instruction, a uniform, a steel comb, and eighteen boxes of products to get started. Additional products would then be available at the wholesale rates paid by Walker agents.[35] It is not known how many colleges Walker contacted, but before the end of spring 1917, at least four schools had signed up, received their donations, and began their renovations.[36]

Madam Walker had had the idea more than a year before when she broached it with A. M. Townsend, the president of Roger Williams University in Nashville, Tennessee. Roger Williams University was founded in 1867 as the Nashville Institute by Daniel W. Phillips, a Welsh Baptist preacher, and was supported by the American Baptist Home Mission Society. It was renamed in 1883 in honor of the founder of Rhode Island.[37] The university focused on educating blacks for ministry and offered the A.B. degree. It had collegiate, theological, music, preparatory, normal, and industrial departments. The industrial department offered sewing, dressmaking, physiology, nursing, printing, carpentry, farming, and gardening.[38]

Walker visited the Nashville campus sometime in early 1916 and addressed students in an exchange that the president described as "a source of great inspiration to all of us and especially our student body."[39] During the visit, Walker shared the curriculum proposal with Townsend and expressed some of her concerns about the idea. Walker felt divine inspiration for the proposal, as Townsend acknowledged: "I am so glad to note that the 'Spirit' is guiding you toward us favorably. I think your plan to have your work established in our schools is a good one."[40] Despite such inspiration, Walker felt some trepidation about the idea when Townsend felt compelled to reply, "I can conceive wherein it is prompted by a motive to make it educative to our people more than directly beneficial to you."[41] Whether a concern that emerged from prior feedback on the idea or a general preoccupation that she maintained because of her status, Walker worried that others would negatively view the initiative and wished to have her motives properly understood.[42] Townsend had attempted to bolster Walker by stating, "Whenever we do those things which we think best, though others may impugn our motives, we can have the assurance of our own conscience that we have done our duty." Townsend then moved from the general to the specific. "That idea of yours is only indicative of the spirit that characterizes your life and desire to do something for your own people in a really developmental and substantial way." He closed by adding "I am willing to cooperate with you in any way to carry out your idea."[43] Walker had found a receptive audience.

As an early adoptee, Roger Williams University received a $500 donation to fund its renovations and preparations. It is not clear why this amount was reduced to $100 for the other colleges who would adopt the program a year later, but it is clear that Townsend viewed the gift positively: "It means so much to us and to me for you to come to our rescue at this particular time, and I am sure that it will mean so much for you also." The funding was definitely attractive, but so were the prospects. Affiliation with Madam Walker as one of the most prominent black women of the time was important for the colleges, but so was the potential for future donations and revenue generation. Freeman B. Ransom negotiated a deal with Roger Williams such that it received a percentage of sales of Walker products used in the training program, and then overall residual profits were divided equally between the school and the instructor, thus lowering the school's exposure.[44] With reduced margins on the wholesale cost of products sold to Roger Williams, meaningful financial gain would have redounded to the benefit of Walker only after program enrollments reached scale across the participating institutions, something she had little control over. Even still, Walker's gospel of giving did not hold business and philanthropy in tension. The two coexisted by design in her company and now in her schools. She could simultaneously bolster black schools, share profits, and advance black women through beauty culture without conflict. The more immediate payoff for Walker came in being able to publicly announce the partnerships to reinforce beauty culture as a respectable profession and hire the graduates.

President Townsend was so enthusiastic about the idea that he began preparations without funding in hand. On January 26, 1917, Townsend acknowledged receipt of the $500 gift for the laboratory and informed Madam Walker that the lab was complete and had been named "The Madame C. J. Walker Laboratory" in appreciation of her generosity and partnership. In the same letter, Townsend reiterated his encouragement from nearly a year earlier: "The idea you have with reference to the placing of your work in institutions for aesthetic training and so on is a proper one and shows that your motive is not a selfish one, but that you are interested in this necessary kind of development for our people."[45] Walker had hoped that other schools would follow suit.

Other black colleges were, indeed, as excited as Roger Williams University and began their preparations. Wiley University in Marshall, Texas, was also an early adopter. It reported near completion of its "Walker Hair Parlor" as a clinical laboratory and storage space for teaching the Walker system in March 1917 and requested additional support to finish. Walker directed Ransom to send an additional $100 to Wiley to help.[46] Arkansas Baptist College in Little Rock quickly agreed to the partnership in early March 1917. The $100 gift was sent to the college by the end of the month, and in acknowledgment, its president, J. A. Booker, endeavored to open the lab by fall and promised "the work will be carried vigourously [sic] and successfully to [Madam Walker's] credit and honor." Guadalupe College in Seguin, Texas, asked for an additional $38 gift to cover painting expenses, and Walker directed Ransom to send $100.[47]

Some schools were more cautious. Mound Bayou Industrial College in Mississippi, whose motto was "Education of the Head, Hands, and Heart," was a logical prospective partner. Its president agreed with the idea, but asked for additional time to consider because of concerns over the costs.[48] Similarly, Walden College in Nashville, Tennessee, considered the proposal and inquired about additional costs; its ultimate decision is unknown.[49]

Another recipient of Walker's proposal letter was of particular note, Mary McLeod Bethune. The black educator, who founded the Daytona Normal and Industrial School for Negro Girls in 1904 in Florida and who would later found the National Council of Negro Women and serve in the administration of President Franklin Delano Roosevelt, responded positively to the offer. The two women had met five years before at the 1912 National Association of Colored Women (NACW) meeting, and Madam was immediately impressed by Bethune. The women had comparable backgrounds and levels of resolve on the problems of the race. Both were born in the post-Emancipation South, but Bethune was formally educated. Both were philanthropists as churchwomen, clubwomen, and educators. Bethune's story of Daytona's founding with less than $2 that she had saved resonated with the $2 that Sarah Breedlove and Lelia had upon their arrival in St. Louis, where their lives changed. At that NACW meeting, Walker volunteered to lead a fundraising campaign to benefit Daytona and sent donations regularly thereafter, as she did for many woman-run schools. Walker's new proposal provided opportunity for the friends to continue to work together. Bethune affirmed it "to be very beneficial indeed and would be very glad to place [the curriculum] in our schools as a course of study."[50] She and some of her students had already been using Walker's hair grower product with great success.

At the time, Bethune's institution offered elementary and industrial curricula that included cooking, sewing, laundering, gardening, poultry raising, and weaving, with increasing attention paid to teacher education. Bethune had more than one hundred students and eleven teachers and largely depended on donations to fund her $10,453 annual budget.[51] The opportunity to receive donations from Walker and develop a potential revenue stream through the Walker product line had to be very attractive to Bethune. But she pressed for more, as the unceasing process of fundraising required black women educators and clubwomen to do. In her reply to Walker, Bethune asked for assistance in housing the employee she would send to Lelia College. Bethune, ever the fundraiser, thanked Walker for her $100 gift of two years past and asked whether such a gift could be renewed annually because "The high cost of living has made this a very anxious year for us. May we hear from you now?"[52] Walker made Bethune's institution a $5,000 legatee to her estate, which confirmed her belief in Bethune and for schools founded and run by black women.

Walker made at least $900 in donations to these black schools that adopted her curriculum.[53] At least five colleges responded positively, and of those, four acknowledged receipt of the seed donations and executed plans. Problems beset some of the programs from the beginning, and most do not appear to have had a long run. Roger Williams University had trouble building up a client base to support the program because of its isolated location. But the proposition remained attractive nonetheless. For most institutions, Walker's gift amounted to 1–2% of their total operating budgets. For Guadalupe College and Roger Williams University, Walker's gifts represented 4% and 10% of their respective annual operating budgets. Further, Walker's gifts were similar in size to the awards made by white industrialist philanthropies such as the Slater Fund and the Phelps-Stokes Fund to the smaller industrial institutes.[54] Having access to such a prominent black donor who could make gifts that matched those of some of the coveted white institutional donors was a boon for the struggling institutes. And for Walker, the initiative with black colleges was one way to use her philanthropy and her approach to industrial education to validate the legitimacy of both the Walker system and beauty culture as a respectable profession while enabling scores of black women to become credentialed.

## Madam C. J. Walker's Gift of Education

Although Madam Walker never achieved her philanthropic dream of building her Tuskegee of Africa, she achieved something more remarkable.[55] Effectively, she had "out-Tuskegeed" Booker T. Washington. She created a more enduring form of industrial education with an appropriate vocational focus on beauty culture that outlasted Booker T. Washington's mode of industrial education. She gave education to black working-class women, and some men, to support themselves, their families, and their communities.[56] Whereas Washington and other purveyors of the Hampton-Tuskegee idea of industrial education promoted an unsustainable method that did not lead to skilled employment nor directly challenge the status quo of race relations, Walker used her own national chain of beauty-culture schools and philanthropic gifts to black schools to advance a brand of beauty culture industrial education appropriate for the times and make opportunities available in segregated black urban economies.

Walker identified with Booker T. Washington's life story and his industrial program at Tuskegee, but she differed greatly from him in her embrace of urbanization and modernization and her understanding of the political economy of black beauty culture.[57] From her firsthand experience as a former migrant, she understood the dynamics of industrialization, modernization, migration, urbanization, and racial segregation and their impact on the evolving black working class. She discerned the possibilities and the implications of harnessing the restricted yet untapped opportunities embedded in these inequitable systems and used them to subvert the same in service to the struggle for liberation. She understood that if black women migrants and local residents were going to find their place, they would have to equip themselves. Walker's brand of beauty culture industrial training provided the opportunity women migrants were looking for and it supported the bottom line of her company by preparing agents and creating ways to get her products to market and compete with others. Using her company as a base for her race work, she created a network of schools to educate black women just as her peers had done elsewhere through churches and clubs. Her gift of education extended her gospel of giving by establishing an accessible pathway to independence for black women.

Walker's embrace of urbanization and industrialization positions her as being with the times, whereas Washington was against migration and was stuck in the fading agricultural economy.[58] Consequently, she, better than he, was able to provide a meaningful educational experience and credential that became a pathway to economic independence for black women while she publicly advocated for continuation of social protest and political action to counter, rather than acquiesce to, Jim Crow.[59] This analysis challenges the notion of what industrial philanthropy accomplished with respect to industrial education in the early twentieth century. The white northern industrial philanthropists, who have received most of the attention in extant historiography, saw black education as a problem, but Walker, ever the race woman and entrepreneur, saw opportunity in that problem. Instead of thinking about how to control the black population, she thought about how to free black women to pursue their own aspirations.

At face value, Walker fits the description of an industrial philanthropist despite not fitting the historical conceptual mold of it. Walker's wealth certainly accrued from industrial enterprise and was largely directed toward educational pursuits. Being neither white, male, nor from the North, however, Walker represented a different kind of industrial philanthropist, one who was not only sympathetic to the black plight, but who had lived it and yearned for the opportunity of formal education. Walker lived close to the issue of black education in a way that none of the white male industrial philanthropists traditionally identified with black education (Carnegie, Rockefeller, Slater) could have ever approximated. She identified with black aspirations for education and had her own resources to put in service to that vision.

In keeping with the dual commercial and philanthropic mission of her race company and black women's record of providing education, Walker emerges as an educator and funder who gives us a different view of what philanthropy and industrial education accomplished when rightly oriented within the context of the social, political, cultural, and economic forces shaping the early twentieth century. She had proven that the beauty culture industrial form of education and training could lead to a gainful career, for she had transformed the lives of thousands of black women and their families through employment in modern, urban economies. She put in place a supportive infrastructure to help black women become credentialed through her training and launch their work through capital investments to set up salons around the country.[60] Further, she demonstrated that the need for continual protest and struggle was not lost on those who were industrially educated, and she advocated in many ways for black civil rights and organized her agents into benevolent clubs, in part, to do the same. She could hardly be labeled an accommodationist. Her business interests did not depend on an appeased white South. The fear of southern backlash that motivated the white industrial philanthropists to act as they did was of no consequence for Walker or her business. Indeed, she was disturbing the social order, and her schools became another platform for her gospel of giving.

Her concept of industrial education was well equipped to deal with the turbulence of early-twentieth-century economic change, while Booker T. Washington's was not. Being financially independent, she did not have to engage in the same kinds of political maneuvering as other black heads of schools like her friends Mary McLeod Bethune, Charlotte Hawkins Brown—even Washington—who had to appease their white industrial funders while implementing their broader visions for black education in somewhat clandestine fashion.[61] She funded and delivered the exact kind of education she thought was needed. It is for these reasons, and more, that we can affirm Walker in responding to historian Darlene Clark Hine's query about whether the era of the turn from the nineteenth to the twentieth century isn't best ascribed to Madam C. J. Walker *and* to Booker T. Washington rather than to Washington alone.[62] Walker is an example of what can happen when philanthropy and industrial education are rightly directed by blacks and focused within the context of the broader set of economic and labor-market forces actually reshaping America. To be sure, it was still industrial education and not classic liberal arts training; but Walker proved its value. In this way, my analysis of Walker's gift of education offers a completely different story and different reading of the history of blacks, philanthropy, and industrial education and further contextualizes Walker's activist engagement of her graduates and employees in the political struggle for freedom through agent clubs.

# 4

# Activism

We must not let our love of our country, our
patriotic loyalty, cause us to abate one whit
in our protest against wrong and injustice.
We should protest until the American sense
of justice is so aroused that such affairs as
the East St. Louis Riot be forever impossible.
—Madam C. J. Walker, 1917[1]

On a hot summer day in late August 1917, Madam Walker stood before an
audience of hundreds of her agents, reportedly from nearly every state
in America, who were packed into the Union Baptist Church of Philadelphia, Pennsylvania. The event was the first national convention of Walker
agents, and Walker delivered an address to them entitled "Women's Duty
to Women." Prior to her speech, local and national dignitaries from politics,
business, and the National Association of Colored Women (NACW) spoke
to the group, as did leadership from Walker Clubs, like local club president
Margaret Thompson. Freeman B. Ransom delivered the charge and purpose
of the meeting of agents, which he had been developing for some time. It
was a glorious triumph for Madam Walker's organizing efforts to bring
her agents together to accomplish significant goals for beauty culture and
for black people.[2]

In her rousing speech, Walker spoke about the courage and bravery of
black soldiers fighting abroad in World War I and advised the agents to hold
fast to their patriotism. It was a message that Walker would increasingly

share as she raised money for black soldiers' needs in the trenches, visited military installations in the Midwest, and encouraged African Americans to purchase liberty bonds to help finance the war.[3] Despite its harshness toward her and its brutality toward her people, Walker referred to the United States as the greatest country under the sun. A growing national sentiment among African Americans reflected their heartfelt hope that black soldiers' valiant fighting and deaths in the theaters of war and black vocal and financial support for the war at home would translate into full recognition of their equality and citizenship after the conflict ended. Perhaps in a foreshadowing of the disappointment that was to come, Madam Walker admonished her agents, "We must not let our love of our country, our patriotic loyalty, cause us to abate one whit in our protest against wrong and injustice. We should protest until the American sense of justice is so aroused that such affairs as the East St. Louis Riot be forever impossible."[4]

Walker was referring to the race riot in East St. Louis, Illinois, a few months earlier that stemmed from the resentment of white factory workers over the increasing presence of black people in their facility. An influx of black migrants had occurred in the city that caused a small black population in 1910 to swell to thirteen thousand by 1917. A strike of white workers at the local aluminum ore factory led the company to hire black and white replacements, which further stirred the racial ire of whites. Rage and rhetoric against black migrants escalated and came to a head on May 28 after a union meeting. For three days, angry whites attacked local black people and destroyed black-owned properties with no resistance from police. In fact, police acted against black people who had armed themselves for protection. The violence quelled somewhat but ultimately continued for several weeks. By July, at least thirty-nine black people had been killed, many black homes and businesses were destroyed, and several blacks had fled the city.[5]

Lynching was part of an American tradition of treatment of African Americans dating back to the earliest days of slavery and slave holders' particular brutality and violence used to police their plantations. With Emancipation, the end of Reconstruction, and the passage of Jim Crow laws came extensive violence against black people in the 1880s. It occurred everywhere with such shocking frequency that today scholars still critique as incomplete at best the available numbers and assessments from traditionally reliable sources such as newspapers. Madam Walker was personally familiar with lynching, for the rumblings of racial violence in Louisiana and

Mississippi in the 1880s were partly what sent her to St. Louis in search of better opportunities and safety as a young widowed mother. Now at St. Louis she was providing a significant voice, and later funding, to a long-standing history of black antilynching resistance that included politics, data, protest, armed self-defense, and activism. White racial violence toward African Americans would continue unabated well into the twentieth century, but Madam Walker did what she could to try to end its reign.[6] To this end, Walker and her agents passed a resolution on the matter and sent it to President Woodrow Wilson.[7]

Black women had long engaged in such political activism. Activism was an important part of black women's philanthropy, and it cut across class differences. Walker's agents were mostly striving working-class women, and through the clubs she gave them a platform for engaging in the larger struggle for equality. Working-class black women had their own brand of activism, which was limited by their available time, that focused on institutions and activities already built into their lives, such as the church. They did not have the leisure time that some of the middle- and upper-class clubwomen, whose full-time work was their voluntary leadership of the clubs, possessed. Nonetheless, many of them were as active as they were able.[8] As an association affiliated with their profession, the Walker clubs became integrated into working-class women's work lives and further facilitated their activism and charity efforts, of which the antilynching resolution was one example.

In a series of scathing critiques, the agents' resolution noted the hypocrisy of US protest of "the wrongs of people and races of people on the other side of the Atlantic" while ignoring its own wrongs against 10 million black people at home. It condemned the mob violence and murderous lynchings as a national disgrace and a threat to America's role and reputation abroad. The resolution depicted black soldiers as demonstrating "a courage and patriotism not surpassed by any other American soldier" and heralded the race's patriotism and women's efforts for equality. Through the resolution, Walker and her agents called on President Wilson to "use your great influence that Congress enact the necessary laws to prevent a recurrence of such disgraceful affairs."[9] Walker and her agents had collectively raised their activist voices to challenge Jim Crow.

Although several scholars have examined Walker's life, few have made her agents focal points for analysis.[10] Madam Walker's agents, by design, were very active in their communities, raising funds, providing services, and speaking out on issues. This agent activism was an outgrowth of Walker's gospel of giving and the ways she engaged the resources of her race company. At times, she encouraged their charitable giving and civic engagement to address community needs. At other times, she asked them to give to specific causes, such as the Booker T. Washington Memorial Fund and the Frederick Douglass Fund, which many of them did.[11] It was through her national network of agent clubs that Madam Walker created a familiar form of associationalism to bond the agents to each other and to the Walker Company. She created a platform for harnessing their collective power as virtuous women to extend her voice and theirs in defense of their profession and in service to their race during Jim Crow. The organizational structure of the Walker clubs drew inspiration from the NACW, but their formal culture quickly evolved to include African American fraternalism. Exploring this combination deepens our understanding of how the clubs pursued their goals of bonding agents together, building their professional identities, and enabling their charity and activism work.

## Madam C. J. Walker's Organization of Agents

There were four articulated purposes for Madam Walker's national association of agents.[12] The association served as a mechanism for generating and sustaining unity among the agents, who were reportedly at or approaching twenty thousand by the end of the decade. It strengthened ties between the agents and the Walker Company, and between the agents themselves. It also protected "all such agents against misrepresentations and false statements of fakes and [impostors], and last, to have this organization, its rules and regulations so strict, and perfect, until it will be utterly impossible for anyone to handle our goods, unless such a one is a regular agent of the Company, and is a member of the National Organization."[13] There was another distinct purpose that, although not articulated in original notices to the agents introducing the concept, was often repeated in company correspondence—charity. Madam Walker envisioned her agents performing charitable work in their communities as they sold products and advanced beauty culture. Ransom urged that the clubs "may by entertainments, dues, etc. accumulate a fund, out of which they can do charitable work."[14] The association was designed to bring the agents together as a cohesive group for the benefit of their profession, their communities, and, ultimately, their race.

The creation of Madam Walker's national association came on the heels of more than a year of Walker's organizing clubs at the local level. In April 1916 Madam Walker informed Freeman B. Ransom of a club she organized in New York City and noted the existence of another in Philadelphia, Pennsylvania.[15] She noted that the New York group would serve to protect agents from counterfeiters and that members decided to contribute to the national Booker T. Washington Memorial Fund. From the beginning, Walker considered the rationale for the clubs to be related to both company and community interests. She also envisioned the local groups connecting through a national body in this early conception and asked of Ransom, "What do you think about having a National organization of the agents?" As her trusted adviser, Ransom would turn the concept into a reality the following year.[16]

It remains unclear how many start-up clubs there were during these early days, but within a decade there would be more than fifty.[17] Clubs operated at local, state, and regional levels. Initially, there were at least six regions organized around the urban centers Chicago, Illinois; Muskogee, Oklahoma; Atlanta, Georgia; Philadelphia, Pennsylvania; Knoxville, Tennessee; and Richmond, Virginia.[18] The company ran promotions to encourage agents to form and join the clubs. The promotions offered monetary incentives to "stimulate this spirit of organization." Such incentives included prizes of $5 to $500 to agents who sold the most goods, recruited the largest number of new agents, and sent the most delegates to the national convention. The company also reduced its usual $25 start-up fee to $10 in order to attract new agents and encourage their involvement in the association.[19]

The national meetings were typically hosted by a church in a major US city and lasted for two to three days. Meetings included speeches, beauty-culture instruction, committee reports, and awarding of incentives and recognition. At the local level, the names of the clubs varied and included Walker Clubs, Walker Benevolent Associations, Walker Beneficial Clubs, and Walker Unions. At the national level, the unifying body was called the National Beauty Culturists' and Benevolent Association of Madam C. J. Walker Agents, Inc.[20]

When seeking to understand Walker's national network of benevolent clubs and associations, scholars have looked to the NACW, the major federation of black women's clubs, for context.[21] There was good reason to do so. In a 1916 letter, Madam Walker acknowledged "Women's Federated clubs" as the inspiration for the creation of the Walker clubs.[22] She was very familiar with NACW's network of local, regional, and national clubs since her first exposure to the group twenty years earlier while living in St. Louis.[23] She had courted the endorsement of the NACW to enhance her credibility, and by this time, she was an accepted member in their ranks.

This recognition was an achievement because Walker did not fit the profile of the leading NACW women, who were mostly highly educated and married. Walker was self-educated and divorced, but she earned respectability through entrepreneurship and philanthropy to gain the NACW's acceptance. Her life was marked by transitions in class consciousness. Born to formerly enslaved parents, Walker's early life was stamped as poor or working-class. But the material wealth she accumulated enabled upward mobility into the middle class and onward to higher status via her mansion in an exclusive New York neighborhood. As scholar Imani Perry noted, however, "to be elite in this group was a modest privilege at best" because black women were still at the bottom of the social world.[24] Further, historian Martin Summers's recognition that black middle- and upper-class consciousness was based less on materiality and more on the strategic positioning of oneself against the poor and working-class black masses is instructive.[25] Rather than positioning herself against the working class, Walker stationed herself between classes as a translational figure, as comfortable in the elite circles occupied by her clubwomen friends like Mary B. Talbert as she was in small Midwestern towns and big southern cities speaking in church basements and lodge halls with local folk. She was able to morph and move among and between black social classes with aplomb, gathering social capital along the way. This ability informed the establishment of these agent clubs, which brought together black women across regions as well as classes. The Walker clubs were modeled after the NACW in their organizational structure, but understanding their bonding across class and social differences requires the insights of another important cultural and social institution, African American fraternalism.

## Black Fraternalism

Initially it may seem that African American fraternalism should be dismissed as a frame of reference for the Walker clubs. In the same letter in which Walker named women's federation clubs as an influence, she specifically stated, "I think you misunderstood my meaning. I didn't mean to organize as a Fraternal Society," in response to Ransom. In further explanation, she continued, "I meant to organize clubs all over the country, and at some time call a meeting of all the agents and form a National. . . . [O]nly there would be no handling of moneys. . . . Each club will handle its own money."[26] The NACW influenced the organization's autonomous structure. At some point in its early development, African American fraternalism exerted influence on the Walker clubs' function too. Within a few years of their initial creation, fraternal ritual was the foundation of the clubs' formal culture, which bonded Walker agents into a cohesive body to reinforce their professionalism and community involvement.

To make this connection, Imani Perry's concept of black formalism is useful. Black formalism or black formal culture is a practice Perry described as "the performance and substance within black associations and institutions." By this she meant the ways of being and doing that constituted participation inside black civic organizations. "Black formalism includes ritual practices within embedded norms, codes of conduct, and routine, dignified ways of doing and being. It includes greetings, sartorial practices [and] oratory, homiletics, traditional songs, and standard ways of structuring events and special occasions." Perry saw black formalism as a distinctive culture that cut across class differences and contrasted with respectability because it was internal to the black community and not focused on acceptance by whites: "It is, in its symbolic meaning, an articulation and expression of grace and identity that existed in refuge from the violence of white supremacy." Black formalism was an omnipresent aspect of black civic life because of the explosion of organizations created after Emancipation and the end of Reconstruction that black people used to express their dignity and aspirations. African American fraternalism was keyed toward such expressions of grace and identity.[27]

Early-twentieth-century American fraternalism was a self-protective, exclusive, and self-segregating form of competitive voluntarism through which Americans bonded within gendered, racial, ethnic, and religious private groups that became increasingly homogeneous over time.[28] Despite their neglect and exclusion in the fraternalism historiography, African Americans were no exception. A significant portion of this historiography has either ignored black fraternal organizations or viewed them largely as imitations of white organizations. But African American fraternalism included both parallel (or imitative) orders and distinctive orders. They were successful and prolific and represented particular cultural expressions and political and social innovations characteristic of the African American experience. Scholars Theda Skocpol and Jennifer Oser read African Americans as "super-joiners" with a "special proclivity for association building in many spheres" and "frequent and intensive use of fraternal forms of organization." With a heritage dating back to 1775, black fraternal organizations in the late nineteenth and early twentieth centuries had memberships composed of higher percentages of the adult population and more lodges per capita than their white counterparts. African Americans created their own lodges after experiencing exclusion by white lodges. Protest of such treatment frequently led them to circumvent their exclusionary white brethren by connecting directly with the originating orders in Europe to appeal for recognition of their lodges, which was typically granted, as in the case of the Prince Hall Masons in 1775 and the Grand United Order of Odd Fellows in 1843. These black "parallel" orders were not simple caricatures of white orders; rather, they were expressive of African Americans' desire for full participation in US society, and they achieved larger memberships, networks, and financial assets than the distinctively black orders.[29]

As an organizational form, African American fraternalism had much to offer the Walker clubs. First, like other voluntary associations of the era, black fraternals were structured as federations of local, state, regional, and national organizations. Black fraternalism consisted of "massive organizational networks" that not only spanned coast to coast, but also extended overseas and included both paid and volunteer workers laboring within the administrative layers. With ties to Europe and lodges frequently located in the Bahamas, Liberia, Bermuda, the West Indies, and Central America, black fraternals had a strong transnational tradition that was highly regarded and far more extensive than white fraternals. Black fraternal orders connected people across widespread geographies and social classes. They operated as "popularly rooted, cross-class associations" that bonded people from different occupations and religious denominations. Rather than scrutinize prospective members based on class, black fraternals focused on individual character and were thus able to create large grassroots memberships composed of everyday people. Women played much more prominent roles in black fraternal organizations than in white orders, which also spoke to the nature of gender relations within the groups. These webs of relations across land, sea, social class, and gender supported Madam Walker's original vision of a dispersed but connected network of women. They also related to her increasing Pan-Africanist consciousness that emerged in the latter years of her life and her desire to engage the middle-class clubwomen of the NACW with her agents, whose circumstances varied but were mostly working-class.[30]

As recounted earlier, beauty culture offered options for women in domestic-service positions. Walker attracted many of these women to work for the company. Several agents could not afford the $25 fee for Walker's first course and required a subsidy or waiver to get started. There were, however, some agents and credentialed beauty-school graduates who were middle-class women of prominence in their communities, like her St. Louis friend Jessie Batts Robinson or Jacqueline Randolph of Harlem, who was the wife of labor leader A. Phillip Randolph. Some were already self-sufficient and used the Walker Method System to further establish themselves, their families, and their status in the community. But most of the agents were working-class women. Walker had a canny ability to connect with women across these differing circumstances, and her philanthropy was a significant part of this translational work.

As a woman who had evolved from being one of the downtrodden to one of the uplifted and then to one who uplifted others, Walker could address the hopes, fears, and frustrations of the black poor and members of the working class and uphold the values and expectations of the black middle and upper classes. Her philanthropy, as a broad platform of resources deployed in numerous ways, enabled her to relate to black struggle and striving across differences. As a simultaneous demonstration of her generosity and respectability, her philanthropy gave her access to—and the eventual ability to become a part of—the black elite social circles pressing for change from both the masses and the powers that be. The clubs allowed her to further promote her brand of respectability that merged middle-class and working-class consciousness in a seamless manner. The formal culture of black fraternal ritual supported the development of a shared identity that blended such stark class differences.

Black fraternals also enhanced economic, philanthropic, and civic participation for their members. The mutual aid fostered by black fraternals was substantial and grew out of their pooling of weekly membership dues or other periodic assessments to fund initiatives. They offered social insurance, an important asset during a time when white insurance companies regularly denied black people coverage. Such social insurance—which could have provided for burial expenses, payouts to decedents' survivors, and benefits in case of inability to work due to sickness—were of particular interest to black women because of their economic roles in their families. Mutual aid led black fraternals to establish social-welfare organizations, such as old folks' homes and orphanages and educational scholarships. They also incubated black entrepreneurship through infusions of capital into local businesses.[31]

Black fraternals provided opportunities for black men and women to exercise civic leadership skills and competencies through officer positions, committee structures, maintenance of financial and organizational records, event coordination, and conduct of meetings. In a society that denied black citizenship, such activities may have seemed futile to distant observers; but to African Americans themselves, they were vital. Black organizations were bastions of self-determination and autonomy. In a racially divided society hostile to black aspirations, black organizations offered existential evidence of black agency, efficacy, and competency. They gave black people a means of declaring and living out their humanity and cultivated avenues for striving and contributing something to the larger good. Black fraternals had more leadership posts than white organizations, which generated more opportunities for service. They also had better systems for promoting local leadership up the ranks into larger governance roles than did their white counterparts. As an example, in the 1880s and 1890s, Jessie Batts Robinson was a member of her local Order of the Court of Calanthe, but by the early 1900s, she had become the Supreme Worthy Inspectrix, the order's national leader. By combining this kind of skill development with regalia and other rituals, black fraternals provided regular time and space for members to publicly assume leadership roles otherwise denied them by the larger society.[32]

The hallmark of black and white fraternal organizational life was ritualism—the initiations, ceremonies, symbolism, dramatizations, and other cultural productions that bonded members together on the basis of shared values, beliefs, and identities. By engaging in ritual, members affirmed their identification with each other and their shared values and belief systems, and they regularly demonstrated the norms of conduct for meetings.[33] There were, nevertheless, differences in the rituals and structures of African American fraternalism.

African American fraternal orders were extremely egalitarian. Degrees, which were ranks of achievement, were earned through completion of collective projects rather than demonstration of individual skill or authority, as in the white male orders. Members bonded to each other through rituals in magnitudes that exceeded those of the white orders. The African American orders also tended to utilize religious imagery, hymns, and stories from the Christian tradition to a far greater extent than their white counterparts.[34]

Another prominent difference between the black and white orders had to do with their conceptions of charity. There were four conceptions of charity in black and white orders: (1) expressive, in which charity was promoted as a virtue; (2) instrumental, in which charity was framed as a reciprocal obligation of membership; (3) world-transformative, in which charity focused on improving the quality of life throughout society beyond the boundaries of the orders; and (4) gendered, in which charity was conceptualized by women's roles in caring for orphans and the sick. The conceptions of charity were fluid and overlapped. African American fraternal orders overwhelmingly focused on the instrumental and world-transformative conceptions and utilized collective practices in pursuit of them, whereas the white orders were more focused on expressive and gendered charity.[35] These distinctive characteristics of African American fraternalism were aligned with Walker's original goal for the clubs of cohesively bonding the agents to simultaneously protect the company brand and serve the community. Also, they were familiar.

Madam Walker was a member of the Order of the Court of Calanthe, the auxiliary of the third-largest black order in the country, the Colored Knights of Pythias. It had a membership of more than two hundred thousand by the 1920s. The motto of the Colored Knights was Friendship, Charity, and Benevolence and the organization focused on supporting members, paying death benefits, and caring for and educating members' widows and children.[36] Freeman B. Ransom was a member of the Colored Knights and achieved the level of Grand State Lecturer in Indiana.[37]

The Calanthes' self-described goal was "a large and liberal charity." The order drew its identity from its birth out of Pythianism, just as the biblical Eve was formed from the rib of Adam. The Calanthes viewed themselves as "helpmates" of the Knights because "man cannot labor alone . . . in a work of Charity, Purity, Fidelity, Harmony and Love." The order had three ritual degrees, Fidelity, Harmony, and Love, which were earned through collective projects. Walker achieved all three. The Calanthes exemplified many of the distinctive features of black fraternalism. The order used mild forms of hazing, employed significant religious symbolism, and directed its charity toward racial uplift. Further, the Calanthes' conception of charity was gendered, instrumental, and world-transformative, which cast helping others as a reciprocal obligation of membership, women's particular responsibility, and an imperative for redressing social wrongs that afflicted members and society at large.[38]

Walker and Ransom had ample experience with fraternalism and access to sacred rituals and other documentation. Features of black fraternal ritualism were evident in the Walker clubs after her death, but perhaps occurred sooner. She may have incorporated ritual with or without persuasion from Ransom. He may have implemented it as company leader after her death. Or the agents may have adopted ritual themselves through the autonomous nature of the clubs and their familiarity with it. Regardless of the origins, early in their existence, the clubs drew on both NACW and black fraternalism, two leading voluntary institutions in black philanthropy. From the perspective of Perry's black formalism, the NACW provided the federation-style organizational structure, and fraternal ritual defined the inner ways of being that unified and empowered agents, who tended not to be members of the NACW, but rather objects of its social and cultural programs. Walker's cross-class engagement of black women in this way contrasts with wealthy white women philanthropists of the day, whose actions tended to foment resentment among working-class women.[39]

Fraternal ritual was a powerful social mechanism for creating purpose, inculcating values, bonding relationships, and promoting harmony in society. Sociologist Émile Durkheim emphasized that ritual created solidarity (connection, belonging) and effervescence (collective joy, exuberance) among people. It instilled a framework for understanding one's sense of self and one's relationship to the broader world. These conceptualizations of ritual provide context for the formal culture of the Walker clubs and how they bonded agents together and developed their sense of identity as respectable professionals and race women responsible for uplifting African Americans from the scourge of Jim Crow. Rather than lower-class objects to be changed, Walker clubwomen became agents of change in their own communities.[40]

## "A Vehicle of Divine Service":
## Formal Culture in the Walker Clubs

Two publications convey the formal culture of the Walker clubs: *The Ritual for the Local Bodies of the National Beauty Culturists' and Benevolent Association of Madam C. J. Walker Agents, Inc.* (ca. 1920) and the *By-laws of the Local Bodies of the National Beauty Culturists' and Benevolent Association of Madam C. J. Walker Agents, Inc.* (1927). Both publications bear similarities with the *Ritualistic Ceremonies of the Order of Calanthe* (1914), a publication of Walker and Ransom's fraternal affiliation.[41]

In these texts, ritual formed the basis for fraternal bonding along with religious and literary allusions. Although it was not as elaborate, colorful, or demonstrative as that of the Colored Knights and the Calanthes, the ritual for the national association of Walker agents prescribed specific procedures for running meetings and conducting business. It outlined movements and scripted recitations for leadership and membership.

According to the ritual, the president called meetings to order by moving into position, donning her badge,[42] striking her gavel three times, and saying, "This being a Fraternal Organization of business people it is meet that we should always on all occasions bear witness that starting on time is absolutely essential to achieving our aims when we should. The possession of ambition, talent, wealth and vision count for nothing if precious moments of our lives slip away while we constantly wait for the next minute. One minute lost is an opportunity, it may be a fortune lost."[43] She then issued a brief recitation of a quotation from William Shakespeare's *Julius Caesar* to reinforce the importance of time and preparedness for opportunity:

> There is a tide in the affairs of men,
> Which, taken at the flood, leads on to fortune.[44]

The officers of the union then moved into their respective positions in the meeting room, movements reminiscent of those prescribed for the Court of Calanthe's leadership in their ritual. The president then summoned the sergeant-at-arms, who was asked to verify that everyone present was "entitled to sit and participate in this meeting."[45] The sergeant-at-arms examined the membership to ascertain whether any were not in good standing and then reported to the president. Good standing meant being accredited by or having no outstanding debts or obligations to the Walker Company. If all were in good standing, the meeting continued. If not, those undeserving of participation were escorted out of the room with "all possible courtesy," and the sergeant-at-arms resumed her watchful position at the door.[46] The rituals of the Court of Calanthe prescribed a similar verification of the membership status of meeting participants.[47]

After a roll call, the president was to strike her gavel one time, signaling for everyone to rise and sing the "Hairdressers' Ode to Madam C. J. Walker Agents," which was performed to the melody of the religious hymn, "Onward, Christian Soldiers":

> Onward, Walker Hair Dressers,
> Outward to the fray;
> Have your combs all sterilized,
> Keep a shining tray;
> Be thou not divided,
> As one body stand;
> Strive to help the Nation,
> In this great demand.
>
> Bring, ye, on your shampoo;
> Bring, ye, on your salve;
> In the name of Walker
> Beautify hair.
>
> Think forever of the one
> In whose name we stand;
> Keep the honor that she won,
> The best one in the land.
> Treat your client courteous,
> Always pleasant be;
> Let your smiles and patience
> Last eternally.[48]

The ode used song and verse to uphold Walker standards of practice with opening references to sterilized and presentable equipment undergirded by unity between agents, pleasant interactions with clients, and welcoming personal presentations and appearances. The ode emphasized Madam Walker's reputation and affirmed the responsibility to maintain it at all cost. The lyrics also laid claim to a larger work. By urging the agents to be out in the "fray" and to strive to "help the Nation," the song linked commerce and philanthropy, beauty culture and racial uplift to national improvement. Within the context of the Julius Caesar reference, the ode proclaimed the agents' opportunity to act on behalf of themselves, their race, and their country to continue Walker's legacy of expanding economic opportunity for black women, giving to their communities, and advocating to make life better for all. By being set to the melody of "Onward, Christian Soldiers," the ode was easy to remember and felt familiar to the members, who would also have been devout church attenders. What is more, the recognizable tune created an aura of triumph as the unforgettable tone of the original lyrics instilled the ode's words with a military-like fervor to further inculcate into agents the commitment to fight for beauty culture as a respectable profession and Madam Walker's legacy.

After the song, the president entered into a lengthy statement of purpose that highlighted each member's responsibility to be loyal to each other, the company, and the association. Such loyalty required

> a deep seated, eradicable willingness to put aside jealousy, envy, petty pride, dishonesty of all kinds and each and every day on all occasions in spite of temptation to do otherwise, think, speak and act to help every Walker Agent to be the best possible representative of said Madam C. J. Walker Mfg. Company, the National Association and her union, ever realizing that every time a Walker Agent does well she builds a foundation for a larger life not only for herself but for all of us, and if she does poor work or conducts herself improperly anywhere, she hurts not only herself but she brings discredit upon all of us.[49]

This statement was an attempt to promote unity and quell any conflicts between the agents. These women did relate well to each other in general, but conflicts were still present.

The experience of Margaret Thompson, a Walker agent and parlor owner in Philadelphia, Pennsylvania, proved the point. Thompson owned the Thompsino Hair Dressing Parlor, through which she offered beauty-culture services and trained women in the Walker method.[50] She was also president of the local Walker club. In 1917 she informed Freeman B. Ransom of two rogue agents, one, whose last name was also Walker, had circumvented the company's distribution line by supplying local agents with products at unauthorized prices, and a second, whose last name was Maginley, had sold counterfeit products. The two women were brought before the local club where they admitted their wrongdoing. To resolve the issue, agent Walker was reassigned to run the local supply station for agents in order to disrupt her own distribution ring, and Maginley was made to pledge loyalty to official Walker products only.[51] Such reprimands seemed mild in comparison with the offenses, but more severe disciplinary action was unknown. The episode took a toll on Thompson, even after her hosting of the triumphant first national meeting of the agents in her city, for she lamented to Ransom, "I am thinking of resigning from the presidency. . . . You are aware of the many perplexing problems existing in Philadelphia. I feel I can better solve these problems as a lay member chair, than by occupying the President's chair."[52] Thompson's ultimate decision was unclear, but her challenges continued as Walker, the rogue agent, disregarded agreements made with her related to the operation of the local supply station, and the Walker Company had logistical problems fulfilling supply orders for agents in Philadelphia more broadly. In defeat, Thompson bemoaned, "I do know I struggled very hard to build up the club and it is paining my heart to see how things are going."[53] Historian Deborah Gray White has meticulously outlined the commonplace interpersonal conflicts among black clubwomen, noting that their history was "about women with missions that varied and often clashed, about women who aimed for progress and unity, but who sometimes fell short, about women who sometimes found the job of representing and fighting for themselves burdensome."[54] These same dynamics clearly existed among the Walker agents as well. The association of Walker agents used the elements of ritual to attempt to address such inevitable interpersonal conflicts and continually pointed to Walker's legacy and the divine for inspiration.

This function of the club was important because the women had to learn to work together. Such discord obviously affected business negatively. It also had implications for the broader philanthropic work, which included activism and charity. Cooperation, collaboration, and conflict resolution were values and skills that had to be nurtured for the clubs to achieve their social goals. Leveraging the meaning and memory of Walker in these efforts meant a lot to these women who identified with her. A statement in the ritual emphasized this point: "Our task as Madam Walker Beauty Culturists is great and our responsibilities awe inspiring. To falter or fail would not only be a disgrace to all of us, but let the greatest name among modern women, the name of the late Madam C. J. Walker that has been given into our hands to magnify and glorify, trail in the dust. Such undertaking requires the conscious receipt of the aid of the all powerful, all wise, ever present God of our Fathers."[55] Delivered by the club president, this statement framed the gravity of their responsibility and the importance of Walker's legacy to them. The group then recited the twenty-third psalm together, a religious remembrance to comfort them and inspire forward movement despite difficulties. The chaplain then prayed for divine assistance for the agents as representatives of Madam Walker so that their speech, thoughts, and actions would align with her ethic of service and self-improvement and flow effortlessly as if part of their natural constitution. The prayer concluded by hailing beauty culture as a "divine art" and "a vehicle of divine service" for translating Christian ideals into practice.[56] In these ways, the women laid claim to more than money making by asserting religious and community aspects of their identities. The members then affirmed this prayer and their unity by reciting the pledge of Madam Walker Agents: "I pledge allegiance to this club and each and every member thereof, the Constitution and By-Laws of the National Beauty Culturists' and Benevolent Association of Madam C. J. Walker Agents and the Madam C. J. Walker Mfg. Company; and I pledge that the name and fame of the late Madam C. J. Walker shall be carried to higher places by my conduct and that it will never suffer the slightest reflection because of my disloyalty or dishonesty. All of this I pledge so help me God."[57]

The president would then strike her gavel, declare the meeting open for business, and follow a format issued in the by-laws for handling business.[58] The by-laws prescribed that members should adhere to strict silence and remain in their seats without disrupting the "harmony" of the meeting.[59] The use of vituperative language or even walking across the meeting hall without the express consent of the president was punishable by expulsion. In order to speak, members had to adorn the proper regalia, which was typically a badge representing her rank in the organization, an important part of the formal culture of the clubs.[60] Only agents in good standing wore the badges, which reinforced identity, belonging, and purpose.

The meeting closed with a striking of the president's gavel and the singing of the hymn "God Be with You Till We Meet Again." Then the president issued a benediction, which proclaimed, "We are now about to disband and again mingle with the so-called rough and inconsiderate world. May we leave this body to live among mankind in so far as we are capable of doing in the manner and with the results as did the immortal Madam C. J. Walker. Although she has shuffled off this mortal coil her spirit is with us here and now to lead, guide and inspire us. Unselfishness was the key to her success. It was the Alpha and the Omega of her life."[61]

In Christian worship, the benediction served the function of closing out formal services by invoking a blessing on congregants to protect and guide them as they left the house of worship to return to their daily lives in the world outside the church. In this practice, the world represented a difficult place that would tempt congregants in ways detrimental to their spiritual salvation and, thus, required divine assistance to navigate faithfully until such a time as they returned to the house of worship to be renewed. In much the same way, the club's benediction depicted the external world as "rough and inconsiderate," one that required Walker agents' adherence to the manner in which Madam Walker herself lived in order to attain the results of success. The hallmark of Walker's manner of living was unselfishness. Such generosity was then celebrated and taught as the group collectively recited a brief poem entitled "The Secret to a Happy Life," said to be Madam Walker's motto:

> Lord help me live from day to day
> In such a self-forgetful way
> That when I kneel to pray
> My prayer shall be for-------------OTHERS.
>
> Help me in all the work I do
> To ever be sincere and true
> And know that all I'd do for you
> Must needs done for---------------OTHERS.[62]

With the ritual now completed, agents had shared an experience that upheld the values and generous lifestyle of Madam Walker, bonded them to each other and to these values, and prepared them for continuing the work of using the "divine art" of beauty culture to uplift the race as women and as agents of change.[63]

In addition to these ritual recitations, songs, and pledges, there were strict rules for the handling of money, including no financial transactions without the presence of a quorum (defined as at least 70 percent of membership) and no loaning of funds to individual members without the express consent of the national president.[64] To ensure continuity of leadership, officers could not vacate their positions upon the ending of their terms until successors were elected, and successors could not assume their elected office unless in good financial standing with the union. Strict provisions were in place to ensure the voices of members were heard before voting and decision making. Members could be removed from the club after reports of misconduct were investigated, but they were given opportunity for a hearing to confront their accusers. Membership criteria included being an active agent of the Walker Company and "a believer in the Supreme Being."[65] Members could belong to only one club at a time and had to present withdrawal cards to their first club if they desired to join another, a practice commonly used by black churches. Members were required to pay membership dues of at least $6 per year. In return, they gained access to sick benefits should they become incapacitated and other assistance, such as burial insurance.[66] The by-laws prescribed a moral code that prohibited intoxication, consistent with Madam Walker's commitment to temperance and the proscription of profane language and the improper use of funds.

Each club had a general fund and a burial fund department. The general fund consisted of fees, dues, fines, donations, and interest, and it was designated for general expenses, payment of sick benefits, payment to members in need, and capital investments, such as hall maintenance. The burial fund department administered payment of burial benefits to families of deceased members and monitored member eligibility for such benefits, which would not be paid if dues were in arrears. For the Calanthes, insurance benefits could range from $300 to $3,000 paid to members' survivors.[67] It is not clear what amounts were paid out by the Walker clubs.

The benefits of fraternal membership for white men had included local and national networking, sickness and burial insurance, charity, social cohesion, and stability, all of which were important in a rapidly changing urban, industrial landscape. The same benefits accrued in black fraternal organizations.[68] As demonstrated by the Walker national by-laws, members enjoyed social insurance and social networks and participated in charity. The point is important because regardless of who introduced fraternal ritual into the clubs, the agents found value in asserting Walker's memory and continued to do so for decades to come. The club's ritual practices and formal culture was for them and not for outside audiences. They demonstrated how the clubs built and supported relations among agents so that they could grow their businesses and uplift their communities through charity and activism—vital components of black women's philanthropy.

## Agents of Change:
## Charity and Activism in the Walker Clubs

Walker's brand of activism involved doing charity work and speaking out on important issues of the day. These behaviors were built into the Walker clubs from the beginning. As a collective activity, charity played a special role in the clubs by bonding club members together and to their communities. Clubs conducted a range of charitable works, keeping with the broad-based nature of African American philanthropy. Some clubs held events to raise money for community organizations, went Christmas caroling, and purchased soap for poor families. Some clubs held revue events to raise money to put food and other items in Christmas baskets for poor families. Some pledged gifts to the National Association for the Advancement of Colored People (NAACP), while others provided educational programs on health and business development. Still other clubs cared for the sick and elderly, supported students, paid housing costs for poor families, and provided furniture to black colleges.

Madam Walker encouraged agent generosity by recognizing the most active clubs with monetary prizes. She put much thought into the prizes she awarded the agents. In preparation for the second national convention in 1918, she set aside $1,000 for multiple awards to inspire more clubs to engage their communities "in order that more people might be benefited." Further, she intended to recognize the club that performed the "most charity work" as well as clubs whose members gave one penny per day for charitable purposes.[69] What is more, any agent could be charitable because of this broad definition not constrained by money. The practice of recognizing club members for their charity work became a key feature of national meetings for decades, as would broader agent efforts to raise up their profession and their people. Madam Walker's and her agents' activism during her lifetime culminated in two important moments.

The first moment was in July 1918. While attending a biennial meeting of the NACW in Colorado, Madam Walker set fire to the $15,000-mortgage papers for the home of Frederick Douglass, the statesman and abolitionist, as her friend and NACW president, Mary B. Talbert, held them. Douglass had died in 1895, but his second wife, Helen Pitts Douglass, wanted to maintain the home, known as Cedar Hill, as a memorial to him. The NACW began making donations to support the house as early as 1914 but in 1916 formally took on the mantle of preserving it. Madam Walker was given the ceremonial honor for having donated the final $500 needed to reach the NACW's fundraising goal so the organization could acquire the beloved abolitionist's home.

This effort was about more than helping Douglass's widow restore a residence. The NACW sought to use Cedar Hill to counter public stereotypes of black women as licentious through its representation of moral and virtuous black womanhood and motherhood. In particular, historian Joan Marie Johnson has argued that the preservation of Cedar Hill, as an inspirational symbol of black success, achievement, and respectability, was an act of protest against negative public representations of black women. This focus on combatting public images and stereotypes of the race was fundamental to black social welfare reform. Since its early days, the NACW had a record of fighting against memorialization of vestigial images of slavery, such as the Black Mammy and the contented slave, and the Lost Cause narrative of the Confederacy, which venerated images and representations of Robert E. Lee and others defeated by the Union. Through their churches, schools, and clubs, African Americans had already been creating publications, curricula, and other means of telling their own history and countering the Lost Cause narrative for the black cultural imagination and for the broader public imagination. Cedar Hill became another tool in their arsenal for waging battle against negative public representations of black humanity. Through Cedar Hill, the NACW staked claims on behalf of black women for their own history, memory, image, and representation.[70]

Helen Pitts Douglass was white, which added further symbolism to the importance of black women saving the home. She wanted Cedar Hill to be held in high esteem, like George Washington's Mount Vernon. The Douglasses had lived in the home for slightly more than a decade before Frederick Douglass's death. When problems arose with the legal execution of Douglass's will, his widow incurred debt in buying out his children's interest in the property. In 1896 she began courting the NACW's interest, but it was not until much later, in 1916, that NACW president Mary B. Talbert created the Douglass Home Committee to raise funds for the building's preservation. The campaign was extensive and included penny drives in which black children participated. Geographically, the home's location gave it an impressive view of Washington, DC, and its Victorian decor gave it a stately aura. The home, according to Johnson, "fit perfectly with the NACW agenda for racial uplift through an emphasis on the family, home life, and respectability that would demonstrate African American progress and ability." It was a great triumph for the NACW and for black women to rescue the home, complete its renovation, and dedicate it for service to the race—and Madam Walker figured prominently in the achievement.[71]

For more than a year, Madam Walker had adopted the cause and dedicated the proceeds of numerous public lectures to the fundraising campaign as a way to generate awareness and revenue. Also, her agents joined her in donating to the fund. Her donation and other supportive advocacy not only connected Walker to the NACW and cemented her relationship with its leadership but also aligned her with the NACW's record of protecting and upholding a virtuous image of black womanhood. Walker's beauty-culture products gave black women more control over their own personal appearance and aesthetics, and her participation as a leading donor for preserving Cedar Hill helped black women gain more control in asserting their collective self-image to the public. The financial gift and her participation were instrumental in facilitating the physical preservation work of Cedar Hill and had an expressive function in publicly uplifting black motherhood and womanhood. Further, the NACW's campaign for Cedar Hill played on themes of patriotism because, for black women, upholding their virtue as wives and mothers was a central element of their strategy for achieving citizenship.[72] Numerous political dignitaries attended the 1918 meeting, including Colorado governor Julius C. Gunter and Denver mayor William F. Mills. Topical sessions were held on lynching, suffrage, temperance, family, and education, and a large audience numbering into the thousands reportedly attended.[73]

Walker's activism had already led her to support and fund the work of A. Phillip Randolph and Marcus Garvey. So it was only natural for her to further use this occasion to remind the elected officials gathered there about the injustice of white mob violence against black people and urge action to end lynching and secure full citizenship for African Americans. Walker was the last speaker on the agenda at the opening exercises for the meeting, which included addresses by the governor, Margaret Murray Washington, and Charlotte Hawkins Brown. With such a large and influential audience, Walker, never one to miss an opportunity, boldly and poignantly declared, "When this war is over and the colored boys have helped to win this democracy we all hear about, we expect the lynching of our people to cease, Gov. Gunter, and we also shall demand that we be given first class privileges on our first class fares whenever we shall find it necessary to ride throughout this country. There are many other things that must be adjusted in this country before we shall be satisfied to live here as American citizens." The governor's reaction was unknown, but Walker was said to "have brought down the house with her wit, humor and sarcasm." This event highlighted Walker's direct style of activism, which combined using her voice, her money, and the collective voice of her agents to speak truth to power about the injustices of Jim Crow and the right to full freedom and equality.[74]

At least since the first national Walker agent convention a year earlier, Walker had been outspoken on such issues. Her approach to activism had developed while on the speaking circuit. Walker traveled widely, delivering lectures to promote her company and "make agents," but she discovered, along the way, the opportunity for deeper impact as she attracted larger crowds. Her standard presentations entitled "The Art of Hair Culture" and "The Negro Woman in Business" provided inspirational messages, including her own life story, and promoted the benefits of affiliating with the Walker Company. In addition, her travelogue presentation enabled her to share pictures from her travels around the country in ways that awed local audience members, who had never ventured far beyond their own cities and towns because of poverty and the threats posed to black people traveling under Jim Crow. It soon became standard practice for Walker to solicit donations from her audiences or dedicate portions of admission fees to specific racial uplift issues important to her. At the time of her NACW speech in Denver, Walker had dedicated lecture proceeds to not only the Frederick Douglass fund but also to the NAACP's legal defense fund for a black dentist charged with murder, to an African Methodist Episcopal church's building renovation fund, and to the American Red Cross's garment fund for black soldiers in World War I. This kind of leveraging of opportunities for greater good became a signature of Walker's activism, which also included her networks, such as the NACW, but especially her agent clubs.

Less than a year later, Madam Walker created the second moment while gravely ill and near death. The NAACP had approached Walker in early

1919 about supporting its upcoming national conference dedicated to the anti-lynching movement scheduled for May. The organization's leadership directly solicited her for a financial contribution. She responded positively with a commitment to give $1,000 and endorsed the convening. On May 5, the event reportedly attracted an interracial audience of more than 2,500 inside New York's Carnegie Hall. The NAACP's 1919 report, *Thirty Years of Lynching in the United States, 1889–1918*, documented more than three thousand lynchings during that period and provided descriptions of one hundred of them in various states to demonstrate the pervasiveness of the problem. The convening's goal was to develop a plan to pursue national legislation to end lynching. The fund to support the campaign, which had a $10,000 goal, was said to help support the work of a committee of lawyers who would lobby for the legislation.

But by the time of the conference, Walker was too sick to attend. She sent her $1,000 check to the event with her friend and NACW president Mary B. Talbert along with a public announcement of a total pledge of $5,000 for the cause of fighting lynching. The gift was received with tremendous applause by the audience, picked up by newspapers, and repeatedly acknowledged by the NAACP. The NAACP increased its campaign to raise money to advocate against lynching and defend blacks in the criminal justice system. These were the first steps that led to various proposals that would be considered in Congress. This $5,000 gift—Walker's last and largest monetary one before death—and its associated activism were extensions and escalations of the gospel of giving that characterized Walker's daily life for years.[75]

By organizing her agents into clubs to bond them together, build a profession, and support and speak out for the community, Madam Walker was doing more than making profits. She was pursuing a social goal to transform society by increasing opportunities for black women to care for their families and work against the system of Jim Crow. NACW-style organization and black fraternal-like rituals were used to nurture the identity of Walker agents by creating a sacred and secure space wherein they could distinguish themselves from agents affiliated with other companies. This feature was particularly important in an environment of competitive voluntarism as Poro and, later, Apex also organized their agents into associations and represented a constant membership-poaching threat.[76] But none of those competitors was affiliated with the national, let alone international, brand

and legacy of Madam C. J. Walker. Her legacy became the basis for bonding her agents.

The pride and identity of being a Walker agent were celebrated, and the concomitant responsibility to serve others was reinforced, through fervent prayer to God for direction and, later, through invocation of Madam Walker. The songs, recitations, rituals, and activities of the national association were part of a formal culture that built social cohesion between the agents and inculcated religious values and Madam Walker's ethic of service, giving, and advocacy. Rather than being the lower-class objects of the black intelligentsia's social agenda, Walker clubwomen were agents of change in their own communities who raised their collective voices in opposition to Jim Crow and extended their gift-filled hands to meet local and national needs, just as their founder had done for decades.

Sarah Breedlove a.k.a.
Madam C. J. Walker (1867–
1919). Courtesy of Madam
Walker Family Archives/
A'Lelia Bundles.

Jessie Batts Robinson took young Sarah
under her wing as part of the Mite
Missionary Society at St. Paul AME
Church in St. Louis, Missouri, during
the 1880s and 1890s. The two women
became lifelong friends, and Robinson
eventually worked for the Walker
Company and provided leadership in
the Walker Clubs. Courtesy of Madam
Walker Family Archives/A'Lelia Bundles.

The Madam C. J. Walker Manufacturing Company of Indiana circa 1911. Courtesy of Madam Walker Family Archives/A'Lelia Bundles.

Telephone Morningside 7883

Wonderful Hair Grower was one of the Walker Company's first products. Courtesy of Madam Walker Family Archives/A'Lelia Bundles.

Madam Walker before and after her wonderful discovery.

One of the earliest product advertisements run by Walker in newspapers around the country featuring herself as the "before" and "after" model. Courtesy of Madam Walker Family Archives/A'Lelia Bundles.

Freeman B. Ransom (1882–1947) was Madam Walker's attorney and general manager. He managed the company's daily operations and administered Walker's philanthropy. He was a prominent civic and political leader in the state of Indiana. His son, Willard, would serve as the company's general manager after his death, and his daughter, A'Lelia Nelson, would serve as President. Courtesy of Madam Walker Family Archives/A'Lelia Bundles.

Alice Burnett was a schoolteacher from Mississippi who became a traveling agent for the Walker Company during the 1910s. She recruited agents and conducted demonstration presentations around the country on how to use the Walker Method. Madam C. J. Walker Papers, Indiana Historical Society.

Madam Walker (seated in center) posing with women who worked in her company, including a young Violet Reynolds (seated next to Madam) whom Walker hired as a teenager around 1915. Courtesy of Madam Walker Family Archives/A'Lelia Bundles.

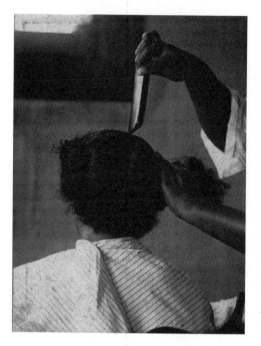

Madam Walker styling a woman's hair (rear view). Courtesy of Madam C. J. Walker Collection, Indiana Historical Society.

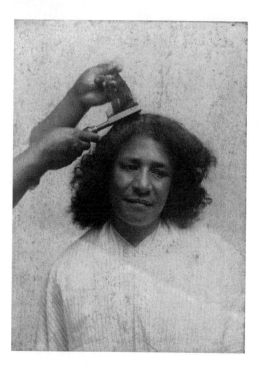

Madam Walker styling a woman's hair (front view). Courtesy of Madam C. J. Walker Collection, Indiana Historical Society.

Madam C. J. Walker with Booker T. Washington (center) at the colored YMCA in Indianapolis. Freeman B. Ransom is standing behind Walker, and George Knox, publisher of the *Indianapolis Freeman*, is to her right. Walker made a $1,000 gift to the campaign for the building, a gift that received national headlines. Washington stayed at Walker's home during his visit to the city to see the facility in 1913. Courtesy of Madam C. J. Walker Collection, Indiana Historical Society.

Madam C. J. Walker (second from left in second row, looking away) with donors who supported the campaign to build the colored YMCA in Indianapolis in 1914, including Sears, Roebuck mogul and philanthropist Julius Rosenwald (front row center with white hat in hand). Rosenwald was unable to attend the grand opening of the YMCA the previous year, but he visited the city in 1914 to great fanfare. Rosenwald provided matching funds to black communities around the country to support the building of YMCAs and schools. George Knox of the *Indianapolis Freeman* is to Rosenwald's right. Courtesy of Madam C. J. Walker Collection, Indiana Historical Society.

A diploma from Lelia College in 1916, part of Walker's national chain of beauty schools, was a respected credential that opened up opportunities for black women to work for the company or strike out on their own as salon owners and entrepreneurs. Courtesy of Madam Walker Family Archives/A'Lelia Bundles.

In Walker's beauty schools, students studied the art and science of beauty culture, including diseases of the scalp, anatomy, hair-dressing techniques, and business and marketing principles. Courtesy of Madam C. J. Walker Collection, Indiana Historical Society.

First National Convention - 1917 - Philadelphia, Pa.

Walker agents with Madam C. J. Walker and Freeman B. Ransom outside First Baptist Church in Philadelphia, Pennsylvania, during the first national convention of Walker agents in August 1917. Courtesy of Madam Walker Family Archives/ A'Lelia Bundles.

Walker agents posing at Villa Lewaro, Madam Walker's thirty-four-room mansion in Irvington-on-Hudson, New York, during a convention meeting. Courtesy of Madam C. J. Walker Collection, Indiana Historical Society.

Madam Walker (right) with daughter Lelia in Madam's automobile outside her Indianapolis home. Walker was fond of giving people rides in her vehicle to share the experience of luxury and being chauffeured. Courtesy of Madam Walker Family Archives/A'Lelia Bundles.

Violet Reynolds joined the Walker Company as Madam's secretary around 1915 at the age of seventeen. Madam Walker bequeathed her $2,000 through her estate. She worked for the company for nearly seventy years, retired from executive leadership there in the early 1980s. Violet is largely responsible for preserving the records that constitute the Walker Papers at the Indiana Historical Society in Indianapolis. Courtesy of Madam C. J. Walker Supplemental Collection, Indiana Historical Society.

Born Lelia McWilliams in 1885 in Vicksburg, Mississippi, Madam Walker's daughter assisted with the company throughout its early development and continued the long line of Walker women who led it into the 1970s. Upon Madam's death, she managed Madam's estate and inherited control of the company until her death in 1931. In the mid-1920s, she changed her name to A'Lelia and became a leading socialite and patron of the Harlem Renaissance. Her adopted daughter, Mae Walker (1898–1945), became president of the company, as did her granddaughter, A'Lelia Mae Perry Bundles (1928–76). Courtesy of Madam C. J. Walker Collection, Indiana Historical Society.

Nettie Ransom, widow of Freeman B. Ransom, lays flowers atop the headstone of her friend, Madam C. J. Walker, during the 1952 memorial ceremony. Nettie was active in Indianapolis organizations such as Flanner House and the Phyllis Wheatley YWCA. She frequently facilitated Madam's gifts to those institutions. Courtesy of Madam C. J. Walker Collection, Indiana Historical Society.

Members of the Chosen 100 preparing to lay their memorial flowers on top of the grave of Madam Walker and A'Lelia Walker during the 1952 national memorial pilgrimage organized by black beauticians to honor Madam Walker. Marjorie Stewart Joyner (far right) was superintendent of the Walker schools and a national leader in the development of beauty culture as a profession. Standing next to her is Willard Ransom, Freeman B. and Nettie Ransom's son, who was an attorney and general manager of the Walker Company at this time. Courtesy of Madam C. J. Walker Collection, Indiana Historical Society.

Race woman, educator, philanthropist, and friend of Madam Walker, Mary McLeod
Bethune (seated center) poses with Marjorie Stewart Joyner (seated first on
left) and other women during the 1952 combined agent convention and national
pilgrimage event. Bethune delivered remarks at the graveside ceremony. Bethune
founded Daytona Normal and Industrial School for Negro Girls in Florida in 1904
(now Bethune-Cookman University), helped to found the United Negro College
Fund, and served in President Franklin Delano Roosevelt's cabinet as an adviser.
She offered Walker's curriculum through her school, and Walker was a regular
donor to and advocate of her work. Courtesy of Madam C. J. Walker Collection,
Indiana Historical Society.

# 5
## Material Resources

I am not and never have been "close-fisted,"
for all who know me will tell you that I am a
liberal hearted woman.
—Madam C. J. Walker, 1913

In 1914 Ella Croker, a black teacher and philanthropist clubwoman in Indianapolis, contacted Freeman B. Ransom to ask for a list of Madam Walker's
philanthropic giving. As a public school teacher, Croker was affiliated with
Mary Cable, a well-known local black civic leader and school principal who
also was a member of Walker and Ransom's church, Bethel AME, and a
founder of the Indianapolis NAACP. Ransom replied to her request with a
three-page letter on November 19, 1914, which described several types of
gifts Walker had made.[1] As the caretaker of Walker's business and image, he
asserted "that Indianapolis ought to know a little more intimately the life
and works of this friend of the poor and needy." The letter included some
phrasing and examples Ransom had previously used to describe Walker's
giving in Walker Company publications and newspaper articles.[2]

He described the list of donations in the letter as being "more or less
chronological" and representative of "some" of Walker's charitable gifts. He
started the list with Walker's 1911 pledge of $1,000 to the building fund of
the colored YMCA in Indianapolis. The list contained a diverse sample of
Walker's gifts from a three-year period. It provided insights into Walker's
thinking about philanthropy at a relatively early point in the life cycle of her

business and experience in acquiring and possessing wealth. Between 1910 and 1913, Walker's annual income tripled, jumping from about $11,000 to more than $32,000 as she became firmly rooted in her Indianapolis neighborhood. This rootedness was new for Walker. Desperation had sent her out of Delta into Vicksburg and St. Louis. Hope and possibility had sent her to Denver and Pittsburgh, but Indianapolis felt welcoming in a different manner. She bonded with several local people and organizations, and her giving reflected these connections.[3]

Scholars have frequently used Ransom's letter and other testamentary documents to illustrate Walker's role as a philanthropist. These documents have formed the basis of our knowledge of the size, number, and recipients of some of Walker's monetary donations. But few scholars have pushed beyond indexing gifts to determine what else about Walker's philanthropy may be learned from them. As Walker's legal adviser, Freeman B. Ransom was empowered to write on Walker's behalf.[4] He advised and administered her giving. He drafted her official correspondence and executed legal documents. In lieu of a direct statement on philanthropy by Walker, this letter about the subject by Ransom, who advised her philanthropic giving, serves as the closest approximation available.[5] The letter provides an important record of Walker's donations, but it also bears witness to Walker's understanding of her community's needs, her responsibilities to others, and the most feasible methods for her to meet such needs and obligations. Closer examination reveals an inconspicuous yet ultimately discernible way of thinking about philanthropy as a versatile, multifaceted tool for uplifting the race against the rising tides of Jim Crow that gave form to Walker's gospel of giving. The letter illustrated the categories of material gifts Walker made, the kinds of recipients and causes she supported, and key motivations behind her gospel of giving. The theme connecting it all was her support for black women.

## Gift Categories

Through Ransom's letter, Madam Walker's gifts can be categorized as monetary, tangible nonmonetary items, employment, and institution-building. The bulk of the letter focused on the typical category of monetary gifts as philanthropy. Ransom presented twelve of Walker's monetary gifts. Amounts were not given for two of the gifts, but the remaining ten ranged from $5 to $1,000 and totaled $1,550 for the three- year period. The $1,000 gift was the famous pledge to the local colored YMCA. It was an outlier on the list because five of the gifts were for $50 or less, and four were for either $100 or $200. It was instructive, however, that Ransom led with this gift because it was clear both he and Walker wanted many people to know about it and the significance of not only its amount, but of its source—a black woman who owned a business and used her resources to uplift the race during Jim Crow. Charitable giving met important needs and demonstrated respectability and virtuous womanhood, too.

Walker tended to make the gifts of $50 or less to smaller, local organizations such as Flanner House in Indianapolis, the Star Christmas Fund, the Mite Missionary Society at St. Paul AME Church in St. Louis, and the St. Louis Colored Orphans' Home. These local organizations were vital to their surrounding communities. Faced with gaps in services created by the discriminatory practices of white mainstream social-service organizations, these black-serving organizations were essential to survival in the black community.[6] In 1916 the *Indianapolis Freeman* reported that Walker had a history of visiting poor families in the city several times per year to "attend to their needs."[7] Her own private visits to families and public gifts to charities represented her efforts to combat poverty. Walker appears to have made several small donations to these organizations over time. Such a pattern likely represented her understanding of the importance of continuous support for vulnerable organizations. A steady stream of smaller gifts better addressed organizations' long-term cash-flow concerns than did one-time gifts of larger sums that often left organizations scrambling to find replacement donations after their expenditure.

Walker had tended to make the gifts of $100 or more to relatively larger organizations with regional, national, or international programs. For instance, such gifts went to Palmer Memorial Institute, which educated students throughout North Carolina and the South; the "State University" in Louisville, Kentucky; and the International YMCA.[8] Her $200 gift to Charlotte Hawkins Brown's Palmer Memorial Institute covered one teacher's salary.[9] The $100 gift to "State University" was made in honor of Alice Kelly, Walker's tutor, assistant, and frequent travel companion, who had worked as a teacher in Kentucky, and Lucy Flint, Walker's bookkeeper.[10] The gifts were commensurate with those made by white northern donors and frequently totaled more than what was given in the aggregate by black donors and southern white donors.[11] These monetary gifts were the most represented type of gift in the letter, but they were complemented by examples of nonmonetary giving that provided added dimension to Walker's gospel of giving.

Walker's gifts of nonmonetary, tangible items represented another way in which she met the needs of individuals and families in her community. She gave baskets of food to the Alpha Home and the Orphans' Home in Indianapolis annually that were worth approximately $50. The Alpha Home had been founded in 1886 to care for elderly black women, especially those who had been enslaved. It offered them an alternative to the alms house because white elder-care facilities denied admissions to aged and infirm blacks. Walker became fond of the organization and hosted the women of the home at a social event around the time of Ransom's letter. In-kind gifts were a significant part of her support and somewhat of an annual tradition. In 1915 the *Indianapolis Freeman* reported that the Walker Company "looked like a grocery store Christmas morning. On the floor were forty well-filled baskets of provisions, which were ready to be given as gifts to the needy. In each basket was a chicken, potatoes, apples, oranges, a head of cabbage, a pound of coffee, sugar, and flour."[12] The gift was consistent with Walker's concern for two of the black population's most vulnerable groups—elderly women and orphans.

The baskets were the beginning of Walker's ongoing support for Alpha Home, which included donating money and chairing a travelogue event in January 1916 after she had returned from the West Coast of the United States. At the event, Walker showed picture slides from her trip to the audience members, who had paid 10 cents admission and had a chance to win $5 in gold from Walker for selling the most event tickets. She narrated her slides, which depicted her travels through Missouri, Colorado, Utah, Montana, Washington, and California and included pictures of the Salt Lake Temple and Cathedral of the Madeleine in Utah as well as geysers from Yellowstone Park. The event attracted Eugene Kinckle Jones of the Urban League and other black leaders. The money from the event was used to clear the Alpha Home's debt, which the local paper described as Walker's final charitable gesture as a resident of the city before moving to New York. Walker's identification with the plight of orphans, arising from her own experience of losing her parents and the day care Lelia received from an orphanage in St. Louis, greatly informed these gifts and involvement with Alpha Home as another way to uphold virtuous black womanhood.[13]

She also gave a "wheeling chair" to a disabled elderly man "who had not been out of his door in sixteen years." It is not clear whether this individual or his representatives solicited Walker, but she gave him the gift of mobility, something she likely had not taken for granted during her extensive travel schedule. Her gift of "milk for sick babies" was an extension of her concern for the vulnerability of youth. Walker gave a ticket to a young man "who was afflicted with an incurable disease that he might go to his home at Knoxville, Tenn." In closing his letter to Croker, Ransom led into this particular gift by classifying it as one of "any number of charitable acts of lesser importance."[14] It was unclear whether Ransom was representing his own sentiments or those of Walker, but, in light of her background, such giving likely held more significance for Walker.

As one who had known the direct generosity of others during her time as a poor, black migrant moving around the South in the late 1800s, Walker had depended on small, interpersonal gifts of support, no matter their constitution, to survive and adjust to her new surroundings. Also, Walker knew the importance of being in the right place at the right time, particularly the place of one's origins or sense of belonging, for it took her a long time to find a place to call home. Helping a sick young man get home when he had no other means for doing so likely was a meaningful act of giving for her.[15]

In addition to giving tangible items, Madam Walker made a nonmonetary gift of another sort that was evident in Ransom's description in the letter of her efforts on behalf of an incarcerated young man:

> One of the more recent charitable acts of Madam Walker, was the securing of a pardon for the only son of aged parents, who had been given a life term in the Miss. state prison for killing a white man. Madam Walker's aide [sic] was sought by the poor boy's mother early in the fall of 1911. . . . [A] certain Mississippi lawyer was employed and after much expense the pardon was denied December 14, 1913. But nothing daunted[,] Madam Walker employed an Indianapolis attorney and the boy was pardoned early in August of this year, and the young man is now working supporting his old mother and father.[16]

The details of this gift were clearly laid out in Ransom's statement about it.[17] The more interesting aspect of it related to what Ransom did not mention. The young man who was incarcerated for murder was Willie Powell, Madam Walker's nephew, the son of her sister Louvenia, who had cared for Walker in her early childhood and adolescent years immediately after the death of their parents. Louvenia asked Walker to assist her son, and Walker obliged by engaging Ransom to secure Norman Allen, an attorney in Mississippi, to pursue a pardon with the governor. Ransom was an excellent adviser to involve in this process because he reportedly had an interest in criminal law and had worked on two other murder cases.[18] In addition to Ransom and Allen, Walker may have hired additional attorneys during the five years it took to accomplish her nephew's release, though it was not clear how much she spent on legal services.[19] The gift's inclusion on this list revealed an interesting facet of African American philanthropy.

Generally, white Western models of giving have viewed gifts as being philanthropic only when given to strangers. By focusing on the other-directedness of giving, these Western models hoped to distinguish altruistic motivations from legal or familial responsibilities. This particular gift by Walker, however, demonstrated the fluidity that has historically defined African American philanthropy, where little distinction exists between gifts to family, friends, and others. Such fluidity emerged from its West African derivations, its formation in the crucible of American racism and sexism, and its orientation toward pragmatism. Because of their shared experience of racial oppression based on skin color, African Americans developed a collective consciousness consisting of a common sense of identity and struggle that tied their liberation to collective effort. W. E. B. DuBois called this collective consciousness a "double consciousness," a "twoness" of simultaneously being American and being black. For black women, the dilemma was more complex; composed of race, gender, and class, which combined into a ternary consciousness.[20] Because philanthropy emanates from the identity of those performing it, personal worldviews, values, interests, and concerns inform the types of voluntary actions taken, whom those actions are directed toward, and the goals sought.

As a result of this shared consciousness and shared status in society, each African American, to the extent that he or she was identified with the black race, was subject to abuse under Jim Crow and, therefore, equally in need of liberation. When directing gifts for the purposes of navigating and overcoming the scourges of racism and sexism, preoccupation with the formal nature of relations between givers and recipients held lesser value in African American philanthropy because African Americans had a broader sense of those to whom they had obligations and maintained responsibilities, especially black women. The African American concept of extended family or fictive kin expanded the boundaries of the nuclear family to embrace distant relatives and unrelated others who were in need.[21] In this context, any form of gift giving for the purposes of liberation was an act of subversion meant to thwart the status quo and bring about justice in an unjust society.

Social justice has historically been important in the tradition of African American philanthropy, which has operated at three levels to fill voids created by racism: (1) meeting individual and community needs for direct relief from suffering; (2) building self-help institutions to pursue social, cultural, religious, political, and economic needs and aspirations; and (3) creating social change through the abolition of public policies and structural barriers that made the United States inhospitable.[22] In this view, Walker's efforts to free her nephew from the criminal justice system, which had long been unfair and hostile to blacks—particularly black men—is considered philanthropy. Walker was fond of her nephew Willie and desperately worked to provide him with opportunities. Later, she made specific provisions in her will to further help him become established. Ransom's listing of her efforts to secure Willie's legal pardon further substantiated the perception of such acts of giving—public expressions of privately held values related to justice and opportunity directed against an onerous legal establishment—as philanthropic in the African American tradition, even if traditional Western ways of thinking would not recognize them as such.

Walker's gifts of nonmonetary items revealed her concern for the suffering of others. It is interesting to note that these types of gifts tended not to be publicized as much as some of Walker's other, monetary gifts. But they represented an important component of her gospel of giving. Walker recognized that there were multiple ways to meet needs. She knew that money was vital for the causes she cared about, but she also knew that other forms of giving would meet felt needs more immediately and directly. Her gifts of Christmas baskets and Thanksgiving turkeys in Indianapolis became annual affairs keenly anticipated by the local community.

The omissions on the list of items Walker gave as nonmonetary gifts to others were equally notable—Walker Company products and services. With a growing manufacturing company and an expanding number of agents around the country, it could have seemed quite reasonable for Walker to make some portion of products available as gifts to others, perhaps to the women at the Alpha Home or the girls at the Orphans' Home. But Violet Reynolds, Walker's long-time employee, recollected that "One of [Walker's] business quirks was that she gave freely of her time and money, but she was never known to give away any of her products."[23] According to Reynolds, Walker was adamant that her goods would never be given away as gifts but rather should always be purchased.

Reynolds attributed this stance to Walker's shrewd understanding of business. She quoted Walker as having said to her, "if any one wants my products, they must buy them. They are for sale."[24] The products generated the income and resulting resources that enabled Walker to be generous on an increasing scale. She was clear that the fundamentals of her business model had to be preserved in order for her to continue her work in its totality. Further, the majority of Walker's charitable giving was made prior to legal changes that began to provide tax benefits to donors, particularly corporations.[25] Even still, there was likely more to Walker's steadfast stance on this issue.

Giving away products would have only addressed one aspect of her philanthropy, namely her desire to improve the self-image and self-esteem of black women by enhancing their personal hygiene and appearance. Product donations would not have advanced Walker's philanthropic interests in social-service and educational organizations. More important, the Walker Company products held special symbolism as representations of Walker's dreams of success and a better life. Product donations would have depreciated those dreams and diminished the dignity of hard work applied in service to them. And so Walker's gospel of giving did not include using her products as gifts, but rather viewed them as part of her overall business model, which she leveraged in multiple ways to be helpful to her community.

In an interesting deviation from the more traditional conceptions of philanthropic giving represented in Ransom's letter to Croker, Ransom noted that Walker had given "employment to one woman Eighty Five years old, to another who is deaf and dumb."[26] In the first instance, Walker employed a very elderly woman whose age and associated frailty left her outside the labor market. As a woman, she was mainly limited to working in domestic positions. While Ransom did not describe the woman's physical build or labor skills, he implied that her age represented a physical limitation that made her undesirable in the workforce. According to Ransom, Walker also employed a person whom he described as "deaf and dumb" (a common reference to muteness at the time).[27] The inability to hear and the associated perceptions of reduced mental capacity imposed on deaf people likely left this individual with few viable employment prospects. It is not clear what kind of positions these two individuals were given. In addition to the sales agents, traveling agents, and salon owners employed by the Walker Company, there were also employees who worked in the main office and on the factory floor of the Indianapolis headquarters, as well as in the beauty schools. These women tended to be Walker's working-class neighbors. Because of their limitations, the two referenced individuals were most likely placed in one of these latter positions within the company.

By employing the unemployable, Walker made at least two gifts. First was the job itself, which was prized in a discriminatory labor market that was hostile to African Americans because of their skin color. Second was the dignity that came with being able to support oneself and one's family, something Walker had diligently searched for when she struggled as a washerwoman in her earlier days in places like Vicksburg and St. Louis. Effectively, Walker gave these gifts not only to the two individuals cited in the letter, but she gave them to all of her employees specifically and to African Americans more generally. Walker was one of an increasing number of black business owners who had created job opportunities for African Americans in a society that had few second thoughts about their welfare and no acceptable plans for their uplift. This concept of employing the unemployable resonated deeply with Walker as representing a form of justice. Implicit in the idea of not employing people because of certain physical limitations or skin color—natural, genetically based characteristics not under the control of any individual—was a sense of unfairness and injustice that needed to be righted. Walker's gifts in this area were aligned with her overall goal of fulfilling her duty as a black woman to help her race.[28]

Her stance contrasted with that of Hetty Green (1834–1916), a wealthy white woman who had turned a multimillion-dollar inheritance into a $100 million fortune through Wall Street investments. Known to have been close-fisted and uncharitable, Green used her provision of jobs as a rationale for *not* engaging in philanthropy.[29] As a black woman, such a position was untenable for Walker. Helping others was fundamental to how she understood herself and her responsibilities to her community. She said as much in a 1916 newspaper interview in which she described the rationale for her use of black workers to build her New York mansion: "My business is largely supported by my own people, so why shouldn't I spend my money so that it will go into colored homes. . . . By giving work to colored men they are thus able to employ others, and if not directly, indirectly. I am generating more jobs for our boys and girls."[30] She felt compelled to use the resources at her disposal to be as helpful to her race as possible. Providing employment through her company, and through her personal consumption, was one way she could give, but doing so did not absolve her from the responsibility to help in other ways. It was part of an array that also included institution building.

As previously discussed, Madam Walker's philanthropic dream was to build an industrial educational institution in South Africa modeled after Booker T. Washington's Tuskegee Institute. Ransom wrote in his letter to Croker that Walker "Established and maintains an Industrial Mission School at Pandoland [sic], South Africa."[31] There was no formal record of Walker having started such a school at that time or later, and so this may refer to a gift to an existing AME school. But it reflected her loyal support of industrial education and the public announcement she had made about it two years earlier before the annual meeting of Booker T. Washington's National Negro Business League (NNBL) in Chicago. Although Walker had a deep yearning for the project, which she called "the real ambition of my life" and an "all-absorbing idea," two years later significant progress had not been made.[32]

Walker's interest in Pondoland, South Africa, likely emerged from her membership in the AME Church. Pondoland was located on the eastern cape of South Africa near the Indian Ocean. It had a long history as an independent kingdom that survived European colonialism in fair fashion. Even legal changes in the early 1900s that gave whites significant ownership of land across South Africa had little effect on the Pondo people, who maintained control of their land.[33] This form of independence may have been the reason for Walker's interest, but so could her religious affiliation.

The AME Church had a presence in South Africa since the early 1890s, when a bishop of the church visited the country for the first time. In 1896 the Ethiopian Church in Pretoria, which was composed of black South African Methodists who fled the white Wesleyan congregations in the country because of their discriminatory racial practices, united with the AME Church and helped to establish church operations in the country. In 1901 the AME Church established a school named Bethel Institute in Cape Town and deployed missionaries. By 1916, the AME Church's involvement with South Africa grew rapidly, to the point that it claimed to have 18,000 members, 1,100 children in schools, 135 buildings, 104 ordained ministers, and 216 preachers and lay helpers in the country.[34]

These numbers included missionaries who had been working in Pondoland since 1898. The AME Church advertised missionary opportunities in South Africa through its publications during the early 1900s and attracted interest. Missionaries on the ground in Pondoland reported vibrant business activity on the part of the local Pondo people, but they also noted a significant need for schools. In 1900 a Pondo chief named Sigcau donated land to the AME Church for an industrial school and asked the church to engage Booker T. Washington for assistance. This particular institute was never built, although another institute modeled after the AME Church's Wilberforce University in Ohio was built in the Transvaal region of northeastern South Africa some years later.[35]

Walker may have learned about Pondoland and its need for education through the AME Church's extensive international communications network. At the start of the AME Church's involvement in Pondoland in 1898, Walker was a member of St. Paul AME Church in St. Louis. In 1914, the time of Ransom's letter, both Walker and Ransom were members of Bethel AME Church in Indianapolis. The church's missionary work was frequently promoted through publications, sermons, and announcements. Regardless of the origins of Walker's idea for building a "Tuskegee in Africa," it was not in existence at the time of Ransom's writing. In 1914 Walker spent time on the Tuskegee campus further researching the idea by observing the institute's classes and operations. In 1916 Walker also offered $1,000 to black religious denominations, including her own AME Church, to start the school, but there were no takers. In 1917 Walker made provisions for the school as part of her last will and testament. But her dream of building a school was never realized.[36]

Despite the fact that the "Tuskegee Institute in Africa" vision never became a reality, Ransom's inclusion of this aspiration on the list of gifts made by Walker revealed important dimensions of her gospel of giving. It represented Walker's desire to make a lasting gift by building an institution that would presumably educate South Africans in perpetuity. Scholarships were useful for assisting particular individuals in acquiring their education. Walker knew and valued that kind of individual support. Building a school, however, could fill an important gap in much needed services and leave a legacy. Much like her own company, which she had set up to endure far beyond her own existence, a school would have stood as a monument to her achievement, as a woman who lacked formal education, and black achievement, as a group once denied the right to learn.

Further, the idea for the school exemplified Walker's shifting attention to global matters and an emerging Pan-African sensibility.[37] In 1913 Walker left the United States to tour Central America and the Caribbean in an effort to open new markets in Costa Rica, Jamaica, Cuba, Panama, and Haiti. This experience exposed her to the success and achievement of the elite people of color in these countries, but it also demonstrated the severe poverty and injustice endured by local people. Particularly, Walker was distressed over the treatment of political prisoners in Haiti and attempted to give food to them.[38] If nothing else, the experience gave her a broader sense of the troubles facing black-skinned people around the world. Well versed in US racial oppression, Walker finally had seen firsthand something she would have heard about through the AME Church's communications network and her increasing interactions with the National Association of Colored Women (NACW) and the NNBL—that people of color were facing racial discrimination and injustice outside the United States, too, and that while their various struggles around the world were in different geographical locations, they were all connected.[39] Walker's travels prefigured her later involvement in cofounding an international advocacy organization for the race. By thinking outside the US context, Walker was beginning to expand her identity and sense of obligation to others; consequently, her gospel of giving was following suit. Her use of gifts of money, tangible items, employment, and institution building demonstrated her sense of how best to be helpful to her people's efforts to survive and overcome Jim Crow and other oppressive systems globally.

## Madam C. J. Walker and Scientific Philanthropy

Walker made philanthropic gifts to both individuals and organizations. The gifts to individuals tended to address immediately felt needs that resulted from poverty or other forms of suffering, such as hunger and lack of mobility. The gifts to institutions had operational or programmatic emphases that addressed various social injustices. This inclusion of both individuals and institutions in Walker's philanthropy was important because, during her lifetime, the emergence of scientific philanthropy as a model for giving became prominent in the United States.

Having started in England in the late nineteenth century with the charity organization movement, scientific philanthropy called for the application of scientific knowledge and methods to eradicate social ills.[40] Anything else was branded a lesser form of charity, which might have been useful for meeting an immediate need, such as ending the severe hunger of a child who had not eaten in days by giving her food, but offered no long-term significant societal impact because the child would be hungry again the following day, thus perpetuating the cycle of need. Scientific philanthropy became a dominant model in the early twentieth century, which was aided by the emerging philanthropic foundations of the period, including the Russell Sage Foundation, Andrew Carnegie's foundations, and John D. Rockefeller's institutions. Among African American organizations, scientific philanthropy's major manifestations were in some elements of the black clubwomen's movement and the National Urban League (NUL).

At the local level, some black clubwomen adopted social science methods in their programming, such as Lugenia Burns Hope, who founded the Neighborhood House in Atlanta, Georgia. Hope conducted social-science surveys of neighborhood conditions, including housing, health, and sanitation, to inform and measure how her organization's programming was meeting the needs of one of Atlanta's most impoverished black neighborhoods.[41] At the national level, these methods were deployed by the NUL and its local affiliates across the country. NUL's cofounder and first executive director was Dr. George Edmund Haynes, the first black graduate of the New York School of Philanthropy, a forerunner of social work and a purveyor of the application of social-science methodologies to social problems. His sister, Birdye Henrietta Haynes, was the first black graduate of Chicago School of Civics and Philanthropy and applied similar methods in her direction of settlement houses in Chicago and New York.[42] As a result, the tenets of scientific philanthropy were not lost on African Americans. During this period of national organizational infrastructure building to advance the struggle for racial uplift, however, African Americans may have had a different interpretation of it because of their firsthand experience with the severity of oppression and their social needs.

For instance, black clubwomen's old folks' homes during the late nineteenth and early twentieth centuries thought about the "worthy poor" differently than did many mainstream white organizations, particularly those influenced by scientific philanthropy.[43] The notion of the "worthy poor" was used to deny services and assistance to those individuals believed to have had a great hand in their own downtrodden condition; thus, they were seen as unworthy of aid because their behavior and lack of moral fortitude was believed to be a cause or contributor to their plight. As a result, it was felt that no infusion of resources could overcome such innate faults. By virtue of their skin color and the concomitant stereotypes that whites imposed on them, African Americans were automatically deemed unworthy of services by many white social agencies. Black old folks' homes, on the other hand, frequently accepted either a good word of reference from a prominent black citizen or membership in a fraternal organization, which typically included social insurance benefits, as proxies for prospective residents' ability to pay for care. Consequently, although black-run organizations had to be prudent in exercising their limited ability to provide assistance, they were more lenient because of the broader situation of the race.[44]

Walker was not greatly influenced by scientific philanthropy. She did not apply formulas to her giving. She did not deploy social-science methods to assess the scope of needs and formulate a strategy to meet those needs. Her giving was rooted in cultural and identity-based perspectives that expected all members of the race, but especially black women, to help as they were able. To be sure, she was concerned with eradicating the suffering of her race and gender and had no desire for temporary measures that offered no long-term solutions. She wanted racial and gender oppression permanently ended and opportunity expanded for people of color. But her approach to philanthropic racial uplift involved supporting black individuals and institutions that she automatically deemed worthy because of the pervasive racial oppression.

Walker was not foolish in her giving. She admitted her great difficulty in turning down appeals when, in 1914, she wrote that public knowledge of her wealth had "caused scores of demands for help. Many of whom are so pathetic that it has been impossible for me to turn them down." Ransom had taken steps to ferret out appeals that were bogus and was diligent in his role to make sure no one took advantage of Walker's generosity and that her benevolence did not lead to problematic alliances that called into question her sincerity or reputation. During the summer of 1915, Walker and a reporter were interrupted several times during an interview by individuals off the street who approached her for financial assistance. Then Walker's staff interrupted the interview to process a donation to a vetted charity as the paper noted, "the faithful secretary ushers in with the check book—everything ready but the signature. She signs, and the secretary glides noiselessly out again. . . . The madam is nowise disturbed by this little reduction of her bank account." Perhaps this was a show for the interviewer, but Walker's giving was not haphazard; rather, it had focus.[45]

## Funding Women, Uplifting the Race

Madam C. J. Walker fundamentally believed that the liberation of black women and girls was intricately tied to the liberation of black men and boys—when one improved, so did the other. For that reason, she funded the race to uplift black women, and she funded black women in order to uplift the race. This distinction is subtle but important and very easy to miss just by looking at Ransom's list because many of her gifts were not overtly for black women. Organizations like Flanner House, the orphans' home, the Star Fund, and Tuskegee broadly met the needs of men and women. On the other hand, organizations like the St. Paul's Mite Missionary Society, Palmer Memorial Institute, and Alpha Home were either founded and run by black women or expressly served black women. In both instances, however, women were served. Whenever she gave, Walker had black women foremost in her mind and said as much about her most widely publicized gift, which seemed to be for men.

In 1911 the *Indianapolis Freeman* praised Walker as the first black woman in the United States ever to give $1,000 to the building fund for the colored YMCA. The white philanthropist Julius Rosenwald had agreed to provide matching funds if the local Indianapolis community could raise sufficient dollars for the project. Walker stepped up and urged everyone to participate even though, as a woman, she could not be a meaningful part of YMCA's programming. Still, of the organization she said, "The Young Men's Christian Association is one of the greatest institutions there is [and] I am very glad to help the association, and I am much interested in its work. I certainly hope that it gets the new building, and I think every colored person ought to contribute to the campaign."[46] Madam Walker was not alone in her staunch and enthusiastic support of the YMCA.

During this period, African Americans believed that, despite its discriminatory practices, the YMCA provided black men and boys with a dedicated space for essential personal and community development. They viewed the YMCA's programs as conducive to racial uplift, and leaders within the YMCA movement created a national network of black-operated YMCAs that served as a source of pride within the community. Black YMCAs provided important vocational and professional training, literacy and educational services, dormitory housing, and recreational and physical activities. Their facilities became community centers and meeting places for black professional, civic, religious, and social organizations that symbolized African Americans' search for cultural self-determination. As independent institutions, the black YMCAs attracted financial support from the community. By making her $1,000 YMCA gift pledge—which almost equaled the total gifts and pledges made by ninety-nine other donors—and subsequent smaller and more regular donations to local, national, and international black YMCAs, Madam Walker expressed the value she placed on the YMCA as a vehicle for uplifting the race and overcoming prejudice. As a multifaceted organization meeting desperate needs at the local level and internationally, it was a unique institution that Walker deemed worthy of support and replication in communities of color across the globe, but there was more to it.[47]

In her view, building the colored YMCA in her city of Indianapolis was critical because "If the association can save our boys [our] girls will be saved, and that's what I am interested in. Some day I would like to see a colored girls' association started."[48] The process had already begun. Colored YWCAs were beginning to open around the country, and the Chapman Branch (later called the Phyllis Wheatley Branch) opened in St. Louis that same year. Walker's mentor and friend, Jessie Batts Robinson, would become affiliated with that branch and later facilitated Walker's giving to it. In Indianapolis, conversations about a colored YWCA had begun a few years earlier, but it would take a few more years to gain traction. When it did, Walker was in the mix, hosting meetings and serving as treasurer of the women's committee, along with her friend Nettie Ransom, that organized the Phyllis Wheatley branch for her city.[49] To Walker, this YMCA gift for black men was ultimately a gift for black women. The Indianapolis campaign was successful, and she later celebrated the grand opening of the YMCA building. YWCAs would benefit additionally from her estate. The theme of funding the race to uplift women, and funding women to uplift the race manifested through her other gifts as well.

Women figured largely in the two primary types of organizational causes that Walker supported, education and social services.[50] She supported schools such as Hannon Industrial Institute, Tuskegee Institute, and Palmer Memorial Institute. The Lomax Hannon Industrial Institute was founded through the AME Zion Church in 1893 in Greenville, Alabama. In 1912, the approximate time when Walker donated a scholarship there, Hannon had 232 students, mainly from Alabama, and annual revenues of $7,360.[51] It had recently built dormitories for girls and boys and was affiliated with nearby Tuskegee Institute. Palmer Memorial Institute, in North Carolina, was led by Walker's NACW friend Charlotte Hawkins Brown. Its program was based on Brown's "triangle of achievement," which emphasized education, culture, and religion through its industrial and agricultural curriculum.[52] Hannon and Palmer had lower profiles than Tuskegee, and fundraising was an ongoing challenge for them. In contrast, Tuskegee Institute served as the archetype of black industrial colleges and was greatly favored among white industrialist funders of black education. Consequently, it boasted an enrollment of 1,527 students from thirty-two states and seventeen countries. It had an operating budget of $270,568 and an endowment worth $1.9 million. The exact dollar value of Walker's scholarships at Hannon and Tuskegee is unknown, but according to Tuskegee's annual report in 1914, a donation of $50 partially covered tuition for one student. For that same calendar year, Walker was listed in Tuskegee's annual report as having given $10.[53] Newspaper accounts indicated that at least one of the Tuskegee students supported by Walker was African and his expenses amounted to $72 per year, which she paid.[54] These gifts demonstrated Walker's concern for education for the race and her specific support for black women educators working in the field to uplift the race.

Walker also made gifts to social services such as Flanner House. It was an Indianapolis community service center founded in 1898 that provided employment, training, social services, recreational programming, health services, child care, and a library. The organization was part of the settlement movement, which was highly segregated because white settlements discriminated against blacks, and it figured largely in the local response to a tuberculosis outbreak in Indianapolis in the 1910s. Ransom may have facilitated the gift to Flanner House as a board member or his associate

Robert Brokenburr and his wife, Alice, who served as superintendent and matron of the Flanner Guild from 1912 to 1914, may have done so.[55] Flanner House and Alpha Home were both very special to Walker and were performing much-needed work in the community for women and the race. Further, Walker's relationships with women were important factors in the affinity she developed for Indianapolis and St. Louis, where her giving was concentrated. These locales represented turning points in her life story that were facilitated by women.

Walker made the vast majority of gifts in Ransom's letter to people and organizations that were in her Indianapolis neighborhood. Walker chose Indianapolis as her place of residence, in part, because of the warm welcome she received from the local black community during a visit to the city in 1910. She was quickly embraced by locals as a favored daughter of the city and of the state by extension.[56] The affinity that the local black community felt for Walker was represented in a resolution presented to her in 1915 to discourage her from leaving the city to reside in New York after rumors had begun circulating about her possible departure. Signed by nearly sixty YMCA leaders, members, and civic leaders, the resolution referred to Walker as the city's "daughter," "sister," "comrade," "benefactor," "gracious sympathizer," and "generous mother" and begged her to "always live among us."[57] The *Indianapolis Freeman* wrote that Walker would be missed not only for her business contributions but also for her charity as "the big-hearted race loving woman that she is," and many of the individuals personally helped by Walker called her or visited her home to express gratitude before her departure in 1916.[58] Walker greatly appreciated the warm hospitality even though other experiences, such as her mistreatment by the local Isis Theater, which charged her a higher price of admission than whites paid for attending a moving picture show, later left her feeling distrustful of the city.[59] Nothing, however, would taint Walker's connection to the people and handful of charities that she held dear. Even after she left for New York, the Indianapolis charities remained important to Walker, and many later received bequests through her estate.

Beyond the obvious ties in being the headquarters of the Walker Company, Indianapolis held significance in her life story. She had formally incorporated her company in the city and had there the first opportunity to establish the kind of community roots long missing in her life. Madam Walker visited her birthplace in October 1916 as part of a southern promotional tour for her company, and she wrote to Ransom, "Went to my home in Delta yesterday and came back to Vicksburg and gave a lecture at Bethel church to a very appreciative audience[. G]oing back Wed. night [*sic*] lecture at Baptist church."[60] Although she may have made some impromptu gifts during her visit to her birthplace, as she was known to do during her travels, Walker did not appear to have ongoing engagement with Delta or Vicksburg. In the early days of her business, Sarah also lived in Denver and Pittsburgh, but she did not stay long in those cities or establish long-term personal relationships with local residents.

By contrast, Madam Walker had numerous women employees in Indianapolis and very close friends like Freeman and Nettie Ransom, Robert and Alice Brokenburr, and Joseph and Zella Ward.[61] As a member of Bethel AME Church, Walker was connected to local churchwomen, clubwomen, and the broader black working- and middle-class communities. She was active in the local Order of the Court of Calanthe. The roots Walker set down in the city gave her not only a base of operation for the company but one for developing the relationships, networks, and engagements necessary to serve the cause of racial and gender uplift against Jim Crow locally and nationally, no matter where her business travels took her. Thus she was able to maintain proximity to the people and the causes she sought to help by residing among them and engaging in philanthropic giving in a very practical and versatile manner based on known and observed local needs. The Indianapolis gifts represented a depth of connection and sense of place that held great meaning for her. Indianapolis may not have been where she started her business, but it was the place where it thrived and where the return on her laborious efforts first became most evident. Indianapolis remained a place of importance to the Walker brand and to Walker herself, and, to this day, her work and attachments in the city form the primary basis for her legacy.[62]

Organizations in St. Louis were recipients of a few gifts that represented Walker's most intimate self-identification. Walker gave $10 annually to both the "colored Orphans Home at Saint Louis" and the Mite Missionary Society of the St. Paul AME Church. She also gave $100 annually to the YMCA of St. Louis. Between 1889 and 1906, the transformation that led Sarah Breedlove to become Madam C. J. Walker largely occurred while she resided in that city. During the seventeen-year period, Sarah, the twenty-two year-old, illiterate, penniless, migrant widow and mother who struggled as a washerwoman to provide for her child, became Sarah, the confident, forward-thinking dreamer who had put her daughter through college and resolved to leave her washtub behind in pursuit of her business idea. The women-run charities named in Ransom's letter had a great hand in this transformation. They socialized her into black women's respectability and modes of service and charitable giving—it was where her gospel of giving first emerged.[63]

During her extensive business travels, Walker continued to visit St. Louis and maintained her friendships there; most notably to Jessie Batts Robinson, who was a member of the Mite Missionary Society that welcomed young Sarah to town in 1889. But Jessie was not only Walker's friend. She became an active employee of the Walker Company, ran a local supply station for Walker agents, served as chair of the Rules of Order Committee of the National Convention of Madam C. J. Walker Agents, and presided over the St. Louis Walker Club.[64] Beyond these involvements, Jessie was Walker's connection to St. Louis and a facilitator of some of her giving to the city. For instance, in December 1912, Robinson wrote to her friend to give her an update on charities. Robinson told Walker that St. Paul AME Church's new pastor had placed the work of a church auxiliary called the Helping Hand Society under the auspices of the Mite Missionary Society. Then, on behalf of the pastor, Robinson asked Walker for a donation to this effort because "we are doing a wonderful work for humanity."[65] She also informed Walker of the election of a new board president at the orphan home, a person she described as "a wonderful woman, a good manager, honest and upright."[66] Robinson noted that the new president was working hard on the Christmas bazaar fundraising event and provided her address to encourage Walker's donation. This relationship illustrated how Walker not only gave *to* women, but *because of* and *through* women. Robinson kept Walker connected to a special place in her life.

In a 1912 newspaper interview, Walker told a reporter that she gave to the orphanage in St. Louis "in remembrance of the kindnesses that were shown her own daughter there" and that she gave to the programs of the St. Paul AME Church because "she was converted" there—a reference to her personal and religious transformation aided by women.[67] Her ongoing support of St. Louis–based charities honored those women and organizations that had helped her and attested to her identification with the effective local efforts that worked to change lives.

Together, Indianapolis and St. Louis, two Midwestern cities in which dramatic developments occurred in the southern-born Walker's life, received the bulk of her gifts between 1911 and 1914 as Ransom recounted in his letter. This pattern continued in subsequent years and Walker's bequest provisions maintained it. Although the letter also mentioned gifts to some black schools across the South, on the whole Walker's affinity for Indianapolis and St. Louis explained a great deal of her gospel of giving and how she expressed her sense of identity and responsibility as a woman dedicated to uplifting the race.

Walker's approach further distinguished her as a representative of black women's giving. During this era, white women recognized as philanthropists were privileged in race and class and were very direct in their emphasis on women's causes, almost to the exclusion of men's. They wrestled with class and gender through their philanthropy, but mostly they left race out of the equation despite some gifts to black causes. Such a contrast was evident with Olivia Russell Sage, who in 1916 reportedly said, "Nothing more for men's colleges," as her educational philanthropy struggled to navigate thousands of university solicitations.[68] Walker could not assume such a stance, because race and gender liberation were intimately connected. Funding one supported the other and vice versa.

⁂

Walker elevated, celebrated, and sought to advance women through her giving. In 1913 she told the audience at the NNBL conference, "I am not and never have been 'close-fisted,' for all who know me will tell you that I am a liberal hearted woman."[69] Ransom's letter presented important dimensions of this liberality during a period in her life when her company was firmly established and her wealth and reputation were on the rise. Her giving took form through multiple channels that included monetary gifts, nonmonetary support, employment, and institution building. It supported black organizations and people in desperate need and emerged from Walker's sense of obligation to be a respectable race woman who served her community. She directed her support for education and racial uplift via social services through women and woman-run charities to the communities with whom she had a special connection and also across the South. In all, the principle of funding the race to uplift women, and funding women to uplift the race, carried through each gift. Overall, Ransom's letter revealed Walker's gospel of giving to be practical, versatile, and responsive to black needs, qualities that continued to play out in the design of Walker's ultimate gift.

# 6

# Legacy

I hope the time will come when I will be able
to do many of these things before I pass
away, as I would get so much pleasure out
of it.
—Madam C. J. Walker, 1919

Mme. Walker lives in the organizations
whose progress she forwarded.
—Willard Ransom, Assistant Manager, the
Walker Company, 1952

At 12 noon on April 21, 1952, the pilgrims took off from West 110th Street
up New York's Seventh Avenue in Harlem in their full regalia. A fleet of
Cadillac limousines decorated in purple and black led them toward their
destination, Woodlawn Cemetery in the Bronx, where their hero lay at
rest. En route, church choirs were staged at strategic points leading them
in song, possibly the "Ode to Hairdressers" keyed to the tune of "Onward
Christian Soldiers," and urging them forward. The pilgrims had come from
as far south as Texas and as far west as Oregon to participate in the Madam
C. J. Walker Memorial Pilgrimage and Convention. They were periodically
greeted by illuminated signs featuring Walker's name and likeness. They
were mostly women. They were beauticians and cosmetologists. Some were
Walker agents and club members, and others were self-employed or affiliated with other companies. They were unified, determined, and proud.[1]

Organizers conceptualized the event nearly a year earlier, after hearing "dramatic facts in the life of Mme. Walker never yet revealed." Mae Thornton Muldrow, a black beautician and national chair of the event, said, "I have been deeply affected by the facts reported to me of the life of the late Mme. C. J. Walker. . . . I am convinced she was a very great woman. She led a blameless life and an unselfish life and gave two-thirds of her estate to Negro charity. I believe that nothing but good can come to the Pilgrims who engage in this pilgrimage." Muldrow's expectation was based on her previous visit to Walker's grave site in November with others from the movement, after which she reported being changed: "We have experienced an advancement along some line since that visit. In a way it was like going to a great church." Muldrow and her colleagues spent months traveling the country raising awareness about the pilgrimage and asking for support. Rallies and organizing meetings were held in Little Rock, Chicago, Indianapolis, St. Louis, Newark, New York, Philadelphia, and Atlanta. The National Beauty Culturist League (NBCL) was the primary sponsor, along with the Walker Company and the *Pittsburgh Courier* newspaper, which ran extensive coverage of the event and published a serial biography of Walker in the weeks leading up to it. Other partners and participants were the United Beauty Schools Owners and Teachers Association, the Pennsylvania State Association of Modern Beauticians and Cosmetologists, the National Council of Negro Women, the National Negro Business League, and numerous Walker agent clubs, reflecting the significant national and regional professional infrastructure that had evolved around beauty culture since Madam Walker's and Annie Malone's early days of pioneering the field.[2]

The event spanned four days and commenced with a Sunday night service at Mother AME Zion Church filled with tributes to Madam Walker and presentations of service awards in her memory. A hairstyle show and fete occurred on Tuesday and the annual Walker agent convention on Wednesday. Its goals were threefold: "1. To pay homage to a Great American Woman; 2. To educate the youth of the nation about her life and her greatness; and 3. To pay off the mortgage on the National Beauticians Home in Washington [DC]." In addition, the event served as the launching of a Hall of Fame for Beauticians with the induction of five new members to join the existing triumvirate of Madam Walker, Annie Malone, and Sarah Spencer Washington as founders of the black beauty-culture industry.[3] Monday's pilgrimage, however, was the centerpiece.

Riding at the front of the procession line in the limousines were the "Chosen 100," women who had qualified for the honor by raising at least $100 toward the mortgage-burning goal. Among their ranks, they wore special starred insignias that displayed the speed with which they raised funds, with five stars representing those first to reach their goals. Adding to the drama, the *Pittsburgh Courier* published a running tally of the Chosen 100 list and photos of many of the women. Behind them were the Platinum, Pearl, Diamond, Gold, Silver, Copper, Blue, Red, and White divisions, marchers who had raised at least $50 each for the campaign.[4] Walker agents also held special position in the line-up as the procession moved into the cemetery.

The pilgrimage was reminiscent of a similar gathering that had occurred thirteen years before at Woodlawn. On August 20, 1939, leaders of the Walker Company, including Freeman B. Ransom, Robert Brokenburr, Mae Walker Perry, and Marjorie Stewart Joyner led a large group composed of Walker employees and agents to the grave site to place a marble headstone for their founder as part of the twenty-second annual Walker Agents Convention.[5] The moment was memorialized in a newspaper photograph featuring Ransom standing behind the headstone as employees and agents draped in white surrounded the grave site. Ransom's son, Willard, had risen to company leadership upon his father's death in 1947, and he now led the procession graveside, where he delivered a memorial address. "Mme. Walker lives in the organizations whose progress she forwarded," he declared. Walter White, the executive secretary of the NAACP, made brief remarks as well. Cordelia Greene Johnson, president of the NBCL, joined Ransom in laying wreaths on Madam's grave, which also was the resting place for her daughter, A'Lelia, who had died in 1931. In solemn fashion, wreaths were passed from hand to hand down a line of pilgrims toward the headstone. The event concluded as each member of the Chosen 100 walked past the grave and dropped a flower on it.[6] Madam Walker had been dead for thirty-three years, but the vision for her legacy was unfolding just as she had planned.

Walker finalized her last will and testament on May 28, 1917, which was shortly after she returned from an extended retreat in Hot Springs, Arkansas, to gain rest and relief from her high blood pressure and chronic kidney problems.[7] In January 1919 Walker had begun creating a codicil to amend her last will and testament with assistance from Ransom. It was finalized on April 29, 1919.[8] During this time, she had taken ill while traveling through the Midwest and visiting St. Louis. Her friend Jessie Batts Robinson and others traveled with her back to New York by train to get her home. She was near death and had taken steps to ensure certain provisions were in place, some of which were making several deathbed pledges to her dearest causes such as the NAACP, Palmer Memorial Institute, and Daytona Normal and Industrial Institute. The seriousness of her medical condition was reflected in the shakiness of Walker's signature on the codicil document. Death did not wait long to come, but Walker had been preparing herself and her testamentary documents for some time.

Wills are social documents for understanding family relations, legal systems, inheritance practices, power relations, and social orders.[9] Wills have particular historical value for understanding the lived experiences and agency of women. Historically, women's wills have been fundamentally different in character from those of men. Such differences are a matter of both content and instrumentality. In terms of content, women's wills have been more likely than those of men to contain nonkin beneficiaries, gift distributions to individuals, itemized personal property, charitable provisions, and an equitable distribution of property to beneficiaries. In terms of instrumentality, women have historically used their wills to portray their respectability, honor, and social status to society, as well as to negotiate their public images. In these ways, women's wills reflected the societal constraints placed on them and served as a powerful form of storytelling through which they managed and asserted their social standing. Across time and cultures, women's wills display the full web of women's relations in all their complexities, including their social roles and identities as mothers, citizens, friends, and employers.[10]

Numerous scholars have studied the role of gender and class in shaping wills, but very little specific research exists on African American testators in any historical period or on their race and wills more generally. As another social status that has been used to establish power relations and assert control in society, race, like class and gender, has historically represented a social constraint with far-reaching implications. Federal and state laws in the United States varied in their recognition of African Americans' humanity, freedom, self-determination, and rights of property ownership over time as reflected in African Americans' centuries-long struggle to transition from being property to owning property. Madam Walker lived during a transitional episode in this history, and the present chapter's analysis of her testamentary documents shows how she navigated her social position with respect to race during a time when women's practices of producing wills were emerging. Women's wills were rare in nineteenth-century America, but they became increasingly common in the early twentieth century.[11] Further, the general use of wills to make charitable bequests also was rare.[12] And so Walker's last will was a historically significant document because of her use of it to assert her identity as an honorable, respectable, God-fearing, and generous black female business owner. It unified her philanthropic motivations, priorities, and hopes for her race, perpetuated her gospel of giving, and told succeeding generations how she wished to be remembered.

## Madam Walker's Last Will and Testament

Wills are not only legal documents, but also personal stories and lasting legacies. They are personal narratives and direct instructions. Their development requires individual confrontation with death, and, as a result, they emerge as personal narrative repositories of the values, relationships, and identities most consequential to testators. The language of wills overwhelmingly focuses on the disposition of property, but testators use them to articulate the value of such property—both material and symbolic—as well as the value of their relationships with the assigned beneficiaries of property. Furthermore, the use of the first-person *I* throughout the narrative further personalizes the story and emphasizes the testator's agency, control, and choice.[13] The personal narrative qualities of wills, even in their formal structure, creates the basis for their commemorative function. As instruments for making legacy, wills contain "direct *memento mori* moments."[14] A Latin phrase meaning "remember you must die," it reflects the burden of confronting one's mortality and the opportunity to consider one's legacy. By providing both onus and occasion, the will-writing process could inspire changes in the testator's remaining lifetime and enable construction of a "post-death identity." From the disposal of their own remains to the care of loved ones and provisions for charity, testators use wills to set the tone for and terms of their legacies. In this way, legal historian Karen Sneddon's description of the will as "a document of the past, written in the present, for the future" is apropos.[15]

This framework is useful for approaching Walker's testamentary documents because it provides a means for a penetrating analysis of the instructions she left behind. Such documents have been used frequently by scholars to illustrate Walker's generosity to charities through her bequests. My analysis, however, reveals that such uses reflect only a preliminary understanding, and that more of the critical elements of Walker's identity, values, and intended legacy can be discerned than previous analyses have done.

Walker's will matched the structural and organizational conventions that were common at the time. Wills generally included an exordium section that introduced the testator and demonstrated her ability to create an authentic document; a listing of provisions to dispose of personal property, cash, stock, other assets, and the residue of the estate; and a testimonium section through which the testator executed the document with date and signature, and witnesses verified that such date and signature were written in their presence by countersigning.[16] Walker's will began with the phrase "In the Name of God, amen," a common invocation that reinforced religious affiliations but mainly served as a signal to interested parties to abide by the terms of the document.[17] As a Christian, Walker would not have started her will in any other manner, especially since she publicly attributed the formula for her hair-growing product to a divine dream. The rest of the exordium was fairly standard: "I, Sarah Walker, better known as Madam C. J. Walker, of Indianapolis, Marion County, State of Indiana, being of sound mind and disposing mind and memory, do make, declare, and publish this my last will and Testament, hereby revoking all former wills by me made."[18] This phrase certified Walker's identity and legal residence.[19] The remainder of the three-page document contained twenty-nine items that represented the provisions of Walker's directions.

Practice allowed for great flexibility in sequencing provisions to best reflect the testator's interests and desires. In general practice, the order of provisions usually started with gifts of personal property, cash, other financial assets, and the residuary of the estate and listed them and their recipients in order of importance to the testator.[20] In the will's first item, after directing that all debts and funeral expenses be paid, Walker bequeathed the title and interest of her company to her daughter and then made a series of cash gifts to friends, family members, and employees before returning to the disposal of tangible personal property and charitable bequests. Walker's most prized relationship and asset formed the second item: Walker gave her daughter Lelia one-third of the Walker Company—no surprise, for she wanted the company to remain in family hands and for her daughter to have the primary benefit. The next four provisions provided financial gifts to two very close friends and two family members. Alice Kelly, Walker's friend, personal tutor and factory foreman, was given $10,000 and a lifetime job at the company provided she "honestly and faithfully" performed her duties.[21] Parthenia Rawlins, Walker's aide and cook, to whom she referred as "grandma," received $5 per week for the rest of her life as well as burial expenses, which reportedly ended up being $14,500 by the time of her death in 1952. Rawlins had been enslaved in Kentucky for the first fifteen years of her life and met Walker after moving to Indianapolis with her children.[22] To her sister, Louvenia, Walker left $50 per month for life plus burial expenses. Louvenia was Walker's only sister, and she had cared for young Sarah after the death of their parents. Walker loved her dearly and made sure she was comfortable. Her nephew, Willie, received $1,000. Having secured Willie's pardon a few years earlier, Walker was deeply concerned that he "have a decent start in life."[23] These first beneficiaries named in the will represented Walker's core concern about caring for her dearest relations and providing a significant source of support that would enable them to lead more secure lives within Jim Crow's hostile constraints. With three marriages behind her and difficult memories of her stressful relationship with one of her brothers-in-law, Walker's personal interactions with men were largely unpleasant, save those in her employ such as Ransom and Brokenburr. Her gift to her nephew Willie, in many ways, may have represented her aspirations for the men of her race—that they be able to rise above their circumstances and lead lives in service to their families and to the race.

In the will, Walker outlined provisions for her philanthropic dream of building of her Tuskegee in Africa.[24] She stipulated that if such a school were in existence at her death, all owned stock and securities were to be directed toward its support. If such school was not in existence, $10,000 was to be given to establish it. This provision was followed by an item to create a trust fund for the maintenance and upkeep of Villa Lewaro, Walker's mansion in New York, and for annual donations to charities. The trust fund was to be overseen by Ransom and four other "colored citizens of Indianapolis" as appointed by the local Marion County Probate Court.[25] Here we see Walker's greatest ambition and greatest achievement on display. The school in Africa signified Walker's unequivocal belief in education, her unrelenting support for industrial education, and her emerging Pan-Africanist consciousness.

Villa Lewaro represented a monument to not only her own success, but to the unlimited possibilities of the race. Walker had showcased the property as a point of pride for the race and opened it up to organizations fighting for liberation, such as the NACW, the International League of Darker Peoples (ILDP), and other racial-uplift organizations. Ultimately, Walker made provisions for the house to go to the NAACP to continue such use assuming her appointed trust fund committee approved of its racial uplift activities.[26]

Walker then turned attention to her tangible personal property, identified broadly as household goods, which she left to Lelia to keep or distribute among friends and family. Walker left $25 per month to Mary Hudson, an elderly friend from St. Louis, and $1,000 to Agnes Prosser, her ex-sister-in-law from Louisville, Kentucky.[27] During Walker's marriage to Agnes's brother, C. J., Agnes, known as Peggy to Walker, had observed C. J.'s business and marital infidelities and the two women became close. This item also identified three other women as friends whom Walker wanted remembered in some fashion, but she did not outline provisions to indicate how.[28]

Walker then made provisions for a child named Sarah Wilson to be given $500 and for four charities: the Colored Orphan Home of St. Louis, the Colored Alpha Home of Indianapolis, and the Mite Missionary Society of St. Paul AME Church in St. Louis were to be given $1,000 each; Tuskegee Institute in Alabama was slated to receive $2,000, undoubtedly in recognition of its founder, Booker T. Washington, whom Walker revered. The $1,000 bequest to the Mite Missionary Society was amended in a subsequent item to be invested as an endowment for continuous support of the society. Through this series of provisions, Walker elevated and affirmed the importance of supporting women's organizations.

Walker had only one child, but she made provisions in her will for other children that may have been natural or adopted.[29] In 1912 Lelia adopted a teenage girl named Fairy Mae Bryant (Mae). Walker loved Mae as if she were related by blood, and this provision suggested that she may once have considered following suit with an adoption of her own, but none occurred.[30] The next provision left more property, another residence in New York, to Lelia. Further, Walker indicated that all remaining property be given to Lelia and that she was to receive life use of the Villa Lewaro property, meaning she could live in it until her death, and then the will's provisions for disposal would take place.

Walker also made provisions for her domestic staff, those individuals who had managed personal aspects of her life such as her residences. She left $5,000 to Louis Tyler, her chauffeur, who diligently drove Walker across the country during her extended tours through various regions, including the Jim Crow South. Owning her automobile and having a driver enabled Walker to avoid the indignities and dangers of segregated trains. She also directed that any other "domestic help" receive the same amount provided they had worked for Walker for five years. This type of conditional bequest was a common tool used by testators to induce certain behaviors in their beneficiaries.[31] In this instance, Walker used it to incentivize good employees to stay in their roles to work for Lelia as heir to the estate. Similar conditional provisions were made for other employees, including Ransom and Brokenburr, who both stayed with the company for many years after Walker's death.

In her next set of provisions, Walker remembered other sets of dear relations. First, there were the children of her friends and advisers. Ransom's son was given a home in Chicago, the son of Walker's physician, Dr. Ward, was given $1,000, and Brokenburr's daughter was given $500. These gifts represented the significance of Walker's relationships with the fathers of these children. Walker continued with provisions for Thirsapen, her niece, to whom she left $1,000 and a home in California. Then she remembered Violet Davis, the company's bookkeeper, and Maggie Wilson, a friend and high-performing agent from Pittsburgh, with $2,000 and $1,000 bequests, respectively.

Among her final provisions, Walker declared that she was "anxious to help members of my Race to acquire modern homes."[32] Walker's love of real estate was well known, as evidenced by the properties she owned and disposed of through the will, as well as her directive that no such properties be liquidated to fulfill the obligations of the will. This provision noted that, if Walker had not taken significant action in the area of making housing more available to African Americans, the committee of trustees should determine a manner in which to do so. Ransom was a member of that committee and had great responsibility for fulfilling her testamentary wishes. Her trust in him was evident in her final provisional item, for him to continue working in her company and receive an annual $1,000 increase in his salary up to $10,000. Ransom served as general manager and legal counsel with the company until his death in 1947, and his children, Willard and A'Lelia, subsequently became Walker executives.

And so, as a document created in 1917, Walker's last will and testament reflected Walker's initial plans for establishing her legacy. Through it, she identified her most treasured relationships and values. The document presented Walker's maternal, familial, social, and business roles and relations. The charities listed in the will were among those present in Ransom's philanthropy letter to Ella Croker[33] and demonstrated that Walker's firm commitment to funding the race to uplift women, and funding women to uplift the race, increased over time. These same elements were reiterated and reinforced in the codicil.

## Madam C. J. Walker's Codicil

In January 1919 Walker had begun drafting a codicil to her last will and testament, a common practice to legally document and amend previous testamentary provisions. Walker directed Ransom to make changes, including several charitable gifts.[34] First, she wanted the "residue and undisposed part of my business, the profits which may accrue from year to year, to be put in a general trust fund for charities." She then required that $100,000 be set aside for the maintenance of her Villa Lewaro so that it and the maintenance fund could be given to the ILDP if it was "measuring up to the satisfaction of the committee," or else the committee would "select an organization doing the most good for the race." Her bequeathing of her house to an organization came with the provision that it never be used as housing for orphans, old folks, or a school, to preserve it as a monument to success and facilitate its further use as a place for convening leaders of the race to discuss problems and devise plans.[35]

In another provision, Walker directed that $50,000 be split evenly between the NAACP and the ILDP, "provided that they are working together toward the same end—for the uplift and benefit of the race." If either organization failed to cooperate, Walker ordered that the bequest be forfeited in an attempt to navigate the difference of opinion between her and Ransom over the ILDP. In a nod to the NAACP, he urged her to reconsider: "In wills people only remember established institutions of standing and of proven worth. Never to an organization in the mere making of the organization, you don't know now whether it will turn out a blessing or a disgrace. Just because you have hopes for the thing does not by any means make it a success. Hope you will get my meaning."[36] His recommendation apparently quelled Madam's fervor, for only the NAACP appeared in the final document. After this provision, Walker wanted any remaining investment income and business profits "to go for educational and uplift work in Africa."[37]

Her revisions focused on increasing the amount of specific bequests to charities run by women. She added a $10,000 bequest for Charlotte Hawkins Brown's Palmer Memorial Institute and made bequests to Mary McLeod Bethune's Daytona Normal and Industrial Institute, Jane Dean's Manassas Industrial School, the Alpha Old Folks Home in Indianapolis, the Old Folks Home in St. Louis, and Lucy Laney's Haines Institute at $5,000 each. She further wrote that the Mite Missionary Society's bequest of $1,000 should be doubled. When it came to Tuskegee Institute, however, Walker felt that Booker T. Washington's institution had sufficient resources: "In view of the fact that Tuskegee has been so bountifully provided for, we will let item #13 stand," which had bequeathed $2,000 to the institute. She knew that her resources would go further at the other institutions, where $5,000 to $10,000 could fund an entire year's budget or at least a significant portion thereof. At Tuskegee, the same amount was not as consequential in light of its nearly $300,000 annual operating budget and endowment of nearly $2 million.[38] Although she revered Washington, her gifts would do more and mean more at the women-run institutions. Some of these women-run schools, like Brown's, had recently suffered fires and experienced lower enrollments and donation levels during wartime. In classic fashion, Madam's provisions were a show of financial and moral support to encourage her sisters in their efforts on behalf of the race.

From these revisions, it was evident where Walker's deepest commitments rested. Walker concluded the letter to Ransom with the following: "I guess you think I am hashing out money, with a very lavish hand, but I am taking into consideration that the business is constantly on the increase and in the next five [years] I will be able to do all that I plan. I hope the time will come when I will be able to do many of these things before I pass away, as I would get so much pleasure out of it."[39] Such sentiment reflected Walker's gospel of giving according to her means and the joy she felt by helping others. Eight days later, Ransom replied to Walker, "I think I have covered everything suggested by you in your codicil." He made the revisions and advised her to sign the document, have two witnesses countersign, and return it to him for placement in a bank vault.[40]

The final codicil that was executed revised only particular sections of the last will while letting the rest of the original document's provisions stand. It contained only eight items. Instead of leaving her Chicago home to her godson, Frank Ransom, she gave him $10,000. Instead of one trust fund set up from the residue of the estate for the purposes of maintaining Villa Lewaro and giving to charity, Walker declared that separate trust funds be established with $100,000 each to serve both purposes. The NAACP won out over the ILDP as the beneficiary of Villa Lewaro, but it still had to prove itself worthy and in good standing according to the executive committee of the estate.

In addition to the aforementioned revised bequest amounts to several industrial schools and social-service agencies run by black women, Walker also adjusted her provisions for the important young people in her life. Her adopted granddaughter Mae was bequeathed $2,000, her godson Hubert Barnes Ross was given $10,000, and Nerrisa Lee Brokenburr, daughter of Walker employee and adviser Robert Brokenburr, was given $1,000.[41] These bequests represented investments in the future of the race, which were well placed. Mae would go on to graduate from Spelman College in Atlanta and assume leadership within the company, and Brokenburr later graduated from Oberlin College with distinction and ahead of schedule. Walker was friends with Ross's mother, Carolyn Barnes, who was from Indianapolis but served as a teacher at Tuskegee Institute. Barnes had died just days after Hubert's birth in April 1916 and Walker felt a keen sense of identification with and responsibility for him as a fellow orphan. The bequest ultimately helped to finance Ross's education at Yale University and Columbia University, where he studied with distinguished sociologists and anthropologists. As a black anthropologist and educator, Ross taught in the Atlanta University system for years and trained an entire generation of black social scientists.[42]

Walker also used the codicil to reinforce her desire to recognize her domestic staff, such as her chauffeur, through gifts of $5,000 each, but also included her friends Jessie Batts Robinson and Ida Winchester from St. Louis as well as Louis George from New York. These relationships were very special to Walker as important parts of her life story of transition from poverty to success. Finally, she ordered that Ransom's salary be increased annually until it reached $10,000 and that Robert Brokenburr's salary be increased to $5,000.[43]

Together, these elements provided a framework for remembrance. In her testamentary documents, we see Walker's concern for her race and gender; her maternal and sisterly connections to women and children; her business relationships; her investment in the next generation; and her commitment to education, racial uplift, and social services. Her aspirations for black men were also evident in her gifts to young male children and the male leaders of her company. Her plans were complete—almost.

## Walker's Estate

Madam Walker died on May 25, 1919. Her death was announced in newspapers around the country and overseas. Her funeral service was held on May 30 at Villa Lewaro. The event was a grand affair and was attended by everyday people from far and wide, as well as leaders from Tuskegee Institute, NAACP, the Urban League, the YMCA, and other organizations. The affidavit of death and proof of will was signed on June 12, 1919, as Lelia confirmed Walker's death.[44] The will was probated in open court in Indianapolis on June 12, 1919, and the appraisal of Walker's estate began on September 11, 1919.[45] One day later, several organizations and individuals who had a claim of interest in Walker's property were given notice of pending appraisal by the State of New York for Walker's properties in that state.[46]

On September 11, 1926, A'Lelia filed her final report as executrix, having changed her name a few years earlier.[47] A'Lelia confirmed receipt of a $10,000 payment for an executrix fee, as well as $11,600 worth of jewelry and additional furniture and goods valued at $53,137.78. The report listed total payments of $458,043.97 to individuals, companies, and charitable organizations to satisfy Walker's debts and legatees. The vast majority of these funds went to the individuals Walker named and the companies to whom she was indebted, but among the legatees were nineteen charities:

| | |
|---|---|
| Home for the Aged and Infirm Colored People (Pittsburgh) | $500 |
| Sojourner Truth House (NY) | $500 |
| Wilberforce University (OH) | $500 |
| People's Hospital (St. Louis) | $500 |
| Pine Street Branch, YMCA (St. Louis) | $1,500 |
| YWCA (St. Louis) | $1,500 |

| | |
|---|---|
| YWCA (Louisville, KY) | $500 |
| YMCA (New York, 135th Street) | $1,500 |
| YWCA (New York, 137th Street) | $1,500 |
| NAACP | $4,000 |
| Manassas Industrial Institute (VA) | $4,755* |
| Colored Orphans' Home (St. Louis) | $955* |
| Tuskegee Institute (Alabama) | $1,905* |
| Daytona Normal and Industrial Institute (FL) | $4,755* |
| Alpha Home (Indianapolis) | $5,000 |
| Mite Missionary Society (St. Louis) | $1,910* |
| Colored Old Folks' Home (St. Louis) | $4,755* |
| Haines Institute (GA) | $4,755* |
| Palmer Memorial Institute | $955*[48] |

Of these nineteen legatees, only nine were specifically named by Walker in her testamentary documents: Alpha Home, Tuskegee Institute, NAACP, Daytona Normal and Industrial Institute, Manassas Industrial Institute, Old Folks' Home in St. Louis, Haines Institute, Palmer Memorial Institute, and the Mite Missionary Society. The rest—the old folks' home in Pittsburgh, Sojourner Truth House, Wilberforce University, People's Hospital in St. Louis, the YMCAs, and the YWCAs—reflected Walker's philanthropic concern for education and racial uplift via social services, and may have been chosen by A'Lelia as executor of the estate.

In total, $42,245 went to these organizations, representing approximately 10 percent of the appraised value of the estate, a far cry from Walker's desired goal of leaving one-third for charitable provisions. This fact has not been included in scholarship that refers to Walker's philanthropy on the basis of her will. The continual omission of the fact prevents a full accounting of Walker's generosity by separating her charitable intent from the execution of it. The discrepancy between Walker's intended charitable provisions and legatees and those actually executed and supported by A'Lelia as executor is explained at least in part by the significant debts Walker incurred, which reduced the total amount of funds available for charities. Also, A'Lelia had taken legal action to have the courts void certain provisions of the will, including the charitable provision for $10,000 to fund the creation of the industrial school in Africa because no specific school was named and A'Lelia did not feel able to create one.[49]

Further, the company struggled under A'Lelia's leadership despite the best efforts of Ransom and others, because postwar economic conditions had changed, competition from other black beauty-culture companies had increased, and her own attentions were more directed toward social matters and the Harlem Renaissance than toward business.[50] She was an extravagant spender, like her mother, and paid nearly $50,000 for her daughter's wedding in 1923. She also enjoyed international travel to Europe. Her Harlem residence, known as the Dark Tower, became the central location for parties that attracted Harlem's elite. Distant family members perturbed at being omitted in Walker's will also made claims against the estate. Because Madam Walker's wealth was largely tied up in the company, her charitable provisions may have been doomed from the start. That said, despite the details of A'Lelia's leadership and the estate's final settlement, significant gifts were made, and these testamentary documents captured the primary philanthropic motivations and intentions for how Walker wanted posterity to remember her.

## Madam C. J. Walker's Legacy

The public outpouring of grief over Madam Walker's death verified recognition of her generosity. The response was immense and palpable. Letters and telegrams flooded the Walker residence and business office as people from around the country expressed their deep sense of loss. The condolence communications contained important themes. Regardless of whether these individuals were close personal friends or admirers from a distance, they shared a common sense of the meaning of Walker's life—they saw her as a race woman who was very generous.

Walker was viewed as an exemplar of the race woman. Letter after letter referred to her significance as a "lover and worker for her race" or "heroine" and "foremost woman of our race."[51] They praised her for the "useful and noble life" she led.[52] The phrase "useful life" appeared repeatedly. Mrs. J. C. Frazier wrote that "Her useful life was a benediction."[53] The Byron brothers agonized that "Death . . . had deprived us of the most useful woman of our race."[54] Part of Walker's usefulness undoubtedly extended from her work ethic, which drove her success. W. P. Curtis, Walker's doctor from St. Louis, acknowledged that Walker had "crowded into the few years a century of achievements."[55] Consequently, many people saw Walker as an example to follow: "Madam Walker was a living example of what one can accomplish."[56] George Harris stated that Walker modeled "the progress of the race and its ability to take advantage of its all too few opportunities."[57]

Florence Garnette, principal of the Florence Garnette Training School for Little Girls in New York, noted that she used Walker as an example for her students at her training school.[58]

The mourners certainly remembered Walker's generosity. R. W. Thompson called her "a genuine philanthropist and a practical benefactor."[59] J. C. Napier remembered her as "Our most progressive and philanthropic woman."[60] It was clear by such sentiments that Walker's desired legacy was already in existence prior to her death. African Americans had looked to Walker as an exemplary race woman who dedicated her life to serving others and providing inspiration and opportunities for a people desperately in need of both because of their social circumstances.

The letters of bereavement eventually ceased coming to the Walker residence, but Walker's legacy continued to pervade the cultural imagination of African Americans for decades after her death. Freeman B. Ransom and Robert Brokenburr certainly did their part to keep her name in the mouths of the people. The Walker Company revered its founder and held her up as an example to employees and customers alike. Walker's likeness and name continued to grace product labels, publications, and advertisements for decades. The rituals of the Walker clubs reinforced her life story as a model for agents to emulate, and the training manuals of the Walker beauty schools opened by recounting Walker's story, celebrating her philanthropy, and challenging new beauty culturists to be loyal to the woman, the brand, and the company. But Walker's legacy did not belong to the company. It became bigger—it belonged to the race.

In the 1920s and 1930s, Revella Hughes, a leading African American soprano and pianist who performed with artists like Paul Robeson, Eubie Blake, and Marian Anderson, sang a popular song named for Madam Walker. In the 1930s and 1940s, African American author Zora Neale Hurston wrote a novel based on Walker's life entitled *The Golden Bench of God.*[61] In the 1930s, Duke Ellington first developed the idea for an opera based on Madam Walker's life. In the 1950s, beauticians converged on her grave site to commemorate their beloved industry legend. In the 1960s, Ellington began working on his opera as a production for public television, but by the time of his death in 1974, *Queenie Pie* was unfinished. Subsequent musicians attempted to finish the opera with various degrees of success, but in 2014 a rendition of it was produced at the Chicago Opera Theater.

*Roots* author Alex Haley was fascinated with Walker's life and began research for a biography in the 1980s. He died without having finished his research or written his book. Tananarive Due, however, an African American fiction writer, resumed Haley's research and published in 2000 a historical novel about Walker based on Haley's research called *The Black Rose*. One year later, Walker's great-great-granddaughter and journalist A'Lelia Bundles, who had begun researching her family's legacy as an undergraduate at Radcliffe in the 1970s and who had initially worked with Haley on his project, published *On Her Own Ground: The Life and Times of Madam C. J. Walker*. Dozens of plays have been produced during the past forty years about Walker's life through local and regional theater companies around the country, including *Madam—A Musical on the Life of Madam C. J. Walker*, which played in New York and Atlanta, Georgia, in the early 2000s. In 2016 Oscar-winning actress Octavia Spencer purchased the movie rights to Bundles's book and later partnered with basketball star LeBron James to produce a Netflix series in 2020 about Walker costarring Blair Underwood and Tiffany Haddish.

Madam Walker's family sold the Walker Company in 1985, and it continued to operate modestly for nearly thirty years. In 2013 the black-owned Sundial Brands purchased the company and relaunched a line of Madam Walker products as part of its beauty-care category for women of color, including SheaMoisture. Sundial was cofounded by Richelieu Dennis, a Liberian entrepreneur, whose grandmothers had been entrepreneurs in Africa and inspired the recipes he, his mother, and college roommate used to launch their business in New York in the 1990s. In 2017 Dennis sold Sundial to the global corporation Unilever, which included control of Sundial and the creation of a multimillion-dollar fund to support women entrepreneurs of color as part of the deal. The Madam Walker product line continues to be sold through Sephora, and Dennis is now a billionaire.[62]

In 2018 Madam Walker's mansion, Villa Lewaro, was reclaimed and rededicated for the uplift of black women by Dennis. During the Great Depression, the property had been sold and its contents auctioned off as maintenance costs soared. The Companions of the Forest bought the home in 1932 and, over the next fifty years, used it expressly for a purpose Walker forbade in her will—an old folks' home. After being in private hands for a few years, the home was purchased in 1993 by US Ambassador Harold and

Ms. Helena Doley, a wealthy black couple who were the first to own a seat on the New York Stock Exchange. The Doleys restored much of the house to its original condition and sold it in 2018 to the billionaire Dennis. After establishing the $100 million New Voices Fund to support businesses by women of color and buying *Essence Magazine*, Dennis dedicated Villa Lewaro as a think tank for advancing black women's entrepreneurship. The mansion has been returned to its roots and restored as a monument of black success and possibility.

In 2019 the Madam Walker Theater building in Indianapolis, which had been built in 1927 by A'Lelia and Ransom and served as the company headquarters until 1979, underwent a major renovation. The project updated the space, modernized technology, and reintroduced the facility to the local community as the Madam Walker Legacy Center. The center will extend Walker's story further into the twenty-first century by offering educational, cultural, artistic, and business-development programming for the Indianapolis community and beyond. That same year, 136th Street near Lennox Avenue in Harlem, New York, was officially renamed Madam C. J. Walker and A'Lelia Walker Place to commemorate the centennial of Madam's death close to where her famous home in the city once stood.

Across all these representations, Walker's generosity has been acknowledged and celebrated as being central to her life and a cornerstone of her legacy. Whether she was a penniless migrant widow who raised money for an indigent neighbor in St. Louis or an internationally known millionaire entrepreneur, Walker gave as she was able to the people, places, and institutions dearest to her, which represented her deepest aspirations for the eventual uplift of black women and the race as a whole.

Walker left a blueprint for her legacy that perpetuated her gospel of giving. Her testamentary documents revealed that her *memento mori* moments enhanced her generosity and led to greater provisions of gifts to individuals and institutions in service to the race. Many of her gifts to individuals included provisions for proper burial, which was historically a use for black philanthropy, as well as cash payments to help her loved ones, business associates, and friends navigate a hostile Jim Crow society that limited opportunities to earn a living and greatly restricted freedoms. Consequently, this analysis of oft-cited primary sources that have previously been used only to provide lists of Walker's giving has yielded far more—a full-circle understanding of Walker's philanthropic legacy on her own terms.

At the 1952 grave-site pilgrimage, Walker's friend, Mary McLeod Bethune, commented that the event served "as a symbol of the great work of all the great Negro women of the past on whose shoulders today's younger women stood."[63] The fitting tribute captured Walker's greatest hopes and ambitions for a legacy. Her company was still operational, employing thousands of women and being run by her great-granddaughter. Her schools were still credentialing women around the country and launching their careers. Her agents were still associating through clubs and doing good works in the community. Beauty culture had become an officially recognized and respected profession. And many of the organizations she had so generously and consistently funded through their nascent years, like the NAACP, were in the midst of mobilizing the national civil-rights movement that would ultimately dismantle de jure Jim Crow and create revolutionary political, social, and economic changes for which young Sarah Breedlove, who knew firsthand the broken promises of Reconstruction, could only have yearned.

# Conclusion

Thus while reaping grandly for herself she
scatters forth, with lavish hand, a part of her
goods.
—*Denver Star*, August 7, 1915[1]

It is urgent that donors, fundraisers, historians, and all who care about philanthropy return to Madam C. J. Walker today—like those beauty pilgrims who gathered at her grave thirty-three years after her death to reconnect with her legacy. When we do, we will emerge with a richer knowledge of who she was and with an enduring, relevant, and accessible model of black generosity at a time when the imagery, public perception, and scholarly discourse on philanthropy are dominated by white elites. Different historical processes gave birth to philanthropy in communities of color, a fact that must be recognized. The instance of venerated white donors of US philanthropy, like Andrew Carnegie and John D. Rockefeller, explains *some* of what is happening on the philanthropic landscape today with elite donors like investment tycoon Warren Buffet and technology moguls Bill and Melinda Gates. They explain the other billionaire, and mostly white, members of the Giving Pledge.[2] But they do not explain Oprah Winfrey or Robert F. Smith, the black billionaire who surprised the 2019 graduating class of Morehouse College in Atlanta, Georgia, by paying off all their and their parents' student loan debt, to the tune of approximately $40 million.[3] They do not account for Osceola McCarty, the black washerwoman who

donated $150,000 to the University of Southern Mississippi in the 1990s.
They do not explain the millions of African American churchwomen and
clubwomen, including my mother, who daily do "the Lord's work" without
great fanfare, or black millennials who leverage their giving and activism
online. But Madam C. J. Walker does explain these black philanthropic
agents of the early twenty-first century and more. Such contemporary expressions of African American philanthropy are Madam Walker's legacy,
and she is their heritage.

Scholars have long called Walker a philanthropist and noted some of her
charity. But their interest never ventured beyond short lists of charitable
gifts and, as a result, her generosity was more of an interesting side note
than an essential character trait. By using philanthropy as a lens through
which to view this prominent American historical figure, this philanthropic
biography has developed and contextualized the motivations for and influences on her giving. Articulating these origins has yielded clear patterns
across her giving that are explained by her early experiences as a poor,
black, female migrant with a young child in St. Louis during the late 1800s,
when she was aided by local black women philanthropists at St. Paul AME
Church.

These churchwomen and clubwomen modeled the traditions and practices of giving, serving, and leading that undergirded the proliferation of
black social institutions that followed Emancipation but was rooted in the
eighteenth century development of black churches, mutual-aid societies,
and other voluntary associations. Whether locally through the Mite Missionary Society or nationally through the NACW, these women shaped their
families and communities in ways that defied the dominant white society's
narratives about black inferiority and helplessness. They socialized Sarah
Breedlove into the manner and being of black women's giving as a way of
life. It was for these reasons that the *Indianapolis Freeman* described these
St. Louis women and organizations as "shareholders in [Walker's] bounty."[4]
Under their tutelage, Sarah, who was an orphan, a widow, and poor—three
of the most vulnerable populations identified in the Bible as deserving of
charity—transitioned from being a recipient to a donor in realization of
her own philanthropic capacity to help others regardless of the extent of
her own resources.[5]

This process was integral because it set the tone for Walker's philanthropic life, a gospel of giving according to which she would give along the

way. That is, she gave gradually and incrementally to help others as she could with what she had, rather than focus only on wealth creation and later, near life's end after she had secured her own means, arrive at a sense of responsibility toward others. The *Denver Star* beautifully captured her characteristic unselfishness in 1915: "Thus while reaping grandly for herself she scatters forth, with lavish hand, a part of her goods."[6] These life experiences explained the making of Madam C. J. Walker the philanthropist. Sarah Breedlove was generous by serving in her church and helping her neighbors. Madam Walker's philanthropy was an extension and escalation of Sarah's giving. Sarah did not have the wherewithal to act in broader, organized ways beyond her local neighborhood; but as Madam Walker she did, and she owed this ability to the dreams, persistence, and liberality of Sarah.

## Thwarting Jim Crow

In many ways, the history of African American philanthropy has been the search for hospitality in a land of hostility. Despite Jim Crow's incessant assaults and traumas inflicted on their humanity and personhood, black men and women of Walker's era used philanthropy in their racialized and gendered project of defining and remaking their senses of self and their communities. Black people used whatever means were available to them to make life more tolerable and navigable during their long-suffering and uncertain trek toward freedom and equality. This response was required because of the surging malevolence of late-nineteenth and early-twentieth-century white-controlled governments, markets, and voluntary associations that created and maintained the social, political, and economic conditions of black life. By denying black people legal protections, economic opportunities, and access to services—among other things—public and private societal actors perpetuated suffering, death, and inequality. With their earlier hopes for Reconstruction demolished, black people had to do for themselves in order to survive, and Madam Walker followed suit.

According to America's plan for black people during Jim Crow, Madam C. J. Walker was not supposed to happen. Her literacy, her giving, her company, her $250,000 mansion, her outspokenness on lynching and equality—none of it! Sarah Breedlove's early life of pain, fear, struggle, and constraint was America's best design for black life. The fact that obtaining these achievements for herself was not sufficient and that she used philanthropy to open up similar opportunities for other African Americans was even more unsettling to the grand design. Jim Crow's commitment was in denying or tightly controlling opportunity, education, activism, and material resources. Black businesses were deliberately targeted for failure by private markets and the edicts of government. Black education was initially illegal, then legal but shoddily provided, significantly underresourced, severely controlled, and deeply contested. Black activism was met with racial terror and other forms of surveillance and suppression. And a signifying feature of black life under Jim Crow was a perpetual state of inadequacy—inadequate housing, schooling, employment, public safety and protections, and other bare necessities of life.

For Walker to use her life and company—a third C alongside the church and the club—to provide such needs and opportunities to her people demonstrates the ultimate effect of her giving. Her legacy was in helping individuals get through the racialized and gendered constraints of daily living and in supporting the institutional infrastructures emerging, during this "era of organization" in black philanthropic history, that were working to dismantle Jim Crow.[7] Organizations that Walker supported, like the NACW, the AME Church, and the NAACP, were operating nationally, building networks, and testing strategies for various ways to topple the system. Her giving, in tandem with the giving of others, helped to keep these organizations going despite fits and starts and other struggles. She did not know when or how Jim Crow would end, but she held onto the goal and did what she could to hasten the day.

She was a highly prized and sought-after black donor by black-serving organizations. Her monetary gifts rivaled some of the white funders of the day, particularly those focused on education, but they did not come with the same kind of strings and social control agendas. Accordingly, my analysis upends the trope of industrial philanthropy and black education that has for far too long obscured black generosity in history. What is more, this articulation of Walker the educator disrupts our thinking about what industrial education achieved for black women under Jim Crow in Walker's hands.

Walker did not live to see the official demise of Jim Crow and the legal expansion of equality, but, through her giving, she had a hand in the process. The temporal bridging influence of Walker's philanthropy was verified in 1952, when Walter White, the storied executive secretary of the NAACP, celebrated her impact at the New York graveside ceremony in her memory: "Mme. Walker's generosity virtually saved the NAACP in the dark days of the depression."[8] His reflection is critical because historians have debated the origins and chronology of the midtwentieth century's civil-rights movement. Scholars have noted the importance of philanthropic infusions of cash directly into the movement by major foundations in the 1960s to support initiatives like voter registration.[9] This book provides insights into the kind of community-based philanthropy that was a critical part of the process of organizing resistance to the legal structures of US racism over decades. Walker represents a generation of black donors who endeavored to build organizations in their ultimate quest for freedom, even though they would not see its consummation. Their backing nurtured such organizations and passed them on to subsequent generations to continue the struggle.

Along the way, there was help. Sympathetic and paternalistic white allies provided much-needed support to black organizations and communities, from money and material items to school buildings and teachers. Such funding streams became very important, and, at times, overcame some of the limitations of direct support from the black community. But somehow these efforts took precedence in public perception and historical interpretation over those of African Americans themselves, who came to be viewed as mere passive recipients of the largesse and beneficence of whites.[10] But black philanthropic agency was present before, during, and after these interventions. Nevertheless, the negative perception remains and infuses the need for more work with even greater urgency, particularly as related to black women.

## Theorizing Black Women's Generosity

Contrary to conventional thinking, American philanthropy is not rooted in Andrew Carnegie and his elite peers. It is rooted in the traditions of giving and sharing that were the stuff of daily family and community life from the country's foundations. As I have observed elsewhere, "there is not a single era in U.S. history in which African Americans were not engaged in their own philanthropic actions as a matter of daily survival, religious and cultural practice, or social change at scale."[11] For that reason, we have much to learn from Madam C. J. Walker and her peers, the generations before, and the generations after. In 1909 W. E. B. DuBois wrote, "Few races are more instinctively philanthropic than the Negro."[12] African Americans not only turned to philanthropy out of necessity for survival, they lived it as an expression of their identity and generosity in spite of all that was being done to them and that had been taken away from them. And black women led the way.

If black women lead intersectional lives, it follows that their philanthropy will be intersectional as well—meaning not limited to one type of gift, institution, societal sector, or approach. Rather, it is diverse, multifaceted, overlapping, interactive, and reflective of their embodied identities. It cannot be discerned by consulting the rules on tax donation deductibility or formal accounting procedures. It is an amalgamation, understood only through their lived experiences. I offer Madam Walker's gospel of giving to continue historicizing and giving voice to black women's generosity, work begun decades ago by black women's historians. My hopes are to encourage the fields of black women's history, Africana studies, and philanthropic studies to fully embrace the call to action for pursuing the instinctiveness DuBois observed by advancing the study of black women, and black people by extension, as philanthropists. To that end, Madam Walker's gospel of giving provides foundational elements for theorizing black women's philanthropy. Specifically, there are five characteristics that bring together various threads and offer directions for future research.

## Proximity

Part of the power of Walker's gospel of giving can be attributed to its grounding in black women's identification with and close proximity to suffering. Virtually all Walker's gifts harkened back to some type of gift she once needed or received. When she employed the unemployable, she was remembering the struggles of being both locked out of jobs and locked into menial, unprofitable work because of racism and sexism. When she organized her agents into clubs, she had already participated in similar networks through the Court of Calanthe, the AME Church, and the NACW. When she gave holiday turkeys to poor families, she had experienced hunger and the accompanying anxieties of not being able to feed her child. When she funded scholarships at schools such as Palmer Memorial Institute, it reflected the pain of her own ignorance she had lived with as a formerly illiterate and unschooled young mother. And, no matter how much money she accumulated nor how many properties she purchased, she was still black, still female, and, therefore, still subject to the racialized norms and gender dynamics of Jim Crow society. Social-welfare historians Iris Carlton-LaNey and Sandra Carlton Alexander remind us that black clubwomen in the early twentieth century had "physical, social and psychological proximity to the individuals for whom they advocated."[13] This "nearness" enabled them "to maintain first-hand information about community problems and issues" and yielded authentic perspectives on local needs.[14] In this manner, Madam Walker had the same philanthropic need for freedom as the most uneducated and unkempt among the newly arrived black migrants in any northern city at that time.

To be sure, wealth gave her some insulation from racialized and gendered insult. For instance, her ownership of automobiles spared her the indignities of segregated train travel during her extensive promotional tours throughout the South. At any time, however, Walker could have been lynched, raped, harangued, belittled, humiliated, discriminated against, or otherwise terrorized just like any other black woman in America.[15] Although many of the leading white male donors of her day had known poverty and ignorance in their earlier lives, they were rescued from that former station by their wealth, and the privileges of race accrued to them in those efforts. For them, such conditions remained only as memories that could be conjured or ignored at will. Her white female philanthropic peers still wrestled with sexism as they were constrained by their husbands and social norms of acceptable public life for women. But they also affirmed white supremacy in their own failure to acknowledge the womanhood of black women in their brand of feminism. Walker could never fully escape the conditions imposed on her life by virtue of her skin color and gender without radical social change.

Proximity also explains the openness of Walker's giving without regard to the question of worthiness. Victorian standards of who among the poor was worthy of receiving aid trickled into America from Europe during the nineteenth century. When compounded with the dynamics of American racism, these institutional notions of worthiness automatically excluded African Americans from many social services. Black social-service organizations were founded with either no definitions of worthiness or far less strict ones to counter this larger practice. As a former migrant, Walker was very liberal in her generosity and did not apply strict standards to guide the administration of her gifts. Walker's giving reflected a diverse range of recipients and gifts determined by notions of worthiness applied to family, friends, and strangers. This is an important dimension to acknowledge because worthiness is a theme in philanthropy across cultures and has particular implications for the American context because of the pervasiveness of need and the larger societal structures of inequality. Taken together, this characteristic broadens historical—and challenges contemporary—definitions of what constitutes a gift.

## Resource-fullness

Madam Walker's giving represents resourcefulness in the traditional sense of "making a way out of no way,"[16] that is, being flexible and creative in meeting needs. But it also reflects a *fuller* notion of the resources that can be given as gifts. Scholars have emphasized that black philanthropy is about more than money and typically includes time as an essential gift. This historical examination pushes that observation further in articulating a broader array of resources beyond time that were given. In the context of the early twentieth century, which predated modern governmental concerns over the tax deductibility of gifts, there was a greater focus on the utility of gifts and how they can help the needy overcome the temporary or long-term obstacles they faced. The circumstances of racial and gender discrimination faced by black people automatically expanded concepts of what counted as a gift because deprivation was a hallmark of systemic oppression. This is why Walker's provisions of employment, education, and activism constituted important gifts in this distinctive practice of generosity.

## Collaboration

Madam Walker's philanthropy was shaped by her role as a translational figure who mediated class differences among black women to engage with both working-class and middle-class African Americans for the benefit of the race. Her philanthropy emerged from four female networks and webs of affiliation that were grounded in collective consciousness and collaborative giving—washerwomen, churchwomen, clubwomen, and fraternal women—amid class distinctions. Sarah Breedlove became a part of these women's networks, and they were consequential in her transition into life as Madam Walker. These networks were defined by their penchant for working together to meet personal and community needs by pooling and sharing resources, supporting each other, and helping others. Through these groups, Sarah was taught the rudiments of black women's ways of giving. She was also given opportunities to practice them while she was yet a struggling migrant with her own troubles to surmount. They brought her into the fold of black women's giving. She observed them accomplishing much in the community, and she was able to contribute as well. Walker would remain collaborative in her giving later in life as she worked through such networks to open up educational and social services for African Americans and in advocating for equality. Whether with her own working-class agents or the NACW's elite leaders, Walker was at home with these women and worked together with them to make a difference.[17]

## Incrementalism

When confronted with an opportunity to give, Madam Walker, as one newspaper interviewer noted, became "the unfolding woman, growing at the approach; not receding, getting smaller in all ways, as so many do."[18] This imagery perfectly captures the gradual nature of her gospel of giving. First, it assumes ability. The ability to give is a simple outgrowth of the fact of existence. She gave because she could. What is more, the specific pervasiveness of need arising from the historical experience of African Americans—particularly black women—extends ability further into the realm of obligation and expectation. She gave because she *must* give under the circumstances of Jim Crow realities. As a result, willingness and obligation became the drivers of giving over ability. Walker's religious and cultural training through the AME Church and her black women mentors inculcated this perspective into her to the point that she felt giving to be a natural inclination, which continued to evolve over time.

This incremental quality of her gospel of giving was not age- or status-dependent, because there was always someone in a worse situation than the ones she faced. She gave while being a struggling, penniless migrant, and so anyone can give regardless of their station. Further, rather than being resource-dependent, this mode of giving was context-dependent. When it came to giving to others, what Breedlove—and then Walker—had at any given time was more important than what she did not have.[19] This approach represents a fundamental shift in traditional thinking about philanthropy and creates a different starting point for defining it and those who practice it. Further, it grounds giving in a kind of creativity, proximity, and *resourcefullness* that opens up possibilities on what to give, to whom to give, and when to give.

## *Joy*

Walker used *joy* to describe her giving. Her word choice is noteworthy within the larger mainstream trend at the time of moving away from emotional approaches to giving and toward more scientifically rational ones. The debate over the effectiveness of charity—impulsive gifts to relieve immediate and observable suffering in the moment—and philanthropy—deliberative gifts made to eliminate the root causes of suffering over the long term—had been raging for decades, and philanthropy was winning out at the moment as the rise of the broader scientific philanthropy movement attested.[20] Such distinctions were not overly critical to Walker; she worked on both fronts. But, in this environment, for Walker to articulate joy as a benefit and motivation for giving is remarkable in that it went against the grain of the times. Hers was a Christian joy, reflective of 2 Corinthians 9:7, "for God loveth a cheerful giver." Walker internalized this idea as part of her duty as a woman of faith and as part of her own natural constitution, which she saw as being inclined toward giving—a trait divinely assigned. There is now a growing body of social-science research confirming the physical and psychological benefits of giving, but more than one hundred years ago, Madam Walker articulated an inherent joy of giving not typically seen in the philanthropic treatises of her white contemporaries. Further research on black women's giving can produce greater illumination of these practices.

## Who Counts and What Counts in Philanthropy?

I have previously observed that "One *cannot* study the history of African Americans without encountering their philanthropy; it is unfortunate that one *can* study the history of philanthropy without meaningfully encountering African Americans."[21] The only way to change this is by doing more work. This philanthropic biography has presented a method for pursuing this agenda to fulfill our need for greater understanding and engagement of the stories of black philanthropists. To be certain, there are numerous biographies of black historical figures, especially many affiliated with the black church, social movements, and black women's clubs. The points of entry into these lives were not philanthropy, however, but rather other pressing historical questions to which fields like Africana studies and black women's history are committed. The philanthropic biography demonstrates the possibilities for answering similar questions about black lives and the black experience historically when philanthropy is invoked as the guiding frame-work. What is more, researching individual black philanthropists provides critical insights that challenge current perceptions and understandings of voluntary action and enriches ongoing historical debates. More specific investigations of black philanthropists—broadly defined—are needed to connect their stories to the fields of Africana studies and philanthropic stud-ies so that the former can advance its project of identifying and examining this neglected experience, and the latter can more accurately comprehend and portray philanthropy as a human—rather than white—phenomenon.

Such an approach will also shed light on how blacks have historically used money as a resource in their philanthropic quest for freedom and in their post-civil-rights-era quest for integration and opportunity. Much of the work that has been done on African American philanthropy has developed under the research rubric of black giving not finding significant expression through money, but rather through other means. The value of this approach has been widely demonstrated, and even this study has emphasized the resource-fullness of Walker's giving beyond money. As archeologist Paul Mullins et al. have observed, wealth was not "white-exclusive."[22] It is tempt-ing to think of Walker as an anomalous figure within her community, but she was not. Walker's giving was black women's giving writ large. We cannot allow her millionaire status to separate her in our minds from her peers or community in this regard. She took the philanthropic practices of her black clubwomen and churchwomen mentors and supporters and amplified them. As Tiffany Gill has observed, "Philanthropy was at the center of the way beauty culturists voiced their strength and dignity to the black com-munity."[23] Viewing Walker as a prototypical black female philanthropist of her time guides us to other philanthropic mesdames of black beauty culture, Annie Malone (1869–1957) and Sarah Spencer Washington (1889–1953).

As a black woman who formally studied chemistry and was also or-phaned as a child, Annie "Madam Poro" Malone created the Poro Company in Lovejoy, Illinois, in 1900 to sell her beauty-culture products and moved the company to St. Louis in 1902. She eventually employed tens of thou-sands of black women as agents, ran a string of beauty schools under the Poro College brand, built a multipurpose factory building that provided educational and community programming, organized her agents into local and national clubs, and donated tens of thousands of dollars in service to racial uplift. Malone financially supported the orphan's home that housed and cared for young Lelia in the 1890s and continued to support it for many decades.[24]

Sarah Spencer Washington, also known as Madam Washington, launched the Apex News and Hair Company in Atlantic City, New Jersey, in 1920 after she had opened a hairdressing business seven years prior. She eventually employed tens of thousands of black women as well and opened beauty schools across the country under the Apex name. Her enterprise included a publishing company, a drug company, and a laboratory for the clinical development of products. Her philanthropy reportedly found expression through the creation of a nursing home for the black aged, a golf course open to all people (after she experienced being denied the opportunity to play because of her skin color), and the provision of coal for poor families to heat their residences.[25] And these examples are just from black beauty culture. The history of black business is replete with examples of black entrepreneurs, such as Thomy LaFon (1810–93) and Maggie Lena Walker (1864–1934), who were generous in ways similar to those explored in this philanthropic biography. Indeed, the history of black business is an underutilized gateway for examining black philanthropists across time, and so are black women. Heretofore, juxtaposing women, such as Walker and Malone, has focused on competition between them or arguments over who was actually the first self-made female millionaire. There is so much more to them and the history they give us access to if we can ask deeper and more substantial historical questions.

By understanding black women as philanthropists, we increase our understanding of women as philanthropists. At present, the experiences and ideologies of elite white women dominate the field of women's philanthropy.[26] Walker's white female philanthropic contemporaries were greatly restricted in their giving by the men in their lives. Many followed the pattern of first inheriting wealth from their husbands or fathers and then stepping into their philanthropic agency after the patriarch's death. Others took action before but required male approval prior to making gifts.[27] For some, their philanthropy was confined by marriage and defined by notions of the responsibility of women of leisure. Having emerged differently from black women's public culture,[28] Walker embraced her philanthropic agency and responsibility from an early age, and her marriages to three husbands were of little consequence for her generosity. She did not seek nor need anyone's approval for giving. Further, she worked every day of her life, and so leisure was not a factor either. She created and pursued her own philanthropic agenda on her own terms.

Theorizing based on white women's philanthropy may be useful for understanding some white women's use of spaces and organizations for their public work outside the home but are of little consequence for Walker's company, schools, or agents clubs.[29] Walker's spaces privileged women but were in direct engagement with men. These spaces enabled her to interact with male political, civic, and economic leaders—such as Booker T. Washington, W. E. B. DuBois, Marcus Garvey, and male competitors in beauty culture—as equals. These differences highlight the need for an expanded view of women's philanthropy because the narratives and experiences of wealthy white women are dominating our conceptions and overshadowing the agency of other women.[30] Continuing failure to grapple with these distinctions will prevent the field of women's philanthropy from being true to its appellation.

Finally, philanthropy has frequently appeared as a villain in Africana studies, particularly in the field of black education. DuBois wrote disparagingly about the manipulation he felt from the philanthropic foundations that funded his scholarly work. A significant portion of the accommodationist interpretation of Booker T. Washington as a pawn for white political interests results from his coziness with white industrial philanthropists. Such examples were illustrations of what scholar William H. Watkins called a "race philanthropy" focused on the social control of black people, which certainly needs reckoning. Indeed, the hegemonic potential and practice of philanthropy is very real and may partially explain Africana studies scholars' apparent reticence in applying the term to black people. Caution is appropriate and necessary; but there's more.[31]

Philanthropy has been an externally imposed force of social control used against African Americans, but it has also been an internally harnessed tool of empowerment central to long-term survival, social change, and expression of human dignity. For Africana studies, exploring philanthropic motivations and actions opens up new possibilities in its intellectual commitment to uncovering the nuances of black life from daily living to direct challenges to power. Racial uplift and self-help are only starting points and do not sufficiently capture the full measure of philanthropy in the black experience; neither do activist, community worker, or fundraiser. This is not a debate over semantics, but about fully recognizing the radical spirit of generosity with which black women did this work and continue to do so. It is self-help, but it is also much more. It's a vital characteristic of black women's lives and a critical perspective and tool for studying them.

Rightly or wrongly, the world is increasingly turning to philanthropy to solve its social problems. If, as I argue, black women are the quintessential American philanthropists, but we do not think about or name them as such, access to important conversations, decisions, resources, and opportunities will be forfeited—as will their heritage. They will not be fully at the table (their own or others), even though they have always been in the trenches.

⚜

Generosity is ultimately a form of hope. We give as an expression of the possibilities to which we aspire and that we want to make real. We give not only because the need is so overwhelmingly great, but in spite of its greatness. We are not deterred, though we might be daunted. Our gift represents the possibility of a different tomorrow. The hope wrapped up in each gift, no matter its size, is the hope of Daniel against Goliath. Over time, when our hope is merged with the hope of others through giving, mountains are moved and rivers are reversed. A gift by an African American during Jim Crow was an act of resistance and hope, an expression of dignity, and a signal that no matter the conditions, as long as one could give, the human soul would not be crushed.

Until now, we have not seen a woman like Walker before in the major historical narratives of philanthropy in America. She gave directly to individuals to alleviate their suffering, and she gave through networks and institutions to foster systemic change and to build, strengthen, and maintain business relationships. Her giving was expressed in multiple ways beyond the typical role of financial donor and volunteer of time. She was an employer, educator, orator, organizer, convener, activist, and sharer. She embodied a gospel of giving as an expression of her character and as a practical matter for overcoming society's racial and gender discrimination.

Walker's gospel of giving was not birthed to rationalize a political and economic system that made substantial wealth creation by the relative few possible or to assuage guilt over having accumulated more resources than most others. This was not a gospel of giving prompted by a new realization that one had more resources than one could possibly consume or by a sudden influx of inheritance that created new possibilities. Hers was a gospel of giving forged directly from the collective experience of black women in confrontation with the absurdity of American racial and gender oppression. As such, it created impact over time, it assumed various forms and functions, and it found its fullest expression and maximum effect in partnership with the giving of others. It expressed black women's identity, dignity, agency, and humanity as they chose their constructive responses to seemingly destructive and impossible circumstances.

In this light, Madam C. J. Walker, as a historical figure, was more than just another rich person who donated money or another African American who fought racism or another woman who helped other women. She was a significant American philanthropist whose giving thwarted Jim Crow in her day and changes the complexion and shape of generosity in ours.

# Epilogue

## Madam C. J. Walker and African American Philanthropy in the Twenty-First Century

Let all the world emulate her.[1]
—*Denver Star*, 1915

"I would like to build a school in South Africa," announced Oprah Winfrey, the African American billionaire philanthropist and multimedia mogul, one morning in 2002 as she sat in the Johannesburg home of Nelson Mandela.[2] She had been reading the local newspaper and discussing with the South African freedom fighter and former national president the country's social problems, including the role of education in addressing poverty. Upon hearing Winfrey's statement, the legendary leader started making telephone calls. By midafternoon, Winfrey was meeting with the country's educational minister and her formal planning had begun. Five years later—and ninety-five years after Madam Walker proclaimed to a Chicago audience her vision of building an industrial school in South Africa—the Oprah Winfrey Leadership Academy for Girls opened in Henley on Klip, South Africa, just outside Johannesburg. The boarding school serves more than four hundred girls in grades 8–12 from across the country.

Winfrey's inadvertent fulfillment of Madam Walker's philanthropic dream is remarkable and only one of many resemblances between them. Winfrey's approach to giving reflects the practices and traditions embodied by Walker. She is very conscious of her proximity to her students. "I chose girls because I am one," Winfrey stated. "I wanted to be able to give back to girls who were like myself."[3] These students, each one of whom was personally interviewed and selected by Winfrey, are high-achieving and from low-income families and high-risk communities still suffering from the remnants of apartheid. Like Winfrey, they came from homes with no running water or electricity, and most, if not all, had experienced multiple traumas, including physical, mental, and sexual abuse. Death and loss are such common occurrences in the girls' lives—because of the AIDS epidemic, violence, and other health crises in the country—that the school has regularly observed grieving rituals. Many had previously endured hours of early-morning and late-evening travel in order to go to schools miles away from their isolated villages. The academy is a different world for them, where no less than excellence is the expectation and every resource is put in service to their personal development as part of Winfrey's commitment to them. The expectation for students to be philanthropic is ever-present through their extensive volunteer and service work and an overall foundational and curricular embrace of the South African philosophy of *ubuntu*, which acknowledges the thread of humanity that connects all people.[4]

After ten years of operation, Winfrey has personally donated more than $140 million to the effort, which funded every aspect of operations, including initial design and construction, faculty and staff, the two-hundred-thread count sheets on each girl's bed, school uniforms, international field trips, and guaranteed college tuition. Graduates have gone on to top universities around the world, such as Spelman College in Atlanta, Stanford University in California, Oxford University, and the University of Cape Town. Winfrey also built two other public schools in South Africa for $3 million and is considering whether to replicate the Leadership Academy in the United States. But in describing her real gift, Winfrey downplayed the money: "My hope was that I would give them an opportunity to see the best of themselves reflected through an open mind, an open heart, to what is possible." She spoke of changing the "trajectory" of each girl's life by providing "options and access."[5] Madam Walker would be smiling.

Winfrey traces the origins of her philanthropy back to her grandmother, who raised her in 1950s Jim Crow Mississippi. Hattie Mae Lee was a churchwoman who only finished the third grade, but she taught her granddaughter to give back and to value education. She taught young Oprah to read the

Bible and, thus, began the eventual mogul's love affair with books and learning. From her grandmother, Oprah learned that "education was the road to freedom" and that she was expected to help others.[6] As a result, education is the central focus of Winfrey's philanthropy, which she has expressed through her companies, her Oprah Winfrey Charitable Foundation, and her personal resources. She has reportedly donated more than $400 million to education since the early days of her success, including providing four hundred scholarships at Morehouse College, a southern historically black institution. Of her giving, Winfrey has noted, "It started out as an emotional give back. . . . It has developed into a way of life for me."[7]

This is further evident in the ways Winfrey integrated philanthropy into her core business, just like Walker. The *Oprah Winfrey Show*, which aired from 1986 to 2011, regularly featured nonprofit causes. Oprah's Angel Network was a corporate philanthropy initiative she launched in 1997 to connect her viewers with opportunities to support causes around the world. Over a twenty-year period, it generated more than $72 million that was distributed internationally. The Angel Network engaged her viewers in funding college scholarships, building Habitat for Humanity homes, constructing sixty schools overseas, providing Christmas gifts and books and school uniforms for children around the world—a diverse range of monetary and nonmonetary gifts.[8] Across the years and her numerous media platforms, Winfrey has raised her voice in support of many issues, among which were being instrumental in the passage of the National Child Protection Act signed into law by President Bill Clinton in 1993 and endorsing candidate Barack Obama for president. She firmly believes that television shows, books, movies, magazines, websites, public lecture events, and other forms of media are not just a business means for making money but can give people insights into how to improve their lives and their communities when designed with that intention. Madam Walker would be smiling.

"True philanthropy comes from the heart of yourself," Winfrey told the Forbes 400 Summit on Philanthropy in 2012. Through the school, she has made her greatest gift, which she described as "the fierce love" that she gives to her students and that they give to her. Whether through her previous television show, her Oprah Winfrey Network, her philanthropic foundations, or her schools, Winfrey is living out a philanthropy that reflects the essential features of black women's giving exemplified by Walker and featured in this text. Walker provides a richer context for engaging Winfrey's life of generosity than an easy wealth-based comparison with Andrew Carnegie or even Olivia Sage. Further, Walker's enduring philanthropic relevance is pertinent not only to the world's current leading African American donor but also to the full spectrum of black generosity as it is practiced in the twenty-first century.

On September 24, 2016, the Smithsonian National Museum of African American History and Culture opened on the National Mall in Washington, DC, thanks in part to a $21 million donation from Oprah Winfrey. It was the highest donation by any individual or company and amounted to nearly 10 percent of the total private fundraising goal. Winfrey's gift as the leading donor edged out black tech and finance mogul Robert F. Smith's $20 million by $1 million.[9] In fact, five of the largest seven gifts from individuals came from African Americans; Winfrey and Smith were joined by television mogul Shonda Rhimes, NBA legend Michael Jordan, and BET founder Robert Johnson. Other black celebrities who supported the project included LeBron James, Denzel and Pauletta Washington, Quincy Jones, Magic Johnson, Samuel L. Jackson and LaTanya Richardson, Hank Aaron, and Colin and Alma Powell.[10]

These and other high-end monetary donors set the tone for the rest of the campaign; reportedly nearly two-thirds of donors over the $1 million level were African Americans, and nearly one-third of institutional donors were African American organizations, such as churches, fraternities, sororities, and small businesses. The black congregation of Alfred Street Baptist Church in Alexandria, Virginia, ran a campaign that collected gifts ranging from a little boy's $2 to an eighty-year-old woman's $20,000 in order to give the museum a total of $1 million. A museum membership giving program attracted more than one hundred thousand charter members, each of whom gave between $25 and $5,000. A special initiative focused on the $5,000 to $25,000 gift range from people under forty secured 770 donors, who were mostly African American. After the museum opened, donors at this level grew to more than one thousand.[11]

As with the rest of African American philanthropy, money is only part of the museum's story. The institution uses its collection of more than 37,000 artifacts to tell the story of more than four hundred years, ranging from Harriet Tubman's bible to the dress First Lady Michelle Obama wore in honor of the fiftieth anniversary of the March on Washington. Many items were donated by everyday people who had held them in basements, attics, and closets for decades—even generations—and wanted to give something special to be a part of history. Retired educator Shirley Burke of West Bloomfield, Michigan, donated her great-grandfather's violin, but it was not simply an instrument. Her ancestor, Jesse Burke, played it while he was enslaved in Arkansas in the mid-1800s. Handed down through four generations, the violin has rested under Burke's bed for nearly forty years. At the grand opening of the museum, it was encased with honor in the Slavery and Freedom gallery for the world to see.

Similarly, while a junior in college, twenty-year old Kayla Owens of Albany, New York, donated her family's collection of playbills from black theatrical productions they have been amassing for more than thirty years. Representing Broadway productions such as *Fences* and *The Wiz*, the playbills were showcased on opening day and allowed young Owens to share her love of art and "see the history of African Americans displayed and given justice."[12] A'Lelia Bundles, Madam C. J. Walker's great-great granddaughter, donated thirteen items, some of which are featured in the permanent display honoring the philanthropic and beauty-culture giant. In making the gift, Bundles noted, "As a people, our story is intentionally not told. And sometimes the only evidence we have is a photograph or a letter or a document. And when those things are gone, there's no way to prove it." It is very clear that the same historical spirit of giving that coursed through the veins of the highest of monetary donors emanated equally from the artifact donors.[13]

In addition, the museum was overwhelmed by requests to volunteer to the point that it stopped accepting applications months before grand opening. The museum had trained more than three hundred volunteers for its inaugural year, whose backgrounds surely reflected the diversity of America but also represented a significant number of African Americans. As docents, these volunteers made two-year commitments to give at least four hours per month to welcome and guide museum visitors and provide empathetic responses and support to those emotionally moved by exhibits. Sixty-seven-year-old Alice Bonner from Silver Spring, Maryland, volunteered for the museum for seven years before its opening by supporting temporary exhibits placed at other Smithsonian installations. "I have been waiting for this museum all of my life," said the retired black media executive. "We were mis-educated about African American history, mostly by omission, by distortion." The gift of her time is one way she corrects these omissions and shares her history.[14]

To be sure, African Americans were not the only donors to the project. The museum captured the imagination of all races, and many people, corporations, and foundations responded positively to its development. But the philanthropic feat of building this museum finds additional meaning in the context of its origins and evolution. The museum was originally proposed by black veterans of the Civil War during Madam Walker's lifetime at the height of Jim Crow, but it would take 101 years to bring it to fruition. After numerous fits and starts, challenges, and defeats, congressional support finally cemented in 2003 and $250 million in public funds was committed to the project with the provision that the remaining half of the projected $500 million needed be raised from private philanthropy. President Barack Obama, the first African American president, led the groundbreaking and grand opening ceremonies. And with the philanthropic goal shattered at more than $300 million, the leading monetary, artifact, and volunteer donors were African Americans from every walk of life imaginable, and black women figured prominently among them. As they signed their checks, artifact donation agreements, and volunteer applications, they rewrote their history. Madam Walker would be smiling.[15]

The museum honors the black past as quintessential US history and projects forward the future of black generosity as characteristic American philanthropy. It stands as monumental evidence of the depth and truth of black giving despite a history of myths and omissions. Whether through a violin, $25, four volunteer hours per month, or $21 million, a full spectrum of African Americans showed, just as Madam Walker had, that giving continues to run deep and long throughout the community. In fact, the museum's variety of black individual and organizational donors reflects the broader rich landscape of African American philanthropy as it has evolved from the days of Madam Walker into the early twenty-first century.

Traditional elements of black philanthropy, from Walker's time and before, have been joined by contemporary manifestations of the same historical ethos of giving. As usual, black women are leading the way. Single black women are more likely to make charitable donations to nonprofit organizations than single black men, and in married or cohabitating black heterosexual couples, the women lead decision making for charitable giving. The black church, which is largely composed of women, is "still the community's primary institution teaching and practicing philanthropic values every day." Nearly three-quarters of African American charitable giving is directed to the black church. Interpersonal and communal giving remains vital within families, networks, and neighborhoods and through organizations. In the past few decades, black giving circles have become a particular area of interest, especially among black women, reminiscent of the resource-pooling and sharing habits of washerwomen, clubwomen, fraternal women, and Walker agents.[16]

Walker used her company as a base for her gospel of giving, but today some high-net-worth African Americans are turning to philanthropic tools like family foundations, donor-advised funds, and community foundation funds to institutionalize their giving.[17] Also, the existing black-founded and black-serving nonprofit organizations across the country in education, health, social services, arts and culture, community development, and international efforts have been joined by social enterprises, which combine for-profit and public-benefit motives to improve the community, much like the Walker Company. One such example is Walker's Legacy, a twenty-thousand-member business collective in Washington, DC, named for Madam and composed of women of color entrepreneurs and civic leaders.

African American professionals in the nonprofit and philanthropy fields advocate for social justice, equity in funding for communities of color, and diversity in their professions through the Association of Black Foundation Executives, the African American Development Officers Network, and a plethora of regional Blacks in Philanthropy affinity groups. Contemporary social movements, such as Color of Change, Black Lives Matter, Black-Led Social Change, and Black Philanthropy Month, have emerged alongside traditional movements and networks, like the NAACP, the National Urban League, and the National Action Network in the face of what has been called the "new Jim Crow"—mass incarceration and police brutality—and other social and economic injustices across the color line. Today's black philanthropy is vibrant, but there's more to do.[18]

For Walker, the challenges were the institutional and concomitant effects of Jim Crow and sexism. Today, though legal equality has been achieved on paper, actual equality remains elusive. African Americans face a combination of residual effects of long-standing racism, sexism, and other problems—poverty, mass incarceration, police brutality, inequities in public education, gentrification of black neighborhoods, racial and gender wealth gaps, the AIDS crisis, inadequate access to physical and mental health care, drug addiction, violence, a technology gap, and the renewed public normalization of white nationalism, to name a few. At times, these issues may seem insurmountable, and they certainly require a range of societal responses to address, especially public policy. Black philanthropy will be a vital part of the solution and an essential vehicle for expressing the humanity, dignity, and generosity of black people along the way. Like Walker, we do not know when or how these issues will ultimately be resolved. Nonetheless, the work continues from one generation to the next, and there is a deep historical tradition of giving to draw on.

Donors of color can embrace their philanthropic heritage through Madam C. J. Walker to ground their giving and their rightful place in the history of private individuals who have taken action to make the world a better place. What is more, all donors can look to Walker with pride and for inspiration because her gospel of giving is so instructive and relevant today. It advances the idea that giving is a personal and community responsibility that begins at birth rather than at some later point in life when one's resources reach surplus status. It recognizes that the giver has received much throughout life and must give back in return. It views the giver and the recipient as one in the same. It holds that no one is too close to or too far from the giver for a philanthropic gift to be made—including blood relations, extended family, and strangers. It does not distinguish between spheres of action to bring about social change because, ultimately, all available means—for-profit, nonprofit, and government—must be pursued because of the pervasiveness and depth of need. It promotes cooperation and collaboration in order to magnify and multiply the impact of giving. It views virtually any resource that has potential to alleviate suffering or bring about meaningful change in overcoming personal or societal obstacles as being useful philanthropic currency—be it time, money, employment, education, beauty, influence, inspiration, or tangible goods. It holds that giving, and the joy it engenders, should be known and celebrated so as to model generosity and inspire others to action.

And, as a highly accessible model of generosity, Madam C. J. Walker's gospel of giving strongly attests that anyone, regardless of their station in life—race, gender, age, or socioeconomic status—can be a donor right now with whatever means they have; therefore, affirming the *Denver Star*'s 1915 editorial declaration, "Let all the world emulate her."[19]

# Notes

## Introduction

1. Madam Walker to Booker T. Washington, May 5, 1914, in *The Booker T. Washington Papers*, ed. Louis Harlan and Raymond Smock (Urbana: University of Illinois Press, 1984), 13: 14.

2. Madam Walker was given this label in 1917 by the *New York Times Magazine*, and other newspapers followed suit. While her income was rising, she was never comfortable with the label and tried to correct it in subsequent interviews. A'Lelia Bundles initially wrote that Walker was not a millionaire and had assets totaling $600,000 at the end of her life, but later orally revised her estimate upward to well over $1 million, noting that the original estimate did not incorporate the value of the Walker Company. See A'Lelia Bundles, *On Her Own Ground: The Life and Times of Madam C. J. Walker* (New York: Washington Square, 2001): 216, 277. After Walker's death, the Walker Company heavily promoted the label and it stuck. There were other wealthy black male and female entrepreneurs before Walker, but Walker's wealth—specifically her millionaire status—is the best documented and verified as of this writing. Based on secondary sources including Bundles's original text, Shomari Wills critiqued Walker as not really being a millionaire and inaccurately asserted that the company fabricated the story out of desperation. See Shomari Wills, *Black Fortunes: The Story of the First Six African Americans to Escape Slavery and Become Millionaires* (New York: Amistad, 2018): 237–38.

3. Bettye Collier-Thomas centered Madam Walker and Annie Malone as philanthropists. See Collier-Thomas, "Sister Laborers: African American Women, Cultural Capital, and Educational Philanthropy, 1865–1970," in *Cultural Capital and Black Education: African American Communities and the Funding of Black Edu-*

*cation, 1865 to the Present,* ed. V. P. Franklin and C. J. Savage, 97–115 (Greenwich, CT: Information Age, 2004).

4. See Leroy Davis, "Madam C. J. Walker: A Woman of Her Time," in *The African Experience in Community Development: The Continuing Struggle in Africa and in the Americas,* ed. Edward W. Crosby, Leroy Davis, and Anne Adams Graves. 2: 37–60 (Needham Heights, MA: Advocate, 1980); Noliwe Rooks, *Hair Raising: Beauty, Culture, and African American Women* (New Brunswick, NJ: Rutgers University Press, 1996); Bundles, *On Her Own Ground;* Tiffany Gill, "'I Had My Own Business . . . So I Didn't Have to Worry': Beauty Salons, Beauty Culturists, and the Politics of African-American Female Entrepreneurship," in *Beauty and Business: Commerce, Gender, and Culture in Modern America,* ed. Philip Scranton (New York: Routledge, 2001): 169–94; Kathy Peiss, "On Beauty . . . and the History of Business," in *Beauty and Business: Commerce, Gender, and Culture in Modern America,* ed. Philip Scranton, 7–22 (New York: Routledge, 2001); Beverly Lowry, *Her Dream of Dreams: The Rise and Triumph of Madam C. J. Walker* (New York: Vintage, 2003); Susannah Walker, *Style and Stylus: Selling Beauty to African American Women, 1920–1975* (Lexington: University Press of Kentucky, 2007); Kate Dossett, *Bridging Race Divides: Black Nationalism, Feminism, and Integration in the United States, 1896–1935* (Gainesville: University Press of Florida, 2008); Erin Chapman, *Prove It on Me: New Negroes, Sex, and Popular Culture in the 1920s* (New York: Oxford University Press, 2012. Gill has developed a significant treatment of Walker's philanthropy. See Tiffany Gill, *Beauty Shop Politics: African American Women's Activism in the Beauty Industry* (Urbana: University of Illinois Press, 2010).

5. Robert L. Payton and Michael P. Moody, *Understanding Philanthropy: Its Meaning and Mission* (Bloomington: Indiana University Press, 2008).

6. Adrienne Lash Jones, "Philanthropy in the African American Experience," in *Giving: Western Ideas of Philanthropy,* ed. J. B. Schneewind (Bloomington: Indiana University Press, 1996), 153–78; Collier-Thomas, "Sister Laborers."

7. Walker to Washington, May 5, 1914; Willingham, Henry. Annual Report of the Superintendent of Education in the State of Alabama (Montgomery, AL: Brown, 1911). Washington's letter to Walker has not survived, but her response to him has survived.

8. This estimate is based on her earnings in 1913, which were rapidly growing as a result of the expansion of the company (Bundles, *On Her Own Ground,* 145).

9. Walker to Washington, May 5, 1914.

10. See chapter 3 for a discussion of Walker's philanthropic gifts to black colleges for adoption of her beauty culture curriculum.

11. Walker to Washington, May 5, 1914.

12. Bundles, *On Her Own Ground,* 166.

13. Booker T. Washington, *Up from Slavery: An Autobiography* (New York: Doubleday, 1901); repr., electronic edition Chapel Hill: University of North Carolina Press, 1997 http://docsouth.unc.edu/fpn/washington/washing.html.

14. "Dr. Booker T. Washington," *Indianapolis Freeman,* July 12, 1913, p. 1.

15. "$600,000 for Tuskegee and B. T. Washington," *New York Times*, April 24, 1903.

16. Washington, *Up from Slavery*, 192; Booker T. Washington to Madam Walker, May 22, 1914, Harlan and Smock, *Booker T. Washington Papers*, 13: 30.

17. Although Washington maintained his resistance to the curriculum proposal, the institute may have relented, for Walker reported in 1917 that Tuskegee had adopted her curriculum after Washington's death. In 2016 Tuskegee archivists were unable to confirm the use of the curriculum.

18. Bundles aligned Walker with Carnegie's views on the responsibilities of wealth (Bundles, *On Her Own Ground*, 97–98).

19. David Nasaw, *Andrew Carnegie* (New York: Penguin Press, 2006); Leslie Lenkowsky, "Andrew Carnegie," Philanthropy Roundtable, accessed January 10, 2020, https://www.philanthropyroundtable.org/almanac/people/hall-of-fame/detail/andrew-carnegie.

20. Andrew Carnegie, "Wealth," *North American Review* 148, no. 391 (June 1889): 653–64. His philosophy of philanthropy has been called "the gospel of wealth."

21. Ruth Crocker, *Mrs. Russell Sage: Women's Activism and Philanthropy in Gilded Age and Progressive Era America* (Bloomington: Indiana University Press, 2006).

22. For two lists of black philanthropists, mostly unrecognized by history, see Benjamin Brawley, *A Short History of the American Negro* (New York: Macmillan, 1929); Joan Marie Johnson, "Philanthropy," in *Black Women in America*, 2nd ed., ed. Darlene Clark Hine, 474–83 (New York: Oxford University Press, 2005).

23. Robert T. Grimm, ed., *Notable American Philanthropists: Biographies of Giving and Volunteering* (Westport, CT: Greenwood, 2002); Dwight Burlingame, ed., *Philanthropy in America: A Comprehensive Historical Encyclopedia* (Santa Barbara, CA: ABC-CLIO, 2004); Karl Zinsmeister, ed., *The Almanac of American Philanthropy* (Washington, DC: Philanthropy Roundtable, 2016).

24. Joseph Frazier Wall, *Andrew Carnegie* (Pittsburgh, PA: University of Pittsburgh Press, 1989); Ron Chernow, *Titan: The Life of John D. Rockefeller, Sr.* (New York: Random House, 1998); Peter Ascoli, *Julius Rosenwald: The Man Who Built Sears, Roebuck and Advanced the Cause of Black Education in the American South* (Bloomington: Indiana University Press, 2006).

25. These generalizations are based on representative works from the historiography on American philanthropy. See, for example, Robert M. Penna, *Braided Threads: A Historical Overview of the American Nonprofit Sector* (New York: Routledge, 2018); David Callahan, *The Givers: Wealth, Power, and Philanthropy in a New Gilded Age* (New York: Alfred A. Knopf, 2017); Olivier Zunz, *Philanthropy in America: A History* (Princeton, NJ: Princeton University Press, 2012); Peter Dobkin Hall, "A Historical Overview of Philanthropy, Voluntary Associations, and Nonprofit Organizations in the United States, 1600–2000" in *The Nonprofit Sector: A Research Handbook*, 2nd ed., ed. Walter W. Powell and Richard Steinberg, 32–65 (New Haven, CT: Yale University Press, 2006); Judith Sealander, *Private Wealth and Public Life: Foundation Philanthropy and the Reshaping of American Social*

*Policy from the Progressive Era to the New Deal* (Baltimore, MD: Johns Hopkins University Press, 1997); Robert H. Bremner, *American Philanthropy*, 2nd ed. (Chicago: University of Chicago Press, 1988).

26. Kathleen McCarthy, ed., *Lady Bountiful Revisited: Women, Philanthropy and Power* (New Brunswick, NJ: Rutgers University Press, 1990); McCarthy, *Women and Philanthropy: Three Strategies in a Historical Perspective*, Working Paper 22 (New York: Center on Philanthropy and Civil Society, 1994); McCarthy, *Women's Culture: American Philanthropy and Art, 1830–1930* (Chicago: University of Chicago Press, 1991); Karen J. Blair, *The Torchbearers: Women and Their Amateur Arts Associations in America, 1890–1930* (Bloomington: Indiana University Press, 1994); Kathryn Kish Sklar, *Florence Kelley and the Nation's Work: The Rise of Women's Political Culture, 1830–1900* (New Haven, CT: Yale University Press, 1997).

27. Blair, *Torchbearers*, 1994; Kathleen Waters Sander, *The Business of Charity: The Women's Exchange Movement, 1832–1900* (Urbana: University of Illinois Press, 1998); Lori Ginzberg, *Women and the Work of Benevolence: Morality, Politics, and Class in the Nineteenth-Century United States* (New Haven, CT: Yale University Press, 1990).

28. Bernice Kert, *Abby Aldrich Rockefeller: The Woman in the Family* (New York: Random House, 1993); Crocker, *Mrs. Russell Sage*, 2006; Kathleen Waters Sander, *Mary Elizabeth Garrett: Society and Philanthropy in the Gilded Age* (Baltimore, MD: Johns Hopkins University Press, 2008); Sylvia D. Hoffert, *Alva Vanderbilt Belmont: Unlikely Champion of Women's Rights* (Bloomington: Indiana University Press, 2012); Joan Marie Johnson, *Funding Feminism: Monied Women, Philanthropy, and the Women's Movement, 1870–1967* (Chapel Hill: University of North Carolina Press, 2017).

29. There were some important interventions as historians specifically critiqued and countered the canonized history of women's associations and American philanthropy through edited collections, new histories, and community studies that offered diverse agents and representations of philanthropy. Representative examples include Anne Firor Scott, "Most Invisible of All: Black Women's Voluntary Associations," *Journal of Southern History* 56, no. 1 (February 1990): 3–22; Lawrence J. Friedman and Mark D. McGarvie, eds., *Charity, Philanthropy, and Civility in American History* (New York: Cambridge University Press, 2003); Laura Tuennerman-Kaplan, *Helping Others, Helping Ourselves: Power, Giving, and Community Identity in Cleveland, Ohio, 1880–1930* (Kent, OH: Kent State University Press, 2001); Andrea Walton, ed., *Women and Philanthropy in Education* (Bloomington: Indiana University Press, 2005); Marybeth Gasman and Katherine V. Sedgwick, eds. *Uplifting a People: African American Philanthropy and Education* (New York: Peter Lang, 2005).

30. Darlene Clark Hine, "We Specialize in the Wholly Impossible:' The Philanthropic Work of Black Women," in McCarthy, *Lady Bountiful*, 70–93; Bettye Collier-Thomas, "Sister Laborers"; Emmett Carson, *A Hand Up: Black Philanthropy and Self-Help in America* (Washington, DC: Joint Center for Political and Economic

Studies Press, 1993); Iris Carlton-LaNey, Jill Hamilton, Dorothy Ruiz, and Sandra Carlton Alexander, "'Sitting with the Sick,' African American Women's Philanthropy," *Affilia* 16 (Winter 2001): 447–66.

31. Mossell wrote under the pen name "Mrs. N. F. Mossell." Joanne Braxton likened Mossell's work to Paula Giddings's classic 1984 text, *When and When I Enter*. See Braxton's introduction to N. F. Mossell, *The Work of the Afro-American Woman* (New York: Oxford University Press, 1988), xxvii.

32. N. F. Mossell, *The Work of the Afro-American Woman* (New York: Oxford University Press, 1988), 27–28.

33. Ibid., 32.

34. Ibid., 30.

35. Ibid., 28.

36. Ibid., 46.

37. See Hine, "We Specialize"; Collier-Thomas, "Sister Laborers"; Collier-Thomas, *Jesus, Jobs, and Justice: African American Women and Religion* (New York: Alfred A. Knopf, 2010); J. Johnson, "Philanthropy"; Gill, *Beauty Shop Politics*.

38. Activism was identified as one of five main themes as part of the Black Women's Studies Booklist intended to further support the development of the field: Stephanie Y. Evans, *The Black Women's Studies Booklist: Emergent Themes in Critical Race and Gender Research*, February 16, 2019, https://bwstbooklist.net/.

39. For representative examples, see Paula Giddings, *When and Where I Enter: The Impact of Black Women on Race and Sex in America* (New York: Bantam, 1984); Dorothy Salem, *To Better Our World: Black Women in Organized Reform, 1890–1920* (Brooklyn, NY: Carlson, 1990); Stephanie Shaw, "Black Club Women and the Creation of the National Association of Colored Women," *Journal of Women's History* 3, no. 2 (Fall 1991): 10–25; Susan Smith, *Sick and Tired of Being Sick and Tired: Black Women's Health Activism in America, 1890–1950* (Philadelphia: University of Pennsylvania Press, 1995; Anne Meis Knupfer, *Toward a Tenderer Humanity and a Nobler Womanhood: African American Women's Clubs in Turn-of-the-Century Chicago* (New York: New York University Press, 1996); Knupfer, *The Chicago Black Renaissance and Women's Activism* (Urbana: University of Illinois Press, 2006); Glenda E. Gilmore, *Gender and Jim Crow: Women and the Politics of White Supremacy in North Carolina, 1896–1920* (Chapel Hill: University of North Carolina Press, 1996); Tera Hunter, *To 'Joy My Freedom: Southern Black Women's Lives and Labors after the Civil War* (Cambridge, MA: Harvard University Press, 1997); Wanda A. Hendricks, *Gender, Race, and Politics in the Midwest: Black Club Women in Illinois* (Bloomington: Indiana University Press, 1998); Deborah Gray White, *Too Heavy a Load: Black Women in Defense of Themselves, 1894–1994* (New York: W. W. Norton, 1999); Megan Taylor Shockley, *"We, Too, Are Americans:" African American Women in Detroit and Richmond, 1940–54* (Urbana: University of Illinois Press, 2004); Martha S. Jones, *All Bound Up Together: The Woman Question in African American Public Culture, 1830–1900* (Chapel Hill: University of North Carolina Press, 2007); Cheryl Hicks, *Talk with You like a Woman: African American Women, Justice, and Reform*

*in New York, 1890–1935* (Chapel Hill: University of North Carolina Press, 2010); Julie A. Gallagher, *Black Women and Politics in New York City* (Urbana: University of Illinois Press, 2012).

40. For representative examples, see Evelyn Brooks Higginbotham, *Righteous Discontent: The Women's Movement in the Black Baptist Church, 1880–1920* (Cambridge: Harvard University Press, 1993); Jualynne E. Dodson, *Engendering Church: Women, Power, and the AME Church* (New York: Rowman and Littlefield, 2002); Collier-Thomas, *Jesus, Jobs, and Justice*.

41. Keisha N. Blain and Tiffany M. Gill, *To Turn the Whole World Over: Black Women and Internationalism* (Urbana: University of Illinois Press, 2019); Keisha N. Blain, *Set the World on Fire: Black Nationalist Women and the Global Struggle for Freedom* (Philadelphia: University of Pennsylvania Press, 2018); Michelle Rief, "Thinking Locally, Acting Globally: The International Agenda of African American Clubwomen, 1880–1940," *Journal of African American History* 89, no. 3 (Summer 2004): 203–22.

42. For representative examples, see Darlene Clark Hine, *When the Truth Is Told: A History of Black Women's Culture and Community in Indiana, 1875–1950* (Indianapolis: National Council of Negro Women, 1981); Giddings, *When and Where I Enter*; Iris Carlton-LaNey, "Old Folks' Homes for Blacks during the Progressive Era," *Journal of Sociology and Social Welfare* 16, no. 3 (September 1989): 43–60; Cynthia Neverdon-Morton, *Afro-American Women of the South and the Advancement of the Race, 1895–1925* (Knoxville: University of Tennessee Press, 1989); Salem, *To Better Our World*; Shaw, "Black Club Women"; Higginbotham, *Righteous Discontent*; Elizabeth Lindsay Davis, *Lifting As They Climb* (New York: G. K. Hall, 1996); Knupfer, *Toward a Tenderer Humanity*; Hendricks, *Gender, Race, and Politics*; Kibibi V. C. Mack, *Parlor Ladies and Ebony Drudges: African American Women, Class, and Work in a South Carolina Community* (Knoxville: University of Tennessee Press, 1999); White, *Too Heavy a Load*; Iris Carlton-LaNey and Sandra Carlton Alexander, "Early African American Social Welfare Pioneer Women: Working to Empower the Race and the Community," *Journal of Ethnic and Cultural Diversity in Social Work* 10, no. 2 (2001): 67–84; Floris Barnett Cash, *African American Women and Social Action: The Clubwomen and Volunteerism from Jim Crow to the New Deal, 1896–1936* (Westport, CT: Greenwood, 2001); Victoria W. Wolcott, *Remaking Respectability: African American Women in Interwar Detroit* (Chapel Hill: University of North Carolina Press, 2001); Earline Rae Ferguson, "African American Clubwomen and the Indianapolis NAACP, 1912–1914," in *Black Women in Africa and the Americas*, ed. Catherine Higgs, Barbara Moss, and Earline Ferguson, 73–84 (Athens: Ohio University Press, 2002); Iris Carlton-LaNey and Vanessa Hodges, "African American Reformers' Mission: Caring for Our Girls and Women," *Affilia* 19, no. 3 (Fall 2004): 257–72; Joan Marie Johnson, *Southern Ladies, New Women: Race, Region, and Clubwomen in South Carolina, 1890–1930* (Gainesville: University Press of Florida, 2004); Collier-Thomas, *Jesus, Jobs, and Justice*.

43. Leith Mullins, *On Our Own Terms: Race, Class, and Gender in the Lives of African American Women* (New York: Routledge, 1997).

44. Higginbotham, *Righteous Discontent*; Hendricks, *Gender, Race, and Politics*; Mack, *Parlor Ladies*; J. Johnson, "Philanthropy"; Knupfer, *Chicago Black Renaissance*, 2006; Knupfer, *Toward a Tenderer Humanity*.

45. As quoted in Hine, "We Specialize," 84. For additional discussion of black women's anxiety over fundraising and how they provided moral and financial support to each other to compensate, see J. Johnson, *Southern Ladies*.

46. It is important to note that the gradual development of fundraising as a noble profession based on the moral authority of a community-supported mission was simultaneously occurring in different places during the early twentieth century, but would not advance in earnest until middle century and beyond. See Scott M. Cutlip, *Fund Raising in the United States: Its Role in America's Philanthropy* (New Brunswick, NJ: Transaction, 1990).

47. Emmett Carson described black philanthropy as a form of self-help and mutual aid (Carson, *Hand Up*). Adrienne Jones thought such labels to be dismissive and objected to their use because they prioritize the motivations for giving over the giving itself, and white philanthropy is not circumscribed in such a manner (A. L. Jones, "Philanthropy").

48. For examples of taking black women seriously, see Gerda Lerner, *Black Women in White America: A Documentary History* (New York: Random House, 1972); Giddings, *When and Where I Enter*; Darlene Clark Hine, *Hine Sight: Black Women and the Re-construction of American History* (New York: Carlson, 1994); White, *Too Heavy a Load*; Brittany Cooper, *Beyond Respectability: The Intellectual Thought of Race Women.* (Urbana: University of Illinois Press, 2017).

49. See Carnegie, "Wealth"; M. Olivia Sage, "Opportunities and Responsibilities of Leisured Women," *North American Review* 181, no. 588 (1905): 712–21; John D. Rockefeller, *Random Remembrances of Men and Events* (New York: Doubleday, Page, 1916). These donors were exceptions; most philanthropists did not publish major declarations about their philosophies of giving.

50. A'Lelia Bundles, personal communication to author, March 5, 2010. In addition, because the black press meticulously covered Walker's travels around the country, including some of her giving, and the white press also typically included her giving in articles about her, she may have felt no need or urgency to write specifically about philanthropy.

51. Jenny Shaw, *Everyday Life in the Early English Caribbean: Irish, Africans, and the Construction of Difference* (Athens: University of Georgia Press, 2013): 8, 10, 12; Marisa J. Fuentes, *Dispossessed Lives: Enslaved Women, Violence, and the Archive* (Philadelphia: University of Pennsylvania Press, 2016): 3.

52. Fuentes, *Dispossessed Lives*, 12.

53. In the 1920s, Lelia changed her name to A'Lelia. Both names will be used throughout the text to refer to her.

## Chapter 1. Making Madam C. J. Walker

Excerpts appear from "The Collectivist Roots of Madam C. J. Walker's Philanthropy" by Tyrone McKinley Freeman on *Black Perspectives* (the blog of the African American Intellectual History Society), May 20, 2019, https://www.aaihs.org/the-collectivist-roots-of-madam-c-j-walkers-philanthropy/. Reprinted by permission of *Black Perspectives*.

1. "Wealthiest Negro Woman's Suburban Mansion," *New York Times Magazine*, November 4, 1917, 4.

2. Carter G. Woodson, "The Negro Washerwoman, a Vanishing Figure," *Journal of Negro History* 15, no. 3 (July 1930): 269.

3. "America's Foremost Colored Woman," *Indianapolis Freeman*, December 28, 1912, 16.

4. Anthropologist Clifford Geertz applied the phrase "the social history of the moral imagination" to describe the ways in which anthropologists interpret and translate their field observations of the different peoples and cultures they study (Clifford Geertz, "Found in Translation: On the Social History of the Moral Imagination," *Georgia Review* 31, no. 4 (1977): 788–810. The concept of moral imagination has philosophical roots in the works of writers such as Plato, Immanuel Kant, Adam Smith, and Edmund Burke. Robert Payton and Michael Moody adapted Geertz's concept of the moral imagination to explain the moral actions and motivations of philanthropists. They described philanthropy as "the social history of the moral imagination" and named philanthropic action as "the exercise of the moral imagination." In this light, philanthropists Benjamin Franklin, Andrew Carnegie, and John D. Rockefeller were said to be "effective entrepreneurs with vivid moral imaginations" because their giving was directed toward an array of social issues. The use of the term *social history* refers to the ways in which people have used their deeply held values to inspire and guide their voluntary actions to improve society over time (Payton and Moody, *Understanding Philanthropy*, 22, 99, 133).

5. This biographical account was drawn from Bundles, *On Her Own Ground*.

6. W. E. B. DuBois, *Black Reconstruction in America 1860–1880* (New York: Atheneum, 1992), 453.

7. "Queen of Gotham's Colored 400," *Literary Digest* 55 (October 13, 1917): 75–76.

8. DuBois, *Black Reconstruction*, 227, 230.

9. Earle H. West, "The Peabody Fund and Negro Education, 1867–1880," *History of Education Quarterly* 6, no. 2 (Summer, 1966): 3–21; John E. Fisher, *The John F. Slater Fund: A Nineteenth Century Affirmative Action for Negro Education* (Lanham, MD: University Press of America, 1987).

10. Carson, *Hand Up*; A. L. Jones, "Philanthropy."

11. For black club women's institution-building efforts around the country after the Civil War into the twentieth century, see Neverdon-Morton, *Afro-American Women*; Knupfer, *Toward a Tenderer Humanity*; Hendricks, *Gender, Race, and Poli-*

tics; Cash, *African American Women*. For particular examples in the Midwest in response to migration, see Charles E. Coulter, *"Take Up the Black Man's Burden:" Kansas City's African American Communities, 1865–1939* (Columbia: University of Missouri Press, 2006); Kimberley L. Phillips, *AlabamaNorth: African-American Migrants, Community, and Working-Class Activism in Cleveland, 1915–45.* (Urbana: University of Illinois Press, 1999).

12. DuBois, *Black Reconstruction*, 57; Eric Foner, *Forever Free: The Story of Emancipation and Reconstruction* (New York: Alfred A. Knopf, 2005), 129 (quote), 134, 173.

13. Henry Louis Gates Jr., *Stony the Road: Reconstruction, White Supremacy, and the Rise of Jim Crow* (New York: Penguin, 2019); Foner, *Forever Free*, 198; Rayford Logan, *The Negro in American Life and Thought: The Nadir 1877–1901* (New York: Dial, 1954); Kenneth Stampp, *The Era of Reconstruction, 1865–1877* (New York: Alfred A. Knopf, 1966), 185.

14. Nell Irvin Painter, *Exodusters: Black Migration to Kansas after Reconstruction* (New York: Alfred A. Knopf, 1977), 16; "Madam C. J. Walker," *Indianapolis Freeman*, November 11, 1911, 1; "America's Foremost Colored Woman," *Indianapolis Freeman*, December 28, 1912, 3; Bundles, *On Her Own Ground*, 36.

15. William H. Davis, *Report of the Thirteenth Annual Convention of the National Negro Business League* (Washington, DC: n.p., 1912), 154; "Wealthiest Negro Woman's Suburban Mansion"; Bundles, *On Her Own Ground*, 46. Brimmer made a distinction between laundresses and washerwomen, with the former being a higher-status job recognized as full-time employment on the premises of a homeowner and the latter involving the management of multiple clients on one's own and washing at communal wells. Such distinctions did not seem readily evident in Madam Walker's usage of the terms. See Brandi C. Brimmer, "Laundresses," in *Black Women in America*, 2nd ed., ed. Darlene Clark Hine (New York: Oxford University Press, 2005): 229–31.

16. Woodson, "Negro Washerwoman," 269.

17. Woodson, "Negro Washerwoman."

18. Pan toting was domestic workers' practice of taking home leftover food from client families to feed their own families.

19. Hunter, *To 'Joy My Freedom*, 67.

20. For more on how working-class black women organized themselves and pursued respectability in different contexts at different times around the country, see Hicks, *Talk with You*; Shockley, *"We, Too, Are Americans"*; Wolcott, *Remaking Respectability*; Mack, *Parlor Ladies*.

21. Hunter, *To 'Joy My Freedom*, 91, 94.

22. "Wealthiest Negro Woman's Suburban Mansion," 4.

23. "Queen of Gotham's Colored 400."

24. Bundles, *On Her Own Ground*, 41.

25. A. L. Jones, "Philanthropy," 162. See aforementioned clubwoman literature, n. 11.

26. Mark Andrew Huddle, "Exodus from the South," in *A Companion to African American History*, ed. Alton Hornsby Jr. (Malden, MA: Blackwell, 2005), 450; Kimberly L. Phillips, *Daily Life during African American Migrations* (Westport, CT: Greenwood, 2012), 2.

27. Painter, *Exodusters*, 256; Phillips, *Daily Life*, 12.

28. Painter, *Exodusters*, 195.

29. Ibid., 225.

30. Ibid., 226.

31. Bundles, *On Her Own Ground*, 44.

32. Many of these same women were active inside and outside church. For representative scholarly treatment of black women's identities as churchwomen and clubwomen, see Higginbotham, *Righteous Discontent*; Collier-Thomas, *Jesus, Jobs, and Justice*, xv–xxxiv.

33. Carlton-LaNey, "Old Folks' Homes."

34. Daniel Levine, "A Single Standard of Civilization: Black Private Social Welfare Institutions in the South, 1880s-1920s," *Georgia Historical Quarterly*, 81, no. 1 (Spring 1997): 52–77; Neverdon-Morton, *Afro-American Women*; Knupfer, *Toward a Tenderer Humanity*; Hendricks, *Gender, Race, and Politics*; Cash, *African American Women*.

35. Virginia and Barry Gilbert, "Annie Malone Children's Organization Will Celebrate 125 Years of Service," *St. Louis Public Radio*, September 23, 2019. https://news.stlpublicradio.org/post/annie-malone-childrens-organization-will-celebrate-125-years-service-0#stream/0.

36. Bundles, *On Her Own Ground*, 46.

37. Daniel Levine, "Single Standard," 63; Pennsylvania Historical and Museum Commission, "African Americans in Pennsylvania: Benevolent, Fraternal and Sororal Societies, and Women's Clubs, 1644–1965," accessed June 27, 2013, https://studylib.net/doc/8864548/chapter-6-benevolent--fraternal-and-sororal-societies--and.

38. Bundles, *On Her Own Ground*, 57.

39. "America's Foremost Colored Woman," *Indianapolis Freeman*, December 28, 1912, 16.

40. Andrew Carnegie, John D. Rockefeller, and Olivia Sage couched their philanthropy in terms of responsibility, not joy.

41. Collier-Thomas, *Jesus, Jobs, and Justice*, xxvi–xxvii.

42. Bundles, *On Her Own Ground*, 56.

43. As previously noted, working-class black women had their own ideas about racial uplift and respectability, and these early experiences with the women of St. Paul's likely shaped Walker's ability to move across class differences and interact in various social circles later in life, especially with the National Association of Colored Women.

44. M. Jones, *All Bound Up Together*, 5.

45. Ibid., 8.

46. The literature disagrees whether Allen was actually accosted along with Jones, but both did protest and leave the congregation. See, e.g., Harry V. Richardson, *Dark Salvation: The Story of Methodism As It Developed among Blacks in America* (Garden City, NY: Doubleday, 1976), 65; Carson, *Hand Up*, 8; Richard Allen, *The Life Experience and Gospel Labours of the Rt. Reverend Richard Allen* (Philadelphia: Martin and Boden, 1833), http://docsouth.unc.edu/neh/allen/allen.html; Richard S. Newman, *Freedom's Prophet: Bishop Richard Allen, the AME Church, and the Black Founding Fathers* (New York: New York University Press, 2008), 90. There are discrepancies in the historiography about the exact date of the founding of the Free African Society.

47. John H. Smith, *Vital Facts concerning the African Methodist Episcopal Church: Its Doctrines, Government, Usages, Polity Progress* (Philadelphia: AME, 1941), 193, 195 198; Richardson, *Dark Salvation*, 82, 83.

48. Julius Bailey, *Race Patriotism: Protest and Print Culture in the AME Church* (Knoxville: University of Tennessee Press, 2012), 17.

49. Bailey, *Race Patriotism*, xii, xv. For black churchwomen's and clubwomen's countering the Lost Cause narrative and developing curricula for children, see J. Johnson, *Southern Ladies*; S. Shaw, "Black Club Women."

50. Reginald F. Hildebrand, *The Times Were Strange and Stirring: Methodist Preachers and the Crisis of Emancipation* (Durham, NC: Duke University Press, 1995), 54.

51. Ibid., 61.

52. J. Smith, *Vital Facts*, 202.

53. Richardson, *Dark Salvation*, 89.

54. Lawrence S. Little, *Disciples of Liberty: The African Methodist Episcopal Church in the Age of Imperialism, 1884–1916* (Knoxville: University of Tennessee Press, 2000), xi–xii.

55. Allen, *Life Experience*, 50–51.

56. Payton and Moody, *Understanding Philanthropy*.

57. J. Smith, *Vital Facts*, 58.

58. "The Life Work of Mme. C. J. Walker," *Indianapolis Freeman*, December 26, 1914, 1. For scriptural context, see 2 Cor. 8 and 9, specifically 2 Cor. 9:7.

59. Collier-Thomas, *Jesus, Jobs, and Justice*; James T. Campbell, *Songs of Zion: The African Methodist Episcopal Church in the United States and South Africa* (New York: Oxford University Press, 1995), 93.

60. Collier-Thomas, *Jesus, Jobs, and Justice*, 189, 195, 202.

61. Dodson, *Engendering Church*, 2.

62. Collier-Thomas, *Jesus, Jobs, and Justice*, 142.

63. Ibid., 120–21; Dodson, *Engendering Church*, 50, 54, 80.

64. Bundles, *On Her Own Ground*, 54. For a discussion of the 1904 World's Fair Exhibition, see pages 70–75.

65. Collier-Thomas, *Jesus, Jobs, and Justice*, 189.

66. M. Jones, *All Bound Up Together*, 17.

67. See Julius H. Bailey, *Around the Family Altar: Domesticity in the African Methodist Episcopal Church, 1865–1900* (Tallahassee: University Press of Florida, 2005); Bailey, *Race Patriotism*; Campbell, *Songs of Zion*; Richardson, *Dark Salvation*); Little, *Disciples of Liberty*); and Clarence Walker, *A Rock in a Weary Land: The African Methodist Episcopal Church during the Civil War and Reconstruction* (Baton Rouge: Louisiana State University Press, 1982).

68. Bundles, *On Her Own Ground*, 59.

69. "Queen of Gotham's Colored 400."

70. "Foremost among the few Women," ca. 1919, box 3, folder 1, Madam C. J. Walker Papers, Indiana Historical Society, Indianapolis, Indiana; "Queen of Gotham's Colored 400." For discussions of Walker's relationship with Malone, see Bundles, *On Her Own Ground*, 64–68, 81–82.

71. Bundles, *On Her Own Ground*, 83, 84, 86.

72. Ibid., 88; "Former Denverite Succeeds," *Denver Statesman*, December 23, 1911, 2.

73. Bundles, *On Her Own Ground*, 92.

## Chapter 2. Opportunity

1. The Madam C. J. Walker Manufacturing Company, *1924 Yearbook and Almanac* (Indianapolis: Madam C. J. Walker Manufacturing Co., 1924), 15, box 13, folder 24, Madam C. J. Walker Papers, Indiana Historical Society, Indianapolis, Indiana (hereafter cited as Walker Papers).

2. "The Negro Woman in Business: Madam C. J. Walker Urges Her Sisters to Rise above the Wash Tub and Cook Kitchen and Make a Place in the Commercial World," *Indianapolis Freeman*, September 20, 1913, 1; Walker Company, *1924 Yearbook*, 10 (Mrs. R. Walker quote), 15, 18, Walker Papers; "Former Denverite Succeeds," *Denver Statesman*, December 23, 1911, 2.

3. See L. Davis, "Madam C. J. Walker." Davis viewed Walker as combining racial cooperation with racial solidarity as black entrepreneurs and black consumers engaged in mutually beneficial exchanges that sustained commercial enterprises and yielded economic and philanthropic value to the community. See also Dossett, *Bridging Race Divides*. Dossett echoed Nicole Biggart's earlier use of "charismatic capitalism" to view Walker as both businesswoman and race woman (Nicole Biggart, *Charismatic Capitalism: Direct Selling Organizations in America* [Chicago: University of Chicago Press, 1989]). See also Chapman, *Prove It on Me*. Chapman presented Walker's ethos of profits and service to the race in relation to the larger New Negro Progressive framework of "race motherhood."

4. P. Hall, "Historical Overview," 55. For a discussion of the evolution of the names and definitions of the nonprofit sector, see Peter Frumpkin, *On Being Nonprofit: A Conceptual and Policy Primer* (Cambridge, MA: Harvard University Press, 2002), 10–16.

5. Kathleen McCarthy, *American Creed: Philanthropy and the Rise of Civil Society 1700–1865* (Chicago: University of Chicago Press, 2003), 4, 5.

6. Cooper, *Beyond Respectability*.

7. Elsa Barkley Brown, "Womanist Consciousness: Maggie Lena Walker and the Independent Order of Saint Luke," *Signs* 14, no. 3 (1989): 610–33.

8. Freeman B. Ransom, Walker's general counsel, called the business a "race company" ("Madam C. J. Walker, Black Business Woman," by A'Lelia Bundles, box 12, folder 19, Walker Papers.

9. For more on the role of the black church, see Marci Bounds Littlefield, "The Black Church and Community Development and Self-Help: The Next Phase of Social Equality," *Western Journal of Black Studies* 29, no. 4 (2005): 687–93; Milton C. Sernett, ed., *Afro-American Religious History: A Documentary Witness* (Durham, NC: Duke University Press, 1985); C. Eric Lincoln, *The Negro Church in America/ The Black Church since Frazier* (New York: Schocken, 1974). The same can be said about other black institutions such as fraternal organizations, which were not just about associationalism; they also engaged in business development, social service provision, education, and political and social activism.

10. Cheryl A. Smith, *Market Women: Black Women Entrepreneurs Past, Present, and Future* (Westport, CT: Praeger, 2005); Juliet E. K. Walker, *The History of Black Business: Capitalism, Race, Entrepreneurship*, 2nd ed. vol. 1, *To 1865* (Chapel Hill: University of North Carolina Press, 2009); Angel Kwolek-Folland, *Engendering Business: Men and Women in the Corporate Office, 1870–1930* (Baltimore, MD: Johns Hopkins University Press, 1994).

11. C. Smith, *Market Women*, 44, 45, 50. Gill, *Beauty Shop Politics*.

12. Sandra Crouse Quinn and Stephen Thomas, "The National Negro Health Week, 1915–1951: A Descriptive Account," *Minority Health Today* 2, no. 3 (March–April 2001): 44–49.

13. Roscoe C. Brown, "The National Negro Health Week Movement," *Journal of Negro Education* 6, no. 3 (July 1937): 553–64; Thomas Monroe Campbell, *The Movable School Goes to the Negro Farmer* (Tuskegee, AL: Tuskegee Institute Press, 1936).

14. For a discussion of the Tuskegee Mother's Club and the Neighborhood Union, see Neverdon-Morton, *Afro-American Women*, 132–37, 145–63; Jacqueline Anne Rouse, *Lugenia Burns Hope, Black Southern Reformer* (Athens: University of Georgia Press, 2004); S. Smith, *Sick and Tired*.

15. For discussions of black clubwomen's work in health and hygiene, see Salem, *To Better Our World*; S. Smith, *Sick and Tired*; Neverdon-Morton *Afro-American Women*; Cash, *African American Women*.

16. For a discussion of the National Urban League's work in hygiene, see Touré F. Reed, *Not Alms but Opportunity: The Urban League and the Politics of Racial Uplift, 1910–1950* (Chapel Hill: University of North Carolina Press).

17. Adrienne Jones identified the connection between hygiene and black women's philanthropy, noting that clubwomen sought to "build pride and self-esteem among the young and to model the social skills which they considered imperative for upward social and economic mobility." She also described these

efforts as providing "a formula for maintaining dignity and self-confidence . . . however distorted their motivations and methods may seem today" (A. L. Jones, "Philanthropy," 164).

18. Dossett, *Bridging Race Divides*, 87.

19. W. E. B. DuBois, *Economic Co-operation among Negro Americans* (Atlanta: Atlanta University Press, 1907): 11. I am using the term in the broad sense that DuBois used it to reflect collaboration and cooperation. Walker did not establish her company as a "cooperative" organization that belonged to its employees or consumers, but she did give shares to her staff. For an updated history of cooperative economics, see Jessica Gordon Nembhard, *Collective Courage: A History of African American Cooperative Economic Thought and Practice* (University Park: Pennsylvania State University Press, 2014).

20. Lynn M. Hudson, *The Making of 'Mammy Pleasant': A Black Entrepreneur in Nineteenth-Century San Francisco* (Urbana: University of Illinois Press, 2003); E. Brown, "Womanist Consciousness."

21. Articles of Incorporation of the Madame C. J. Walker Manufacturing Company of Indiana, box 7, folder 1, Walker Papers.

22. "Madam C. J. Walker, Black Business Woman" by A'Lelia Bundles, box 12, folder 19, Walker Papers.

23. Madam C. J. Walker Manufacturing Company, *The Madam C. J. Walker Beauty Manual: A Thorough Treatise Covering all Branches of Beauty Culture*, 1st ed. (Indianapolis, IN: Madam C. J. Walker Manufacturing Company, 1924): 212–14, Indianapolis Special Collections Room, Indianapolis–Marion County Public Library, Indianapolis, Indiana. Over time, the product array included as many as sixteen products.

24. For statistics on black business ownership in late nineteenth and early twentieth centuries, see J. Walker, *History of Black Business*, 272.

25. Steven A. Reich, *A Working People: A History of African American Workers since Emancipation* (New York: Rowman and Littlefield, 2013); Enobong Hannah Branch, *Opportunity Denied: Limiting Black Women to Devalued Work* (New Brunswick, NJ: Rutgers University Press, 2011).

26. Sharon Harley, "When Your Work Is Not Who You Are: The Development of a Working-Class Consciousness among Afro-American Women," in *Gender, Class, Race, and Reform in the Progressive Era*, ed. Noralee Frankel and Nancy Dye (Lexington: University Press of Kentucky, 1991), 43–44.

27. Claudia Goldin, "Female Labor Force Participation: The Origin of Black and White Differences, 1870–1880," *Journal of Economic History* 37, no. 1 (March 1977): 92. Despite black women's significant presence in the labor market, they experienced tensions with their husbands and other men about their role in the home. For discussions, see Sharon Harley, "For the Good of Family and Race: Gender, Work and Domestic Roles in the Black Community, 1880–1930," *Signs* 15, no. 2 (Winter 1990): 336–49; Bailey, *Around the Family Altar*. Madam Walker was apparently largely unaffected by these tensions possibly because she could not trust or rely on her husbands for subsistence, since her first husband died

shortly after their marriage, her second husband did not work, and her third husband was unfaithful.

28. Harley, "When Your Work Is Not Who You Are," 43.

29. Mullings, *On Our Own Terms*, 48.

30. Evelyn Nakano Glenn, "Racial Ethnic Women's Labor: The Intersection of Race, Class, and Gender Oppression," *Review of Radical Political Economics* 17, no. 3 (1985): 96. See also Giddings, *When and Where I Enter*; Hunter, *To 'Joy My Freedom*, 106–7.

31. Giddings, *When and Where I Enter*, 144; Leah Platt Boustan and William J. Collins, "The Origin and Persistence of Black-White Differences in Women's Labor Force Participation," in *Human Capital in History: The American Record*, edited by Leah Platt Boustan, Carola Frydman, and Robert A. Margo, 205–40 (Chicago: University of Chicago Press, 2014), www.nber.org/chapters/c12902.pdf. There were a small number of black female nurses and teachers (Harley, "For the Good of Family and Race"; Glenn, "Racial Ethnic Women's Labor."

32. Sociologist Robert Boyd used the terms "ethnic niche economy" and "protected market" to describe black beauty culture (Robert Boyd, "The Great Migration to the North and the Rise of Ethnic Niches for African American Women in Beauty Culture and Hairdressing, 1910–1920," *Sociological Focus* 29, no. 1 [February 1996]: 33–45; quotes on 37).

33. Mullings, *On Our Own Terms*, 62 (quote); Johnson, *Southern Ladies*; Harley, "For the Good of Family and Race," 348. For discussions of the class differences in the amount of time and resources available to do the work of the "triple day" and regional differences in how the work was done, see Shockley, "*We, Too, Are Americans*," 2004; Wolcott, *Remaking Respectability*.

34. Payroll Statements, 1915–1917, box 27, folder 2, Walker Papers; Payroll Statements, June 24, 1916, box 27, folder 3, Walker Papers; G. S. Olive to FBR [Ransom], September 15, 1919, box 27, folder 6, Walker Papers.

35. Notice of Meeting to Increase Stock, July 7, 1919, box 7, folder 7, Walker Papers.

36. Special Agent's Contract 1916, box 7, folder 11, Walker Papers; Contracts with Special Agents 1917–1919, box 7, folder 18, Walker Papers; letter from A. C. Burnett, June 8, 1918 box 9, folder 16, Walker Papers.

37. Madam Walker to Freeman B. Ransom, April 18, 1918, box 1, folder 10, Walker Papers.

38. Walker Manufacturing Company Order Form, box 30, folder 1, Walker Papers; The rates agents may have charged for other beauty culture services—such as hairdressing, massage, or manicures—are not discernible from the company's records.

39. Madam Walker to Freeman B. Ransom, March 2, 1918, box 1, folder 9, Walker Papers.

40. Madam Walker to Freeman B. Ransom, March 6, 1918, box 1, folder 9, Walker Papers.

41. It is difficult to corroborate that Walker had twenty thousand agents, though the number was widely circulated through newspapers and company literature.

42. Madam Walker to Freeman B. Ransom, March 11, 1918, box 1, folder 9, Walker Papers.

43. Madam Walker to Freeman B. Ransom, April 6, 1918, box 10, folder 1, Walker Papers.

44. A. C. Burnett to Freeman B. Ransom, May 28, 1918, box 9, folder 16, Walker Papers; A. C. Burnett to Freeman B. Ransom, June 22, 1918, box 9, folder 16, Walker Papers.

45. Madam Walker to Robert Brokenburr, April 11, 1918, box 1, folder 10, Walker Papers.

46. Madam Walker to Freeman B. Ransom, April 18, 1918, box 10, folder 1, Walker Papers. This use of *charity* appears to be a rare instance in the Walker Papers in which Walker used it in a pejorative sense. Usually, *charity* and *philanthropy* were used interchangeably to describe Walker's efforts to uplift the race.

47. Floyd Snelson, "Slave Cabin to Queen's Palace," ca. 1940, box 12, folder 4, Walker Papers. For a biography of Snelson, see Richard R. Wright Jr., *Centennial Encyclopaedia of the African Methodist Episcopal Church, 1816–1916* (Philadelphia: AME Church, 1916), 210.

48. "First Negro Woman Millionaire Manufacturer," *Beauticians Journal*, 1951, p. 3, box 12, folder 8, Walker Papers.

49. Freeman B. Ransom to E. T. Rouzeau, September 25, 1931, box 6, folder 1, Walker Papers.

50. Ibid.

51. "A Memorial Service for Freeman B. Ransom," box 6, folder 6, Walker Papers; "F. B. Ransom, Indianapolis," *Indianapolis Freeman*, December 25, 1915.

52. Ransom press release (no date shown), box 6, folder 2, Walker Papers.

53. Ibid.; "Memorial Service for Freeman B. Ransom."

54. Bundles, *On Her Own Ground*, 248; Freeman B. Ransom to E. T. Rouzeau, September 25, 1931, box 6, folder 1, Walker Papers.

55. Ransom to Rouzeau, September 25, 1931.

56. Chernow, *Titan*; Crocker, *Mrs. Russell Sage*; Ascoli, *Julius Rosenwald*; and Wall, *Andrew Carnegie*.

57. "Memorial Service for Freeman B. Ransom."

58. Freeman B. Ransom to Madam Walker, February 20, 1918, box 1, folder 8, Walker Papers.

59. In 1913 Walker made $32,000 during the first eight months of the year. By 1917, she was making $175,000 per year (Bundles, *On Her Own Ground*, 149, 248).

60. Freeman B. Ransom to Lelia Walker Robinson, May 27, 1913, box 4, folder 6, Walker Papers.

61. Freeman B. Ransom to Lelia Walker Robinson, November 20, 1914, box 4, folder 6, Walker Papers.

62. Lelia Walker Robinson to Freeman B. Ransom, July 30, 1915, box 4, folder 7, Walker Papers.

63. Lelia Walker Robinson to Freeman B. Ransom, May 18, 1918, box 4, folder 10, Walker Papers.

64. George S. Olive to Freeman B. Ransom, September 15, 1919, box 27, folder 3, Walker Papers.

65. Madam Walker to Freeman B. Ransom, March 2, 1918 box 1, folder 9, Walker Papers.

66. Madam Walker to Freeman B. Ransom, December 12, 1918, box 1, folder 14, Walker Papers.

67. Madam Walker to Freeman B. Ransom, December 19, 1918, box 1, folder 14, Walker Papers.

68. Freeman B. Ransom to Madam Walker, January 17, 1919, box 1, folder 15, Walker Papers.

69. Freeman B. Ransom to Madam Walker, February 1, 1919, box 1, folder 16, Walker Papers.

70. Freeman B. Ransom to Madam Walker, December 24, 1918, box 1, folder 14, Walker Papers.

71. E. D. Thomas to Mrs. Blackwell, November 21, 2918, box 9, folder 4, Walker Papers.

72. I mostly deal with Ransom's advice to Walker about the ILDP. For full discussions about the ILDP and Walker's internationalism, see Bundles, *On Her Own Ground*, 250–65; and Dossett, *Bridging Race Divides*, 118–25.

73. "Will Look to the Needs of the Poor and Homeless during the Winter Months," *Indianapolis Freeman*, September 14, 1912, 12, Walker Papers. It is not clear whether the organization ever in fact was created or what may have happened to it.

74. "In Club Circles," *Indianapolis Recorder*, December 12, 1914, 2.

75. "National Organizer W.C.T.U.," *Indianapolis Recorder*, January 23, 1915, 1.

76. This account of the ILDP is drawn from Bundles, *On Her Own Ground*, 250–65; Gill, *Beauty Shop Politics*, 58; David Levering Lewis, *W. E. B. DuBois: The Fight for Equality and the American Century, 1919–1963* (New York: Owl, 2000), 114. For discussions of the international efforts of black organizations and black clubwomen, see Yuichiro Onishi, "The New Negro of the Pacific: How African Americans Forged Cross-Racial Solidarity with Japan, 1917–1922," *Journal of African American History* 92, no. 2 (Spring 2007): 191–213; Rief, "Thinking Locally, Acting Globally."

77. Freeman B. Ransom to Madam Walker, January 25, 1919, box 1, folder 15, Walker Papers. For tension between these groups, see Blain, *Set the World on Fire*.

78. Ransom to Walker, January 25, 1919; Lewis, *W. E. B. DuBois*, 59. The Military Intelligence Division of the US Army conducted surveillance of Walker because of her involvement with ILDP and its efforts to engage Japan and other countries in

the African American struggle. Walker was successful in connecting with publishers of a Japanese newspaper, and this raised the concern of government officials who feared the sympathy of foreign governments could be cultivated. For a discussion, see Onishi, "New Negro of the Pacific."

79. Martin Summers, *Manliness and Its Discontents: The Black Middle Class and the Transformation of Masculinity, 1900–1930* (Chapel Hill: University of North Carolina Press, 2004).

80. White, *Too Heavy a Load*, 59.

81. Summers, *Manliness and Its Discontents*, 147.

82. Freeman B. Ransom to E. T. Rouzeau, September 25, 1931, box 6, folder 1, Walker Papers.

83. Freeman B. Ransom to Madam Walker, December 21, 1918, box 1, folder 14, Walker Papers.

84. Madam Walker to Freeman B. Ransom, December 28, 1918, box 1, folder 14, Walker Papers.

85. "The World's Famous Hair Culturist Puts New Toilet Articles on the Market," *Dallas Express*, March 29, 1919, 5.

86. Ibid.

87. For an example of Walker Company ads and competitor ads, see "Mme. CJ Walker Tells How to Have and to Keep a Bright and Beautiful Complexion," *Richmond Planet*, May 17, 1919, 11; "World's Famous Hair Culturist," 5.

88. S. Walker, *Style and Stylus*, 64–70; Cash, *African American Women*, 51; Rooks, *Hair Raising*; Gill, "'I Had My Own Business"; Giddings, *When and Where I Enter*, 187–89; Treva B. Lindsey, *Colored No More: Reinventing Black Womanhood in Washington, D.C.* (Urbana: University of Illinois Press, 2017); Kathy Peiss, "On Beauty," 19.

89. For a history of direct-selling organizations, see Biggart, *Charismatic Capitalism*, 20–38; Katina Manko, "'Now You Are in Business for Yourself': The Independent Contractors of the California Perfume Company, 1886–1938," *Business and Economic History*, 26, no. 1 (1997): 5–26.

90. Edward J. Balleisen, *Fraud: An American History from Barnum to Madoff* (Princeton, NJ: Princeton University Press, 2017): 144, 165–66. See Bundles, *On Her Own Ground*, 211–12, for a brief discussion of agent complaints.

91. "Former Denverite Succeeds," *Denver Statesman*, December 23, 1911, 2.

92. C. Smith, *Market Women*; J. Walker, *History of Black Business*.

## Chapter 3. Education

I thank James D. Anderson for reading and commenting on an earlier version of this chapter for the 2015 annual meeting of the History of Education Society in St. Louis.

1. Walker's relationship with Washington has been widely recounted by her biographers and scholars. Faced with Washington's initial rejection in 1911, a con-

sequence of his complicated views on women, hairdressing, and cosmetics, Walker eventually overcame his stubbornness through a relentless campaign involving personal letter writing, networking with mutual acquaintances, and gift giving to Tuskegee. Within four years, the once evasive Washington was posing in pictures with Walker and even made beauty culture a theme of his NNBL conference in 1915 (Darlene Clark Hine, *Speak Truth to Power: Black Professional Class in United States History* [Brooklyn: Carlson, 1996]: 95–104; Bundles, *On Her Own Ground*; Lowry, *Her Dream of Dreams*; Dossett, *Bridging Race Divides*; Chapman, *Prove It on Me*).

2. Davis, *Report of the Thirteenth Annual Convention*, 154–55.

3. See Davis, "Madam C. J. Walker," 37–60; Bundles, *On Her Own Ground*; Lowry, *Her Dream of Dreams*; Dossett, *Bridging Race Divides*; Chapman, *Prove It on Me*. Gill developed a significant treatment of Walker's beauty schools and curricula (Gill, *Beauty Shop Politics*).

4. Michael Scott Bieze and Marybeth Gasman, *Booker T. Washington Rediscovered* (Baltimore, MD: Johns Hopkins University Press, 2012) 67, 93.

5. For alternative historiography on Washington, see Bieze and Gasman, *Booker T. Washington*; Robert J. Norrell, *Up from History: The Life of Booker T. Washington* (Cambridge, MA: Harvard University Press, 2009); Kenneth M. Hamilton, *Booker T. Washington in American Memory* (Urbana: University of Illinois Press, 2017).

6. For discussion of African Americans' efforts to educate themselves during and after slavery, see Heather Andrea Williams, *Self-Taught: African American Education in Slavery and Freedom* (Chapel Hill: University of North Carolina Press, 2007).

7. Booker T. Washington, *Up from Slavery: An Autobiography*, electronic edition (Chapel Hill: University of North Carolina Press, 1997), 30.

8. This system of second-class education framed the well-known debates between Booker T. Washington and W. E. B. DuBois on the form and function of education for blacks in the early twentieth century, as well as Carter G. Woodson's famous formulation of the deliberate and calculated misuse of education as a form of social control of blacks (Carter G. Woodson, *The Miseducation of the Negro* [Washington, DC: Associated Publishers, 1933]). See also James D. Anderson. *The Education of Blacks in the South, 1860–1935* (Chapel Hill: University of North Carolina Press, 1988), 2, 17.

9. For discussions of education as philanthropy, see Payton and Moody, *Understanding Philanthropy*, 23; Frances Huehls, "Teaching as Philanthropy: Catharine Beecher and the Hartford Female Seminary," in *Women and Philanthropy in Education*, ed. Andrea Walton, 39–59 (Bloomington: Indiana University Press, 2005); Tyrone McKinley Freeman, "Beyond Hegemony: Reappraising the History of Philanthropy and African-American Higher Education in the Nineteenth Century," *International Journal of Educational Advancement* 10, no. 3 (December 2010): 148–65.

10. For discussion of how black individuals connected their philanthropy with educational pursuits, see Gasman and Sedgwick, *Uplifting a People*; Carson, *Hand Up*, 13. In viewing education as philanthropy, the teaching and learning transaction becomes a philanthropic exchange through which teachers and learners create and share knowledge, skills, and information that can be life-changing when applied in pursuit of personal, professional, or social goals. The knowledge, skills, and information effectively become philanthropic gifts that promote the public good by supporting individual self-determination and enhancing civic life. For more on the community and philanthropic engagements of black women teachers, see Adam Fairclough, *A Class of Their Own: Black Teachers in the Segregated South* (Cambridge, MA: Belknap, 2007); Vanessa Siddle-Walker, *Their Highest Potential: An African American School in the Segregated South* (Chapel Hill: University of North Carolina Press, 1996); Sharon Harley, "Beyond the Classroom: The Organizational Lives of Black Female Teachers in the District of Columbia, 1890–1930," *Journal of Negro Education* 51, no. 3 (Summer 1982): 254–65. For representative discussions of black churchwomen's and clubwomen's use of education, see Giddings, *When and Where I Enter*; Neverdon-Morton, *Afro-American Women*; Charles W. Wadelington and Richard F. Knapp, *Charlotte Hawkins Brown and Palmer Memorial Institute: What One Young African American Woman Could Do* (Chapel Hill, NC: University of North Carolina Press, 1999); Joyce A. Hanson, *Mary McLeod Bethune and Black Women's Political Activism* (Urbana: University of Illinois Press, 2003).

11. Gilmore, *Gender and Jim Crow*, 14.

12. I have argued for a more nuanced view of the historical relationship between philanthropy and black education that moves "beyond hegemony" by urging for scholarly investigations of black donors and fundraisers affiliated with the nineteenth-century black colleges (Freeman, "Beyond Hegemony").

13. DuBois, *Black Reconstruction*, 57; Anderson, *Education of Blacks*.

14. James D. Anderson, "The Historical Development of Black Vocational Education," in *Work, Youth, and Schooling: Historical Perspectives on Vocationalism in American Education*, ed. Harvey Kantor and David B. Tyack, 180–222 (Stanford, CA: Stanford University Press, 1982); Booker T. Washington, "Relation of Industrial Education to National Progress," *Annals of the American Academy of Political and Social Science* 33, no. 1 (January 1909): 5.

15. Anderson, "Historical Development," 186–87; Donald Spivey, *Schooling for the New Slavery: Black Industrial Education, 1868–1915* (Westport, CT: Greenwood, 1978): 74; Roy E. Finkenbine, "'Our Little Circle': Benevolent Reformers, the Slater Fund, and the Argument for Black Industrial Education, 1882–1908," in *African Americans and Education in the South, 1865–1900*, ed. Donald G. Nieman, 70–86 (New York: Garland, 1994).

16. Anderson, "Historical Development"; Spivey, *Schooling for the New Slavery*.

17. Robert G. Scherer, *Subordination or Liberation? The Development and Conflicting Theories of Black Education in Nineteenth Century Alabama* (Tuscaloosa: University of Alabama Press, 1977): 59; Anderson, "Historical Development," 195.

18. Finkenbine, "Our Little Circle," 72, 77; William H. Watkins, *The White Architects of Black Education: Ideology and Power in America, 1865–1954* (New York: Teachers College Press, 2001): 19; 23. Such critiques were not reserved for the specific case of black industrial education in the South; scholars have emphasized that even the broader vocational education movement of the era, which began around the beginning of the twentieth century, was "aimed at socializing workers to stabilize American industrial society" and assume their place in the capitalist system of production. But the history of race in America makes the case of black industrial education a unique area of interest because of the stakes at that moment in history. The Hampton-Tuskegee idea was operationalized differently from the vocational philosophies debated by the likes of John Dewey and David Snedden in the larger national discussion on how to educate the "nonacademic" white populace. See Emery J. Hyslop-Margison, "An Assessment of the Historical Arguments in Vocational Education Reform," *Journal of Career and Technical Education* 17, no. 1 (2000): 24; Howard R. D. Gordon, *The History and Growth of Vocational Education in America* (Boston: Allyn and Bacon, 1999); Harvey Kantor and David Tyack, Introduction to *Work, Youth, and Schooling: Historical Perspectives on Vocationalism in American Education*, ed. Harvey Kantor and David Tyack (Stanford, CA: Stanford University Press, 1982). Eric Anderson and Alfred A. Moss Jr., *Dangerous Donations: Northern Philanthropy and Southern Black Education, 1902–1930* (Columbia: University of Missouri Press, 1999): 4; Anderson, *Education of Blacks*; Gasman and Sedgwick, *Uplifting a People*.

19. Hine, *Speak Truth to Power*.

20. Gill, *Beauty Shop Politics*, 25.

21. There were Lelia College locations in Pittsburgh, Harlem, and Indianapolis. It is not clear where other locations may have been or exactly when and why the Walker Beauty School moniker replaced it ("Special to the Freeman," *Indianapolis Freeman*, October 23, 1915, 1).

22. "Madam CR Walker's New Discovery," *Indianapolis Recorder*, December 30, 1916. A black woman from Utah who was trained at Poro College (Annie Malone's school) set up shop in Indianapolis and called herself "Madam CR Walker." She recruited agents and canvassers to sell cosmetics in close proximity to the Walker Company.

23. Boyd, "Great Migration."

24. Walker did not live to see the national recognition that beauty culture would receive in the middle of the twentieth century, but her early efforts in starting beauty schools and organizing national associations for beauty culture contributed to that recognition, as did the individual efforts of her education director, Marjorie Stewart Joyner, who continued the push long after Walker's death ("Learn to Grow Hair and Make Money," *Indianapolis Freeman*, September 25, 1915, 2; Gill, *Beauty Shop Politics*, 5; "Special to the Freeman," *Indianapolis Freeman*, October 23, 1915, 1).

25. Walker's approach to equality was pragmatic and reflected versatility in moving between and simultaneously embracing seemingly competing strategies.

She valued industrial education and sought to offer it to others, but she also employed her own personal tutor and filled her personal library with the kind of classical literature W. E. B. DuBois espoused and voraciously read it. She financially supported Tuskegee Institute, the Daytona Normal School, Haines Normal Institute, and other industrial education institutions, but she was a significant donor to the National Association for the Advancement of Colored People.

26. *The Madam C. J. Walker Beauty Manual: A Thorough Treatise Covering All Branches of Beauty Culture*, 1st ed. (Indianapolis, IN: Madam C. J. Walker Manufacturing Company, ca. 1928), Indianapolis Special Collections Room, Indianapolis–Marion County Public Library, Indianapolis, Indiana.

27. The name *Lewaro* was created by combining the first two letters of Walker's daughter's first, middle, and last names, *Lelia Walker Robinson*. Another industrial philanthropist, John D. Rockefeller Sr., also lived in the area.

28. *Madam C. J. Walker Beauty Manual*, 15.

29. Ibid., 16.

30. Ibid., 21.

31. Ibid., 16.

32. The Students of the Walker College of Beauty Culture, *The Madame C. J. Walker College of Beauty Culture Yearbook* (Kansas City, MO: n.p., 1946), 13–14, box 13, folder 20, Madam C. J. Walker Papers, Indiana Historical Society, Indianapolis, Indiana (hereafter cited as Walker Papers).

33. Ibid., 7.

34. Walker's known scholarship gifts also went to Hannon Industrial Institute, Palmer Memorial Institute, and Daytona Normal and Industrial Institute. Walker also made estate provisions for several black schools. For a discussion, see chapter 6 in this volume. See Executrix's Final Report, September 11, 1926, box 3, folder 7, Madam C. J. Walker Papers, Indiana Historical Society, Indianapolis, Indiana (hereafter cited as Walker Papers); Madam Walker to Normal Industrial and Agricultural College of Pensacola, Florida, March 27, 1917, box 1, folder 7, Walker Papers. Archival evidence of such course offerings was not available. For income, see Bundles, *On Her Own Ground*, 248.

35. Walker to Normal Industrial and Agricultural College of Pensacola, March 27, 1917, box 1, folder 7, Walker Papers.

36. Gill and Bundles accounted for a few additional schools that adopted the curriculum.

37. Eugene TeSelle, "The Nashville Institute and Roger Williams University: Benevolence, Paternalism, and Black Consciousness, 1867–1910," *Tennessee Historical Quarterly* 41, no. 4 (Winter 1982): 360–79.

38. Roger Williams University, *Catalogue of the Officers and Students of Roger Williams University* (Nashville, TN: Wheeler, Osbourne and Duckworth, 1885), https://archive.org/details/catalogueofofficooroge.

39. A. M. Townsend to Madam Walker, May 12, 1916, box 1, folder 4, Walker Papers.

40. Ibid.

41. Ibid.

42. Madam Walker felt that her competitor, Annie Malone of the Poro Company, repeatedly misunderstood her motives and actions. She was bothered by Malone's representation of Walker's charitable gifts as a competitive challenge to Poro (Madam Walker to David Jones, n.d., box 1, folder 18, Walker Papers).

43. Townsend to Walker, May 12, 1916.

44. Freeman B. Ransom to Mabel Marble, January 17, 1917, box 9, folder 2, Walker Papers. In the case of two institutions, Roger Williams University in Nashville, Tennessee, and Guadalupe College in Seguin, Texas, Walker provided an instructor, a Walker agent named Mabel Marble. Marble traveled between the campuses and worked to develop markets in their locales. The other schools seemed to have provided their own instructors by sending representatives to be trained at Lelia College.

45. A. M. Townsend to Madam Walker, January 26, 1917, box 1, folder 7, Walker Papers.

46. M. W. Dogan to Madam Walker, March 6, 1917, box 1, folder 7, Walker Papers; Freeman B. Ransom to M. W. Dogan, March 27, 1917, box 9, folder 2, Walker Papers.

47. J. Washington to Madam Walker, March 20, 1917, box 1, folder 7, Walker Papers; Freeman B. Ransom to J. Washington, March 24, 1917, box 9, folder 2, Walker Papers.

48. P. M. Smith to Madam Walker, August 25, 1917, box 1, folder 7, Walker Papers.

49. E. A. White to Freeman B. Ransom, October 4, 1917, box 9, folder 2, Walker Papers.

50. Bundles, *On Her Own Ground*; Hanson, *Mary McLeod Bethune*; Mary McLeod Bethune to Madam Walker, April 5, 1917, box 1, folder 7, Walker Papers.

51. Thomas Jesse Jones, *Negro Education: A Study of the Private and Higher Schools for Colored People in the United States* (Washington, DC: US Government Printing Office, 1917), 2: 179.

52. Mary McLeod Bethune to Madam Walker, April 5, 1917, box 1, folder 7, Walker Papers.

53. It is not clear how many colleges received Walker's proposal and how many accepted. Surviving correspondence is limited to the institutions covered in this chapter. In her proposal letter, Walker stated that Tuskegee Institute offered the curriculum, but there is no other supporting documentation for it in the Walker Collection or in Tuskegee's archives.

54. For profiles of black colleges and industrial institutes, including their operating budgets and sources of income, see Jones, *Negro Education*. Between 1912 and 1913, these entities made awards in the range of $200 to $600 to the smaller industrial institutes. Their larger gifts of $10,000 or more went to Tuskegee Institute.

55. Walker offered black religious denominations funding to establish the school on her behalf, but there were no takers. She also asked Booker T. Washington for

his advice on how to proceed because of his experience with placing Tuskegee students in Togo. She made provisions for the school in her will to the tune of $10,000, but her daughter, as executor of the estate, later abandoned the idea as impractical and too complicated (Bundles, *On Her Own Ground*; Executrix's Final Report, September 11, 1926, box 3, folder 7, Walker Papers).

56. Walker was not alone in this endeavor. Other black women beauty-culture entrepreneurs established schools and credentials during this time, which lasted beyond the middle of the century and trained thousands of women. The black beauty-culture industry certainly faced struggles later, but it was strong and thriving at the time of Walker's death and became recognized as a field with the rise of several professional associations. The Walker Company struggled through the Great Depression but emerged and continued well into the late 1970s under control of Walker's heirs. The family sold the company in the 1980s to a local businessman named Raymond Randolph, and it remained headquartered in Indianapolis until 2016. Sundial Brands, a black-owned corporation, purchased the company that year and reintroduced Walker products as a special line sold through Sephora. In 2017 Unilever announced its acquisition of Sundial Brands and continued the sale of the Walker product line. Richelieu Dennis, the Sundial CEO, was retained as head of the product lines. As part of the deal, Unilever and Sundial started a $100 million investment fund to support women entrepreneurs of color. The Walker schools ceased operations in the 1970s.

57. Hine, *Speak Truth to Power*.

58. For Washington's antimigration stance, see Washington, "Relation of Industrial Education to National Progress"; Scherer, *Subordination or Liberation*, 59. For Samuel Chapman Armstrong's antimigration sentiments, see James D. Anderson, "The Hampton Model of Normal School Industrial Education, 1868–1900," in *New Perspectives on Black Educational History*, ed. Vincent Franklin and James Anderson, 61–96 (Boston: G. K. Hall, 1978).

59. In 1917 Walker organized her agents into local clubs and annually convened national meetings. The clubs raised money for local black organizations fighting Jim Crow. That same year, Walker and her agents sent a resolution to President Woodrow Wilson denouncing the lynchings of the East St. Louis riots. As an ongoing project, Walker asked all her agents to be very deliberate in helping the arriving black migrants in their respective cities.

60. The most prominent example of a successful Walker beauty-school graduate and agent was Lucille Randolph, wife of the civil-rights and labor leader A. Philip Randolph. After graduating, she opened a beauty salon in Harlem, New York, that was part of the Walker system and allowed her to support her husband and family so he could engage in his civil-rights work. Her husband credited her finances with supporting his subversive newspaper and other activities. She was good friends with Madam Walker and her daughter Lelia. See Andrew Kersten, *A. Phillip Randolph: A Life in the Vanguard* (New York: Rowman and Littlefield, 2006).

61. See Hanson, *Mary McLeod Bethune*; Wadelington and Knapp, *Charlotte Hawkins Brown*.

62. See Hine, *Speak Truth to Power*.

## Chapter 4. Activism

1. First National Meeting of Madam Walker Agents, press release, August 1917, box 12, folder 1, Madam C. J. Walker Papers, Indiana Historical Society, Indianapolis, Indiana (hereafter, Walker Papers).

2. "Hair Culturists' First Convention," *New York Age*, September 6, 1917, 1.

3. See Bundles, *On Her Own Ground*, for a full account of Walker's activism surrounding black soldiers in World War I.

4. "Press Release from the First National Meeting of Madam Walker Agents," August 1917, box 12, folder 1, Walker Papers.

5. John Hope Franklin and Alfred A. Moss Jr., *From Slavery to Freedom: A History of Negro Americans* (New York: McGraw-Hill, 1988), 307; Christopher Waldrep, *African Americans Confront Lynching: Strategies of Resistance from the Civil War to the Civil Rights Era* (Lanham, MD: Rowman and Littlefield, 2009); Colin A. Palmer, *Passageways: An Interpretive History of Black America* (New York: Harcourt Brace, 1998), 2: 119–20.

6. Palmer, *Passageways*. For a discussion of the changing definitions of lynchings and the problem with data, see Waldrep, *African Americans Confront Lynching*.

7. "Walker Agent Convention Resolution," 1917, box 12, folder 1, Walker Papers.

8. For histories of black women's public culture and activism, see M. Jones, *All Bound Up Together*; Gilmore, *Gender and Jim Crow*. For working-class black women's activism, agency, and conceptions of respectability, see Hicks, *Talk with You*; Shockley, *"We, Too, Are Americans"*; Wolcott, *Remaking Respectability*; Mack, *Parlor Ladies*; Hunter, *To 'Joy My Freedom*.

9. Walker traveled to Washington, DC, as part of a delegation to meet with Wilson at the White House, but he did not meet with them (Bundles, *On Her Own Ground*, 207–9).

10. Kate Dossett (*Bridging Race Divide*) analyzed Walker's and her daughter's use of the company to promote a vision of respectable womanhood that merged commercial and community interests, and, in the process, gave them political access to circles of power within black America. Dossett paid particular attention to the Walker clubs as part of this influence and the clubs' role in engaging agents in their communities. Gill discussed the training and activism of Walker agents and presented Walker's philanthropy as a tool for legitimizing both herself, her agents, and the profession of beauty culture. Gill connected Walker's giving to racial uplift by noting that "Philanthropy was at the center of the way beauty culturists voiced their strength and dignity in the black community" (Gill, *Beauty Shop Politics*, 45).

11. For a discussion of the fund and the many ways Washington's life was commemorated, see Hamilton, *Booker T. Washington*.

12. Such associations would eventually become commonplace in black beauty culture, but Madam Walker and her rival, Annie Malone, were among the first to organize them.

13. "Notice to the Agents of the Madam C. J. Walker Manufacturing Company," box 7, folder 3, Walker Papers.

14. Freeman B. Ransom to A. C. Burnett, September 9, 1918, box 9, folder 10, Walker Papers.

15. Madam Walker to Freeman B. Ransom, April 10, 1916, box 1, folder 4, Walker Papers. When corresponding with Ransom while traveling, Walker was consistent in noting her location at the top of her letters. This letter did not have a location handwritten on it as was her usual convention, but she used Lelia College and Walker Hair Parlor stationery with New York City addresses. Therefore, the new club was most likely organized in New York.

16. Walker to Ransom, April 10, 1916.

17. In 1918 Walker suggested that there may have been as many as 125 clubs in 25 states (Madam Walker to Freeman B. Ransom, January 14, 1918, box 1, folder 8, Walker Papers). Her number seems to have been an aspiration rather than a fact. The company regularly reported 50 clubs in its yearbooks in the 1920s. See Madam C. J. Walker Manufacturing Company, *1924 Yearbook and Almanac* (Indianapolis: Madam C. J. Walker Manufacturing Company, 1924), 17, box 13, folder 24, Walker Papers.

18. Walker Company, *1924 Yearbook*, 17.

19. For promotions, see "Notice to the Agents of the Madam C. J. Walker Manufacturing Company," box 7, folder 3, Walker Papers. Although it appears that membership in the association was voluntary, at least one memo template in the Madam C. J. Walker Collection at the Indiana Historical Society indicates the company expected each agent to join and that it would not view "any agent as loyal and regular who refuses to become a member of the Union." It is not clear whether this became policy or how it may have been monitored or enforced. See "To the Agents of the Madam C. J. Walker Mfg. Company" memo, box 7, folder 3, Walker Papers.

20. Both the national conventions and local clubs continued to exist well into the 1960s.

21. Dossett (*Bridging Race Divides*, 130) has shown the similarities between the organizational structure of the Madam Walker Benevolent Association and the NACW, which included producing a newsletter, holding conventions, and offering rewards for charitable work. She also likened Walker's well-known "Hints to Agents" document, which emphasized the importance of cleanliness and personal appearance, to clubwomen propaganda. Gill (*Beauty Shop Politics*, 47) related the group to other professional associations emerging at the time for black nurses and cosmetologists. Chapman (*Prove It on Me*, 86) likened Walker's network of women to the NACW and connected Walker's beauty products to clubwomen's prevailing interest in promoting the respectability of black women and the race.

22. Madam Walker to Freeman B. Ransom, April 17, 1916, box 1, folder 4, Walker Papers.

23. See chapter 1 for Madam Walker's early life in St. Louis and initial exposure to the NACW.

24. Imani Perry, *May We Forever Stand: A History of the Black National Anthem* (Chapel Hill: University of North Carolina Press, 2018), 14.

25. Martin Summers, *Manliness and Its Discontents*.

26. Madam Walker to Freeman B. Ransom, April 17, 1916, box 1, folder 4, Walker Papers.

27. Perry, *May We Forever Stand*, 7–8, 12.

28. Jason Kaufman viewed black fraternals largely as imitations of white orders and described African American fraternal orders, in general, as unsuccessful in creating sustained economic cooperation and social cohesion because of their position within broader societal discrimination, their status as "high exit" organizations that frequently lost members to competing groups, and their fostering of divisions among African Americans rather than the requisite unity for securing civil rights. He characterized American fraternalism as "competitive voluntarism" because members frequently moved between orders as a result of aggressive recruiting practices (Jason Kaufman, *For the Common Good? American Civic Life and the Golden Age of Fraternity* [New York: Oxford University Press, 2002], 7).

29. Theda Skocpol and Jennifer Oser, "Organization despite Adversity: The Origins and Development of African American Fraternal Associations," *Social Science History*, 28, no. 3 (September 2004): 402, 418, 372. The term "super-joiners" is a reference to historian Arthur Schlesinger's pronouncement of the United States as a "nation of joiners" because voluntary associations have been prevalent throughout its history (Arthur Schlesinger, "Biography of a Nation of Joiners," *American Historical Review* 50, no. 1 [October 1944]: 1–25).

30. Theda Skocpol, Ariane Liazos, and Marshall Ganz, *What a Mighty Power We Can Be: African American Fraternal Groups and the Struggle for Racial Equality* (Princeton, NJ: Princeton University Press, 2006), 14 ("massive organizational networks" quote), 92–93, 59 ("popularly rooted" quote), 88. Skocpol and Oser, "Organization despite Adversity," 372. For a discussion of Walker's Pan-Africanism, see Dossett, *Bridging Race Divides*, 118–25. For a discussion of Walker's efforts to engage working-class women in the NACW, see Gill, *Beauty Shop Politics*, 44.

31. Skocpol et al., *What a Mighty Power*.

32. Voluntary associations' penchant for incubating civic leadership skills has caused them to be characterized as "schools of citizenship" through which average people learn how to become active citizens. For a general discussion of schools of citizenship, see Elisabeth Clemens, "The Constitution of Citizens," in *The Nonprofit Sector: A Research Handbook*, 2nd ed., ed. Walter Powell and Richard Steinberg, 207–20 (New Haven, CT: Yale University Press, 2006). For descriptions of black fraternals as schools of citizenship, see Skocpol and Oser, "Organization despite Adversity," 419; Skocpol et al., *What a Mighty Power*, 80.

33. Mark C. Carnes, *Secret Ritual and Manhood in Victorian America* (New Haven, CT: Yale University Press, 1989). Skocpol et al., *What a Mighty Power*, 4.

34. Bayliss Camp and Orit Kent, "'What a Mighty Power We Can Be': Individual and Collective Identity in African American and White Fraternal Initiation Rituals," *Social Science History* 28, no. 3 (2004), 448.

35. Ibid., 448–49. The Calanthes deviated from Camp and Kent's generalization: read on.

36. "Order of Calanthe Withdrawal Card" box 2, folder 15, Walker Papers. The Calanthes had three degrees, Fidelity, Harmony, and Love (Charity). Marilyn T. Peebles, *The Alabama Knights of Pythias of North America, South America, Europe, Asia, Africa, and Australia: A Brief History* (New York: University Press of America, 2012), 12. See also W. Fitzhugh Brundage, *The Southern Past: A Clash of Race and Memory* (Cambridge, MA: Belknap, 2005), 65–73. Brundage argued that African American public processions and festivals in the late nineteenth and early twentieth centuries were forms of protest to commandeer prominent public assembly spaces normally used by whites, test the "boundaries of racial etiquette," and "symbolize the ideal of black masculine leadership" in the face of Jim Crow oppression. The military-style parades of black fraternals in the early 1900s, like those of the Colored Knights of Pythias, were reactions to the legal abolition of black militia companies in the South. The response of southern whites to these public events ranged from withdrawal to their homes to "overt intimidation" and "open violence." The two largest black fraternal groups were the Prince Hall Masons and the Grand United Order of Odd Fellows (Skocpol et al., *What a Mighty Power*, 34–38; Peebles, *Alabama Knights of Pythias*, 11).

37. Indiana Historical Society, Ransom Family Papers, 1912–2001 (Indianapolis: Indiana Historical Society, 2015), https://indianahistory.org/wp-content/uploads/ransom-family-papers.pdf.

38. Order of Calanthe, *Ritualistic Ceremonies of the Order of Calanthe* (Chicago: Fraternal Press, 1914), 4–5. Camp and Kent, "What a Mighty Power," 471.

39. J. Johnson, *Funding Feminism*.

40. Catherine Bell, *Ritual: Perspectives and Dimensions* (New York: Oxford University Press, 1997); Barry Stephenson, *Ritual: A Short Introduction* (New York: Oxford University Press, 2015), 38, 41.

41. *Ritual for the Local Bodies of the National Beauty Culturists' and Benevolent Association of Madam C. J. Walker Agents, Inc.* (ca. 1920), Beinecke Rare Books and Manuscript Library, Yale University, Call # JWJ Zan W1505+ N920R (hereafter cited as *Ritual*); *By-laws for the Local Bodies of the National Beauty Culturists' and Benevolent Association of Madam C. J. Walker Agents, Inc.* (1927), Beinecke Rare Books and Manuscript Library, Yale University, Call # JWJ Zan W1505 927be (hereafter cited as *By-laws*); Calanthe, *Ritualistic Ceremonies*.

42. The official regalia and insignia was the National Convention Badge, which came in either yellow or purple fabric with gold frills hanging at the bottom and a cameo of Madam Walker wrapped in a gold color casing and chained to a placard with the word *member* printed on it.

43. *Ritual*, 1.

44. Ibid. (*Julius Caesar*, Act IV, Scene iii, ll. 217–18).

45. Ibid.

46. Ibid., 2.

47. Calanthe, *Ritualistic Ceremonies*, 9–10.

48. Walker Company, *1924 Yearbook*, 20.

49. *Ritual*, 3.

50. Margaret Thompson to Freeman B. Ransom August 9, 1917, box 9, folder 2, Walker Papers.

51. Margaret Thompson to Freeman B. Ransom, September 25, 1917, box 9, folder 2, Walker Papers; Margaret Thompson to Freeman B. Ransom, October 2, 1917, box 9, folder 2, Walker Papers.

52. Thompson to Ransom, September 25, 1917.

53. Thompson to Ransom, October 2, 1917.

54. White, *Too Heavy a Load*, 17.

55. *Ritual*, 3.

56. Ibid.

57. Ibid., 4.

58. *By-laws*, 3–4.

59. Ibid., 5.

60. Ibid., 6.

61. *Ritual*, 4–5; the Court of Calanthe's ritual ends with the Worthy Inspectrix, the organizational leader, declaring "Alpha and Omega" (Order of Calanthe, *Ritualistic Ceremonies*, 59).

62. *Ritual*, 5.

63. Ibid., 3.

64. *By-laws*, 29.

65. Ibid., 23.

66. The *By-laws* (p. 27) guaranteed that sick benefits would not be less than $1 per week but did not prescribe an upper limit on payment.

67. Ibid., 36, 38; Luther E. Hall III, *Rochelle Court #14 Order of Calanthe Record, 1906–1933* (Indianapolis: Indiana Historical Society, 2011), 3.

68. Carnes, *Secret Ritual and Manhood*; Skocpol et al., *What a Mighty Power*.

69. *Walker News* 2, no. 2 (December 1928), Walker Papers; *Walker News* 2, no. 1 (November 1928), Walker Papers; *Walker News* 1, no. 5 (March 1928), Walker Papers; *Walker News* 1, no. 6 (April 1928), Walker Papers; Walker Company, *1924 Yearbook*, 21, Walker Papers; Madam Walker to Freeman B. Ransom, January 14, 1918, box 1, folder 8, Walker Papers.

70. Joan Marie Johnson, "'Ye Gave Them a Stone': African American Women's Clubs, the Frederick Douglass Home, and the Black Mammy Monument," *Journal of Women's History* 17, no. 1 (Spring 2005): 62–86.

71. J. Johnson, "Ye Gave Them a Stone," 65; Cash, *African American Women*; E. Davis, *Lifting As They Climb*.

72. J. Johnson, "Ye Gave Them a Stone."

73. *Nashville Globe*, July 19, 1918, 2.

74. Ibid.

75. NAACP, *Thirty Years of Lynching in the United States, 1889–1918* (New York: National Association of Colored People, 1919); "Mme. Walker Contributes $5,000 to Anti-lynching Fund," *Dallas Express*, May 17, 1919, 1. For a discussion of Walker's broader involvement with the NAACP's conference, see Bundles, *On Her Own Ground*, 270–72. Although the NAACP's lobbying efforts made strides at different times, such federal legislation was never fully passed into law. For a discussion of the NAACP's efforts to pass federal antilynching laws starting in 1919 and continuing for several decades, see Waldrep, *African Americans Confront Lynching*.

76. Kaufman, *For the Common Good*, 7.

## Chapter 5. Material Resources

Portions of this chapter are from Tyrone McKinley Freeman, "The Big-Hearted Race Loving Woman: Madam C. J. Walker's Philanthropy While Living in Indianapolis, Indiana, 1911–1914," in *Hoosier Philanthropy: Understanding the Past, Planning the Future*, ed. Greg Witkowski (Bloomington: Indiana University Press, forthcoming). Reprinted by permission.

1. For information about Croker, see Ferguson, "African American Clubwomen," 80; Ella Croker to Freeman B. Ransom, November 19, 1914, box 9, folder 1, Madam C. J. Walker Papers, Indiana Historical Society, Indianapolis, Indiana (hereafter, Walker Papers); Matt Arant, "Historic School Torn Down at IUPUI," *NUVO*, January 18, 2006, https://www.nuvo.net/news/news/remembering-history/article_4adee7c0-fabf-5f90-85f9-fecc8ba1362a.html; Freeman B. Ransom to Ella Croker, November 19, 1914, box 9, folder 1, Walker Papers.

2. Ransom to Croker, November 19, 1914. See also "America's Foremost Colored Woman," *Indianapolis Freeman*, December 28, 1912, 16; "The Negro Woman in Business," *Indianapolis Freeman*, September 20, 1913, 1; "The Life Work of Mme. C. J. Walker," *Indianapolis Freeman*, December 26, 1914, 1; Robert Lee Brokenburr, "A Negro Woman's Success," *Southern Workman* 47 (December 1918): 70–74.

3. Ransom to Croker, November 19, 1914. For income, see Bundles, *On Her Own Ground*, 107, 122.

4. See chapter 2 for a discussion of Ransom's professional and personal relationships with Walker.

5. Karen Sneddon has noted that the counsel provided by attorneys while advising their clients enables them to produce legal documentation that formally meets the language requirements of the law and substantively presents their clients' voices (Karen Sneddon, "The Will as Personal Narrative," *Elder Law Journal* 20 [2013]: 356–410).

6. Edyth L. Ross, ed., *Black Heritage in Social Welfare, 1860–1930* (Metuchen, NJ: Scarecrow, 1978); Joanne Martin and Elmer Martin, *The Helping Tradition in the Black Family and Community* (Silver Spring, MD: National Association of Social Workers, 1985). The Star Christmas Fund was established by the *Indianapolis Star* newspaper ("Hearts Touched by Call for Aid," *Indianapolis Star*, March 29, 1913, 9).

7. "Madam Walker Leaves Scene of Her Labor and Success," *Indianapolis Freeman*, February 12, 1916.

8. "State University" referred to the State Colored Baptist University/State University in Louisville, Kentucky, which operated from 1881 to 1918. As a black higher-education institution, it offered professional degrees in theology, law, and medicine and was supported by black Baptists in Kentucky. The state reference in its title reflected its origins in legislation that created Kentucky's separate, but unfunded, public system of schools for blacks. See "Towards Louisville Municipal College," last modified 2005, https://louisville.edu/lmc/history1.html.

9. "Life Work of Mme. C. J. Walker."

10. "Walker Leaves Scene."

11. Wadelington and Knapp, *Charlotte Hawkins Brown*, 80. Wadelington and Knapp reported that Charlotte Hawkins Brown, the founder of Palmer Memorial Institute, raised $5,600 from donors between 1914 and 1915, which included less than $100 each from "African Americans and southern whites" as aggregate groups and gifts of $150 to $500 from white individuals and county school boards.

12. *Indianapolis Freeman*, "City and Vicinity," January 2, 1915, 8.

13. I am indebted to Paul Mullins for the founding information about Alpha Home; *Indianapolis News*, "Mrs. Merritt's Generous Gift," June 29, 1886. For discussions of the vulnerability of black orphans and the elderly, see Carlton-LaNey, "Old Folks' Homes"; "Local," *Indianapolis Freeman*, January 1, 1915, 8. For a description of the event, see "For Sweet Charity," *Indianapolis Freeman*, December 25, 1915, 8; "MMe. C. J. Walker's Travelogue a Success," *Indianapolis Freeman*, January 22, 1916, 4; "Walker Leaves Scene."

14. Ransom's use of this phrasing may have been an attempt to preempt a solicitation from Croker because the volume of requests for assistance to Walker was steadily increasing. Ransom and Walker referred to these requests as begging letters. Ransom would eventually develop an internal office procedure for processing such requests and keeping them away from Walker because she felt stressed by them and had difficulty rejecting them.

15. Ransom to Croker, November 19, 1914.

16. Ibid.

17. Ransom may have taken license in describing this gift because other correspondence shows that the pardon had not yet been granted in 1914, the time of his letter. Rather, the pardon was granted sometime between August 1915 and January 1916, as the Mississippi governor's term was ending and clemency was being granted to the young man. See Freeman B. Ransom to Norman Allen, December 6, 1911, box 9, folder 1, Walker Papers.

18. "Freeman B. Ransom," *Indianapolis Freeman*, December 25, 1915.

19. A $15 travel expense was mentioned shortly before the pardon was granted. But that expense did not encompass the entire effort (Norman Allen to Freeman B. Ransom, August 31, 1915, box 9, folder 1, Walker Papers).

20. For discussions of Western models of philanthropy, see Payton and Moody, *Understanding Philanthropy*; Cheryl Hall Russell and Robert H. Kasberg, *African*

*American Traditions of Giving and Serving: A Midwest Perspective* (Indianapolis: Indiana University Center on Philanthropy, 1997), 11–22; A. L. Jones, "Philanthropy," 153–78. For a discussion of double consciousness, see W. E. B. DuBois, *The Souls of Black Folk* (Chicago: A. C. McClurg, 1903), 3. For a discussion of ternary consciousness, see White, *Too Heavy a Load*).

21. For discussions of fictive kin in the African American community, see Carol B. Stack, *All Our Kin: Strategies for Survival in a Black Community* (New York: Harper and Row, 1975), 58–61; Herbert G. Gutman, *The Black Family in Slavery and Freedom, 1750–1925* (New York: Pantheon, 1976), 20; Martin and Martin, *Helping Tradition*, 5; Andrew Billingsley, *Climbing Jacob's Ladder: The Enduring Legacy of African-American Families* (New York: Simon and Schuster, 1992), 31.

22. Carson, *Hand Up*, 2.

23. Violet Reynolds, "The Story of a Remarkable Woman," p. 10, box 12, folder 15, Walker Papers.

24. Ibid.

25. Paul Arnsberger et al., "A History of the Tax-Exempt Sector: An SOI Perspective," in *The Nature of the Nonprofit Sector*, 2nd ed., ed. J. Steven Ott and Lisa A. Dicke (Boulder, CO: Westview, 2012), 126–27. The Revenue Act of 1917 created an individual tax deduction for charitable gifts, and corporations were not able to claim charitable deductions until the Revenue Act of 1936.

26. Ransom to Croker, November 19, 1914.

27. The term is currently viewed as derogatory.

28. See chapter 2 for a discussion of the Walker Company as a vehicle for providing the gift of opportunity and employment.

29. Susan M. Yohn, "Crippled Capitalists: The Inscription of Economic Dependence and the Challenge of Female Entrepreneurship in Nineteenth-Century America," *Feminist Economics* 12, nos. 1–2 (January–April 2006): 91.

30. "Walker Leaves Scene."

31. Ransom to Croker, November 19, 1914. See chapter 3 for a discussion of Walker's role in education and her dream of a school in South Africa.

32. Davis, *Report of the Thirteenth Annual Convention*, 155.

33. "Pondoland," *South African History Online*, accessed February 15, 2020, https://www.sahistory.org.za/place/pondoland.

34. Richard R. Wright Jr., *Centennial Encyclopaedia of the African Methodist Episcopal Church 1816–1916* (Philadelphia: AME Church, 1916), 287, 288.

35. J. Campbell, *Songs of Zion*, 199.

36. Bundles, *On Her Own Ground*, 250. See chapter 1 for a review of the AME Church's publications, educational activities, and international missions work. For more information on the handling of Walker's testamentary provisions for establishing the school in Africa, see chapter 6.

37. For a discussion of Madam Walker's interest in Pan-Africanism, see Dossett, *Bridging Race Divides*, 118–34.

38. Walker's tour of Haiti occurred prior to the US occupation of the country in 1915. For coverage of Walker's international trip, see "Short Flights," *Indianapolis*

*Freeman*, January 3, 1914, 2; "Madam C. J. Walker of Indianapolis Seeing the Islands of the Southern Seas," *Indianapolis Freeman*, January 17, 1914.

39. Establishing a school in Africa also represented an opportunity for Walker to open new markets for her products on the continent. Although Walker did not publicly discuss the possibility, her school, if built, would have undoubtedly offered her training curriculum, which would have facilitated development of markets by preparing a workforce, much as her beauty schools were doing in the United States.

40. For a discussion of scientific philanthropy, see Bremner, *American Philanthropy*, 85–99; Sealander, *Private Wealth and Public Life*.

41. Rouse, *Lugenia Burns Hope*; Neverdon-Morton, *Afro-American Women*, 145–63.

42. Iris Carlton-LaNey, "The Career of Birdye Henrietta Haynes, a Pioneer Settlement House Worker," *Social Science Review* 68, no. 2 (June 1994): 254–73; Reed, *Not Alms but Opportunity*.

43. See Carlton-LaNey, "Old Folks' Homes." In their research, Hall-Russell and Kasberg found that "The concept of the 'deserving poor' does not exist in the African-American community as a whole" (Hall-Russell and Kasberg, *African American Traditions of Giving*, 4). The statement may have evolved to be true for African Americans in the twentieth century, but more research is necessary to determine how African Americans have historically viewed worthiness.

44. The influence and role of scientific philanthropy in black-run organizations is beyond the scope of this book. In fact, it represents an area in need of research. To be sure, the class conflict inherent among African Americans during this time reflected the range of biases from the larger Victorian milieu and moral code that informed much of scientific philanthropy. These complexities and nuances, and their specific influences on black philanthropy, also need further attention.

45. Harlan and Smock, *Booker T. Washington Papers*, 13: 14; "The Life Work of Mme. C. J. Walker," *Denver Star*, August 7, 1915, 1.

46. "Mme. C. J. Walker Who Subscribed $1,000 to the Y.M.C.A. Building Fund," *Indianapolis Freeman*, October 28, 1911, 7.

47. Nina Mjagkij, *Light in the Darkness: African Americans and the YMCA, 1852–1946* (Lexington: University Press of Kentucky, 1994), 84, 129. "Colored Subscribers to the Building Fund of the Colored Men's Branch Y.M.C.A.," *Indianapolis Freeman*, May 10, 1913, 8.

48. "Mme. C. J. Walker Who Subscribed $1,000."

49. Madam Walker to Nettie Ransom, June 22, 1918, box 1, folder 11, Walker Papers; Dorothy Guinn to Madam Walker, March 28, 1918, box 1, folder 9, Walker Papers.

50. Walker had a philanthropic interest in the arts. Ransom did not include gifts to the arts in his letter to Croker because such gifts seemed to have started shortly after he had written the letter. According to newspaper reports, she patronized at least three black artists: John Wesley Hardrick (painter), William Edouard Scott (painter), and Frances Spencer (harpist). Spencer turned out to be

an impostor who took advantage of Walker's generosity. See "Another Chapter of the Mme. Walker-Frances Spencer Incident," *Indianapolis Freeman*, August 28, 1915. Walker also served on the board of the Music Settlement House, an arts organization in Harlem, New York. There is insufficient evidence in the Walker archives to substantiate claims for the overall role of the arts in Walker's giving. Further investigation is necessary. See, for example, "Life Work of Mme. C. J. Walker," *Indianapolis Freeman*; "Mme. C. J. Walker Thanks Public for Support," *Indianapolis Freeman*, February 27, 1915.

51. Henry Willingham, *Annual Report of the Superintendent of Education*, 316, 320. Hannon eventually became a two-year junior college, but it closed in 1984.

52. Wadelington and Knapp, *Charlotte Hawkins Brown*, 133.

53. Tuskegee Institute, *Annual Report of the President*, 1915, 5, 8, 13, 165. In a letter to Madam Walker, Booker T. Washington indicated that students did not pay tuition and that her $50 donations would cover students' other expenses. Nevertheless, the annual report lists $50 as covering tuition.

54. "America's Foremost Colored Woman"; "Life Work of Mme. C. J. Walker," *Indianapolis Freeman*.

55. Indiana Historical Society, "Flanner House Records, CA 1906–1979" (Indianapolis: Indiana Historical Society, 2006), https://indianahistory.org/wp-content/uploads/flanner-house-records.pdf.

56. To this day, Madam Walker is considered by many people in Indiana to have been a "Hoosier," the colloquial term for natives of the state of Indiana. She was posthumously honored with many distinctions, including placement of a sign representing her likeness on the Cultural Trail in downtown Indianapolis.

57. Resolution from Indianapolis YMCA, 1915, box 2, folder 7, Walker Papers.

58. "Walker Leaves Scene."

59. Walker ultimately sued the theater for the discriminatory treatment and never quite felt the same about Indianapolis afterward.

60. Madam Walker to Freeman B. Ransom, October 30, 1916, box 1, folder 5, Walker Papers.

61. For Walker's relationship with Ransom's family, see chapter 2. The Wards befriended Walker when they hosted her first visit to Indianapolis. Dr. Joseph Ward became her physician and cared for her on her deathbed. The Brokenburrs attended church with Walker and were dear to her as well. For discussion of these friendships, see Bundles, *On Her Own Ground*, 162, 223.

62. Indianapolis is the primary site of Walker's historic legacy because the Madam C. J. Walker Legacy Center in the city occupies the building that housed her company from 1927 until its sale in the 1980s. It was built on land purchased by Walker that was adjacent to her home and first factory. Today, the center operates a range of cultural, artistic, and educational programming for the local community. The neighborhood in which the center sits is called Ransom Place in honor of Walker's friend and trusted adviser, who also lived there.

63. See chapter 1 for a review of Walker's experiences in St. Louis and details on the roles of these organizations in her life.

64. Madam C. J. Walker Manufacturing Company *Yearbook and Almanac 1929*, 22, Walker Papers.

65. Jessie B. Robinson to Madam Walker, December 9, 1912, box 1, folder 1, Walker Papers.

66. Ibid.

67. "America's Foremost Colored Woman."

68. Ruth Crocker, "'Nothing More for Men's Colleges': The Educational Philanthropy of Mrs. Russell Sage," in *Women and Philanthropy in Education*, ed. Andrea Walton, 257–80 (Bloomington: Indiana University Press, 2005).

69. William H. Davis, ed., *Report of the Fourteenth Annual Convention of the National Negro Business League* (Washington, DC: National Negro Business League, 1913), 212.

## Chapter 6. Legacy

1. "Walker 'Pilgrims' Ready to March," *Pittsburgh Courier*, April 19, 1952, 5; "Top Beauticians Qualifying for March," *Pittsburgh Courier*, March 8, 1952, 3; "Pilgrimage to Madam Walker's Grave to Be Colorful," *Pittsburgh Courier*, March 8, 1952, 3; "Decks Clear for Gala 'Pilgrimage Parade to Mme. C. J. Walker Grave," *Pittsburgh Courier*, April 5, 1952, 3; Board of Directors Minutes, March 28, 1952, box 1, folder 7, Madam C. J. Walker Papers Addition, Indiana Historical Society, Indianapolis, Indiana (hereafter, Walker Papers Addition); Board of Directors Minutes, April 23, 1952, box 1, folder 2, Walker Papers Addition.

2. "Pilgrimage to Madame Walker Grave Finds Beauticians Rallying in Support," *Pittsburgh Courier*, December 8, 1951, 20; "Beauticians to Make Pilgrimage to Grave of Mme. C. J. Walker," *Pittsburgh Courier*, November 24, 1951, 2; "Pilgrimage Plans Are Speeded Up by Beauticians," *Pittsburgh Courier*, February 16, 1952, 2.

3. National Beauty Culturists League and Mme. C. J. Walker Mfg. Company, "Madame C. J. Walker Memorial Pilgrimage and Convention New York City April 20–22, 1952," MSJ 92/09, box 5, folder 18, Marjorie Stewart Joyner Papers, Vivian G. Harsh Collection, Chicago Public Library, Chicago, Illinois (hereafter, MSJ). Sarah Spencer Washington founded the Apex News and Hair Company in Atlantic City, NJ, after Madam Walker's death. For discussion, see Conclusion in this volume.

4. "Top Beauticians Qualifying for March," *Pittsburgh Courier*, March 8, 1952, 3.

5. "Historic Symbol," *Pittsburgh Courier*, January 19, 1952, 20.

6. "Leaders in Pilgrimage to Mme. Walker's Grave," *Pittsburgh Courier*, May 3, 1952, 5; National Beauty Culturists League and Mme. C. J. Walker Mfg. Company, "Madame C. J. Walker Memorial Pilgrimage and Convention New York City April 20–22, 1952," MSJ 92/09, box 5, folder 18, MSJ.

7. Last Will and Testament of Sarah Walker, May 28, 1917, box 3, folder 4, Madam C. J. Walker Papers, Indiana Historical Society, Indianapolis, Indiana (hereafter, Walker Papers).

8. Codicil to Sarah Breedlove's Last Will and Testament, April 29, 1919, box 3, folder 4, Walker Papers.

9. Janet Finch, Lynn Hayes, Jennifer Mason, Judith Masson, and Lorraine Wallis, *Wills, Inheritance, and Families* (Oxford, UK: Clarendon, 1996); Ray D. Madoff, *Immortality and the Law: The Rising Power of the American Dead* (New Haven, CT: Yale University Press, 2010); Lawrence M. Friedman, *Dead Hands: A Social History of Wills, Trusts, and Inheritance Law* (Stanford, CA: Stanford Law Books, 2009); Carole Shammas, Marylynn Salmon, and Michel Dahlin, *Inheritance in America from Colonial Times to the Present* (New Brunswick, NJ: Rutgers University Press, 1987); Marvin B. Sussman, Judith N. Cates, and David T. Smith, *The Family and Inheritance* (New York: Russell Sage Foundation, 1970); Lawrence M. Friedman, "Patterns of Testation in the 19th Century: A Study of Essex County (New Jersey) Wills," *American Journal of Legal History* 8, no. 1 (January 1964): 34–53; Sandra Cavallo, *Charity and Power in Early Modern Italy: Benefactors and Their Motives in Turin, 1541–1789* (New York: Cambridge University Press, 1995).

10. Daphna Hacker, "The Gendered Dimensions of Inheritance: Empirical Food for Legal Thought," *Journal of Empirical Legal Studies* 7, no. 2 (June 2010): 322–54; Maria Isabel Martinez Mira, "Female Testaments as Social Discourse: A Textual Analysis under Critical Discourse Analysis Approach," *Mediterranean Journal of Social Sciences* 2, no. 2 (May 2011): 101–10; Giovanna Benadusi, "Investing the Riches of the Poor: Servant Women and Their Last Wills," *American Historical Review* 109, no. 3 (June 2004): 805–26. Benadusi presented the example of how domestic servant women in seventeenth-century Italy used their wills to assert their identities despite their grave poverty. Benadusi also demonstrated how female employers used gift provisions for staff in their wills not only to express gratitude for loyal service, but also to reinforce their own dominant social status, and in the process—perhaps unintentionally—they reified existing social inequities.

11. L. M. Friedman, "Patterns of Testation," 36.

12. Ibid., 34–53; Lawrence M. Friedman, Christopher Walker, and Ben Hernandez-Stern, "The Inheritance Process in San Bernardino County, California, 1964: A Research Note," *Houston Law Review* 43, no. 5 (January 2007): 1445–74. In these studies of randomly selected wills, one on New Jersey testators from the late nineteenth and very early twentieth century and another on California testators from the midtwentieth century, charitable giving provisions were found to be extremely uncommon.

13. Sneddon, "Will as Personal Narrative." Sneddon has developed a methodology of analyzing wills that is useful for understanding Walker's testamentary documents. She viewed the will as "the most important and personal legal document an individual ever executes" (359). She argued that despite being drafted by

an attorney, the will contains the voice of the testator as represented through a persona crafted to merge the testator's wishes with the required legalisms. She has conceptualized the will as a legal document, personal story, and lasting legacy that "is the last words spoken by the testator" (740) and further noted that attention to voice in wills began in the 1960s, but she deployed her method to wills from various historical periods from colonial to present (Sneddon, "Speaking for the Dead: Voice in Last Wills and Testaments," *St. Johns Law Review* 85, no. 2 [2011]: 683–754).

14. Karen Sneddon, "Memento Mori: Death and Wills," *Wyoming Law Review* 14, no. 1 (2014): 235.

15. Ibid., 212, 240, 252.

16. Sneddon, "Speaking for the Dead," 740; Karen Sneddon, "In the Name of God, Amen: Language in Last Wills and Testaments," *Quinnipiac Law Review* 29, no. 3 (2011): 687.

17. Sneddon, "In the Name of God," 699.

18. Last Will and Testament of Sarah Walker.

19. Even though Walker had moved from Indianapolis to New York in 1916, she maintained Indianapolis as her legal residence.

20. Sneddon, "Speaking for the Dead," 740–41.

21. Last Will and Testament of Sarah Walker. The provision for Kelly also included $500 for George O. Barnes Jr., Walker's self-described "little friend," a term she used for children. The nature of her relationship with Barnes is unclear.

22. *Appeal* (St. Paul, MN), June 21, 1919, "Walker Will," http://chronicling america.loc.gov/lccn/sn83016810/1919–06–21/ed-1/seq-2/; *Indianapolis Recorder*, "Local Woman, age 107, Passes in Home Here," November 1, 1952, 1. I am indebted to Paul Mullins for information about Rawlins.

23. Last Will and Testament of Sarah Walker.

24. See chapter 3 for discussion of Walker's goal of building a school in South Africa modeled after Booker T. Washington's Tuskegee.

25. Last Will and Testament of Sarah Walker.

26. See chapter 2 for discussion about Walker and Ransom's conflict over the ILDP and NAACP.

27. *Appeal*, "Walker Will."

28. The women were Ella Scott Dunovant, Viola Evans, and Annie Caldwell. The nature of their relations to Walker is unclear.

29. Last Will and Testament of Sarah Walker.

30. According to a newspaper account, Walker considered adopting the African male student she supported through a scholarship at Tuskegee Institute ("America's Foremost Colored Woman," *Indianapolis Freeman*, December 28, 1912, 16).

31. Madoff, *Immortality and the Law*, 72.

32. Last Will and Testament of Sarah Walker.

33. See chapter 5.

34. Madam Walker to Freeman B. Ransom, January 10, 1919, box 1, folder 15, Walker Papers.

35. Ibid.

36. Freeman B. Ransom to Madam Walker, January 26, 1919, box 1, folder 15, Walker Papers.

37. Walker to Ransom, January 10, 1919.

38. Ibid.; Tuskegee Institute, *Annual Report*, 5, 8, 13, 165.

39. Walker to Ransom, January 10, 1919.

40. Freeman B. Ransom to Madam Walker, January 18, 1919, box 1, folder 15, Walker Papers.

41. Sarah Wilson was given $1,000, but her relationship to Walker is unclear.

42. Ira E. Harrison, "Hubert B. Ross, the Anthropologist Who Was," in *African-American Pioneers in Anthropology*, ed. Ira E. Harrison and Faye V. Harrison, 265–73 (Urbana: University of Illinois Press, 1999).

43. It is interesting to note that, in many cases, Walker's bequests to men were significantly larger than those to women. The meaning and implications of this need more attention.

44. Affidavit of Death and Proof of Will, June 12, 1919, box 3, folder 4, Walker Papers.

45. Appraiser's Notice, September 11, 1919, box 3, folder 5, Walker Papers.

46. Opening of Probate, September 11, 1919, box 3, folder 5, Walker Papers; Report of Appraiser, October 1919, box 3, folder 6, and box 3, folder 7, Walker Papers.

47. Executrix's Final Report, September 11, 1926, box 3, folder 7, Walker Papers.

48. Ibid.; entries marked with an asterisk reflect posttax gift amounts.

49. Memorandum on Construction of Walker Will, n.d., box 3, folder 10, Walker Papers.

50. For information about Lelia and the Walker Company after Madam Walker's death, see Bundles, *On Her Own Ground*, 278–92.

51. Gertrude Johnson to Freeman B. Ransom, May 31, 1919, box 2, folder 25, Walker Papers; Gina Shelly to Lelia Walker Robinson, May 29, 1919, box 2, folder 28, Walker Papers; W. F. Cozart to Lelia Walker Robinson, May 26, 1919, box 2, folder 23, Walker Papers.

52. Lillie P. Barnes to Lelia Walker Robinson, May 26, 1919, box 2, folder 22, Walker Papers.

53. Mrs. J. C. Frazier to Lelia Walker Robinson, May 27, 1919, box 2, folder 24, Walker Papers.

54. The Byron brothers to Lelia Walker Robinson, May 27, 1919, box 2, folder 22, Walker Papers.

55. W. P. Curtis to Lelia Walker Robinson, May 25, 1919, box 2, folder 23, Walker Papers.

56. R. Black to Lelia Walker Robinson, May 29, 1919, box 2, folder 22, Walker Papers.

57. George Harris to Lelia Walker Robinson, June 6, 1919, box 2, folder 24, Walker Papers.

58. Florence Garnette to Lelia Walker Robinson, n.d., box 2, folder 24, Walker Papers.

59. R. W. Thompson to Freeman B. Ransom, May 26, 1919, box 2, folder 28, Walker Papers.

60. J. C. Napier to Freeman B. Ransom, May 28, 1919, box 2, folder 27, Walker Papers.

61. Robert Wayne Croft, *A Zora Neale Hurston Companion* (Westport, CT: Greenwood, 2002), 53. The novel was never published and its manuscript was reportedly lost in a fire.

62. *Rockland/Westchester Journal News*, "Billionaire Richelieu Dennis of SheaMoisture and Essence Shares Vision for Irvington Mansion," December 19, 2018 (updated December 20), https://www.lohud.com/story/news/local/westchester/irvington/2018/12/19/african-american-billionaire-richelieu-dennis-buys-irvington-mansion/2304770002/.

63. "Leaders in Pilgrimage to Mme. Walker's Grave," *Pittsburgh Courier*, May 3, 1952, 5.

## Conclusion

Excerpts appear from "The Collectivist Roots of Madam C. J. Walker's Philanthropy" by Tyrone McKinley Freeman on *Black Perspectives* (the blog of the African American Intellectual History Society), May 20, 2019, https://www.aaihs.org/the-collectivist-roots-of-madam-c-j-walkers-philanthropy/. Reprinted by permission of *Black Perspectives*.

1. "The Life Work of Mme. C. J. Walker," *Denver Star*, August 7, 1915, 1.

2. The Giving Pledge is a group of billionaires founded in 2010 who agreed to give away 50 percent of their wealth to charitable purposes. The group was spearheaded by Bill and Melinda Gates and Warren Buffet. For more information, see Kelly LeRoux and Mary K. Feeney, *Nonprofit Organizations and Civil Society in the United States* (New York: Routledge, 2015), 170–71.

3. See Tyrone McKinley Freeman, "400 Years of Black Giving: From the Days of Slavery to the 2019 Morehouse Graduation," The Conversation (blog), August 22, 2019, https://theconversation.com/400-years-of-black-giving-from-the-days-of-slavery-to-the-2019-morehouse-graduation-121402.

4. "The Life Work of Mme. C. J. Walker," *Indianapolis Freeman*, December 26, 1914, 1.

5. Deuteronomy 10:18; Isaiah 1:17; Psalms 68:5; Psalms 82:3; Galatians 2:10; 1 Timothy 5:3; James 1:27.

6. "The Life Work of Mme. C. J. Walker," *Denver Star*, August 7, 1915, 1.

7. Adrienne Jones dubbed the period from the immediate post-Reconstruction period to the end of World War I "the era of organization" in African American

philanthropic history because existing black organizations, such as churches and fraternal orders, were expanding in membership and reach, while new organizations were emerging, particularly at the national level, for example, the NACW and the NAACP. See A. L. Jones, "Philanthropy," 162–70.

8. "Leaders in Pilgrimage to Mme. Walker's Grave," *Pittsburgh Courier*, May 3, 1952, 5.

9. For the debate over the "long civil rights movement," see Jacquelyn Hall Dowd, "The Long Civil Rights Movement and the Political Use of the Past," *Journal of American History* 91, no. 4 (March 2005): 1233–63; Sundiata Keita Cha-Jua and Clarence Lang, "The 'Long Movement' as Vampire: Temporal and Spatial Fallacies in Recent Black Freedom Studies," *Journal of African American History* 91, no. 2 (2007): 265–88; Angela Jones, *African American Civil Rights: Early Activism and the Niagara Movement* (Denver, CO: Praeger, 2011); Shawn Leigh Alexander, *An Army of Lions: The Civil Rights Struggle before the NAACP* (Philadelphia: University of Pennsylvania Press, 2013). For the role of philanthropic foundations in funding the civil-rights movement, see Claude A. Clegg III, "Philanthropy, Civil Rights Movement, and the Politics of Racial Reform," in *Charity, Philanthropy, and Civility in American History*, ed. Lawrence J. Friedman and Mark D. McGarvie, 341–61 (New York: Cambridge University Press, 2003); Zunz, *Philanthropy in America*.

10. A. L. Jones, "Philanthropy," 153, 159; Jayne R. Bielke, "Nineteenth-Century Traditions of Benevolence and Education: Toward a Conceptual Framework of Black Philanthropy," in *Uplifting a People: African American Philanthropy and Education*, ed. Marybeth Gasman and Kathrine Sedgwick (New York: Peter Lang, 2005), 10.

11. Tyrone McKinley Freeman, "7 Ways to Read around the History of Philanthropy's Diversity Problem This Black History Month," Histphil (blog), February 25, 2019, https://histphil.org/2019/02/25/7-ways-to-read-around-the-history-of -philanthropys-diversity-problem-this-black-history-month/.

12. W. E. B. DuBois, *Efforts for Social Betterment among Negro Americans* (Atlanta: Atlanta University Press, 1909), 37.

13. Carlton-LaNey and Alexander, "Early African American Social Welfare Pioneers," 77.

14. Ibid., 77 ("nearness"), 82 ("to maintain first-hand information").

15. See chapter 5 for a brief discussion of Walker's experience being discriminated against at the Isis Theater in Indianapolis, Indiana, and her subsequent lawsuit against the company.

16. A. L. Jones, "Philanthropy," 177.

17. For more on webs of affiliation, see Iris Carlton-LaNey, "African American Social Work Pioneers' Response to Need," *Social Work* 44, no. 4 (July 1999): 311–21; Freeman, "The Collectivist Roots of Madam C. J. Walker's Philanthropy," Black Perspectives (blog), May 20, 2019, https://www.aaihs.org/the-collectivist-roots -of-madam-c-j-walkers-philanthropy/.

18. "America's Foremost Colored Woman," *Indianapolis Freeman*, December 28, 1912.

19. I am grateful to Rev. Roscoe D. Cooper Jr. for this observation.

20. See chapter 5 for discussion of scientific philanthropy.

21. T. M. Freeman, "7 Ways."

22. Paul R. Mullins, Modupe Labode, Lewis Jones, Michael Essex, Alex Kruse, and G. Brandon Muncy, "Consuming Lines of Difference: The Politics of Wealth and Poverty along the Color Line," *Historical Archeology* 45, no. 3 (2011): 148.

23. Gill, *Beauty Shop Politics*, 45.

24. John H. Whitfield, *"A Friend to All Mankind": Annie Turbo Malone and Poro College* (Charleston, SC: CreateSpace, 2015); Poro College, *"Poro in Pictures": With a Short History of Its Development* (St. Louis, MO: Poro College, 1926); Virginia Gilbert and Barry Gilbert, "Annie Malone Turns 125," *St. Louis American*, February 7, 2013, http://www.stlamerican.com/black_history/article_1de145fc-70bf-11e2 -b7f2-0019bb2963f4.html#.URQfiirZflU.gmail. Today, that institution still exists in St. Louis and is named the Annie Malone Children and Family Service Center. The legal name of Lovejoy, Illinois, is now Brooklyn, Illinois.

25. "Sarah Spencer Washington," accessed August 4, 2014, http://www.atlanticcity experience.org/index.php?option=com_content&view=article&id=13:madame -washington&catid=6&Itemid=11; Mattie L. McHollin, "Washington, Sarah Spencer," in *Encyclopedia of African American Business*, ed. Jessie Carney Smith, 2: 819–22 (Westport, CT: Greenwood); Gladys L. Porter, *Three Negro Pioneers in Beauty Culture* (New York: Vantage, 1966). Annie Malone's papers are located in the Robert O. French Papers of the Vivian G. Harsh Research Collection at the Chicago Public Library in Illinois. French was Malone's nephew and worked at her company for a time. He preserved many of Malone's original documents. Collections and exhibits related to Sarah Spencer Washington are located at the Atlantic City Free Public Library in New Jersey.

26. Kert, *Abby Aldrich Rockefeller*; McCarthy, *Women's Culture*; Crocker, *Mrs. Russell Sage*; Hoffert, *Alva Vanderbilt Belmont*.

27. J. Johnson, *Funding Feminism*.

28. M. Jones, *All Bound Up Together*.

29. Kathleen McCarthy, "Women and Political Culture," in *Charity, Philanthropy, and Civility in American History*, ed. Lawrence J. Friedman and Mark D. McGarvie (New York: Cambridge University Press, 2003), 179; McCarthy, "Parallel Power Structures: Women in the Voluntary Sphere," in *Lady Bountiful Revisited: Women, Philanthropy, and Power*, ed. Kathleen McCarthy (New Brunswick, NJ: Rutgers University Press, 1990): 23.

30. This is not new and follows a larger and unfortunate pattern that casts the history of feminism and women's suffrage as primarily a white women's endeavor. To be sure, white women experienced sex discrimination as Walker did, but their wealth and agency were extensions of their white and marital privileges.

This is why educational scholar Cheryl Smith's observation that "gender is not always unifying" is so poignant (C. Smith, *Market Women*, 9). Walker, and the black women she represents—the poor working class and the entrepreneurial class—had different ways of being that greatly challenge the dominant patterns and approaches of her white female contemporaries.

31. William H. Watkins, *The White Architects of Black Education: Ideology and Power in America, 1865–1954* (New York: Teachers College Press, 2001), 19; Freeman, "Beyond Hegemony."

## Epilogue

Excerpts appear from "The Collectivist Roots of Madam C. J. Walker's Philanthropy" by Tyrone McKinley Freeman on *Black Perspectives* (the blog of the African American Intellectual History Society), May 20, 2019, https://www.aaihs.org/the-collectivist-roots-of-madam-c-j-walkers-philanthropy/. Reprinted by permission of *Black Perspectives*.

1. "The Life Work of Mme. C. J. Walker," *Denver Star*, August 7, 1915, 1.

2. Forbes Live, "A Conversation with Oprah Winfrey," *Forbes 400 Summit on Philanthropy*, YouTube video, 15:29 minutes. Posted September 12, 2012. www.youtube.com/watch?v=8RKm93-BQ2Q.

3. Ibid.

4. In 2007 Winfrey received widespread criticism when a female employee was accused of sexually and physically abusing students on campus. The employee was fired but not convicted by the legal system, and she later sued Winfrey. The suit was settled out of court. Winfrey fired all staff and personally oversaw the rebuilding of the school's processes and reputation.

5. Malina Saval, "Oprah Winfrey Leadership Academy for Girls Marks 10 Years," *Variety.com*, August 3, 2017, www.variety.com/2017/biz/news/oprah-winfry-leadership-academy-for-girls-10-year-anniversary-1202510605/; Forbes Live, "Conversation with Oprah Winfrey," and Forbes Live, "Conversation with Oprah Winfrey," Associated Press Archive. "Oprah Winfrey Talks about Her Academy for Girls," YouTube video, 3:27 minutes. Posted August 4, 2015. www.youtube.com/watch?v=hNKF_F9SvL4.

6. Forbes Live, "Conversation with Oprah Winfrey."

7. Clare O'Connor, "The Education of Oprah Winfrey: How She Saved Her South African School," *Forbes.com*, September 18, 2012, https://www.forbes.com/sites/clareoconnor/2012/09/18/the-education-of-oprah-winfrey-how-she-saved-her-south-african-school/#6cf49d217a45.

8. Harpo Productions, "History of Angel Network," accessed January 20, 2020, http://www.oprah.com/angelnetwork/the-history-of-oprahs-angel-network.

9. In 2016 Smith gave $50 million to his alma mater, Cornell University, to support black and female students in the college of engineering. The college was named for him as a result of the gift. In 2019 Smith also made international

headlines when he announced a gift to pay off all the student debt of Morehouse College's graduating class that same year.

10. Peggy McGlone, "A Diverse Foundation," *Washingtonpost.com*, August 5, 2016, https://www.washingtonpost.com/graphics/lifestyle/national-museum-of -african-american-history-and-culture/biggest-museum-donors/?noredirect=on; Smithsonian Institution, "Founding Donors," last modified September 13, 2016, https://nmaahc.si.edu/about/founding-donors; Carissa Dimargo, "Major Celebri- ties Donate to Smithsonian National Museum of African American History," *NBC-Washington.com*, May 5, 2016, https://www.nbcwashington.com/entertainment/the -scene/Major-Celebrities-Donate-to-Smithsonians-National-Museum-of-African -American-History-378302941.html. The list includes gifts made through family foundations. The other two major individual donors were Bill and Melinda Gates and David Rubenstein.

11. Keith A. Owens, "Black Donors Made New African American Museum a Reality," *Michigan Chronicle*, September 26, 2016, https://michiganchronicle.com/ 2016/09/26/black-donors-made-new-african-american-museum-a-reality/; Anna Barber, personal communication to the author, June 4, 2018. Barber served on the fundraising staff for the museum's campaign.

12. Jennifer Patterson, "Donations Add to the New Museum of African Ameri- can History and Culture," *Timesunion.com*, October 12, 2016, https://www.times union.com/tuplus-local/article/Donations-add-to-new-National-Museum-of -African-9968098.php.

13. Ellen Creager, "Detroit Treasure to Star at U.S. African-American Museum," *Detroit Free Press*, September 14, 2016, https://www.freep.com/story/news/nation/ 2016/09/14/metro-detroiters-violin-star-national-african-american-museum/ 90004988/; Ashleigh Joplin, "Families Reflect on Donations to African Ameri- can Museum," *Washingtonpost.com*, September 14, 2016, https://www.washington post.com/video/local/family-members-reflect-on-donations-to-african-americans -museum/2016/09/14/37cfbb10–7a2a–11e6–8064–c1ddc8a724bb_video.html?utm _term=.23df2e225b92.

14. Peggy McGlone, "300 volunteers for African American Museum: 'We're Ready,'" washingtonpost.com, June 8, 2016, https://www.washingtonpost.com/ entertainment/museums/300-volunteers-for-african-american-museum-were -ready/2016/06/07/bd590f0e-21cc-11e6-aa84–42391ba52c91_story.html?utm _term=.0f1499f2a23d.

15. Patricia A. Banks, *Diversity and Philanthropy at African American Museums: Black Renaissance* (New York: Routledge, 2019).

16. Women's Philanthropy Institute, *WomenGive 2019: Gender and Giving across Communities of Color*, accessed April 5, 2019, from https://scholarworks.iupui.edu/ bitstream/handle/1805/18629/women-give2019–1.pdf; Tyrone McKinley Free- man, "Donors of Color Are Not 'New' or 'Emerging,'" *Chronicle of Philanthropy*, Au- gust 13, 2018, https://www.philanthropy.com/article/Opinion-Donors-of-Color

-Are/244252; Freeman, "Diversity and Fundraising," webinar, Indiana University Lilly Family School of Philanthropy at IUPUI, Indianapolis, IN, February 8, 2018. In giving circles, members make regular donations at a set amount and then collectively decide how the resulting total of dollars will be used. Amounts to join can range from a few hundred to several thousands of dollars. But the central feature of giving circles is the social aspect of working with others to engage community issues and needs.

17. Donor-advised funds are typically held by private nonprofit financial institutions or community foundations and allow donors to receive immediate tax deductions for gifts made to them and disburse the funds for charitable causes in the future. The funds manage the money and administration of gifts on behalf of the donors.

18. Freeman, "Donors of Color."

19. "The Life Work of Mme. C. J. Walker," *Denver Star*, August 7, 1915, 1.

# Bibliography

## Collections

Beinecke Rare Books and Manuscripts Library, Yale University, New Haven, Connecticut

Madam C. J. Walker Papers, Indiana Historical Society, Indianapolis, Indiana

Madam C. J. Walker Papers Addition, Indiana Historical Society, Indianapolis, Indiana.

Marjorie Stewart Joyner Papers, Vivian G. Harsh Collection, Chicago Public Library, Chicago, Illinois

Indianapolis Special Collections Room, Indianapolis–Marion County Public Library, Indianapolis, Indiana

## Newspapers

*Dallas Express*
*Denver Star*
*Denver Statesman*
*Indianapolis Freeman*
*Indianapolis Recorder*
*Nashville Globe*
*New York Age*
*New York Times*
*Pittsburgh Courier*
*Richmond Planet*

## Secondary Sources

Alexander, Shawn Leigh. *An Army of Lions: The Civil Rights Struggle before the NAACP*. Philadelphia: University of Pennsylvania Press, 2013.

Allen, Richard. *The Life Experience and Gospel Labours of the Rt. Reverend Richard Allen*. Philadelphia: Martin and Boden, 1833. http://docsouth.unc.edu/neh/allen/allen.html.

Anderson, Eric, and Alfred A. Moss Jr. *Dangerous Donations: Northern Philanthropy and Southern Black Education, 1902–1930*. Columbia: University of Missouri Press, 1999.

Anderson, James D. *The Education of Blacks in the South, 1860–1935*. Chapel Hill: University of North Carolina Press, 1988.

———. "The Hampton Model of Normal School Industrial Education, 1868–1900." In *New Perspectives on Black Educational History*, edited by Vincent Franklin and James Anderson, 61–96. Boston: G. K. Hall, 1978.

———. "The Historical Development of Black Vocational Education." In *Work, Youth and Schooling: Historical Perspectives on Vocationalism in American Education*, edited by Harvey Kantor and David Tyack, 180–222. Stanford, CA: Stanford University Press, 1982.

Arnsberger, Paul, Melissa Ludlum, Margaret Riley, and Mark Stanton. "A History of the Tax-Exempt Sector: An SOI Perspective." In *The Nature of the Nonprofit Sector*, 2nd ed., edited by J. Steven Ott and Lisa A. Dicke, 125–39. Boulder, CO: Westview, 2012.

Ascoli, Peter. *Julius Rosenwald: The Man Who Built Sears, Roebuck and Advanced the Cause of Black Education in the American South*. Bloomington: Indiana University Press, 2006.

Bailey, Julius H. *Around the Family Altar: Domesticity in the African Methodist Episcopal Church, 1865–1900*. Tallahassee: University Press of Florida, 2005.

———. *Race Patriotism: Protest and Print Culture in the AME Church*. Knoxville: University of Tennessee Press, 2012.

Balleisen, Edward J. *Fraud: An American History from Barnum to Madoff*. Princeton, NJ: Princeton University Press, 2017).

Banks, Patricia A. *Diversity and Philanthropy at African American Museums: Black Renaissance*. New York: Routledge, 2019.

Bell, Catherine. *Ritual: Perspectives and Dimensions*. New York: Oxford University Press, 1997.

Benadusi, Giovanna. "Investing the Riches of the Poor: Servant Women and Their Last Wills." *American Historical Review* 109, no. 3 (June 2004): 805–26.

Bielke, Jayne R. "Nineteenth-Century Traditions of Benevolence and Education: Toward a Conceptual Framework of Black Philanthropy." In *Uplifting a People: African American Philanthropy and Education*, edited by Marybeth Gasman and Kathrine Sedgwick, 9–24. New York: Peter Lang, 2005.

Bieze, Michael Scott, and Marybeth Gasman. *Booker T. Washington Rediscovered*. Baltimore: Johns Hopkins University Press, 2012.

Biggart, Nicole. *Charismatic Capitalism: Direct Selling Organizations in America*. Chicago: University of Chicago Press, 1989.

Billingsley, Andrew. *Climbing Jacob's Ladder: The Enduring Legacy of African-American Families*. New York: Simon and Schuster, 1992.

Blackwelder, Julia Kirk. *Styling Jim Crow: African American Beauty Training during Jim Crow*. College Station: Texas A&M University Press, 2003.

Blain, Keisha N. *Set the World on Fire: Black Nationalist Women and the Global Struggle for Freedom*. Philadelphia: University of Pennsylvania Press, 2018.

Blain, Keisha N., and Tiffany M. Gill. *To Turn the Whole World Over: Black Women and Internationalism*. Urbana: University of Illinois Press, 2019.

Blair, Karen J. *The Torchbearers: Women and Their Amateur Arts Associations in America, 1890–1930*. Bloomington: Indiana University Press, 1994.

Boustan, Leah Platt, and William J. Collins. "The Origin and Persistence of Black-White Differences in Women's Labor Force Participation." In *Human Capital in History: The American Record (2014)*, edited by Leah Platt Boustan, Carola Frydman, and Robert A. Margo, 205–40. Chicago: University of Chicago Press, 2014. http://www.nber.org/chapters/c12902.pdf.

Boyd, Robert L. "The Great Migration to the North and the Rise of Ethnic Niches for African American Women in Beauty Culture and Hairdressing, 1910–1920." *Sociological Focus* 29, no. 1 (February 1996): 33–45.

Branch, Enobong Hannah. *Opportunity Denied: Limiting Black Women to Devalued Work*. New Brunswick, NJ: Rutgers University Press, 2011.

Brawley, Benjamin. *A Short History of the American Negro*. New York: Macmillan, 1929.

Bremner, Robert H. *American Philanthropy*. 2nd ed. Chicago: University of Chicago Press, 1988.

Brimmer, Brandi C. "Laundresses." In *Black Women in America*. 2nd ed., edited by Darlene Clark Hine, 229–31. New York: Oxford University Press, 2005.

Brown, Elsa Barkley. "Womanist Consciousness: Maggie Lena Walker and the Independent Order of Saint Luke." *Signs* 14, no. 3 (1989): 610–33.

Brown, Roscoe C. "The National Negro Health Week Movement." *Journal of Negro Education* 6, no. 3 (July 1937): 553–64.

Brundage, W. Fitzhugh. *The Southern Past: A Clash of Race and Memory*. Cambridge, MA: Belknap, 2005.

Bundles, A'Lelia. *On Her Own Ground: The Life and Times of Madam C. J. Walker*. New York: Washington Square, 2001.

Burlingame, Dwight. ed. *Philanthropy in America: A Comprehensive Historical Encyclopedia*. Santa Barbara, CA: ABC-CLIO, 2004.

Byrd, Ayana, D., and Lori L. Tharps. *Hair Story: Untangling the Roots of Black Hair in America*. New York: St. Martin's Griffin, 2001.

Calanthe, Order of. *Ritualistic Ceremonies of the Order of Calanthe*. Chicago: Fraternal Press, 1914.

Callahan, David. *The Givers: Wealth, Power, and Philanthropy in a New Gilded Age*. New York: Alfred A. Knopf, 2017.

Camp, Bayliss, and Orit Kent. "'What a Mighty Power We Can Be': Individual and Collective Identity in African American and White Fraternal Initiation Rituals." *Social Science History* 28, no. 3 (2004): 439–83.

Campbell, James T. *Songs of Zion: The African Methodist Episcopal Church in the United States and South Africa*. New York: Oxford University Press, 1995.

Campbell, Thomas Monroe. *The Movable School Goes to the Negro Farmer*. Tuskegee, AL: Tuskegee Institute Press, 1936.

Carlton-LaNey, Iris. "African American Social Work Pioneers' Response to Need." *Social Work* 44, no. 4 (July 1999): 311–21.

———. "The Career of Birdye Henrietta Haynes, a Pioneer Settlement House Worker." *Social Service Review* 68, no. 2 (June 1994): 254–73.

———. "Old Folks' Homes for Blacks during the Progressive Era." *Journal of Sociology and Social Welfare* 16, no. 3 (September 1989): 43–60.

Carlton-LaNey, Iris, and Sandra Carlton Alexander. "Early African American Social Welfare Pioneer Women: Working to Empower the Race and the Community." *Journal of Ethnic and Cultural Diversity in Social Work* 10, no. 2 (2001): 67–84.

Carlton-LaNey, Iris, Jill Hamilton, Dorothy Ruiz, and Sandra Carlton Alexander. "'Sitting with the Sick': African American Women's Philanthropy." *Affilia* 16, no. 4 (Winter 2001): 447–66.

Carlton-LaNey, Iris, and Vanessa Hodges. "African American Reformers' Mission: Caring for Our Girls and Women." *Affilia* 19, no. 3 (Fall 2004): 257–72.

Carnegie, Andrew. "Wealth." *North American Review* 148, no. 391 (June 1889): 653–64.

Carnes, Mark C. *Secret Ritual and Manhood in Victorian America*. New Haven, CT: Yale University Press, 1989.

Carson, Emmett D. *A Hand Up: Black Philanthropy and Self-Help in America*. Washington, DC: Joint Center for Political and Economic Studies Press, 1993.

Cash, Floris Barnett. *African American Women and Social Action: The Clubwomen and Volunteerism from Jim Crow to the New Deal, 1896–1936*. Westport, CT: Greenwood, 2001.

Cavallo, Sandra. *Charity and Power in Early Modern Italy: Benefactors and Their Motives in Turin, 1541–1789*. New York: Cambridge University Press, 1995.

Cha-Jua, Sundiata K., and Clarence Lang. "The 'Long Movement' as Vampire: Temporal and Spatial Fallacies in Recent Black Freedom Studies." *Journal of African American History* 91, no. 2 (2007): 265–88.

Chapman, Erin D. *Prove It on Me: New Negroes, Sex, and Popular Culture in the 1920s*. New York: Oxford University Press, 2012.

Chernow, Ron. *Titan: The Life of John D. Rockefeller, Sr*. New York: Random House, 1998.

Clegg, Claude E. III "Philanthropy, the Civil Rights Movement, and the Politics of Racial Reform." In Friedman and McGarvie, *Charity, Philanthropy, and Civility*, 341–61.

Clemens, Elisabeth. "The Constitution of Citizens." In *The Nonprofit Sector: A Research Handbook*. 2nd ed., edited by Walter W. Powell and Richard Steinberg, 207–20. New Haven, CT: Yale University Press, 2006.

Collier-Thomas, Bettye. *Jesus, Jobs, and Justice: African American Women and Religion*. New York: Alfred A. Knopf, 2010.

———. "Sister Laborers: African American Women, Cultural Capital, and Educational Philanthropy, 1865–1970." In *Cultural Capital and Black Education: African American Communities and the Funding of Black Education, 1865 to the Present*, edited by V. P. Franklin and C. J. Savage, 97–115. Greenwich, CT: Information Age, 2004.

Cooper, Brittany. *Beyond Respectability: The Intellectual Thought of Race Women*. Urbana: University of Illinois Press, 2017.

Coulter, Charles E. *"Take Up the Black Man's Burden:" Kansas City's African American Communities, 1865–1939*. Columbia: University of Missouri Press, 2006.

Crocker, Ruth. *Mrs. Russell Sage: Women's Activism and Philanthropy in Gilded Age and Progressive America*. Bloomington: Indiana University Press, 2006.

———. "'Nothing More for Men's Colleges': The Educational Philanthropy of Mrs. Russell Sage." In *Women and Philanthropy in Education*, edited by Andrea Walton, 257–80. Bloomington: Indiana University Press, 2005.

Croft, Robert Wayne. *A Zora Neale Hurston Companion*. Westport, CT: Greenwood, 2002.

Cutlip, Scott M. *Fund Raising in the United States: Its Role in America's Philanthropy*. New Brunswick, NJ: Transaction, 1990.

Davis, Elizabeth Lindsay. *Lifting As They Climb*. New York: G. K. Hall, 1996.

Davis, Leroy. "Madam C. J. Walker: A Woman of Her Time." In *The African Experience in Community Development: The Continuing Struggle in Africa and in the Americas*, edited by Edward W. Crosby, Leroy Davis, and Anne Adams Graves, 2: 37–60. Needham, MA: Advocate, 1980.

Davis, William H., ed. *Report of the Fourteenth Annual Convention of the National Negro Business League*. Washington, DC: National Negro Business League, 1913.

———, ed. *Report of the Thirteenth Annual Convention of the National Negro Business League*. Washington, DC: National Negro Business League, 1912.

Dodson, Jualynne E. *Engendering Church: Women, Power, and the AME Church*. Lanham, MD: Rowman and Littlefield, 2002.

Dossett, Kate. *Bridging Race Divides: Black Nationalism, Feminism, and Integration in the United States, 1896–1935*. Gainesville: University Press of Florida, 2008.

Dowd, Jacquelyn H., "The Long Civil Rights Movement and the Political Use of the Past." *Journal of American History* 91, no. 4 (March 2005): 1233–63.

DuBois, W. E. B. *Black Reconstruction in America 1860–1880*. New York: Athenaeum, 1992.

———. Economic *Co-operation among Negro Americans*. Atlanta: Atlanta University Press, 1907.

———. *Efforts for Social Betterment among Negro Americans*. Atlanta: Atlanta University Press, 1909.

———. *The Souls of Black Folk*. Chicago: A. C. McClurg, 1903.

Evans, Stephanie. *The Black Women's Studies Booklist: Emergent Themes in Critical Race and Gender Research*. Retrieved July 7, 2019, from https://bwstbooklist.net/.

Fairclough, Adam. *A Class of Their Own: Black Teachers in the Segregated South*. Cambridge, MA: Belknap, 2007.

Ferguson, Earline Rae. "African American Clubwomen and the Indianapolis NAACP, 1912–1914." In *Black Women in Africa and the Americas*, edited by Catherine Higgs, Barbara Moss, and Earline Ferguson, 73–84. Athens: Ohio University Press, 2002.

Finch, Janet, Lynn Hayes, Jennifer Mason, Judith Masson, and Lorraine Wallis. *Wills, Inheritance, and Families*. Oxford, UK: Clarendon, 1996.

Finkenbine, Roy E. "'Our Little Circle': Benevolent Reformers, the Slater Fund, and the Argument for Black Industrial Education, 1882–1908." In *African Americans and Education in the South, 1865–1900*, edited by Donald G. Nieman, 70–86. New York: Garland, 1994.

Fisher, John E. *The John F. Slater Fund: A Nineteenth Century Affirmative Action for Negro Education*. Lanham, MD: University Press of America, 1987.

Foner, Eric. *Forever Free: The Story of Emancipation and Reconstruction*. New York: Alfred A. Knopf, 2005.

Franklin, John Hope, and Alfred A. Moss Jr. *From Slavery to Freedom: A History of Negro Americans*. 6th ed. New York: McGraw-Hill, 1988.

Freeman, Tyrone McKinley. "Beyond Hegemony: Reappraising the History of Philanthropy and African-American Higher Education in the Nineteenth Century." *International Journal of Educational Advancement* 10, no. 3 (2010): 148–65.

———. "The Collectivist Roots of Madam C. J. Walker's Philanthropy." Black Perspectives (blog), May 20, 2019. https://www.aaihs.org/the-collectivist-roots-of-madam-c-j-walkers-philanthropy/.

———. "Donors of Color Are Not 'New' or 'Emerging': We've Been Giving All Along." *Chronicle of Philanthropy*, August 13, 2018. https://www.philanthropy.com/article/Opinion-Donors-of-Color-Are/244252.

———. "400 Years of Black Giving: From the Days of Slavery to the 2019 Morehouse Graduation." The Conversation (blog), August 22, 2019. https://theconversation.com/400-years-of-black-giving-from-the-days-of-slavery-to-the-2019-morehouse-graduation-121402.

———. "7 Ways to Read around the History of Philanthropy's Diversity Problem This Black History Month." HistPhil (blog), February 25, 2019. https://histphil.org/2019/02/25/7-ways-to-read-around-the-history-of-philanthropys-diversity-problem-this-black-history-month/.

Friedman, Lawrence J. "Philanthropy in America: Historicism and Its Discontents." In Friedman and McGarvie, *Charity, Philanthropy, and Civility*, 1–21.

Friedman, Lawrence J., and Mark D. McGarvie, eds. *Charity, Philanthropy, and Civility in American History*. New York: Cambridge University Press, 2003.

Friedman, Lawrence M. *Dead Hands: A Social History of Wills, Trusts, and Inheritance Law*. Stanford, CA: Stanford Law Books, 2009.

———. "Patterns of Testation in the 19th Century: A Study of Essex County (New Jersey) Wills." *American Journal of Legal History* 8 (1964): 34–53.

Friedman, Lawrence M., Christopher Walker, and Ben Hernandez-Stern. "The Inheritance Process in San Bernardino County, California, 1964: A Research Note." *Houston Law Review* 43, no. 5 (January 2007): 1445–74.

Frumpkin, Peter. *On Being Nonprofit: A Conceptual and Policy Primer*. Cambridge, MA: Harvard University Press, 2002.

Fuentes, Marisa J. *Dispossessed Lives: Enslaved Women, Violence, and the Archive*. Philadelphia: University of Pennsylvania Press, 2016.

Gallagher, Julie A. *Black Women and Politics in New York City*. Urbana: University of Illinois Press, 2012.

Gasman, Marybeth, and Katherine V. Sedgwick, eds. *Uplifting a People: African American Philanthropy and Education*. New York: Peter Lang, 2005.

Gates, Henry Louis Jr. *Stony the Road: Reconstruction, White Supremacy, and the Rise of Jim Crow*. New York: Penguin, 2019.

Geertz, Clifford. "Found in Translation: On the Social History of the Moral Imagination." *Georgia Review* 31, no. 4 (1977): 788–810.

Giddings, Paula. *When and Where I Enter: The Impact of Black Women and Race and Sex in America*. New York: Bantam, 1984.

Gilbert, Virginia and Barry. "Annie Malone Children's Organization Will Celebrate 125 Years of Service." *St. Louis Public Radio*, September 23, 2019. https://news.stlpublicradio.org/post/annie-malone-childrens-organization-will-celebrate-125-years-service-0#stream/0.

Gill, Tiffany M. *Beauty Shop Politics: African American Women's Activism in the Beauty Industry*. Urbana: University of Illinois Press, 2010.

———. "'I Had My Own Business . . . So I Didn't Have to Worry': Beauty Salons, Beauty Culturists, and the Politics of African-American Female Entrepreneurship." In *Beauty and Business: Commerce, Gender, and Culture in Modern America*, edited by Philip Scranton, 7–22. New York: Routledge, 2001.

Gilmore, Glenda E. *Gender and Jim Crow: Women and the Politics of White Supremacy in North Carolina, 1896–1920*. Chapel Hill: University of North Carolina Press, 1996.

Ginzberg, Lori. *Women and the Work of Benevolence: Morality, Politics, and Class in the Nineteenth-Century United States*. New Haven, CT: Yale University Press, 1990.

Glenn, Evelyn Nakano. "Racial Ethnic Women's Labor: The Intersection of Race, Class, and Gender Oppression." *Review of Political Economics* 17, no. 3 (1985): 86–108.

Goldin, Claudia. "Female Labor Force Participation: The Origin of Black and White Differences, 1870–1880." *Journal of Economic History* 37, no. 1 (March 1977): 87–108.

Gordon, Howard R. D. *The History and Growth of Vocational Education in America*. Boston: Allyn and Bacon, 1999.

Grimm, Robert T., ed. *Notable American Philanthropists: Biographies of Giving and Volunteering*. Westport, CT: Greenwood, 2002.

Gutman, Herbert G. *The Black Family in Slavery and Freedom, 1750–1925*. New York: Pantheon, 1976.

Hacker, Daphna. "The Gendered Dimensions of Inheritance: Empirical Food for Legal Thought." *Journal of Empirical Legal Studies* 7, no. 2 (June 2010): 322–54.

Hall, Luther E. III. *Rochelle Court #14 Order of Calanthe Record, 1906–1933*. Indianapolis: Indiana Historical Society, 2011.

Hall, Peter Dobkin. "A Historical Overview of Philanthropy, Voluntary Associations, and Nonprofit Organizations in the United States, 1600–2000." In *The Nonprofit Sector: A Research Handbook*. 2nd ed., edited by Walter W. Powell and Richard Steinberg, 32–65. New Haven, CT: Yale University Press, 2006.

Hall-Russell, Cheryl, and Robert H. Kasberg. *African American Traditions of Giving and Serving: A Midwest Perspective*. Indianapolis: Indiana University Center on Philanthropy, 1997.

Hamilton, Kenneth M. *Booker T. Washington in American Memory*. Urbana: University of Illinois Press, 2017.

Hanson, Joyce A. *Mary McLeod Bethune and Black Women's Political Activism*. Columbia: University of Missouri Press, 2003.

Harlan, Louis, and Raymond Smock, eds. *The Booker T. Washington Papers*, Vol. 13, *1914–15*. Urbana: University of Illinois Press, 1984.

Harley, Sharon. "Beyond the Classroom: The Organizational Lives of Black Female Teachers in the District of Columbia, 1890–1930." *Journal of Negro Education* 51, no. 3 (Summer 1982): 254–65.

———. "For the Good of Family and Race: Gender, Work and Domestic Roles in the Black Community, 1880–1930." *Signs* 15, no. 2 (Winter 1990): 336–49.

———. "When Your Work Is Not Who You Are: The Development of a Working-Class Consciousness among Afro-American Women." In *Gender, Class, Race, and Reform in the Progressive Era*, edited by Noralee Frankel and Nancy S. Dye, 42–55. Lexington: University Press of Kentucky, 1991.

Harrison, Ira E. "Hubert B. Ross, the Anthropologist Who Was." In *African-American Pioneers in Anthropology*, edited by Ira E. Harrison and Faye V. Harrison, 265–73. Urbana: University of Illinois Press, 1999.

Hendricks, Wanda A. *Gender, Race, and Politics in the Midwest: Black Club Women in Illinois*. Bloomington: Indiana University Press, 1998.

Hicks, Cheryl. *Talk with You like a Woman: African American Women, Justice, and Reform in New York, 1890–1935*. Chapel Hill: University of North Carolina Press, 2010.

Higginbotham, Evelyn Brooks. *Righteous Discontent: The Women's Movement in the Black Baptist Church 1880–1920*. Cambridge, MA: Harvard University Press, 1993.

Hildebrand, Reginald F. *The Times Were Strange and Stirring: Methodist Preachers and the Crisis of Emancipation*. Durham, NC: Duke University Press, 1995.

Hine, Darlene Clark. *Hine Sight: Black Women and the Re-construction of American History*. New York: Carlson, 1994.

———. *Speak Truth to Power: Black Professional Class in United States History*. Brooklyn: Carlson, 1996.

———. "We Specialize in the Wholly Impossible': The Philanthropic Work of Black Women." In McCarthy, *Lady Bountiful*, 70–93.

———. *When the Truth Is Told: A History of Black Women's Culture and Community in Indiana, 1875–1950*. Indianapolis, IN: National Council of Negro Women, 1981.

Hoffert, Sylvia D. *Alva Vanderbilt Belmont: Unlikely Champion of Women's Rights*. Bloomington: Indiana University Press, 2012.

Huddle, Mark Andrew. "Exodus from the South." In *A Companion to African American History*, edited by Alton Hornsby Jr., 449–62. Malden, MA: Blackwell, 2005.

Hudson, Lynn M. *The Making of 'Mammy Pleasant': A Black Entrepreneur in Nineteenth-Century San Francisco*. Urbana: University of Illinois Press, 2003.

Huehls, Frances. "Teaching As Philanthropy: Catharine Beecher and the Hartford Female Seminar." In *Women and Philanthropy in Education*, edited by Andrea Walton, 39–59. Bloomington: Indiana University Press, 2005.

Hunter, Tera W. *To 'Joy My Freedom: Southern Black Women's Lives and Labors after the Civil War*. Cambridge, MA: Harvard University Press, 1997.

Hyslop-Margison, Emery J. "An Assessment of the Historical Arguments in Vocational Educational Reform." *Journal of Career and Technical Education* 17, no. 1 (2000): 23–30.

Johnson, Joan Marie. *Funding Feminism: Monied Women, Philanthropy, and the Women's Movement, 1870–1967*. Chapel Hill, NC: University of North Carolina Press, 2017.

———. "Philanthropy." In *Black Women in America*. 2nd ed., edited by Darlene Clark Hine, 474–83. New York: Oxford University Press, 2005.

———. *Southern Ladies, New Women: Race, Region, and Clubwomen in South Carolina, 1890–1930*. Gainesville: University Press of Florida, 2004.

———. "Ye Gave Them a Stone: African American Women's Clubs, the Frederick Douglass Home, and the Black Mammy Monument." *Journal of Women's History* 17, no. 1 (Spring 2005): 62–86.

Jones, Adrienne Lash, "Philanthropy in the African American Experience." In *Giving: Western Ideas of Philanthropy*, edited by J. B. Schneewind, 153–78. Bloomington: Indiana University Press, 1996.

Jones, Angela. *African American Civil Rights: Early Activism and the Niagara Movement*. Denver, CO: Praeger, 2001.

Jones, Martha S. *All Bound Up Together: The Woman Question in African American Public Culture, 1830–1900*. Chapel Hill: University of North Carolina Press, 2007.

Jones, Thomas Jesse. *Negro Education: A Study of the Private and Higher Schools for Colored People in the United States*, vol. 2. Washington, DC: US Government Printing Office, 1917.

Kantor, Harvey, and David Tyack. Introduction to *Work, Youth, and Schooling: Historical Perspectives on Vocationalism in American Education*, ed. Harvey Kantor and David Tyack. Stanford, CA: Stanford University Press, 1982.

Kaufman, Jason. *For the Common Good? American Civic Life and the Golden Age of Fraternity*. New York: Oxford University Press, 2002.

Kersten, Andrew. *A. Philip Randolph: A Life in the Vanguard*. Lanham, MD: Rowman and Littlefield, 2006.

Kert, Bernice. *Abby Aldrich Rockefeller: The Woman in the Family*. New York: Random House, 1993.

Knupfer, Anne Meis. *The Chicago Black Renaissance and Women's Activism*. Urbana: University of Illinois Press, 2006.

———. *Toward a Tenderer Humanity and a Nobler Womanhood: African American Women's Clubs in Turn-of-the-Century Chicago*. New York: New York University Press, 1996.

Kwolek-Folland, Angel. *Engendering Business: Men and Women in the Corporate Office, 1870–1930*. Baltimore, MD: Johns Hopkins University Press, 1994.

Lerner, Gerda. *Black Women in White America: A Documentary History*. New York: Random House, 1972.

LeRoux, Kelly, and Mary K. Feeney. *Nonprofit Organizations and Civil Society in the United States*. New York: Routledge, 2015.

Levine, Daniel. "A Single Standard of Civilization: Black Private Social Welfare Institutions in the South, 1880s-1920s." *Georgia Historical Quarterly* 81, no. 1 (Spring 1997): 52–77.

Lewis, David Levering. *W. E. B. DuBois: The Fight for Equality and the American Century, 1919–1963*. New York: Owl, 2000.

Lincoln, C. Eric, ed. *The Black Experience in Religion*. New York: Doubleday, 1974.

———. *The Negro Church in America/The Black Church since Frazier*. New York: Schocken, 1974.

Lindsey, Treva B. *Colored No More: Reinventing Black Womanhood in Washington, D.C.* Urbana: University of Illinois Press, 2017.

Little, Lawrence S. *Disciples of Liberty: The African Methodist Episcopal Church in the Age of Imperialism, 1884–1916*. Knoxville: University of Tennessee Press, 2000.

Littlefield, Marci Bounds. "The Black Church and Community Development and Self-Help: The Next Phase of Social Equality." *Western Journal of Black Studies* 29, no. 4 (2005): 687–93.

Logan, Rayford. *The Negro in American Life and Thought: The Nadir 1877–1901*. New York: Dial, 1954.

Lowry, Beverly. *Her Dream of Dreams: The Rise and Triumph of Madam C. J. Walker*. New York: Vintage, 2003.

Mack, Kibibi V. C. *Parlor Ladies and Ebony Drudges: African American Women, Class, and Work in a South Carolina Community.* Knoxville: University of Tennessee Press, 1999.

Madoff, Ray D. *Immortality and the Law: The Rising Power of the American Dead.* New Haven, CT: Yale University Press, 2010.

Manko, Katina. "'Now You Are in Business for Yourself": The Independent Contractors of the California Perfume Company, 1886–1938." *Business and Economic History*, 26, no. 1 (1997): 5–26.

Martin, Joanne M., and Elmer P. Martin. *The Helping Tradition in the Black Family and Community.* Silver Spring, MD: National Association of Social Workers, 1985.

McCarthy, Kathleen D. *American Creed: Philanthropy and the Rise of Civil Society 1700–1865.* Chicago: University of Chicago Press, 2003.

———, ed. *Lady Bountiful Revisited: Women, Philanthropy, and Power.* New Brunswick, NJ: Rutgers University Press, 1990.

———. "Parallel Power Structures: Women in the Voluntary Sphere." In McCarthy, *Lady Bountiful*, 1–31.

———. *Women, Philanthropy and Civil Society.* Bloomington: Indiana University Press, 2001.

———. *Women and Philanthropy: Three Strategies in a Historical Perspective.* Working Paper 22. New York: Center on Philanthropy and Civil Society, 1994.

———. "Women and Political Culture." In Friedman and McGarvie, *Charity, Philanthropy, and Civility*, 179–97.

———. *Women's Culture: American Philanthropy and Art, 1830–1930.* Chicago: University of Chicago Press, 1991.

McHollin, Mattie L. "Washington, Sarah Spencer." In *Encyclopedia of African American Business*, edited by Jessie Carney Smith, 2: 819–23. Westport, CT: Greenwood, 2006.

Mira, Maria Isabel Martinez. "Female Testaments as Social Discourse: A Textual Analysis under Critical Discourse Analysis Approach." *Mediterranean Journal of Social Sciences* 2, no. 2 (May 2011): 101–10.

Mjagkij, Nina. *Light in the Darkness: African Americans and the YMCA, 1852–1946.* Lexington: University Press of Kentucky, 1994.

Mossell, N. F. *The Work of the Afro-American Woman.* New York: Oxford University Press, 1988.

Mullings, Leith. *On Our Own Terms: Race, Class, and Gender in the Lives of African American Women.* New York: Routledge, 1997.

Mullins, Paul R., Modupe Labode, Lewis Jones, Michael Essex, Alex Kruse, and G. Brandon Muncy. "Consuming Lines of Difference: The Politics of Wealth and Poverty along the Color Line." *Historical Archaeology* 45, no. 3 (2011): 104–50.

NAACP. *Thirty Years of Lynching in the United States, 1889–1918.* New York: National Association of Colored People, 1919.

Nasaw, David. *Andrew Carnegie.* New York: Penguin, 2006.

Nembhard, Jessica Gordon. *Collective Courage: A History of African American Cooperative Economic Thought and Practice*. University Park: Pennsylvania State University Press, 2014.

Neverdon-Morton, Cynthia. *Afro-American Women of the South and the Advancement of the Race, 1895–1925*. Knoxville: University of Tennessee Press, 1989.

Newman, Richard S. *Freedom's Prophet: Bishop Richard Allen, the AME Church, and the Black Founding Fathers*. New York: New York University Press, 2008.

Nieman, Donald G. *African Americans and Education in the South, 1865–1900*. New York: Garland, 1994.

Norrell, Robert J. *Up from History: The Life of Booker T. Washington*. Cambridge, MA: Harvard University Press, 2009.

Onishi, Yuichiro. "The New Negro of the Pacific: How African Americans Forged Cross-Racial Solidarity with Japan, 1917–1922." *Journal of African American History* 92, no. 2 (Spring 2007): 191–213.

Painter, Nell Irvin. *Exodusters: Black Migration to Kansas after Reconstruction*. New York: Alfred A. Knopf, 1977.

———. *Standing at Armageddon: The United States 1877–1919*. New York: W. W. Norton, 1987.

Palmer, Colin A. *Passageways: An Interpretive History of Black America*. Vol. 2, *1863–1965*. New York: Harcourt Brace, 1998.

Payton, Robert L., and Michael P. Moody. *Understanding Philanthropy: Its Meaning and Mission*. Bloomington: Indiana University Press, 2008.

Peebles, Marilyn T. *The Alabama Knights of Pythias of North America, South America, Europe, Asia, Africa, and Australia: A Brief History*. New York: University Press of America, 2012.

Peiss, Kathy. *Hope in a Jar: The Making of America's Beauty Culture*. New York: Metropolitan, 1998.

———. "On Beauty . . . and the History of Business." In *Beauty and Business: Commerce, Gender, and Culture in Modern America*, edited by Philip Scranton, 7–22. New York: Routledge, 2001.

Penna, Robert M. *Braided Threads: A Historical Overview of the American Nonprofit Sector*. New York: Routledge, 2018.

Pennsylvania Historical and Museum Commission. *Communities in Common: Black History in Pennsylvania Study*. Accessed June 27, 2013, https://archive.org/details/CommunitiesInCommonBlackHistoryInPennsylvaniaStudy/mode/2up.

Perry, Imani. *May We Forever Stand: A History of the Black National Anthem*. Chapel Hill: University of North Carolina Press, 2018.

Phillips, Kimberley L. *AlabamaNorth: African-American Migrants, Community, and Working-Class Activism in Cleveland, 1915–45*. Urbana: University of Illinois Press, 1999.

———. *Daily Life during African American Migrations*. Westport, CT: Greenwood, 2012.

Poro College. *"Poro in Pictures": With a Short History of Its Development.* St. Louis, MO: Poro College, 1926.

Porter, Gladys L. *Three Negro Pioneers in Beauty Culture.* New York: Vantage, 1966.

"Queen of Gotham's Colored 400." *Literary Digest* 55 (October 13, 1917): 75–76.

Quinn, Sandra Crouse, and Stephen Thomas. "The National Negro Health Week, 1915–1951: A Descriptive Account." *Minority Health Today* 2, no. 3 (March–April 2001): 44–49.

Reed, Touré F. *Not Alms but Opportunity: The Urban League and the Politics of Racial Uplift, 1910–1950.* Chapel Hill: University of North Carolina Press, 2008.

Reich, Steven A. *A Working People: A History of African American Workers since Emancipation.* Lanham, MD: Rowman and Littlefield, 2013.

Richardson, Harry V. *Dark Salvation: The Story of Methodism As It Developed among Blacks in America.* Garden City, NY: Doubleday, 1976.

Rief, Michelle. "Thinking Locally, Acting Globally: The International Agenda of African American Clubwomen, 1880–1940." *Journal of African American History* 89, no. 3 (Summer 2004): 203–22.

Rockefeller, John D. *Random Reminiscences of Men and Events.* New York: Doubleday, Page, 1916.

Roger Williams University. *Catalogue of the Officers and Students of Roger Williams University.* Nashville, TN: Wheeler, Osbourne and Duckworth, 1885. http://archive.org/details/catalogueofofficoroge.

Rooks, Noliwe. *Hair Raising: Beauty, Culture, and African American Women.* New Brunswick, NJ: Rutgers University Press, 1996.

Ross, Edyth L., ed. *Black Heritage in Social Welfare, 1860–1930.* Metuchen, NJ: Scarecrow, 1978.

Rouse, Jacqueline Anne. *Lugenia Burns Hope, Black Southern Reformer.* Athens: University of Georgia Press, 2004.

Sage, M. Olivia. "Opportunities and Responsibilities of Leisured Women." *North American Review* 181, no. 588 (November 1905): 712–21.

Salem, Dorothy. *To Better Our World: Black Women in Organized Reform, 1890–1920.* Brooklyn, NY: Carlson, 1990.

Sander, Kathleen Waters. *The Business of Charity: The Women's Exchange Movement, 1832–1900.* Urbana: University of Illinois Press, 1998.

———. *Mary Elizabeth Garrett: Society and Philanthropy in the Gilded Age.* Baltimore, MD: Johns Hopkins University Press, 2008.

Scherer, Robert G. *Subordination or Liberation? The Development and Conflicting Theories of Black Education in Nineteenth Century Alabama.* University: University of Alabama Press, 1977.

Schlesinger, Arthur. "Biography of a Nation of Joiners." *American Historical Review* 50, no. 1 (October 1944): 1–25.

Scott, Anne Firor. "Most Invisible of All: Black Women's Voluntary Associations." *Journal of Southern History* 56, no. 1 (February 1990): 3–22.

Sealander, Judith. *Private Wealth and Public Life: Foundation Philanthropy and the Reshaping of American Social Policy from the Progressive Era to the New Deal.* Baltimore, MD: Johns Hopkins University Press, 1997.

Sernett, Milton C., ed. *Afro-American Religious History: A Documentary Witness.* Durham, NC: Duke University Press, 1985.

Shammas, Carole, Marylynn Salmon, and Michel Dahlin. *Inheritance in America from Colonial Times to the Present.* New Brunswick, NJ: Rutgers University Press, 1987.

Shaw, Jenny. *Everyday Life in the Early English Caribbean: Irish, Africans, and the Construction of Difference.* Athens: University of Georgia Press, 2013.

Shaw, Stephanie. "Black Club Women and the Creation of the National Association of Colored Women." *Journal of Women's History* 3, no. 2 (Fall 1991): 10–25.

Shockley, Megan Taylor. *"We, Too, Are Americans": African American Women in Detroit and Richmond, 1940–54.* Urbana: University of Illinois Press, 2004.

Siddle-Walker, Vanessa. *Their Highest Potential: An African American School in the Segregated South.* Chapel Hill: University of North Carolina Press, 1996.

Sklar, Kathryn Kish. *Florence Kelley and the Nation's Work: The Rise of Women's Political Culture, 1830–1900.* New Haven, CT: Yale University Press, 1997.

Skocpol, Theda, Ariane Liazos, and Marshall Ganz. *What a Mighty Power We Can Be: African American Fraternal Groups and the Struggle for Racial Equality.* Princeton, NJ: Princeton University Press, 2006.

Skocpol, Theda, and Jennifer Oser. "Organization despite Adversity: The Origins and Development of African American Fraternal Associations." *Social Science History* 28, no. 3 (September 2004): 367–437.

Smith, Cheryl A. *Market Women: Black Women Entrepreneurs: Past, Present, and Future.* Westport, CT: Praeger, 2005.

Smith, Eleanor. "Black American Women and Work: A Historical Review, 1619–1920." *Women's Studies International Forum* 8, no. 4 (1985): 343–49.

Smith, John H. *Vital Facts concerning the African Methodist Episcopal Church: Its Doctrines, Government, Usages, Polity Progress.* Philadelphia: AME, 1941.

Smith, Susan. *Sick and Tired of Being Sick and Tired: Black Women's Health Activism in America, 1890–1950.* Philadelphia: University of Pennsylvania Press, 1995.

Sneddon, Karen J. "In the Name of God, Amen: Language in Last Wills and Testaments." *Quinnipiac Law Review* 29, no. 3 (2011): 665–727.

———. "Memento Mori: Death and Wills." *Wyoming Law Review* 14, no. 1 (2014): 211–52.

———. "Speaking for the Dead: Voice in Last Wills and Testaments." *St. Johns Law Review* 85, no. 2 (2011): 683–754.

———. "The Will as Personal Narrative." *Elder Law Journal* 20, no. 2 (2013): 355–410.

Spivey, Donald. *Schooling for the New Slavery: Black Industrial Education, 1868–1915.* Westport, CT: Greenwood, 1978.

Stack, Carol B. *All Our Kin: Strategies for Survival in a Black Community.* New York: Harper and Row, 1975.

Stampp, Kenneth M. *The Era of Reconstruction 1865–1877*. New York: Alfred A. Knopf, 1966.

Stanfield, John H. *Philanthropy and Jim Crow in American Social Science*. Santa Barbara, CA: Praeger, 1985.

Stephenson, Barry. *Ritual: A Short Introduction*. New York: Oxford University Press, 2015.

Summers, Martin. *Manliness and Its Discontents: The Black Middle Class and the Transformation of Masculinity, 1900–1930*. Chapel Hill: University of North Carolina Press, 2004.

Sussman, Marvin B., Judith N. Cates, and David T. Smith. *The Family and Inheritance*. New York: Russell Sage Foundation, 1970.

TeSelle, Eugene. "The Nashville Institute and Roger Williams University: Benevolence, Paternalism, and Black Consciousness, 1867–1910." *Tennessee Historical Quarterly* 41, no. 4 (Winter 1982): 360–79.

Tuennerman-Kaplan, Laura. *Helping Others, Helping Ourselves: Power, Giving, and Community Identity in Cleveland, Ohio, 1880–1930*. Kent, OH: Kent State University, 2001.

Tuskegee Institute. *Annual Report of the President*. Tuskegee, AL: Tuskegee Institute Press, 1915.

Wadelington, Charles W., and Richard F. Knapp. *Charlotte Hawkins Brown and Palmer Memorial Institute: What One Young African American Woman Could Do*. Chapel Hill, NC: University of North Carolina Press, 1999.

Waldrep, Christopher. *African Americans Confront Lynching: Strategies of Resistance from the Civil War to the Civil Rights Era*. Lanham, MD: Rowman and Littlefield, 2009.

Walker, Clarence E. *A Rock in a Weary Land: The African Methodist Episcopal Church during the Civil War and Reconstruction*. Baton Rouge: Louisiana State University Press, 1982.

Walker, Juliet E. K. *The History of Black Business: Capitalism, Race, Entrepreneurship*. 2nd ed. Vol. 1, *To 1865*. Chapel Hill: University of North Carolina Press, 2009.

Walker, Susannah. *Style and Status: Selling Beauty to African American Women, 1920–1975*. Lexington: University Press of Kentucky, 2007.

"Walker Will." *The Appeal* (St. Paul), June 21, 1919. http://chroniclingamerica.loc.gov/lccn/sn83016810/1919-06-21/ed-1/seq-2/.

Wall, Joseph Frazier. *Andrew Carnegie*. Pittsburgh, PA: University of Pittsburgh Press, 1989.

Walton, Andrea, ed. *Women and Philanthropy in Education*. Bloomington: Indiana University Press, 2005.

Warren, Stephen. "Rethinking Assimilation: American Indians and the Practice of Christianity." In Friedman and McGarvie, *Charity, Philanthropy, and Civility*, 107–27.

Washington, Booker T. "Relation of Industrial Education to National Progress." *Annals of the American Academy of Political and Social Science* 33, no. 1 (January 1909): 1–12.

———, *Up from Slavery: An Autobiography*. New York: Doubleday, 1901; repr., electronic edition, Chapel Hill: University of North Carolina Press, 1997. http://docsouth.unc.edu/fpn/washington/washing.html.

Watkins, William H. *The White Architects of Black Education: Ideology and Power in America, 1865–1954*. New York: Teachers College Press, 2001.

West, Earle H. "The Peabody Education Fund and Negro Education, 1867–1880." *History of Education Quarterly* 6, no. 2 (Summer 1966): 3–21.

White, Deborah Gray. *Too Heavy a Load: Black Women in Defense of Themselves 1894–1994*. New York: W. W. Norton, 1999.

Whitfield, John H. *"A Friend to All Mankind": Annie Turnbo Malone and Poro College*. Charleston, SC: CreateSpace, 2015.

Williams, Heather Andrea. *Self-Taught: African American Education in Slavery and Freedom*. Chapel Hill: University of North Carolina Press, 2007.

Willingham, Henry. *Annual Report of the Superintendent of Education in the State of Alabama*. Montgomery, AL: Brown, 1911.

Wills, Shomari. *Black Fortunes: The Story of the First Six African Americans to Escape Slavery and Become Millionaires*. New York: Amistad, 2018.

Wolcott, Victoria W. *Remaking Respectability: African American Women in Interwar Detroit*. Chapel Hill: University of North Carolina Press, 2001.

Woodson, Carter G. *The Miseducation of the Negro*. Washington, DC: Associated Publishers, 1933.

———. "The Negro Washerwoman, a Vanishing Figure." *Journal of Negro History* 15, no. 3 (July 1930): 269–77.

Wright, Richard R. Jr. *Centennial Encyclopaedia of the African Methodist Episcopal Church 1816–1916*. Philadelphia: AME Church, 1916.

Yohn, Susan M. "Crippled Capitalists: The Inscription of Economic Dependence and the Challenge of Female Entrepreneurship in Nineteenth-Century America." *Feminist Economics* 12, nos. 1–2 (January–April 2006): 85–109.

Zinsmeister, Karl. *The Almanac of American Philanthropy*. Washington, DC: Philanthropy Roundtable, 2016.

Zunz, Olivier. *Philanthropy in America: A History*. Princeton, NJ: Princeton University Press, 2012.

# Index

Page numbers in *italics* indicate photographs.

Aaron, Hank, 204
activism, 16–17, 48–50, 105–7; black fraternalism and, 110–16; and charity in the Walker Clubs, 124–29; East St. Louis riot and, 106; formal culture in the Walker Clubs and, 117–24; Madam C. J. Walker's organization of agents and, 108–10. *See also* African American philanthropy; philanthropy of Madam C. J. Walker
African American businesses: dual motives of, 58–62; growth of, 62–63; white hostility toward, 58–59
African American Development Officers Network, 207
African American philanthropy, 3–9; definitions of, 3, 7, 62, 82; in education, 86–87; giving circles, 207; intersectional, 19; modern day, 185–86, 201–4, 206–9; reclaiming and naming black women as philanthropists and, 14–19; scholarship on, 9–14; theorizing, 189–94; through business, 58–62; as tool against Jim Crow, 144–45, 148–49, 154, 187–89, 198; West African origins

of, 148; who counts and what counts in, 194–99. *See also* activism; philanthropy of Madam C. J. Walker
African Americans: activism by (*see* activism); as agents of philanthropy, 3, 16; black beauty culture and, 64–66; education of (*see* education, black); fraternalism among, 110–16; hostility toward businesses owned by, 58–59; lynchings of, 29, 33, 106–7, 128; migration out of the South, 33–40; old folks' homes for, 155–56; philanthropy of Madam C. J. Walker in uplifting, 157–63; race riots and, 106; in the Reconstruction era, 27–30; as soldiers in World War I, 105–6, 107. *See also* black women
Africana studies, 190, 194–95, 197
African Methodist Episcopal (AME) church, 2; Christian charity and, 45–46; educational efforts of, 44; establishment of, 41–42; history of self-help and voluntary action in, 40–41; leadership of, 41–46; philanthropy of Madam C. J. Walker and, 152–54, 188; publications of, 43–44; women's work in, 37–38, 47–50. *See also* St. Paul African Methodist Episcopal (AME) Church
Alexander, Sandra Carlton, 191

Allen, Richard, 41–42, 44–46
Alpha Home, 146, 150, 157, 160, 172, 175, 178
*AME Church Review*, 43
American Baptist Home Missionary Society, 97
Anderson, James, 86, 88–89
Anderson, Marian, 180
Angel Network, 203
Apex News and Hair Company, 196
archives, historical: difficulties of working in, 19–21; silences and absences of, 21
Arkansas Baptist College, 99
Armstrong, Samuel Chapman, 88
associationalism, 23, 42, 108
Association of Black Foundation Executives, 207
Avon Cosmetics, 80–81

Bailey, Julius, 43
Baldwin, William, 90
Barnes, Carolyn, 176
*Beauticians Journal*, 69
beauty schools, 91–96, 137
Belmont, Alva Vanderbilt, 12
Benevolent Association of Madam C. J. Walker Agents, Inc., 23, 109
Bertram, James, 71
Bethel AME Church, 41, 70, 143, 161
Bethune, Mary McLeod, 17–18, 23, 81, 100–101, 104, 142, 175, 183
black beauty culture, 64–66, 79–80; fraternalism and, 113
black bodies, 14
black formalism, 111
black identity, 14, 17
Black-Led Social Change, 207
Black Lives Matter, 207
black philanthropy. *See* African American philanthropy
Black Philanthropy Month, 207
*Black Rose, The*, 181
Blackwell, Florence Moss, 68
black women: as agents for the Walker Company, 55–56, 65–68; black beauty culture and, 64–66, 79–80, 113; community work of, 7–8, 13, 17–18, 87;

desolate economic landscape for, 62–69; fundraising by, 17–18; generosity of, 20–21, 94, 208; hygiene work by, 60–61; institution-building of, 12, 17, 28, 40, 144, 152, 154, 163; intersectional philanthropy by, 19, 190–94; Mite Missionary Society and, 37–38, 47–49, 50, 51; philanthropy of Madam C. J. Walker funding for, 157–63; political and social work by, 16–17, 48–50, 105–7; public culture of, 40–41, 44, 49, 196; as "race women," 57, 94, *142*; religious institutions and culture of, 40–41; respectability of, 15–16, 22, 51, 52, 113, 125, 145, 162, 168; tradition of philanthropy among, 14–19, 185–86, 189–94; as washerwomen, 25, 30–32. *See also* African Americans
black women's history, 14, 16, 19, 190, 194
Blake, Eubie, 180
Bonner, Alice, 205–6
Booker, J. A., 99
Booker T. Washington Memorial Fund, 108, 109
Breedlove, Alexander, 27, 39
Breedlove, James, 27, 35, 39
Breedlove, Louvenia (Powell), 1, 27, 30, 39, 147–48, 171
Breedlove, Minerva, 1, 26–27
Breedlove, Owen, 1, 26–27
Breedlove, Owen, Jr., 27, 35, 39
Breedlove, Sarah, *130*; as budding philanthropist, 45–50; early years of, 1–2, 26–33, 93; enrollment in night school, 40; marriage to John Davis, 39; marriage to Moses McWilliams, 32–33; move to St. Louis, 36, 161–62; St. Paul African Methodist Episcopal (AME) Church and, 35–38, 40–50; transformation into Madam C. J. Walker, 52–53; as washerwoman, 25, 30–32, 52. *See also* Walker, Madam C. J.
Breedlove, Solomon, 27, 35, 39
Brokenburr, Alice, 160
Brokenburr, Nerrisa Lee, 176
Brokenburr, Robert, 160, 167, 173, 176–77, 180

Brown, Charlotte Hawkins, 18, 23, 74, 104, 126, 145, 159, 175
Brown, Clara, 11
Brown, Elsa Barkley, 57
Brown, Hallie Quinn, 49
Bryant, Fairy Mae, 172, 176
Buffet, Warren, 185
Bundles, A'Lelia, 19, 181, 205
Bureau of Refugees, Freedmen, and Abandoned Lands, 27
Burke, Jesse, 205
Burke, Shirley, 205
Burnett, Alice, 66, 68, 133
Burney plantation, 26–27, 40
Burroughs, Nannie Helen, 18, 81
By-laws of the Local Bodies of the National Beauty Culturists' and Benevolent Association of Madam C. J. Walker Agents, Inc., 117

Cable, Mary, 143
California Perfume Company, 80
Carlton-LaNey, Iris, 13, 191
Carnegie, Andrew, 6, 9–10, 71, 85, 155, 185, 189, 204
Carson, Emmett, 13
Carter, Lavinia, 49
charity: by African Americans, 90, 107–8; Christian, 45–47; effectiveness of, 194; of Madam C. J. Walker, 24, 68, 157, 160, 166, 186; remembered in last wills and testaments, 169; scientific philanthropy and, 155; by Walker Clubs, 23, 107–8, 115–16, 124–29; in will of Madam C. J. Walker, 176
Chicago School of Civics and Philanthropy, 155
Chicago Urban League, 60
Christian Recorder, 43
churchwomen, 36, 41, 100; collaborative giving by, 192; community institutions built by, 17, 31–32; countering the Lost Cause narrative, 43; embracing commitment to religion and racial uplift, 49; influence on Sarah Breedlove/Madam C. J. Walker, 14, 22, 53, 61, 161, 195; race women as, 81; racial uplift and, 15; tra-

ditions and practices of giving, serving, and leading modeled by, 49, 186
Civil War, 26, 27
Clinton, Bill, 203
clubwomen, 13, 81, 100, 110, 113, 120, 161, 207; as agents of change, 116, 129; collaboration by, 192; community institutions built by, 17, 31–32, 60; countering the Lost Cause narrative, 43; educational programs set up by, 86–87; influence on Sarah Breedlove/Madam C. J. Walker, 14, 22, 195; local programming by, 155; old folks' homes and, 155–56; orphanages founded by, 36; political and social work by, 16, 107; proximity to those they served, 191; racial uplift and, 15, 61; traditions and practices of giving, serving, and leading modeled by, 49, 186
Cohron, Sarah Newton, 36–37
Collier-Thomas, Bettye, 13, 16, 39, 48, 49
Colored Relief Board, 35
Colored Young Men's Christian Association (YMCA), 70
Color of Change, 207
Companions of the Forest, 181
Croker, Ella, 143, 147, 150, 174
Curtis, W. P., 179

Davis, John, 39
Davis, Violet, 65, 173
Daytona Normal and Industrial School for Negro Girls, 100, 168, 175, 178
Dean, Jane, 175
de Forest, Robert, 71
Delta (La.), 1–2, 26–30, 34–35, 37–38, 40, 93, 144, 161
Dennis, Richelieu, 181, 182
Denver, 2, 51–52, 93, 144, 161; Madam C. J. Walker's speech to the NACW in, 127
Denver Star, 185, 187, 201, 208
Denver Statesman, 56
Doley, Harold, 181–82
Doley, Helena, 182
Dossett, Kate, 61
Douglass, Frederick, 42, 124–25
Douglass, Helen Pitts, 125

Dr. Perkins' Foot Soap Manufacturing
    Company, 70
DuBois, W. E. B., 28, 43, 61, 85, 189–90,
    197
Due, Tananarive, 181

East St. Louis Riot, 106
education, black: aspirations and denial
    of, 85–86; industrial, 88–90, 96–101,
    152; Madam C. J. Walker Beauty
    Schools and, 91–96, 137; Madam C. J.
    Walker's gift of, 101–4, 152–54; as me-
    lioristic act, 86; problem of, post–Civil
    War, 88–90; viewed as philanthropy,
    86–87; Walker's philanthropy to south-
    ern black industrial schools for, 96–101
Ellington, Duke, 180
Emancipation Proclamation, 26
Embree, Edward Rogers, 71
Equal Suffrage Association of Indiana, 75
Essence Magazine, 182
Evans, Harry D., 66
"exodusters," 33–34

Fifteenth Amendment, 27
Finkenbine, Roy, 89
Flanner House, 145, 157, 159–60
Flint, Lucy, 145
Foner, Eric, 28
formalism, black, 111, 116
Fourteenth Amendment, 27
Franks, Robert, 71
fraternalism, black, 110–16
Frazier, Mrs. J. C., 179
Frederick Douglass Fund, 108
Frederick Douglass Life Insurance Asso-
    ciation, 70
Free African Society, 41, 42
Freedmen's Bureau, 27–28
Fuentes, Marisa, 20

Garnette, Florence, 180
Garrett, Mary Elizabeth, 12
Garvey, Marcus, 76–77, 126, 197
Gates, Bill and Melinda, 185
Gates, Frederick T., 71
generosity, 2–3, 20–21; of agents of the
    Walker Company, 124; of black life,

94–95, 185, 188, 204; of black washer-
    women, 31; of black women, 18–19;
    Christian charity and, 46, 122; early
    experiences in life of Madam C. J.
    Walker and her, 25–26, 147, 196–97; as
    form of hope, 198; legacy of Madam
    C. J. Walker's, 10, 96, 99, 170, 178,
    179–80, 182, 186, 189, 199; Madam C. J.
    Walker as foremother of black, 9, 113;
    Madam C. J. Walker's gospel of giving
    and, 6–8; origins in Africa, 15; sincerity
    of Madam C. J. Walker's, 156–57; theo-
    rizing black women's, 189–94; through
    lens of leisure, 12
George, Louis W., 66, 176
Gill, Tiffany, 16, 59, 195
Gilmore, Glenda, 87
giving circles, 207
Giving Pledge, 185
Golden Bench of God, The, 180
gospel of giving of Madam C. J. Walker,
    3–9, 198–99
Grand United Order of Odd Fellows, 33,
    112
Great Black Migration, 33–40
Green, Hetty, 151–52
Guadalupe College, 99, 101
Gunter, Julius C., 126, 127

Habitat for Humanity, 203
Haddish, Tiffany, 181
Haines Institute, 175, 178
Haley, Alex, 181
Hampton-Tuskegee model, 88–89, 101–2
A Hand Up: Black Philanthropy and Self-
    Help in America, 13
Hannon Industrial Institute, 159
Harris, Carrie B., 68–69
Harris, George, 179
Hayes, Rutherford B., 29
Haynes, Birdye Henrietta, 155
Haynes, George Edmund, 155
Hine, Darlene Clark, 13, 15–16, 83
Hope, Lugenia Burns, 60, 155
Hudson, Mary, 172
Hughes, Revella, 180
Hunter, Edna, 18
Hunter, Tera, 32

Huntington, Collis P., 5
Hurston, Zora Neale, 180

incrementalism, 193
Independent Order of St. Luke, 62
Indianapolis, 2, 73, 78, 91, 170–71, 176,
    182; colored YMCA of, 3, 5, 75, 143,
    158–59; Flanner House in, 145, 157,
    159–60; Freeman B. Ransom in,
    69–72; incorporation of the Walker
    Company in, 62, 82, 160–61; Madam
    C. J. Walker's philanthropy in, 144,
    146, 149, 160–63, 172, 175; NAACP of,
    143; settlement house in, 70; Walker
    Company factory in, 93, 151; Walker's
    estate settled in, 177–78
*Indianapolis Freeman*, 25, 46, 55, 70, 92,
    135–36, 145, 146, 157
industrial education, 88–90, 96–101, 152
industrial philanthropy, 23, 87, 90, 102–3,
    188; black racial oppression through,
    86, 90; by Booker T. Washington, 85,
    197; dominated by white men, 71, 81,
    86, 88; race philanthropy and, 197
International League of Darker Peoples
    (ILDP), 75–77, 172, 174
intersectional philanthropy, 19, 190–94
*Inter-State Tattler*, 69

Jackson, Samuel L., 204
James, LeBron, 181, 204
Jim Crow society, 1–3, 6–8, 20, 23, 40, 52,
    53, 82, 83, 102, 161, 182; black activism
    and, 108, 127–28; black fraternalism
    and, 116; denial of education for Afri-
    can Americans in, 86; establishment
    and expansion of, 28–29; gender dy-
    namics of, 191; hygiene work in, 61;
    lynchings and, 29, 33, 106–7; "new Jim
    Crow," 207–8; philanthropy as tool for
    uplifting the race in, 144–45, 148–49,
    154, 187–89, 198
Johnson, Cordelia Greene, 167
Johnson, Janet, 66
Johnson, Joan Marie, 16, 125–26
Johnson, Magic, 204
Johnson, Robert, 204
Jones, Absalom, 41

Jones, Adrienne Lash, 13
Jones, Eugene Kinckle, 146
Jones, Martha S., 40–41, 49
Jones, Quincy, 204
Jordan, Michael, 204
Joyner, Marjorie Stewart, *141, 142,* 167
joy of giving, 25, 38, 46, 175, 194
*Julius Caesar,* 117

Kelly, Alice, 65, 145, 171
Knights of Pythias, 70
Knights of the White Camelia, 29
Knox, George, *135–36*
Ku Klux Klan, 29

LaFon, Thomy, 11
Laney, Lucy, 23, 175
Lee, Hattie Mae, 202–3
Lee, Robert E., 125
legacy of Madam C. J. Walker, 1–3, 182–83;
    codicil of 1919, 174–77; last will and
    testament, 167–74; Madam C. J. Walker
    Memorial Pilgrimage and Convention,
    165–67; ongoing influence, 179–82;
    Villa Lewaro estate, 171–72, 174, 177–79,
    181–82
Lelia College, 91–96, 97, 100, 137
Lewaro, Villa, 76
Lincoln, Abraham, 26
Little, Lawrence, 45
Logan, Rayford, 29
lynchings, 29, 33, 106–7, 128

*Madam—A Musical on the Life of Madam
    C. J. Walker,* 181
Madam C. J. Walker and A'Lelia Walker
    Place, 182
*Madam C. J. Walker Beauty Manual: A Thor-
    ough Treatise Covering all Branches of
    Beauty Culture,* 93–95
Madam C. J. Walker Beauty Schools,
    91–96, *137*
Madam C. J. Walker Manufacturing Com-
    pany of Indiana. *See* Walker Company
Madam C. J. Walker Memorial Pilgrimage
    and Convention, *141–42,* 165–67
Madam Walker Legacy Center, 182
Madam Walker Theater, 182

Malone, Annie, 11, 50–52, 62–63, 67, 91, 195–96
Manassas Industrial School, 175
Mandela, Nelson, 201
Marble, Mabel, 92
Mary Kay Cosmetics, 80
McCarty, Osceola, 185–86
McKee, John, 11
McWilliams, Moses, 32–33
Mills, William F., 126
Mite Missionary Society, 37–38, 47, 50, 51, 161–62, 172, 186; Walker's monetary gifts to, 145; in will of Madam C. J. Walker, 175, 178
moral imagination, 18, 22; Madam C. J. Walker's, 30, 32, 40, 44, 46, 82; shaping of Madam C. J. Walker's, 26, 52–53; Walker Company and, 56, 69
Morehouse College, 185
Mossell, Gertrude E. H. Bustill, 14–15, 18
Mother AME Zion Church, 166
Mound Bayou Industrial College, 99–100
Mullins, Paul, 195
mutual aid, 18–19, 31, 42, 61, 113–14, 186
mutual aid organizations, 113–14

Napier, J. C., 180
National Action Network, 207
National Association for the Advancement of Colored People (NAACP), 70, 75, 76, 124, 127–28, 168, 188–89, 207; in will of Madam C. J. Walker, 172, 174–75, 178
National Association of Colored Women (NACW), 15–16, 48–49, 60, 76, 100, 116, 188; activism and, 105, 108, 124–26; black fraternalism and, 110; philanthropy of Madam C. J. Walker and, 154, 172; Walker Clubs and, 109–10
National Beauty Culturists, 23, 109
National Child Protection Act, 1993, 203
National Council of Negro Women, 100
National Negro Business League (NNBL), 5, 30, 152, 163; Walker's speech to, 83–85
National Negro Health Week, 60
National Race Congress, 75

National Urban League (NUL), 60, 155, 207
Negro Masons, 33
"Negro Problem," 42
Neighborhood House, 155
"new Jim Crow," 207–8
New Voices Fund, 182
New York, 2, 10, 73, 75–78, 181–82, 189; Florence Garnette Training School for Little Girls in, 180; Lelia College and, 91, 93, 97; Madam C. J. Walker's home in (see Villa Lewaro estate); New York Urban League of, 60; settlement houses in, 155; Walker Club in, 109
New York Urban League, 60

Obama, Barack, 203, 206
Obama, Michelle, 204
Ogden, Robert, 90
old folks' homes, 155–56; in will of Madam C. J. Walker, 175, 178
Olive, George S., 74
On Her Own Ground: The Life and Times of Madam C. J. Walker, 181
opportunity, as gift, 22, 56, 64, 78, 81–82
Oprah Winfrey Charitable Foundation, 203
Oprah Winfrey Leadership Academy for Girls, 201–2
Oprah Winfrey Show, The, 203
Order of Colored Knights of Pythias, 33, 115
Order of the Court of Calanthe, 37–38, 51, 70, 114, 115–16, 117–18, 161
orphans, black, 36–37, 49, 145
Orphans' Home, Indianapolis, 146, 150, 157
Oser, Jennifer, 112
Overton, Anthony, 82
Overton Hygienic Manufacturing, 82, 91
Owens, Kayla, 205

Palmer Memorial Institute, 145, 157, 159, 168, 175, 178
Paris Peace Conference, 75–76
Payne, Daniel, 44
Peabody Education Fund, 28

People's Hospital, St. Louis, 178
Perry, Imani, 110, 111, 116
Perry, Mae Walker, 167
Peterson, Eliza, 75
Phelps-Stokes Fund, 101
philanthropic biography of Madam C. J. Walker, 19–24, 186, 194, 196
philanthropic studies, 13, 21, 190, 195
philanthropy: business/commerce and, 22, 62, 82, 118–19; education as, 86–87, 96; history of, 11, 194; Western conceptions of, 46
"Philanthropy in the African American Experience," 13
philanthropy of Madam C. J. Walker, 19–24, 81–82; AME Church and, 152–53; to black industrial schools, 96–101, 152; collaboration and, 192–93; compared to Hetty Green, 151–52; education and, 101–4, 152–54; Freeman B. Ransom as de facto philanthropic adviser on, 69–78, 143–44, 147–48; funding women and uplifting the race, 157–63; gift categories in, 144–54; gospel of giving in, 3–9, 198–99; incrementalism and, 193; joy and, 194; as mentored migrant and budding philanthropist in St. Louis, 33–40; as model for modern day philanthropy, 185–87, 201–2, 206–9; monetary gifts in, 144–46; nonmonetary gifts in, 146–50; proximity and, 190–92; resource-fullness and, 192; scholarship on, 19; scientific, 154–57; social justice and, 149; through hiring unconventional employees, 150–51; as tool for uplifting the race, 144, 145, 148–49, 154, 187–89; Walker Company giveaways in, 149–50. See also activism
philanthropy scholarship, 9–14
Phillips, Daniel W., 97
Pittsburgh, 2, 55, 72, 91, 93, 144, 161, 173, 178
Pittsburgh Courier, 167
Pleasant, Mary Ellen, 61–62
Pollard, Curtis, 27
Pollard Church of Delta, Louisiana, 27
Pope-Turnbo Company, 50, 51

Poro College, 91
Powell, Adam Clayton, Sr., 76
Powell, Colin and Alma, 204
Powell, Jesse, 27, 30, 33
Powell, Willie, 147–48, 149, 171
Poynton, John, 71
Progressive Era, 12
Prosser, Agnes, 172
proximity, 38, 161, 190–92, 202

Queenie Pie, 180

race riots, 106
"race women," 57, 94, 142, 163, 179–80
racial uplift, 2, 3, 197; AME Church and, 43, 53; Annie Malone and, 195–96; beauty culture and, 61; by church and clubwomen, 15–17, 49, 155–56; emphasis on personal health and hygiene in, 59; ideology of, 22; industrial education strategy for, 87; Madam C. J. Walker's work for, 8, 22, 23, 64, 75, 77, 96, 119, 163, 172, 177; NACW and, 126, 127; Order of Calanthe and, 116; YMCA and, 158
Randolph, A. Phillip, 76–77, 113, 126
Ransom, A'Lelia, 174
Ransom, Frank, 176, 182
Ransom, Freeman B., 20, 23, 57–58, 82, 105, 109, 110, 132, 135, 138, 150, 160–61, 173, 180; as attorney for Walker Company, 62, 65, 67–69; civic and philanthropic activities of, 70–71; close friendship with Madam C. J. Walker, 78; as de facto philanthropic adviser to Walker, 69–78, 143–44, 147–48; education of, 70; last will of Madam C. J. Walker and, 173–77; management of Walker's finances by, 72–74; Margaret Thompson and, 119–20; as member of Order of the Colored Knights of Pythias, 115–16; protection of Walker by, 74–77; Roger Williams University and, 98–99; at the Walker Agents Convention, 1939, 167
Ransom, Nettie, 140, 158, 161
Ransom, Willard, 141, 165, 174
Rawlins, Parthenia, 171

Reconstruction Acts, 27

Reconstruction era, 27–29; African American education in, 85–86, 88–90; demise of, 29–30

resource-fullness, 192, 193, 195

respectability: black formalism and, 111; black fraternalism and, 77; black women's understanding of, 16–17; Cedar Hill estate as symbol of, 125–26; connected to philanthropy, 15; Madam C. J. Walker and, 22, 51, 52, 110, 113; Richard Allen and, 42; virtuous womanhood and, 16–17, 145, 162, 168

Reynolds, Violet, *133, 139,* 150

Rhimes, Shonda, 204

Richardson, LaTanya, 204

*Ritual for the Local Bodies of the National Beauty Culturists' and Benevolent Association of Madam C. J. Walker Agents, Inc., The,* 117

*Ritualistic Ceremonies of the Order of Calanthe,* 117

Robeson, Paul, 180

Robinson, Christopher K., 37

Robinson, Jessie Batts, 37, 74, 113, 114, *130,* 158, 162, 168; in will of Madam C. J. Walker, 176

Rockefeller, Abby Aldrich, 12

Rockefeller, John D., 2, 6, 9, 18, 71, 90, 155, 185

Roger Williams University, 97–99, 101

Roosevelt, Franklin D., 100

*Roots,* 181

Rosenwald, Julius, 6, 71, *136,* 157

Ross, Hubert Barnes, 176

Ross, John, 71

Russell Sage Foundation, 155

Sage, Olivia Margaret Slocum, 10, 12, 71, 81, *163,* 204

scholarship on philanthropy, 9–14

scientific philanthropy, 154–57

Sears and Roebuck, 81

self-help, 18, 22, 33, 37, 49, 53, 57, 149, 197–98; African American ideology of, 58–59; AME churchwomen and, 40–42

Sephora, 181

Shakespeare, William, 117

Shaw, Jenny, 20

Shaw, Lord of Dunfermline, 71

Shepard, Helen Miller Gould, 2

Shorter Chapel AME Church, 51

Skocpol, Theda, 112

Slater Fund, 28, 90, 101

slavery: Breedlove family and, 1, 26–27; denial of education for African Americans in, 85–86

Smith, Cheryl A., 59

Smith, Robert F., 185, 204

Smithsonian National Museum of African American History and Culture, 204–6

Sneddon, Karen, 169

Snelson, Floyd, 69

social justice, 149, 207

Sojourner Truth House, 178

Spencer, Octavia, 181

Spivey, Donald, 89

Stampp, Kenneth, 29

Star Christmas Fund, 145

St. Louis, 7, 30, 51, 62, 67, 74, 91, 144; black churchwomen and clubwomen of, 14, 22; black washerwomen community of, 32; influence on Madam C. J. Walker's gospel of giving, 25, 33–40, 45–46; race riots of 1917 in, 76, 105, 106; Sarah Breedlove's arrival in, 2, 4, 33, 105

St. Louis Colored Orphan's Home, 36–37, 49, 161, 172; Walker's monetary gifts to, 145

*St. Louis Post-Dispatch,* 38

Stokes, Anson Phelps, 90

St. Paul African Methodist Episcopal (AME) Church, 153, 161–62, 172, 186; ministries of, 35–38; Sarah Breedlove as evolving AME churchwoman with, 40–50; Walker's monetary gifts to, 145. *See also* African Methodist Episcopal (AME) church

St. Paul's Mite Missionary Society, 37–38, 47–49, 50, 51

Summers, Martin, 110

Sundial Brands, 181

Talbert, Mary B., 110, 124–25, 128

Tandy, Charlton H., 34–35

Thirteenth Amendment, 26, 27

*Thirty Years of Lynching in the United States*, 128
Thompson, Margaret, 105, 119–20
Thompson, R. W., 180
Townsend, A. M., 97–99
Trotter, William Monroe, 85
Tubman, Harriet, 204
Turnbo, Annie. *See* Malone, Annie
Tuskegee Institute, 5–6, 88, 101–2, 159; in Africa, 83, 85, 101, 153; emphasis on health and hygiene at, 59–60; in will of Madam C. J. Walker, 175, 178

Underwood, Blair, 181
Unilever, 181
Union Baptist Church, Philadelphia, 105
Universal Negro Improvement Association, 77
*Up from Slavery*, 5
Urban League, 146

Vicksburg (Miss.), 30–38, 144, 151, 161
Villa Lewaro estate, 93–94, *138*, 171–72, 174, 177–79, 181–82
voting rights, 29

Walden College, 100
Walker, A'Lelia, 2, 24, 33, 53, 71, *139–40*, 172, 177, 182, 196; arrival in St. Louis, 36, 37; death of, 167; Freeman B. Ransom and, 72–73; as leader of the Walker Company, 178–79; as officer of Walker Company, 62; turbulent life in St. Louis, 39–40; work in the Walker Company, 52
Walker, Charles Joseph, 2, 39, 52, 62
Walker, Madam C. J., *135–36*; on activism, 105; advocacy for education, 83–88; beauty schools established by, 91–96; charity of, 24, 68, 157, 160, 166, 186; close friendship with Freeman B. Ransom, 78; death of, 2, *140*; Delta (La.) and, 1–2, 26–30, 34–35, 37–38, 40, 93, 144, 161; demonstrations by, *134*; Denver and, 2, 51–52, 93, 127, 144, 161; early years of, 1–2, 26–33; on education, 83; emergence from Sarah Breedlove, 52–53; fraternalism and, 112–13; Freeman B. Ransom as de facto

philanthropic advisor to, 69–78; gospel of giving of, 3–9, 198–99; on her own generosity, 1, 143; on her pleasure in giving, 165; Indianapolis and (*see* Indianapolis); International League of Darker Peoples (ILDP) and, 75–77; last will and testament of, 167–74; legacy of generosity of, 1–3, 165–83; moral values of, 25–26; New York and (*see* New York); on patriotism and love of country, 105–6; personal identity of, 8–9; physical appearance of, 79–80; Pittsburgh and, 2, 55, 72, 91, 93, 144, 161, 173, 178; as "race woman," 57, 94, 163, 179–80; speech at the Union Baptist Church of Philadelphia, 105–6; speech to the National Negro Business League, 83–85; spending by, 72–74; in St. Louis (*see* St. Louis); on uplifting her race, 55; Vicksburg (Miss.) and, 30–38, 144, 151, 161; Villa Lewaro home of, 93–94, *138*, 171–72, 174, 177–79, 181–82; as virtuous woman entrepreneur, 50–53; as washerwoman, 25, 30–32; wealth of, 2, 4–5, 25, 83, 93, *139*. *See also* Breedlove, Sarah; philanthropy of Madam C. J. Walker
Walker, Maggie Lena, 57, 62
Walker, Mrs. Robert, 55
Walker Beneficial Clubs, 109
Walker Benevolent Associations, 109
Walker Clubs, 108–11; charity and activism in, 23, 107–8, 115–16, 124–29; formal culture in, 117–24
Walker Company, *131*; advertising by, *132*; agents of, 55–56, 65–68, 81, 108–10, *138* (*see also* Walker Clubs); black women's desolate economic landscape and, 62–69; critiques of, 78–81; dual motives of, 58–62; early advertising by, 51–52; employees of, 65, *133*, 150–51; founding of, 2; giveaways by, 149–50; incorporation of, 62; national organization of agents of, 108–10, *138*; scholarly analysis of success of, 56–58; sold in 1985, 181; Walker's process in developing products for, 50–51
Walker Method System, 113
Walker's Legacy, 207

Walker Unions, 109
Ward, Joseph, 161, 173
Ward, Zella, 161
washerwomen, 25, 30–32
washing societies, 32
Washington, Booker T., 5–7, 30, 42, 43,
    88, 104, *135*, 153; emphasis on health
    and hygiene by, 59–60; legacy of
    Madam C. J. Walker and, 172, 175, 197;
    National Negro Business League and,
    83–84, 152; Tuskegee Institute and, 83,
    101–2
Washington, Denzel and Pauletta, 204
Washington, Margaret Murray, 49, 60, 126
Washington, Sarah Spencer, 11, 62, 195,
    196
Watkins, William H., 90
Wells, Ida B., 14–15, 76, 81
"We Specialize in the Wholly Impossible,"
    13
*When and Where I Enter,* 14
White, Deborah Gray, 77
White, Walter, 167, 188–89
white American philanthropy, 9–14, 71,
    151–52, 163, 189, 197, 204
White Brotherhood, 29
Wilberforce University, 178
Wiley University, 99

will of Madam C. J. Walker: codicil of 1919
    to, 174–77; contents of, 169–74; Villa
    Lewaro estate in, 171–72, 174, 177–79;
    writing of, 167–69
Wilson, Maggie, 55, 173
Wilson, Sarah, 172
Wilson, Woodrow, 76, 107
Winchester, Ida, 176
Winfrey, Oprah, 185, 201–4
women's benevolent work and associa-
    tions, 12
Women's Christian Temperance Union
    (WCTU), 75
Women's Parent Mite Missionary Society
    (WPMMS), AME, 47
women's philanthropy: history of, 11–12;
    inheritance and, 3, 10, 12; leisure and,
    3, 12, 107. *See also* African American
    philanthropy; black women; church-
    women; clubwomen
Woodson, Carter G., 25, 31
*Work of the Afro-American Woman, The,* 14
worthy poor, 155–56

YMCA, 3, 5, 75, *135–36*, 143, 157–59; in will
    of Madam C. J. Walker, 178
YWCA, 71, 75, 158; in will of Madam C. J.
    Walker, 177–78

**Tyrone McKinley Freeman** is an assistant professor of philanthropic studies at the Indiana University Lilly Family School of Philanthropy.

# The New Black Studies Series

Beyond Bondage: Free Women of Color in the Americas
  *Edited by David Barry Gaspar and Darlene Clark Hine*
The Early Black History Movement, Carter G. Woodson,
  and Lorenzo Johnston Greene   *Pero Gaglo Dagbovie*
"Baad Bitches" and Sassy Supermamas: Black Power Action Films   *Stephane Dunn*
Black Maverick: T. R. M. Howard's Fight for Civil Rights and Economic
  Power   *David T. Beito and Linda Royster Beito*
Beyond the Black Lady: Sexuality and the New African American Middle
  Class   *Lisa B. Thompson*
Extending the Diaspora: New Histories of Black People   *Dawne Y. Curry,*
  *Eric D. Duke, and Marshanda A. Smith*
Activist Sentiments: Reading Black Women in the Nineteenth Century
  *P. Gabrielle Foreman*
Black Europe and the African Diaspora   *Edited by Darlene Clark Hine, Trica Danielle*
  *Keaton, and Stephen Small*
Freeing Charles: The Struggle to Free a Slave on the Eve of the Civil War
  *Scott Christianson*
African American History Reconsidered   *Pero Gaglo Dagbovie*
Freud Upside Down: African American Literature and Psychoanalytic
  Culture   *Badia Sahar Ahad*
A. Philip Randolph and the Struggle for Civil Rights   *Cornelius L. Bynum*
Queer Pollen: White Seduction, Black Male Homosexuality, and the
  Cinematic   *David A. Gerstner*
The Rise of Chicago's Black Metropolis, 1920—1929   *Christopher Robert Reed*
The Muse Is Music: Jazz Poetry from the Harlem Renaissance to Spoken
  Word   *Meta DuEwa Jones*
Living with Lynching: African American Lynching Plays, Performance,
  and Citizenship, 1890—1930   *Koritha Mitchell*
Africans to Spanish America: Expanding the Diaspora
  *Edited by Sherwin K. Bryant, Rachel Sarah O'Toole, and Ben Vinson III*
Rebels and Runaways: Slave Resistance in Nineteenth-Century Florida
  *Larry Eugene Rivers*
The Black Chicago Renaissance   *Edited by Darlene Clark Hine*
  *and John McCluskey Jr.*
The Negro in Illinois: The WPA Papers   *Edited by Brian Dolinar*
Along the Streets of Bronzeville: Black Chicago's Literary Landscape
  *Elizabeth Schlabach*
Gendered Resistance: Women, Slavery, and the Legacy of Margaret Garner
  *Edited by Mary E. Fredrickson and Delores M. Walters*
Racial Blackness and the Discontinuity of Western Modernity   *Lindon Barrett,*
  *edited by Justin A. Joyce, Dwight A. McBride, and John Carlos Rowe*
Fannie Barrier Williams: Crossing the Borders of Region and Race
  *Wanda A. Hendricks*

The Pekin: The Rise and Fall of Chicago's First Black-Owned Theater
  *Thomas Bauman*
Grounds of Engagement: Apartheid-Era African American and
  South African Writing  *Stéphane Robolin*
Humane Insight: Looking at Images of African American Suffering
  and Death  *Courtney R. Baker*
Word Warrior: Richard Durham, Radio, and Freedom  *Sonja D. Williams*
Funk the Erotic: Transaesthetics and Black Sexual Cultures  *L. H. Stallings*
Spatializing Blackness: Architectures of Confinement and Black Masculinity
  in Chicago  *Rashad Shabazz*
Painting the Gospel: Black Public Art and Religion in Chicago  *Kymberly N. Pinder*
Radical Aesthetics and Modern Black Nationalism  *GerShun Avilez*
Sex Workers, Psychics, and Numbers Runners: Black Women in New York City's
  Underground Economy  *LaShawn Harris*
Slavery at Sea: Terror, Sex, and Sickness in the Middle Passage
  *Sowande' M. Mustakeem*
Booker T. Washington in American Memory  *Kenneth M. Hamilton*
Black Post-Blackness: The Black Arts Movement and Twenty-First-Century
  Aesthetics  *Margo Natalie Crawford*
Archibald Motley Jr. and Racial Reinvention: The Old Negro in New
  Negro Art  *Phoebe Wolfskill*
Building the Black Metropolis: African American Entrepreneurship
  in Chicago  *Edited by Robert E. Weems Jr. and Jason P. Chambers*
Jazz Internationalism: Literary Afro-Modernism and the Cultural Politics of
  Black Music  *John Lowney*
Black Public History in Chicago: Civil Rights Activism from World War II
  to the Cold War  *Ian Rocksborough-Smith*
Building the Black Arts Movement: Hoyt Fuller and the Cultural Politics
  of the 1960s  *Jonathan Fenderson*
Black Sexual Economies: Race and Sex in a Culture of Capital
  *Edited by Adrienne D. Davis and the BSE Collective*
Reimagining Liberation: How Black Women Transformed Citizenship
  in the French Empire  *Annette K. Joseph-Gabriel*
Autochthonomies: Transnationalism, Testimony, and Transmission
  in the African Diaspora  *Myriam J. A. Chancy*
Pleasure in the News: African American Readership and Sexuality
  in the Black Press  *Kim T. Gallon*
Roots of the Black Chicago Renaissance: New Negro Writers, Artists,
  and Intellectuals, 1893—1930  *Edited by Richard A. Courage
  and Christopher Robert Reed*
From Slave Cabins to the White House: Homemade Citizenship
  in African American Culture  *Koritha Mitchell*
Laughing to Keep from Dying: African American Satire in the
  Twenty-First Century  *Danielle Fuentes Morgan*
Madam C. J. Walker's Gospel of Giving: Black Women's Philanthropy during
  Jim Crow  *Tyrone McKinley Freeman*